History of Sport and Physical Education in the United States

History of Sport and Physical Education in the United States

Third Edition

Betty Spears
University of Massachusetts-Amherst

Richard A. Swanson
University of North Carolina-Greensboro

Edited by Elaine T. Smith
Mount Holyoke College

wcb
Wm. C. Brown Publishers
Dubuque, Iowa

CONSULTING EDITOR

Physical Education
  Aileene S. Lockhart
  Texas Woman's University

Copyright © 1978, 1983, 1988 by Wm. C. Brown Company Publishers. All rights reserved

Library of Congress Catalog Card Number: 88–70323

ISBN 0–697–07417–X

Printed in the United States of America
10 9 8 7 6 5 4 3 2 1

Contents

3

Pastimes, Sport, and the Beginnings of Physical Education in a Developing Country, 1776–1840

4

From Games to Sport, and from Exercise to Physical Education, 1840–1885

5

**The Organizing of Sport and
Physical Education, 1885–1917**

8

**The Olympic Games, Ancient and
Modern**

List of Illustrations

Preface

The history of sport and physical education in the United States is a vivid story of the American people pursuing vigorous physical activities for their own pleasure and satisfaction, for health and fitness, and for the entertainment of others. In the early days of this country, neither sport nor physical education existed as we know them today. Dramatic changes have led to the modern world of amateur, professional, and recreational sport. Sport has also become the dominant component in physical education. Schools and colleges early incorporated exercise programs to improve the health of their students, at the same time that reformers extolled the benefits of exercise and fitness to the society at large. As educational philosophy changed and as organized sport became an integral part of everyday life in the United States, sport was added to school physical education programs. Dance, which was part of the early social life of this country and of the professional world of entertainment, also became an activity in school physical education. The history of these developments is the subject of this book.

Lists of scores from every Rose Bowl and major league baseball game are not included in this history, nor are precise changes in gymnastic apparatus recorded. Historians are necessarily selective in their choice of materials; we have tried, therefore, to select important information that both *describes* and *explains* the vast shift from yesterday's pastimes and concerns about health to today's complex institutionalized sport and physical education. We have endeavored to include data that furnish a comprehensive picture of sport and physical education in the United States, including men, women, whites, blacks, native Americans, and others of the diverse ethnic groups that make up the United States population. Literally thousands of sources were consulted. Wherever possible we have used primary rather than secondary sources. In some original documents, including some nineteenth-century handwritten journals, we found new and sometimes contradictory evidence. We have attempted to construct a reasonable and accurate history of sport and physical education in the United States, based on a careful selection and synthesis of the available evidence, viewed from the context of the times.

The first chapter focuses on the history of sport and physical education as part of history itself, examining basic historical assumptions and principles. Major themes, developed throughout the book, are also presented. The second chapter analyzes the beginnings of sport and physical education in the United States by examining the activities of the native Americans, the sports and pastimes of the Europeans whose descendants settled in American colonies, as well as the activities of the Africans who came to this country. American sport characteristically began with the changes brought about in each culture as people lived and worked with one another, adapting their customs and pastimes to the new life and environment in the colonies. Little, if any, physical education existed at that time.

Chapters 3, 4, and 5 trace the evolution of the relatively unorganized, spontaneous pastimes and exercise programs of the eighteenth century through the first two decades of the twentieth, highlighting the emergence of structured, institutionalized programs in professional and amateur sport, public recreation, and physical education in the schools. Throughout this section the major themes continue to be analyzed to help explain the changes in the sport, educational, and recreational life of the people.

Chapters 6 and 7 deal with the influence of the Jazz Age, the Great Depression, affluence, technology, and the beginnings of a postindustrial society on sport and physical education in the United States from the first World War until the present. The major themes of the book are developed in these chapters. The final chapter examines the ancient Olympic Games in order to provide a perspective for the modern Games; it also traces the establishment of the modern Olympic Games and reviews the special character of each Olympiad from 1896 to 1984.

Sport history, like most other aspects of human activity, is affected by wars, depressions, leaders, and all that we call *history*. We have therefore treated the material chronologically, in a broad sweep from the origins of athletics, through a study of the country's evolving attitude toward sport and physical education up until the present. The Olympic Games, however, in the growing sense of American sport as part of the international scene, are treated separately.

Students will find several features of this book helpful: comparative timelines of historical events and sport history events; commentaries on the subject matter of each chapter, relating sport history to sport theory; and provocative suggestions for further reading. The extensive bibliography at the end of the book should be helpful to students and teachers alike.

The title of the third edition of *History of Sport and Physical Activity in the United States* has been changed to *History of Sport and Physical Education in the United States*. Today, sport is a pervasive force in contemporary society, both in and out of educational institutions. In schools and colleges sport is often related to physical education. Although most of the first physical education programs did not include sport, over the years sport and physical education have become inextricably intertwined. Therefore we have chosen to shift the emphasis of this edition slightly. The latest scholarship in the history of sport and physical education is incorporated, and the material on dance has been woven into appropriate sections. The additions and revisions highlight the change in title.

The *History of Sport and Physical Education in the United States* is planned as an undergraduate textbook. It is suitable for use in advanced classes and graduate classes if supplemented by theoretical and specialized works in history, sociology, anthropology, history of sport, sport sociology, sport philosophy, education, and other relevant fields. We urge students to purchase and refer to a standard American history text. A study of the annals of American sport and physical education is even more absorbing when seen in the framework of the times, just as the political and economic history of a society is enhanced by knowing what activities people pursued for their own pleasure and benefit.

An enterprise of this nature is not the work of two people. We are indebted to many who have aided us in gathering material and preparing the manuscript. Librarians and archivists in universities, colleges, museums, cities, and towns have patiently helped us dig out facts and track down leads to new information. We greatly appreciate the time and efforts of friends, colleagues, and students who reviewed portions of the manuscript and made many worthwhile comments. The reviewers were Professors Alex G. Ober (Western Maryland College), Chet Buckley (St. Cloud State University), Sonia R. Green (University of Nebraska–Omaha), and Judith A. Davidson (University of Iowa). Finally, we are deeply indebted to Elaine T. Smith, who carefully and skillfully synthesized our individual writing styles, made valuable suggestions, and explored archives to produce still more evidence of the history of sport and physical education in the United States.

Betty Spears
Richard A. Swanson

1 History and the Study of Sport and Physical Education

If several hundred years from now archaeologists were investigating our civilization, they would find innumerable examples of sport in United States society: stadiums, swimming pools, running shoes, hockey sticks, skis, baseball gloves, tennis rackets, turnstiles, rolls of tickets, and pictures of sport stars. Today even a superficial survey of our country reveals sport and physical education everywhere: Little League baseball, gym classes, Special Olympics for the handicapped, neighborhood basketball, jogging in city streets, as well as the televised professional games which mesmerize millions in their homes across the land. Many forms of dance, from ballet to jazz, attract thousands to the theaters and dance halls of the country. Sport, dance, and physical education are accepted as a part of everyday life in and out of schools, as much by the average American as by the sport entrepreneur and the professional performer.

In sharp contrast, when Columbus discovered the New World and the first settlers landed in Virginia and Massachusetts the only "sports" were those of the Indians. As the early settlers struggled for survival they found little time for games and amusements; but as life became easier and values slowly changed, the people of the new country engaged in pastimes and later became concerned about health and fitness. The development of these simple amusements and vigorous pastimes into modern sport and fitness activities that are now such pervasive forces in our society comprises the history of sport and physical education in the United States of America.

History means different things to different people. To many it is predominantly the study of political and economic events—the conquests of Cortez, English naval supremacy in the Elizabethan age, the building of American railroads, and the causes of the Great Depression. For some, history is primarily a study of the men and women who have shaped the events of their times. For others, history is something more than the story of leaders, wars, economics, and power. History has also come to mean social history, that is, the study of persons as social beings, living, working, and playing together. Historians now study the social groups in which people live and investigate what it meant to be rich or poor in some historical epoch—or to be old, or female, or a member of a minority group. Social historians ask many questions about the everyday lives of people. What did the men, women, girls and boys do from day to day? How did social forces affect their manners and customs? How were marriage partners chosen? What ceremonies were celebrated in their lives? Did they have leisure time? Did they play games? What, for example, did ancient Greek athletes do when they were not competing or training? Did they, like most other Greek citizens, attend the theater to watch the great dramas of Euripides and Aristophanes? Why did the medieval tournaments persist long after gunpowder was invented? When a little leisure time existed in colonial America, how did the settlers spend this time? What influence did the Indians and the frontier families have on each others' lives? Did college students one hundred years ago have time for recreation? If African slaves on southern plantations had any leisure, what activities did they enjoy? What games, sports, and amusements have the people of the United States participated in for over three hundred years? What dances have they danced? How have they exercised? This aspect of history seems relatively new in its emphasis, yet in 1531 Sir Thomas Elyot wrote, "Finally so large is the compase of that which is named historie, that it comprehendeth all thynge that is necessary to be put in memorie."[1]

Many of the memories people have relate to their games, sports, amusements, pastimes, and dance. Sportlike activities and dance are age-old endeavors in which people participate for a variety of reasons. Men in ancient Greece challenged each other in footraces and contests seeking honor for themselves, their families, and their cities. Women at that time danced in the rituals and ceremonies that were a part of daily life. Today, games and sport provide a sense of community: as spectators rooting for a team, as members of a team, as a group with a central interest, or as part of ceremonial activities. In this sense sport becomes a means of bringing people together, rather than dividing them. Other activities, such as exercise, are undertaken to improve the participants, either in a specific sense or to benefit their general health.

Not everyone defines sport, exercise, and physical education in the same way. Over the centuries, sport has had a variety of meanings. Samuel Johnson's 1775 *Dictionary of the English Language* defined it as "play, diversion, game, frolick and tumultuous merriment,"[2] but by 1968 it had become useful to examine sport as "a highly ambiguous term," and to "discuss sport as a game occurrence, as a social institution, and as a social situation or social system."[3] Sport in public schools is sometimes equated with physical education, while athletics is usually considered as organized inter-institutional sport. Frequently, physical education also includes exercise and dance activities as well as sport. To further complicate the picture, nineteenth-century exercise programs were known as gymnastics; thus, nineteenth century *gymnastics* does not mean today's Olympic gymnastic events but rather, *exercise* systems. Also, in the late nineteenth century *physical training* was sometimes used to mean either gymnastics or physical education. This complex situation is also part of the history of sport and physical education in this country. For the purposes of this book several terms need to be defined.

Sport
Sport will be considered to be activities involving physical prowess and skill, competition, strategy and/or chance, and engaged in for the enjoyment and satisfaction of the participant and/or others. This definition includes both organized sport and sport for recreational purposes. It includes sport as entertainment and also encompasses professional sport.

Physical Education
Physical education is referred to as a program of physical activities, usually in educational institutions, including dance, exercise, bodily development activities, and sport.

Exercise
Exercise (or an *exercise system*) is defined as a prescribed, formalized pattern of bodily movements of one or more parts of the body, engaged in for particular reasons, with expected specified outcomes. These reasons could range from cardiovascular fitness to postoperative physical therapy.

Dance
Dance is one of the earliest human rhythmic aesthetic activities, and it is woven into many aspects of our daily lives. Dance ranges from country dance to ballet and jazz dance; it exists both within and without educational institutions.

As you study the unfolding drama of sport and physical education in the United States, several concepts related to the study of history would be helpful to understand. These deal with people, time, and curiosity. If you habitually organize ideas into *who, what, when, where, how,* and *why,* think of the concepts related to people as *who* and *what;* the concepts related to time as *when* and *where;* and the concepts related to curiosity as *how* and *why.*

The first and most important concept to remember is that history is about people—real women and men, real girls and boys. As you study this text, imagine yourself in the place of one of the people who affected sport. Would you as a slave owner have freed a winning boxer? Would you have played the new "girls" basketball in the 1890s? Would you have agreed, in the 1950s, to falsify your high school academic record to compete in college athletics? The historian Carl Becker illuminates this point by reducing history to the simplest terms, "History is the memory of things said and done."[4] Human beings are unique in their sustained ability to remember and interpret past and present actions, making it possible to know and understand events and their influence on people. Being human means having desires, hopes, and ideas, and knowing fear, elation, and disappointment. Humans also know respect, love, contempt, and hate. For example, many athletes have the perseverance to undergo years of grueling practice in hopes of making the Olympic team. If the athlete makes the team, fear is undoubtedly present before the trials; she or he will experience disappointment if the event is lost and elation if it is won. Many of us have had coaches and teachers whom we respected, and perhaps some for whom we have had contempt or hate.

Men and women, their deeds, both bad and good, and the effect of these deeds on their lives and the lives of others are the components of the drama of sport and physical education. In sport history, over 2700 years ago Nestor gave his son advice on how to win a chariot race, and over 2500 years ago Lycurgus decreed exercise for girls so that they would bear strong babies. In more modern times, Pierre de Coubertin, who was barely thirty years of age when he revived the ancient Olympic Games, designed them for men and stubbornly refused to consider women in the modern Games. Jack Johnson, an early black heavyweight champion, shocked middle-class Americans with his three white wives. In the 1940s lively debates among Charles McCloy, Jesse Feiring Williams, Jay B. Nash, and Delbert Oberteuffer over physical education theories dominated professional physical education meetings. The "battle of the sexes" was waged through tennis in 1973 when feminist Billie Jean King defeated avowed male chauvinist Bobby Riggs. In the wake of the drug-related death of basketball star Len Bias in 1986, University of Maryland Chancellor John Slaughter ordered an outside review of the athletic department and replaced the athletic director and head basketball coach. Throughout the history of sport and physical education, real men and real women with human strengths and weaknesses have created significant events that influenced sport history.

A second concept, *time,* includes several important ideas. First, in history there is *only* the past. Although we speak of present-day problems and seek solutions to present issues, it is important to realize that literally speaking there is no "present." Rowse reminds us of this truth in speaking of history as a continuum: "History shows there is no break between the past and the future. While I write this sentence, what was the future has already become the past. . . . All is continuous."[5] History, then, derives meanings from a continuum of events. For example, the original Olympic Games, 776 B.C. to 393 A.D., provided the stimulus for Coubertin's model of the modern Olympic Games. To determine the background of today's problems in the Olympic Games we must study them on a continuum from 776 B.C. to about 400 A.D. and then on a second continuum from the late nineteenth century to the present.

Thus history relates and analyzes events of the past to help explain the changes that have occurred and to aid us in understanding both the past and the present. Although it is impossible to view an event exactly as it happened, it is essential to know and comprehend the period in which an event took place. For example, the invention of gunpowder and the ensuing adaptations in warfare tactics changed the original purpose of the medieval tournament from preparation for war to a "sport spectacular" for the aristocracy. Late nineteenth-century industrial technology prompted many young men to move to the cities and, in an effort to occupy their time, basketball was promoted as an indoor sport. Today, with a television set in almost every home in the United States, marketing demands for advertising and prime-time needs within the television industry heavily influence professional sport.

Another challenge in dealing with *time* is to avoid superimposing today's ideas or standards on those of a former period. We are all creatures locked into our own age, into our own place in the long sequence of events. We are the products of our own past—our family, our town, our country, our decade, and our century—influenced or formed by its education, food, songs, flag, expectations, sports, and language. The unstated beliefs and assumptions that we all share—unstated because these are "perfectly obvious" and unthinkable to argue about—are particularly strong. Ordinarily, this condition is not one to struggle against; but when studying other ages, other countries, and other civilizations, it poses a problem. As students of sport history, we should try with heightened imagination and increased knowledge to understand other persons and the "unstated beliefs and assumptions" of their society, although they may be quite alien to and remote from ours. For example, to understand athletics in ancient Greece, it is useful to know that the Greeks accepted slavery as a necessary part of their society and that being a slave was a normal way of life for some people. Another example from sport history is the attitude of the native American Indians toward dance and games. They did not separate work, play, dance, and games as we do, but made these activities part of their rituals and ceremonies that took place in the normal course of their lives. Many Puritans believed literally in an everlasting hellfire which awaited sinners; therefore they attempted to keep themselves and their neighbors on the narrow path to righteousness, which did *not* include games or sport on Sunday. It would be improper to condemn the New England Puritans' ideas on sport and pastimes on the Sabbath without understanding their "narrow path to righteousness." Today women enter colleges and universities freely, but only one hundred years ago they were excluded from major universities and colleges, partly because they were considered too delicate for the rigors of college life. It would be incorrect to blame the men's colleges and universities for excluding them, without studying the views of women's health prevalent at that time. For each period of history of sport and physical education, it is essential to understand the major events of the time, the scientific and general knowledge that was available then, the prevailing attitudes and values as well as the ways in which the various social groups viewed contemporary problems. Historical events must be studied and understood as a part of the period in which they occurred.

The final idea related to *time* is that the farther away a historical period is from the present, and the more years the period tends to embrace, the easier it is to make generalizations. We speak of the period of the ancient Olympics and about the early Games in general terms. Actually, the ancient Olympics covered approximately twelve hundred years, from 776 B.C. to 393 A.D. Imagine how a historian would be ridiculed for speaking of "recent sport" from 787 A.D. to 1987 A.D. As historians of sport and physical education, we should be careful not to develop false generalizations about a period of time or events that occurred thousands of years ago. The closer we come to our contemporary age, the shorter is the time period that we consider to be significant. As we look back at a series of events of the past, it becomes perilously easy to make generalizations. We often feel that "we can only establish contact by imposing upon people, art, and events a retrospective order that is quite another thing than the rich disorder of involvement. History for us has whitened actuality into abstraction."[6] At the same time, it is easy to become so sensitive to differences and so chary of generalizations that we become tongue-tied historians, incapable of brilliant clarifying generalizations. We must also know that "the card index is not knowledge. It is only the beginning of knowledge, and the accumulation of facts is useless until they are related to each other and seen in proportion."[7]

The third concept to remember is that historians are curious. They seek answers to significant questions that add to our knowledge in sport and physical education. Earlier, history was defined as the memory of things said and done; however, not *everything* that has been said and done can be included in history. Many historians believe that an event is not history until it has been studied and written down: that is, investigated, placed in an accurate context, its significance explained, and the event interpreted.

In seeking answers to questions it is essential to discover as much evidence as is possible to support these answers. In fact, historians use many techniques of the detective in mystery stories.[8] If you enjoy detective stories, you may have a head start in becoming a sport historian. The best evidence for solving a mystery or answering a historical question is called *primary* evidence, consisting of indisputable first-hand evidence that the event occurred. Frequently it is difficult or impossible to locate primary evidence about an event, and then *secondary* evidence must be used, consisting of references derived from a first-hand or other account of the event. For example, we have little primary evidence for the ancient Olympics other than the actual stadium at Olympia, the ruins of the wrestling grounds, the practice tracks, and the gymnasium; however, we have numerous examples of secondary evidence in references to the Games in contemporary writings.

Regardless of whether the evidence is primary or secondary, it must meet certain criteria to be acceptable. It must be relevant, authoritative, consistent with other sources, and fit logically with the other evidence. Furthermore, the historian should understand the period from which the evidence was procured and know its source. Sometimes historical questions seem to defy answers. Historians search and search to find the one piece of unquestionable evidence to answer a particular question. In such instances, curiosity, imagination, a guess, or a hunch may provide the key to the mystery. Under these circumstances applying the detective's approach works well. A logical but unexpected lead to an answer can help direct the historian to a much sought after solution. History, thus, is a continuous search for information about significant events that happened in the past.

To summarize this brief introduction, the three concepts essential to the study of the special history of sport and physical education are:

1. **Who and What**
   History is about real men and women who have both desirable and undesirable characteristics, and about their deeds, both good and bad.
2. **When and Where**
   In history there is only the past. The present is a "fleeting moment of reality," but we can study the past because we have records and memories of events. The historian should understand as thoroughly as possible the period in which an historical event occurred; however, the historian should not transpose contemporary ideas, values, and judgments on earlier periods, and must be careful not to alter the essential truths of the past.
3. **How and Why**
   History asks significant questions, locates evidence, and seeks answers.

The importance of asking the right questions should not be underestimated. Your question may already be answered in sport history literature or it may not be able to be answered because the necessary data do not exist. Beginning sport historians should keep three criteria in mind when asking questions: 1) Does evidence exist that permits me to answer the question? 2) Does evidence exist that allows me to place the question and answer in the proper social, economic, and political contexts? and 3) What will I know after I have answered the question? Is it significant? Will it add to the body of knowledge in the history of sport?

Throughout this discussion you may have been asking the questions, "Why study the history of sport and physical education at all?" "How can the knowledge of history help solve contemporary problems?" This chapter has hinted at answers to these questions, but let us focus on three major reasons for studying the history of sport and physical education.

First, we study such history to enrich our understanding of our civilization, our nation, and our world. For many people this is the most convincing reason for undertaking any study. The more we know about every aspect of our lives, the better we are able to foster humanistic values in our social institutions and to acknowledge the worth of each individual in our society. The roots of sport and physical education in the United States lie in other cultures, some existing twenty-five hundred years ago. To understand such a modern phenomenon as the Olympic Games, the student of sport and physical education should be familiar with the ancient Games as well as the modern ones.

Second, sport historians should understand the historical background of today's problems. For example, until about five hundred years ago many sports were conducted primarily to prepare men for war. Today, sport is conducted for the benefit and pleasure of the performer and/or spectator. A century ago, physical education in colleges was directed by medical doctors to maintain and improve students' health. Today, while physical education specialists retain health as an objective, they also teach the value of lifetime sports and fitness activities. In determining policies to comply with the 1975 federal regulations of Title IX of the Educational Amendments of 1972, both women and men should understand the vastly different philosophies on which men's and women's sport and physical education were established. To explain the reasons for these changes one must know and understand the events of the past. Finally, many people study sport history because they are interested in sport and enjoy knowing more about it.

The history of sport and physical education—the investigation, analysis, synthesis, and interpretation of events—is a relatively recent phenomenon. Although Homer and Virgil describe spectacular sport events, the author of *Beowulf* presents a memorable swimming experience, and many medieval manuscripts depict sporting scenes, these accounts and pictures "show-and-tell" but do not explain the meaning of sport and physical education in the lives of people. The current trend to interpret and explain sport as cultural phenomena began in the early years of the twentieth century. In 1915 Fred E. Leonard provided insights into the origin of men's intercollegiate sport, exercise programs, and early leaders of college physical education, but his work did not have the impact of Frederic L. Paxson's seminal article in 1917, "The Rise of Sport." E. Norman Gardiner's *Athletics of the Ancient World* and John Allen Krout's *Annals of American Sport* have become classics in modern sport history. Foster Rhea Dulles' *America Learns to Play* added important interpretations to the place of sport in American life. John Rickards Betts' *America's Sporting Heritage* is recognized as a major influence on contemporary sport history. His wealth of detail, perceptive insights, and interpretation of relationships between sport and industrialization in the United States mark this work as a major contribution to sport history. Deobold B. Van Dalen and Bruce L. Bennett's textbook, *A World History of Physical Education,* added significantly to the understanding of physical education and sport in educational institutions.

In recent years the number of books, monographs, review essays, and specialized articles focusing on the history of sport and physical education has grown, providing overwhelming evidence of sport and physical education throughout the history of the United States and other countries. For example we now know of contests on remote western military outposts in the late nineteenth century, how workers in Worcester, Massachusetts, spent their leisure time at the turn of the century, more about the Spanish legacy in early rodeos, details about physical education in elementary schools in earlier decades, and something of women's leisure activities in the South. As knowledge has increased many scholars have proposed helpful theoretical constructs to explain the history of sport and physical education in the United States. Differing approaches to causation and varying interpretations of the same events expand a reader's consciousness, and therefore we urge you to read widely in sport history. Two journals will be especially helpful, the *Journal of Sport History* and the *Canadian Journal of History of Sport.* Other scholarly journals, which may be found in most libraries, also publish articles on sport history and physical education.

This *History of Sport and Physical Education in the United States* examines the intricate web of interacting forces in United States history, as these have affected the development of contemporary sport and physical education. The titles of Chapters 2 through 7 set forth briefly the central focus of this book, the transformation of colonial pastimes and diversions to contemporary sport for everyone and the change from nineteenth-century gymnastics to the present physical education program of fitness activities, dance, and sport. Chapter 2 examines the place of pastimes and recreational activities in the lives of the people who influenced the period of exploration and colonization of the North American continent: the European settlers, American Indians, and Africans. In the title of Chapter 3 *pastimes* comes before *sport,* suggesting that pastimes were more prevalent than organized sport, but that some sport did exist. This was also the period of the first attempts to include physical education in schools. Chapter 4, "From Games to Sport and From Exercise to Physical Education," tells of the transformation of early pastimes to organized sport and the beginnings of sport as we know it today. This chapter then deals with the change of exercises to physical education in schools.

The title of Chapter 5, "The Organizing of Sport and Physical Education," reflects the development of structures which govern professional, amateur, recreational, and educational sport. The commissioner form of governance for professional sport, national and international sport federations, and the professional physical education associations all began in this period. Chapter 6 tells of "The Growth of Sport and Physical Education During Social Change," the boom of the 1920s, the depression of the 1930s, and World War II in the 1940s. Finally, Chapter 7 recounts the rapid growth of sport and physical education since World War II, "Sport and Physical Education for Everyone."

Six major themes that affected the history of sport and physical education in this country are developed throughout the book. It should be noted that these themes do not unfold evenly from chapter to chapter. Each theme looms large or recedes according to the realities of the period. Hence, in some chapters certain themes will be treated more fully while others will receive less attention.

The first theme is the American expectation of "the good life." When the authors of the Declaration of Independence sought a rallying cry for a heterogeneous group of colonists, they wrote some extraordinarily dynamic words: "We hold these truths to be self-evident, that all men are created equal, that they are endowed by their Creator with certain inalienable Rights, that among these are Life, Liberty and the pursuit of happiness." This last phrase, which still resonates in American ears, provides this book with its first theme. The "pursuit of happiness" has come to be equated with the "good life," and for many Americans this includes watching and participating in sport. Included in the "good life" are health, education, satisfactory work and income, together with leisure time to pursue and enjoy personal interests. In the United States the conception of the "good life" has increasingly come to include everyone, regardless of sex, color, or handicapping condition.

The next theme is the number and diversity of contributions to our American culture from the customs of many countries and societies. From the beginning, daily life in the new land necessitated changes from old ways; and daily lives in many neighborhoods, towns, states, and regions blended ideas and customs from various sources. To understand today's sport and physical education it is necessary to explore why the colonists came to this country, what the later immigrants expected, and what continues to draw people to the United States. The pastimes and amusements of these people had to be adapted to many different living patterns in America, from the stern life of New England Puritan villages to the rough and tumble survival of the frontier. The process of learning to be an American—games on city streets, factory life, cattle ranch customs, different daily foods, going to school every day—must also be examined.

United States citizens have come from more than fifty principal countries. Over the years ethnic groups, particularly the first and second generations, have attempted to maintain their traditional customs and, at the same time, absorb American behaviors and values. Ethnic groups clearly influenced sport and physical education in the United States, but easily recognizable "American" patterns have evolved. At the 1889 Conference on the Interest of Physical Training the great plea was to devise an *American* system of exercise. The three most popular sports in the United States—football, baseball, and basketball—have either been modified to be *American* or were invented in this country.

The first two themes lead to the third—the perceived values that guide and influence the daily lives of the people in this country. The values of the New England Puritans which reinforced the characteristics necessary for survival in the new country determined the early moral principles from which the American work and achievement ethic evolved. This influence has been pervasive. Sunday was set aside as a day of worship and even now in many states, laws regulate commercial and social activities on Sunday. Just as the Puritan and, later, Protestant morality changed to nineteenth-century tenets of "faith and good works" and the "social gospel," attitudes toward sport and physical education changed, until both were considered beneficial and were absorbed into mainstream American culture.

The pattern of daily living has greatly affected sport. For example the number of hours at work has decreased, the time for leisure has increased, more holidays have been observed, and discretionary income for fitness activities, sport, and amusement has become more widely available. Again, one must remember that not all Americans have the same values. Throughout the history of this country certain sports have been questioned on the basis of brutality, lack of honesty, and gambling. Today some forms of professional wrestling and boxing raise concerns as to whether or not they are competitive or should even be considered sport. In the past cockfighting and other "blood" sports have raised similar questions.

The fourth theme in the history of sport and physical education in the United States is the pattern of social organization which has developed in this country, including gender role expectations and social stratification. Throughout history society has assigned specific roles and tasks to men and women. Traditionally, men were the providers and defenders of the family and community and women were the homemakers, caring for the husband and rearing the family. With the impact of modernization on society, these roles have been reexamined and somewhat altered. These changes and their effect on sport and physical education will be examined throughout the text.

The effect of social stratification on sport will also be studied. In spite of the founders' high ideals and the optimistic expectations of the settlers and immigrants, the realities of economic and social life have led to social classes in this country. Many of the early arrivals soon became the entrenched or "upper" class, and over the years social stratification has been evident, reflecting in varying degrees birth, education, wealth, and personal achievement. A certain ambivalence characterizes our attitude toward social class. We may admire the wealthy and famous, but we applaud both political and sport heroes who come from humble or modest beginnings. We accept social mobility and economic mobility, both of which have profoundly affected United States' sport and physical education history.

For much of this country's history, sport was considered the province of upper-class men and boys. Gradually, sport reached middle-class men, working-class men, upper-class women, blacks, middle-class women, other minorities, and persons with special needs. Education, and thus physical education, followed a similar pattern. The diffusion of sport and physical education to all sectors of society is an important development in the United States.

The fifth major theme is the intermixing of technology, industrialization, immigration, and urbanization, as they have influenced the development of sport and physical education. From the beginning the settlers had to adapt the old ways of Europe to the new life in this country; thus contriving, adapting, "making-do" became a part of our self-knowledge. Americans have traditionally liked "tinkering," which sometimes led to inventions and then to important contributions to transportation, communication, and industrialization. During our history more and more immigrants learned new ways of earning their livelihood, occupying their time, and pursuing their ideas of happiness, and for many this included sport, exercise, physical activities, and dance. The railroad enabled the Cincinnati Red Stockings to make an extended baseball tour in 1869. In the late nineteenth century the bicycle changed women's fashions. Television now brings sport into almost every home in this country. The equipment and clothing required for many modern sports are the result of inventions and manufacturing innovations.

The sixth and last theme is the changing conceptualization and justification of sport and physical education. Earlier in this chapter sport was defined as those activities involving physical prowess and skill, competition, strategy and/or chance, and engaged in for the enjoyment and satisfaction of the participant and/or others. Sport fulfills the human need for physical challenge and competition. It also provides a sense of community, a sharing of common rituals, symbols, and ceremonies. In addition, identification with a group or team enables one to glory in vicarious achievements of victory or empathize with defeat. This is modern sport. The simple pastimes and leisure activities of colonial times were very different and it is the forces that created modern sport that will be examined.

Sport scholars VanderZwaag and Sheehan have identified specific characteristics of modern sport.[9] A careful comparison of today's sport with these characteristics shows that colonial pastimes and diversions changed to become "modern" sport by the middle of the nineteenth century, but that it still was not a major cultural force at that time. Justification for sport also changed. Early horse racing was considered important to improve the breed. By the 1870s the nonutilitarian purpose of sport was evident as men cheered for their city's baseball team and upper-class women enjoyed the recently imported game of tennis. Since that time sport has expanded and become more complex. Sport in the 1980s is accepted as a major component of popular culture and a pervasive force in American society. Changes in the conceptualization and justification of what had previously been games and diversions to modern sport is one aspect of this final theme.

Another aspect is the conceptualization and justification of physical education and sport in educational institutions. Today's physical education has been defined as a program of physical activities, usually in educational institutions, including exercise, dance, and sport. These activities represent a marked change from the separate men's and women's gymnastics programs of the 1880s, instituted to improve students' health. At about the same time that sport was becoming "modern," reformers, medical doctors, and educators promoted health through exercise. Schools and colleges adopted exercise programs as physical "training" or "education." As educational theory changed, so did the curriculum which slowly evolved into the present broad program of exercise, dance, and sport.

One aspect of the program, intercollegiate athletics, also required justification. For men, intercollegiate athletics began as informal student challenges between institutions. As the contests became more intense and popular, problems arose that led to students' sports being placed under the control of the institutions. A century later women's sport in schools and colleges moved to intercollegiate athletics through legislation banning discrimination on the basis of sex. Today, men's and women's intercollegiate athletic programs are governed by the same national associations. A single association also governs both the boys' and girls' programs at the high school level. These changes in the conceptualization and justification of physical education and sport in educational institutions, some taking place slowly and others rapidly, complete the final theme of this book.

These themes—the expectations of "the good life" for every citizen, the diversity in which American culture is grounded, the perceived values that govern daily living, social organization, the intermixing of technology and urbanization, and the conceptualization of today's sport and physical education—help us understand the history of sport and physical education in the United States.

The History of Sport and Physical Education in the United States traces and explains the changes that have occurred in this country to make sport a pervasive influence in United States society. It also shows how physical education has become an important component of education. It focuses on the modifications and adaptations of these activities to eventually include everyone. It is an exciting story that deepens our understanding of the United States of America.

Suggestions for Further Reading

1. Adelman, Melvin L. "Academicians and American Athletics: A Decade of Progress." *Journal of Sport History* 10, No. 1 (Spring 1983):80–106.
2. Handlin, Oscar. *Truth in History*. Cambridge: Harvard University, 1979.
3. Loy, John W., Jr. "The Nature of Sport: A Definitional Effort." *Quest* 10 (May 1968):1–15.
4. Morison, Samuel Eliot. *The Oxford History of the American People*. New York: Oxford University Press, 1965.
5. Struna, Nancy L. "E. P. Thompson's Notion of 'Context' and the Writing of Physical Education and Sport History." *Quest* 38, No. 1 (1986):22–32.

Notes

1. Sir Thomas Elyot, *The Boke Named the Governour,* vol. II, ed. H. H. S. Croft (London: C. Kegan Paul & Co., 1880), 387.
2. Samuel Johnson, *A Dictionary of the English Language* (Dublin: Thomas Ewing, 1775).
3. John W. Loy, Jr. "The Nature of Sport: A Definitional Effort," *Quest* 10 (May 1968):1.
4. Carl Becker, *Everyman His Own Historian* (Chicago: Quadrangle Books, 1966), 235.
5. A. L. Rowse, *The Use of History* (New York: Collier Books, 1963), 24.
6. Joseph Kerman, *The Beethoven Quartets* (New York: Alfred A. Knopf, 1967), 4.
7. C. V. Wedgwood, *The Sense of the Past* (New York: Collier Books, 1960), 91.
8. Robin W. Winks, *The Historian as Detective* (New York: Harper & Row, 1968).
9. Harold J. VanderZwaag and Thomas J. Sheehan, *Introduction to Sport Studies* (Dubuque, IA: Wm. C. Brown, 1978), 17–27.

Time Line

HISTORY

1400–1519
Aztec Empire
1438–1538
Inca Empire
1492
Columbus landed on American shores
1517
Reformation began with Luther
1565
Spanish founded St. Augustine
1580
Drake landed near San Francisco
1607
First permanent colony in Virginia
1609
Spanish founded Santa Fe
1619
First Africans landed in America
1620
First permanent colony in
Massachusetts
1633
Massachusetts Bay laws requiring work
1636
Harvard College opened
1639
First printing press, at Harvard
1704
First newspaper, Boston
1730s–1740s
Great Awakening

1769
James Watt patented the steam engine
1776
Declaration of Independence

SPORT AND PHYSICAL EDUCATION

1424
Margot, Frenchwoman, hand tennis
champion

1564
LeMoyne painted Indian life
1598–1599
Shakespeare used "tennis" reference

1618
English King James' *Book of Sport*

1643
Account of Indian football
1665
Horse racing in New York
1732
Schuylkill Fishing Company, Philadelphia
1736
Admission charged to horse race
1762
Little Pretty Pocket Book
1766
Jockey Club founded in Philadelphia
1768
Horse racing, Long Island

2 Peoples That Influenced American Sport and Physical Education, 1492–1776

Overview

The written history of sport and physical education in the United States of America begins with the first accounts of Columbus and other early explorers of the fifteenth and sixteenth centuries. These accounts were only the beginning of information about America, for "the New World was revealed: not suddenly with the news of Christopher Columbus's landfall, but very gradually over the course of more than half a century."[1] Early explorers described exotic plants and extraordinary birds and animals in the new land which conjured up for many Europeans a mystical, mythical country filled with marvels. "We found the people most gentle, loving, and faithfull, voide of all guile and treason, and such as live after the maner of the golden age."[2] Where everything was strange, perhaps the strangest of all were the inhabitants. The natives differed in many ways from the explorers—in their dwellings, language, color, religious beliefs, and also in their dances, games, and pastimes.

Cortés, in 1528, demonstrated these differences when he took back with him to Europe Mexican jugglers and ball players to exhibit at the Spanish court. LéMoyne, an artist who accompanied the explorer Laudonniere on an early voyage, depicted Indians playing a ball game, and John White, another seventeenth-century artist, painted the natives of Virginia fishing and dancing. Later Torquemada described a ball, made of a "strange, resilient material" which bounced, and much later a traveler in the South recounted a ball game in which players carried "in their hands two wooden spoons, curiously carved, not unlike our large iron spoons."[3] Frobisher's mariners in 1576 saw "a number of small things fleeting in the Sea a farre off, whyche he supposed to be Porposes, or Ceales, or some kind of a strange fishe"[4] but were Eskimos in kayaks. These reports of a rubber ball, lacrosse, and kayaks, all unknown in Europe at that time, provide evidence of sport and sport-like activities among indigenous inhabitants of the newly discovered continent.

These native Americans or Indians were one of three very different groups of people, each of which has had a distinctive influence on sport and physical education in the United States. In addition to the native Americans, there were Europeans and Africans. The early European settlers, mostly English, brought with them a rich heritage of pastimes, games, and sport, which are still to be seen on playgrounds and sports fields today. The Africans, most of whom came to this country as slaves, carried with them a heritage of games and dances which survived through their persistence and their devotion to far-off memories. Today Americans of African descent play a significant role in all forms of sport.

This chapter will examine briefly these three major contributors to colonial American culture—and hence sport and physical education—and then consider life in early America. First we will look at the culture, sports, and games of the native Americans whom the explorers found living on the new continent. Next we will investigate the games and pastimes of seventeenth-century England, the homeland of many of the early settlers. This will be followed by a survey of life in the West African countries, from which Africans were enslaved and brought to this continent.

Life on the new continent changed dramatically from the midsixteenth century when a group of Spaniards settled St. Augustine, Florida, and the early seventeenth century when English people founded the Virginia and Massachusetts colonies to the beginning of the American Revolution. In the more than 150 years of colonization immigrants came not only from Spain and England, but also from most of the western European and western African countries. In the 1770s the colonial population numbered a little more than two million, located largely along the eastern seaboard. Most of the people were Protestant, either Puritan or Anglican, but among the settlers were some forty thousand Roman Catholics and a small number of Jewish people. Although this country has always known a variety of religions, many of the colonial leaders were Protestant, and therefore Protestant views dominated public policy and daily life.

Settlers came to this country for a variety of reasons—to escape religious discrimination, to establish their own religious communities, to make fortunes, to better their lives and their families' lives, and some because they were forced into slavery. All found the new land drastically different from the homes they had left. Survival was the first order of business. Many died because of famine, disease, or hygienic practices of the period. After the settlements had become permanently established, a peculiarly American mode of life developed. Economically, the colonists depended on the natural environment for native crops such as tobacco and on the sea for products such as fish. Of necessity, they developed a practical bent, tinkering and inventing what was needed. Although women had no legal or political rights, their services were valued. The relatively few women in the colonies cared for their homes and gardens, saw to the education of their children, and when necessary performed a variety of tasks ranging from tavern keeper to printer. Sometimes children were taught in the home and sometimes they attended a local school. The need for an educated citizenry was recognized early.

Life varied considerably from colony to colony. When the colonists found time for diversion, they participated in "useful" recreations such as fishing and hunting or group efforts known as "bees" to raise a house or barn. The children played games, probably adaptations from early English and European pastimes. Many men, proud of their horses, raced them to prove their speed and worth, noting that improving the breed of horse was worthwhile. Everyone—children, women and men—enjoyed simple pastimes such as sleigh rides, picnics, bees, horse races, and Muster Days when men gathered to practice riflery and other skills necessary for the community's defense.

Sport and physical education as we know them today and as they are defined in the previous chapter did not exist in this period, 1492–1776. However, a social and cultural climate which led to sport and physical education did exist. The purpose of this chapter is to establish the conditions in colonial America and the pastimes from which sport and physical education evolved. To understand these conditions it is necessary to know something about each culture, as well as to understand how the people of each culture lived their daily lives, and why they engaged in their chosen pastimes. This chapter provides an important background for the history of sport and physical education in the United States.

The Native Americans

Authorities estimate that when Columbus reached the New World, about one million people, speaking some 600 dialects, inhabited the area of what is now the United States of America. Scholars theorize that ages ago the native Americans or Indians wandered east across the Bering Strait to Alaska and traveled southeast, fanning out over the continent. Hundreds of cultures developed and lived side by side, each with its own language, customs, and means of livelihood. These cultures can be grouped according to geographical areas— northeast, southeast, plains and prairies, southwest, basin and plateau, California, and northwest.

The northeast Indians occupied the land north of Tennessee and east of the Mississippi River. Some time between 1570 and 1600 five tribes, later six, including the Iroquois and Algonquian, banded together in the Iroquois League of Five Nations. During the colonial period the League controlled much of the area north of Albany, New York, up to Canada. The Indians lived in tribes in which strong family ties usually existed. In their villages the women farmed and managed the households while the men hunted and, at times, engaged in warfare with neighboring tribes. By the time the explorers arrived, weaving, braiding, carving, and pottery had been developed.

In the southeast the Indians honored warriors who engaged in war for the thrill and prestige of the kill. They lived in small villages or settlements, farmed, hunted, and fought with nearby tribes. With the invasion of the white man along the eastern seaboard, many Indian groups were pushed westward until the prairies west of the Mississippi River accommodated a number of different Indian cultures. Many established villages, raised crops, and lived a settled life, as did a number of the prairie Indian tribes. Other nomadic tribes, using the horse recently introduced by the Spaniards and the guns brought by the explorers, developed the characteristic culture we think of as "typical" of the plains Indian, galloping in eagle-feathered headdress and leather leggings, shooting buffalo.

Among the southwest Indians were pueblo dwellers and nomads, both of whom traded with the permanent settlers for their food and other needs. Many of the southwest tribes were peaceful, fighting only to protect their property or themselves. From the southern part of Colorado north to Canada, the Indians hunted and roamed in bands rather than as permanent tribes.

The plateau and basin Indians were seminomadic, moving about their loosely defined territories, fishing, hunting, and gathering food. Their tribal life lacked some of the complex organization of other Indians, but generally they were peaceful and industrious. One of the more simple social subcultures was that of the Indians who lived in California's ideal climate. Their tribal organization was informal, their homes modest, and their crafts limited.

Perhaps the wealthiest of the native Americans were the experienced sailors and fishermen who fished along the northwest coast. Fish was plentiful, and wealth in the form of food, baskets, and blankets, easy to acquire. Slaves from captured tribes helped in the everyday work. For these northwest Indians, life centered around the villages and the "potlatch," a feast during which the host Indian gave his guests many gifts and thus redistributed the wealth among the group.

In spite of their cultural diversity, the Indians had certain common beliefs and practices regarding religion, myths, and rituals. The native Americans organized their daily life around tribal needs and around the natural rhythms of days and seasons. They did not separate their time into arbitrary periods for work, play, and worship. Our eight-hour day, our weekends, our Saturday or Sunday worship observances would seem incomprehensibly narrow to them.

Most tribes worshipped a great spirit as the central force in the universe. They also ascribed supernatural powers to natural objects such as trees. The Indians observed the sky and the earth, sun and moon, day and night, male and female, and expressed these dualities as the Divine Twins in many of their myths and legends. According to Culin these twins were the patrons of play and were pleased when men played their games.[5] Implements like a lacrosse stick were derived from sacred objects ascribed to the twins; they included a throwing club, bow and arrow, lance, and a netted shield.

Rituals reflected the beliefs of the Indians' daily lives and provided rules of action to be followed in almost every situation. Some rituals, repeated accurately, assured the continuation of the tribe through the proper recognition of controlling forces and the observance of certain ceremonies. Others acted out taboos such as that described in the lacrosse game (p. 22). Rituals, and the games played as rituals, usually celebrated a particular time of month, year, or a special occasion. Usually a medicine man or specially designated person presided at tribal ceremonies and rituals. These had to be performed in a precise way to assure fertility in the tribe, an adequate food supply, victory in war, and to prevent disaster from striking the tribe. Children learned their culture and the behavior expected of them by observing the rituals and ceremonies and hearing legends and myths; they were thus initiated into the daily, seasonal, and yearly life of the tribe.

Ritualistic rhythmic movement or dancing was central to the Indian cultures. Nicholas Cresswell took part in one Indian dance:

> Painted by my Squaw in the most elegant manner. Divested of all my clothes, except my Calico short breechclout, leggings, and Mockesons. A fire was made which we danced round with little order, whooping and hallooing in a most frightful manner. I was but a novice at the diversion and by endeavouring to act as they did made them a great deal of sport and ingratiated me much in their esteem. This is the most violent exercise to the adepts in the art I ever saw. No regular figure, but violent distortion of features, writhing and twisting the body in the most uncouth and antic postures imaginable. Their music is an old Keg with one head knocked out and covered with a skin and beat with sticks which regulates their times. The men have strings of Deer's hoofs tied round their ankles and knees, and gourds with shot or pebblestones in them in their hands which they continually rattle. The women have Morris bells or Thimbles with holes in the bottom and strung upon a leather thong tied round their ankles, knees and waists. The jingling of these Bells and Thimbles, the rattling of the Deer's hoofs and gourds, beating of the drum and kettle, with the horrid yells of the Indians, render it the most unharmonious concert, that human idea can possibly conceive. It is a favourite diversion, in which I am informed they spend a great part of their time in Winter.[6]

The early explorers observed many activities which resembled European games and hence identified them as games. However, the "games" of the native Americans, like their dances, may have been ceremonial rather than for entertainment or pleasure. Men and women played the same games, but each had separate games also. Men played lacrosse and other ball games as well as target games, while women engaged in shinny and double-ball.

Games of the Native Americans

While many different games have been discovered, four ball games are of special interest in the history of sport.

Lacrosse

When a French Jesuit missionary saw a game played by Indians with objects resembling a bishop's crosier, he called the game "lacrosse," but other early explorers and travelers referred to the game as rackets. The Indians knew the game as baggataway. It was played throughout the country—by the Algonquians and Iroquoians in the east, the Dakotas in the west, the Muskhogeans in the south, the Chinook and Salish in the northwest, and occasionally the Californians in the far west. For their games native Americans did not use standardized playing fields and equipment, a prescribed number of players on a team, or official rules. The tribal customs, the occasion, the weather, and other factors determined these facets of the game. The playing area or "field" might be the size of the men's modern lacrosse field (60 × 110 yards) for small teams or it might be the distance between two villages when the men of one tribe challenged those of another tribe to a game. For some games tall poles a few feet apart marked the goals, while in other games posts were the goals. The object of all the games was to advance a ball across the opponent's goal or hit the goal post with the ball by throwing and catching the ball with one or two sticks. Balls made of skin and stuffed with hair, or knots of wood burned round, might be used in the Indian game. The sticks varied from about eighteen inches in length to four feet, with a netted portion at one end for catching and throwing the ball. Figure 2.1 illustrates a racket game in which each player, dressed ceremoniously, carries two sticks.

Games marked many occasions. Originally, baggataway is thought to have had deep religious significance and healing powers. Games were played at special seasons in connection with certain festive or religious rites. Also, they were played to please the gods, secure fertility, produce rain, prolong life, cure illness, insure victory, or expel demons. Special dances, ceremonies, and rituals preceded and accompanied the games. Characteristic of most native American games was heavy betting. Many myths evolved around the game, such as the one reported by Culin:

> Some old people say the moon is a ball which was thrown up against the sky in a game a long time ago. They say that two towns were playing against each other, but one of them had the best runners and had almost won the game when the leader of the other side picked up the ball with his hand—a thing that is not allowed in the game—and tried to throw to the goal, but it struck against the solid sky vault and was fastened there, to remind players never to cheat. When the moon is small and pale, it is because some one has handled the ball unfairly, and for this reason they formerly played only at the time of a full moon.[7]

Figure 2.1   Lacrosse or racket game of native Americans, by George Catlin. Courtesy of Department of Library Services, American Museum of Natural History.

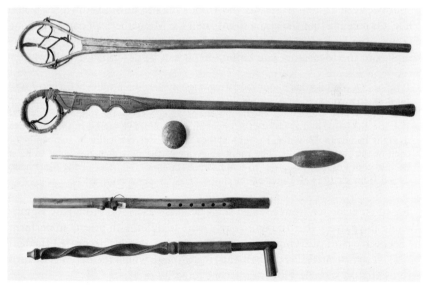

Figure 2.2   Lacrosse sticks and balls (with other artifacts) used in native American games. Courtesy of Department of Library Services, American Museum of Natural History.

Figure 2.3   Terra cotta model of a Mexican ball court, 1000–1500 A.D. Courtesy of the Worcester Art Museum, Worcester, Massachusetts.

Other Games and Sports

Two games without names have been discovered. One is similar to the Mesoamerican rubber ball game. Courts like those in Mexico have been found in southwestern United States at the Hohokam site in Snaketown, Arizona. While it is possible that the game stems from the Mesoamerican game of about 1500 B.C., the Hohokam courts are dated about 800 A.D. Assuming the game is similar to the Mesoamerican ball game, it can be described as follows:

> It is . . . a combination of our modern games of basketball, volleyball, soccer, and *jai-alai.* It was played in a high-walled, paved court (usually 100 to 125 feet long and 20 to 50 feet wide) . . . the floor plans of which were in the shape of a "capital I" . . . the game had as its key the knocking of a solid, five-pound rubber ball, five to eight inches in diameter, through stone "hoops" set vertically in the center of each of the two long walls. The main objective of the play does not seem to have been to gain ground, . . . but to score. Since the inner diameter of the stone hoop varied from six to twelve inches, making a "goal" was no easy task.[8]

Based on evidence from Mexico some scholars ascribe a ritualistic significance to the game. Near the ball courts were temples with priests to perform the necessary rites. Carvings of sacred objects and animals decorated the ball courts. At some court sites the ball and ring through which the ball was thrown were treated as sacred, with rituals conducted by priests.

Another ball game was reported by Laudonniere, on a sixteenth-century visit to Florida, but it does not appear to have been played elsewhere: "They exercise their young men to become excellent runners, and they give prizes to those who have the greatest endurance. They often practice at archery. They

Figure 2.4   Basketball-type game of Florida Indians, by Jacques LeMoyne. Courtesy of Department of Library Services, American Museum of Natural History.

play ball in the following fashion: They use a tree standing in an open place, a tree eight or nine armlengths in height. At the top of the tree there is a square made from wood strips, and the scorer is the one who hits the square."[9] Other ball games included a "football" game in which the hands could not be used to advance the ball toward the opponents' goal. The object of the game was to get the ball across the opposing team's goal posts, which were about a mile from the defenders' goal. Men played hoop-and-pole, which consisted of throwing a spear or shooting an arrow at a rolling hoop or ring. Tribes differed in the way they rolled or shot at the hoops, which also varied in size and design.

The Indians used bows and arrows in wars with other tribes, in competitions, and in hunting for food. LeMoyne, the artist accompanying a sixteenth-century French expedition to Florida, described how the Indians hunted:

The Indians have a way of hunting deer which we never saw before. They manage to put on skins of the largest which have previously been taken, in such a manner, with the heads on their own heads, that they can see out of the eyes as through a mask. Thus accoutred, they can approach close to the deer without frightening them. They take advantage of the time when the animals come to drink at the stream, and having their bows and arrows all ready, easily shoot them, as they are plentiful in those regions.[10]

Figure 2.5   Game of tchungkee or hoop and pole, by George Catlin. Courtesy of Department of Library Services, American Museum of Natural History.

Figure 2.6   Florida Indians hunting deer, by Jacques LeMoyne. Courtesy of Department of Library Services, American Museum of Natural History.

Men played shinny, a game like field hockey, with an unlimited number on each side. Women also played shinny, but never with the men. Each player used a long-handled wooden stick, from two to four feet long and curved at the bottom. The game began when a medicine man or umpire put the ball in the middle of the field by tossing it in the air, putting it in a hole, or covering it with dirt. At a signal the players rushed toward their opponents' goal. Ordinarily the first team to score four goals won the game.

Besides playing shinny, women also played a game known as "double-ball," which used two balls or two blocks—of wood or other material—connected by a rawhide thong about six to twelve inches long. Using sticks from two to six feet long, the players caught the cord between the two balls and passed these double-balls forward over the opponents' goal line, a "line" of posts or piles of dirt. The goals might be anywhere from six hundred feet to a mile apart. Ordinarily five to ten women played the game, but any number might join in. The game started by tossing the double-ball up in the air, after which the teams attempted to pass the double-ball between the goal posts or over the goal line. As in many games, the double-ball could not be touched with the hands.

Our Legacy from the Native Americans

The native American games that the explorers and early settlers first viewed had several common characteristics. First, adults and not children played these games. Second, the teams were large, sometimes consisting of an entire village or a segment of a tribe, and the playing area often ranged over the countryside from village to village. Lacrosse, football, and shinny were contested by two teams intent on attacking each team's territory to determine a winner. Third, these large teams created a mass excitement or frenzy. Fourth, heavy betting generally accompanied all sport events or games.

The explorers did not and perhaps could not realize that these activities may not have been "games" in the European sense of the word. In the sixteenth and seventeenth centuries the native Americans' view of life may have called for activities which were ritualistic in nature to propitiate their gods and secure the continued survival of the tribe or village.

Evidence of Indian sport and games abound in today's sport world. While double-ball has not survived and shinny is relegated to informal neighborhood contests, lacrosse is played in schools and colleges. It should be noted that few women in any other society at that time played such vigorous games. Today canoes and kayaks, used by Indians for transportation and fishing, provide recreation for millions and intensive competition for special enthusiasts. Hiking and backpacking remind us even more of the wilderness that the country has inherited from those who lived on this continent and welcomed the settlers with gifts and without guile.

The European Settlers

Although European explorers had probed the North American continent as early as the eleventh century, not until the early seventeenth century were permanent settlements established in what is now the United States. During that period European countries emerged from medieval feudalism into recognizably modern forms of government with a national identity. Radically different ways of thinking about the world were demonstrated in their separate ways, by Copernicus, Shakespeare, Michelangelo, and Calvin.

As people's lives changed, their ways of amusing themselves changed. During this period the word "sport" referred broadly to field sports such as hunting, diversions such as games and contests, and recreations such as dancing. When Columbus discovered America, the nobility still jousted in tournaments and enjoyed hawking parties. The peasants were restricted to the land and lived according to the whims of the nobility or large landowners. Their amusements, pastimes, and sport followed the seasonal patterns and festivals of the agricultural and religious year. The middle class or town dwellers grew both in number and influence, but as far as sport and social graces were concerned, they emulated the aristocracy.

Sport and Pastimes of the Nobility

The nobleman was the head of his family and his main responsibilities consisted of looking after his estate, his family, and his vassals. However, much of his time was spent either in fighting real battles or mock battles in tournaments.

The early tourneys served to develop and maintain the military, economic, and social aspects of chivalry. As the nobility emerged from the medieval feudal system of inherited authority, titles, and land, the aristocracy saw themselves as a social group with a distinctive way of life. A chivalric code of honor was adhered to in which the "true" knight was admired for his honor, bravery, fair treatment of his foe, and his protection of ladies. At its height, in the fourteenth and into the fifteenth century, a tournament might be part of almost any occasion—a wedding, a victory, settling a grudge, or simply the desire to test a knight's strength. With the increasing use of gunpowder and its effect on the fighting style in warfare, however, the purpose of the tournament became largely social, reaffirming the traditional codes of chivalry and membership in the aristocracy.

Along with tournaments and jousting, chivalry and feudalism made way for the new mercantile world. However, vestiges of knightly codes of honor could be found in the specialized appurtenances of games—rules, referees, fields, players—as these established the norms of the social behavior of "gentlemen." The legacy of the tournament, which had died out by the seventeenth century, was the identification of sport as a status symbol that helped set the aristocracy apart from the other classes. Further, the pomp and pageantry of the medieval "sport spectacular" can be seen in the use of terms today such as the Tournament of Roses. Another use of the word *tournament,* meaning a series of competitions such as a tennis tournament, reflects the jousts found in the medieval tournaments.

Hunting and Hawking

Both hunting and hawking were favorite sports of the nobility. Everyone of "gentle" birth hunted and hawked—the nobles, the clergy, the ladies, and the young people. Highly bred dogs and carefully tended falcons or hawks, ornately hooded, were the constant companions of noblemen and noblewomen. Queen Elizabeth I, always fond of outdoor pursuits, was reported by a courtier to enjoy hunting when she was seventy-seven years of age. A hawking party was an all-day occasion for sport and merriment:

> Assuredly it is an exhilarating sight to see the castle folk go hawking on a fine morning. The baron, baroness, and all their older relatives and guests, each with bird on gauntlet, are on tall horses; the squires and younger people have sparrow hawks to send against the smaller prey, but the leaders of the sport will wait until they can strike a swift duck or heron. Dogs will race along to flush the game. Horns are blowing, young voices laughing, all the horses prancing. . . . Away they go— racing over fences, field and fallow, thicket and brook, until fate sends to view a heron. Then all the hawks are unhooded together; there are shouts, encouragement, merry wagers, and helloing as the birds soar in the chase. The heron may meet his fate far in the blue above. Then follow more racing and scurrying to recover the hawks. So onward, covering many miles of country, until, with blood tingling, all canter back . . . in a determined mood for supper.[11]

Hunting and hawking epitomized the carefully nurtured idea of the aristocracy—a specially defined way of life requiring a specific code of conduct. Owning dogs, hawks, and horses, all of which were expensive and required trained servants to feed, tend, and train them properly, was further evidence of being a member of the aristocracy. The restrictions placed on land or the defining of hunting preserves by the noblemen or clergy, who were often of noble birth, were made on the basis of social position.

A study of the medieval nobility reveals that the nobleman's sport fulfilled both the function of a necessary daily activity and that of sport. Hunting and hawking provided meat for the table, but both were also engaged in for enjoyment and the satisfaction of handling the hawks and the horses. Those few

Figure 2.7   Early sixteenth-century tournament in Europe. Reproduced by permission of the British Library Board.

Figure 2.8   Medieval tennis court. Reproduced by permission of the British Library Board.

members of the aristocracy who emigrated to America settled in Maryland and Virginia. After the early years when everyone struggled for survival, they emulated the lives of the English aristocracy. With their large estates and luxurious style of living, the plantation owners or gentry hunted, hawked, and enjoyed life much like their English counterparts.

Other Sports
Diversions such as court tennis also absorbed the time and attention of the nobles. By the thirteenth century the well-developed game of court tennis (*tenetz* or *tenes*) provided them with a favorite pastime. Its basic action, hitting a ball back and forth between two persons, links it to modern tennis, but in other respects it differed. The tennis court is said to have evolved from the rectangular monastery courtyards where clerics indulged in a form of tennis or handball. Called *jeu de paume,* the game of the palm of the hand, it was something like handball played in a court, with the ball hit over a net and also bounced against the walls and roof of the court. In the course of centuries the game passed from monasteries into secular life, where it became a favorite with men and women of the nobility, who often enjoyed a game in elaborate courts within their castle walls. Court tennis provided Shakespeare with a memorable scene: the French court could think of nothing more expressive of

their contempt for the "frivolous playboy" Henry V of England than to bring him, ceremoniously, a "treasure" of a trunk of tennis balls. Infuriated, the English king responds with ironic restraint:

> We are glad the Dauphin is so pleasant with us.
> His present and your pains we thank you for.
> When we have match'd our rackets to these balls,
> We will, in France, by God's grace, play a set
> Shall strike his father's crown into the hazard.
> Tell him he hath made a match with such a wrangler
> That all the courts of France will be disturb'd
> With chaces. . . .
> And tell the pleasant prince this mock of his
> Hath turn'd his balls to gun-stones. . . .[12]

Cricket, although played by all classes in its earliest forms, developed along class lines, inasmuch as its pace suited the leisured wealthy. They enjoyed wagering on cricket matches and also on horses. Although for centuries horses had been used for hunting, their use for racing appears to have been an early seventeenth-century development, again as a sport for the aristocracy. By the middle of the seventeenth century rules had been established, and within a few decades betting had developed. But at the time of the early English migrations to this country, horse racing was not yet a popular sport. English gentlemen enjoyed betting on cockfights and on their favorite pugilist or boxer. These sports cut across class lines, for the middle class and town dwellers enjoyed them as much as did the gentry and nobility.

Sport and Pastimes of the Common People

The pleasurable life of the nobility was made possible by the hard work of the lower classes. The serf was literally part of the noble's holdings. The lord set aside a small portion of land for a serf, who in return for protection shared part of his crop with the lord or worked for him. An Act of 1495, just three years after Columbus discovered America, defined the working day from March to September from 5 A.M. to 7 or 8 P.M., and in the winter, as the daylight hours. Each day was largely filled with the same drudgery, with life restricted to the routine of work and church. However, there were times for pastimes and merriment, for contests and dancing—snatched a few hours at a time on Sundays, holy days, and at weddings, fairs, and festivals. The Church prohibited some kinds of work on holy days, which occurred frequently, and people appear to have made the most of these occasions. Stow and other writers recount boisterous, rough games, dancing, and gatherings at fairs and "church-ales." Evidence of rowdiness connected with these events also comes from court records, which document many attempts to control sport.

By the time of the seventeenth century migrations to New England, the traditions of the peasant existing at the behest of the nobleman had given way to an emerging society of yeomen with a wide variety of occupations. Men learned to assume some responsibility for governing themselves and to engage in trade and manufacturing. As Trevelyan points out, "The medieval serf would never have planted the free and self-sufficient townships of New England . . . the English colonial movement was the migration of a modern society, self-governing, half-industrial, awake to economic and intellectual change."[13]

Ball Games
Perhaps the most important legacies from the common people to our sport today are the ball games, the precursors to baseball, football, soccer, golf, and bowling. Although these sports and pastimes of the people may seem meager compared to those of the nobility, it is important in the history of sport that commoners did on occasion participate in amusements and sport. It is one of the first times in the history of sport that there is *evidence* that sport was not reserved for the highest social group in a country.

Although manuscripts depict villagers playing with balls and bats or sticks, and references are made to such games in the literature, we have no written, contemporary descriptions of *how* the games were played. The club or bat appears to be a straight piece of wood intended to strike the ball, which was usually made of leather filled with material such as wool or hemp. Most of the evidence suggests that men played baseball-type games, sometimes parish against parish or married men against unmarried men. Occasionally there are reports of young women playing these games. At least one precursor of baseball can be identified.

Stool-ball, played near Windsor, England, as early as 1330, is thought to be the medieval game most closely resembling baseball. Strutt reconstructs the game as follows:

> [It] consists in simply setting a stool upon the ground, and one of the players takes his place before it, while his antagonist, standing at a distance, tosses a ball with the intention of striking the stool; and this it is the business of the former to prevent by beating it away with the hand, reckoning one to the game for every stroke of the ball; if, on the contrary, it should be missed by the hand and touch the stool, the players change places. I believe the same also happens if the person who threw the ball can catch and retain it when driven back, before it reaches the ground. The conqueror at this game is he who strikes the ball most times before it touches the stool.[14]

Stool-ball is theorized to have developed from one stool to two stools or "home" and one "base," then three stools or "home" and two "bases," and then to "home" and three "bases." During this period the game became known as "rounders," the forerunner of baseball. Men played other ball games that were more similar to our soccer or football than baseball. They kicked the ball instead of batting it with a stick or with the hands. The major element of the games, two teams battling to transport the ball across the opponents' goal line, often made for exceedingly dangerous encounters. A ball game resembling our hockey, in which the players hit the ball on the ground with a club or stick in an effort to advance it across the opponents' goal, was called "hurling" in Cornwall, "knappan" in Wales, and "shinty" in Scotland. Fields of play in today's sense did not exist, and the entire countryside became the area of play. In spite of bruises, black eyes, and scuffed shins, large teams of men continued to compete in these games.

"Goff," the name of a golflike game played in the sixteenth century, was unlike other ball games in that each player hit his own ball. It may have developed from shinty when players started depositing—or trying to deposit—their balls into a series of holes.

Other Games and Pastimes

Not only did the villagers play at ball games, but they also held contests in footracing, wrestling, hurling, and shooting. At fairs, on holy days, "church-ales," weddings, and festivals, contests were part of the festivities. Wrestling, especially in the early medieval period, took place at funerals, possibly as a vestige of pagan funeral games. In tavern or pub yards, bowling, quoits, and simple challenge games such as pitching pennies were enjoyed. Many forms of bowling developed around the idea of rolling a ball for accuracy or knocking down a series of upright sticks or pins. The games, varying from locale to locale, were most popular with the men. Amusements that we consider suitable for children were indulged in by adults, as depicted by manuscripts that show adult men walking on stilts, twirling rattles, and riding hobbyhorses.

Other ball games undoubtedly were adapted from those described above or from games ordinarily thought of as games for the nobility. However, in manuscript after manuscript, in woodcuts, and in the literature of the period, there are numerous references to the lower classes of town dwellers playing ball games. By the eighteenth century many of these same people had brought their games to the early colonies of North America, where they eventually developed into our modern ball sports.

Sport and Pastimes of the Town Dwellers

In early seventeenth-century England the only sizeable city was London, numbering about two hundred thousand, including the nearby areas. In comparison to today's standards, most towns were small. Towns were created from villages where tradespeople joined together for protection and commercial advantages. Still, agriculture was as basic to the life of the towns as were the growing trades, crafts, and industries. Contemporary accounts tell of hunting and hawking in nearby forests and, while London seemed congested, other towns blended into the countryside. The seventeenth-century town, much like today's, encompassed a variety of life styles and occupations. Artisans, craftsmen, and skilled workers formed guilds, much like today's labor organizations. At the height of the guilds' strength, almost every conceivable occupation had its own organization, training apprentices, controlling the occupation, and also living in a particular section of town. Merchants and their families, as they acquired wealth, became the upper echelons of town society, but in spite of the fact that money permitted them to live better than many noblemen, they were never considered true "aristocrats."

The variety of social groups—rich merchants or burghers, the guild members, artisans, students, and laborers—led to adaptations of the country sports of the nobility and the commoners. The town dwellers, with their lives regulated by their trade and by the Church, found occasions for sport and dance on Sundays, holy days, and at festivals. Stow describes the pastimes in the language of the day:

Stage playes.

But London for the shows upon Theaters, and Comicall pastimes, hath holy playes, representations of myracles which holy Confessours have wrought, or representations of torments wherein the constancie of Martyrs appeared. Every yeare also at Shrovetuesday, that we may begin with childrens sports, seeing we al have beene children, the schoole boyes do bring Cockes of the

Cock fighting.

game to their master, and all the forenoone they delight themselves in Cockfighting: after dinner all the youthes go into the fields to play at the bal. The schollers of every schoole have their

Ball play.

ball, or baston, in their hands: the auncient and wealthy men of the Citie come foorth on horsebacke to see the sport of the yong men, and to take part of the pleasure in beholding their agilitie.

Exercises of warlike feates on horsebacke with disarmed Launces.

Every Fryday in Lent a fresh company of young men comes into the field on horseback, and the best horseman conducteth the rest. Then march forth the Citizens sons, and other yong men with disarmed launces and shields, and there they practise feates of warre. Many Courtiers likewise when the king lieth nere, and

Battailes on the water.

attendants of noble men doe repaire to these exercises, and while the hope of victorie doth inflame their minds, do shew good proofe how serviceable they would bee in martiall affayres. In Easter holy dayes they fight battailes on the water, a shield is hanged upon a pole, fixed in the midst of the stream, a boat is prepared without oares to bee caried by violence of the water, and in the fore part thereof standeth a young man, readie to give charge upon the shield with his launce: if so be hee breaketh his launce

Leaping, dancing, shooting, wrestling.

against the shield, and doth not fall, he is thought to have performed a worthy deed. If so be without breaking his launce, he runneth strongly against the shield, downe he falleth into the

Dauncing, Fighting
of Boars, bayting
of Beares and
Bulles.

water, for the boat is violently forced with the tide, but on each side of the shielde ride two boates, furnished with yong men, which recover him that falleth as soone as they may. Upon the bridge, wharfes, and houses, by the rivers side, stand great numbers to see, & laugh therat. In the holy dayes all the Summer the youths are exercised in leaping, dancing, shooting, wrastling, casting the stone, and practising their shields: the Maidens trip in their Timbrels, and daunce as long as they can well see. In Winter every holy day before dinner, the Boares prepared for brawne are set to fight, or else Buls and Beares are bayted.

The Moorefield
when there was no
ditch by the wall
of the Citie.
sliding on the yce.

When the great fenne or Moore, which watereth the wals of the Citie on the North side, is frozen, many yong men play upon the yce, some striding as wide as they may, doe slide swiftly: others make themselves seates of yce, as great as Milstones: one sits downe, many hand in hand doe draw him, and one slipping on a sudden, all fall togither: some tie bones to their feete, and under their heeles, and shoving themselves by a little picked

Hauking and hunt-
ing

Staffe, doe slide as swiftly as a bird flieth in the ayre, or an arrow out of a Crossebow. Sometime two runne togither with Poles, and hitting one the other, eyther one or both doe fall, not without hurt: some breake their armes, some their legges, but youth desirous of glorie in this sort exerciseth it selfe agaynst the time of warre. Many of the Citizens doe delight themselves in Hawkes, and houndes, for they have libertie of hunting in Middlesex, Hartfordshire, all Chiltron, and in Kent to the water of Cray.[15]

Stow's description reveals not only sportlike activities which Londoners enjoyed, but also the place of these activities in their lives. Londoners played on holy days—Shrove Tuesday, Lent, and Easter—when people were free. There were football games and informal contests between teams such as we might see on today's playgrounds. Obviously, everyone thoroughly enjoyed the mock battles in boats in which some of the contestants might be thrown in the water and all was in good fun.

Spectators clearly were part of the sporting scene in Stow's London. Men came from the city to watch the games and in "great numbers" gathered on "bridges and wharfes." Stow writes of winning as an integral and expected part of the contests. He also depicts winter sports, which were enjoyed on "frozen water." Most activities were solely for the pleasure of the participants and spectators. Some, however, such as hunting and hawking were necessary to provide food.

Members of all classes enjoyed blood sports, including cockfighting and animal baiting. Not only did school boys "delight themselves on Cockfighting" as described by Stow, but people of all classes were cockfighting enthusiasts. Cocking remained popular, and eighteenth-century England cockfight accounts refer to specially built cockpits, the careful grooming of the cocks, and the heavy wagering that accompanied the sport.

Animal baiting exhibitions frequently took place on Sunday afternoons and the forenoon of holy days. Dogs were trained to attack, torment, and perhaps kill a bear, a bull, badger, or other animal, chained and confined within a pit. While this vicious practice does not seem sport by today's standards, Strutt points out that such "barbarous diversions . . . [were] universally practised on various occasions, in almost every town or village throughout the kingdom, and especially in market towns, where we find it was sanctioned by the law."[16]

Universities were located in the towns or cities, and unlike universities in modern United States, they had neither recreational nor athletic facilities. Universities consisted of clusters of young scholars, all male, gathered in huge cold halls for lectures. Students attended only if they wished, and lived where and how they could, throughout the town or city. They became part of the city life and its activities, and like other young men they wrestled and fenced, played ball, and indulged in rowdy street play. They snatched time from studies to play children's games, to swim in available streams, and to ice skate in the winter. Following the local pattern of amusements, the students entered into the town's revelries.

Influence of the Church on Sport

Some of our knowledge of early sport comes from written laws. Because governments needed better prepared archers, they forbade men from playing football and required them to practice archery. As local governments desired tranquility, they forbade games which led to rioting in the streets. Moreover, church documents show that differing religious doctrines led to diverse attitudes toward sport. During this period in English history, the Catholic and then, after the middle of the sixteenth century, the Anglican Church, was largely tolerant of pastimes and sport and saw no harm in Sunday amusements. The English sovereign, who was also the titular head of the Church of England, greatly influenced people's attitude toward sport. Elizabeth I enjoyed riding, hunting, and watching jousts. On occasion she entertained her visitors with animal baiting. "On the 25th of May, 1559, soon after her accession to the throne, [she] gave a splendid dinner to the French ambassadors, who afterwards were entertained with the baiting of bulls and bears, and the queen herself stood with the ambassadors looking on the pastime till six at night."[17] Not only did the court enjoy these pastimes and spectacles, but the countryside and the town also shared these amusements. "The Citizens and Peasants have Hand-ball, Football, Skittles, or Nine Pins, Shovel-Board, Stow-ball, Goffe, Trol Madam, Cudgels, Bear-baiting, Bull-baiting, Bow and Arrow, Throwing at cocks, Shuttle-cock, Bowling, Quoits, Leaping, Wrestling, Pitching the Barre, and Ringing of Bells, a Recreation used in no other Country of the World."[18] In general, Elizabeth I accommodated sport for her subjects if it did not interfere with her general policies. However, during the latter part of Elizabeth's reign the Puritan movement gained power and it presented problems to her successor, James I, regarding appropriate Sunday behaviors.

By the beginning of the seventeenth century the latent strains of Puritanism and of Protestant reform became more powerful, culminating in the English Civil War. Puritans, predominantly either mercantile or laboring class, wished to reform and purify the church and society; one method used to achieve these ends was to eliminate the many "holydays" so that "idolatry" would cease and the world's work could go on. Economic conditions, technological changes, and the beginning of manufacturing rewarded qualities which the Puritans also prized. Industrious, pious, sober, and thrifty Puritans condemned idleness, impiety, levity, and lavishness, which they equated with the merriment, diversions, imbibing, and amusements at fairs, weddings, and "holydays."

Puritan theology was based on discovering truth and authority in religious matters through a direct interpretation of the Bible rather than through church authorities or sacraments. Essentially Calvinistic, they preached predestination and salvation through conversion and a blameless life of piety and hard work. While a virtuous life might lead to salvation, certainly a life of idleness and debauchery did not. Basic to their beliefs was observing Sunday as a day devoted to God. The strict Puritan observance of Sunday envisioned a family attending two church services with long sermons, and also engaging in family prayers and Bible readings. Children might be allowed a few suitably moral tales or Bible games. In this view of life, sport might be tolerated elsewhere in the week, but on Sunday it was banned, along with business, theater, concerts, and even travel.[19]

King James I found himself caught in the middle of this growing controversy. While traveling through Lancashire, he was handed a petition from citizens complaining that they were barred from all amusements on Sunday. Exceedingly fond of sports himself, the King issued a *Book of Sport* in 1618 expressly approving sport after church services on Sunday:

> Our pleasure likewise is, That, after the end of Divine Service, Our good people be not disturbed, letted, or discouraged from any lawful recreations, Such as dancing, either of men or women, Archery for men, leaping, vaulting or any other such harmlesse Recreation, nor from haveing of May Games, Whitson Ales, and Morris-dances, and the setting up of Maypoles, and other sports therewith used, so as the same be had in due and convenient time, without impediment or neglect of Divine service.[20]

His Declaration was only sporadically enforced; and after King Charles I reissued the *Book of Sport* in 1633, the Puritan Parliament, growing stronger, formally ordered it burned.

Colonial American history reflects this dichotomy in English history. Settlers in Jamestown and later in the South generally were adventurers from the upper classes or else well-off landowners who tended to belong nominally to the Church of England. In the bleak North, however, the rigorous views of the Puritans prevailed; and the work ethic of our society, the Sunday laws, and many restraints on amusements and sport can be traced to Puritan beliefs.

The European settlers who came to this country left behind turbulent times in which the aristocracy was gradually losing its influence on the growing number of merchants and other middle-class persons. It was from these latter groups that many of the first pioneers came to this country, and it was their amusements and attitudes toward sport that shaped the pastimes and sport activities in the new country.

The Africans Who Came to America

Most Europeans came to this country for religious and economic reasons, but most Africans came because they had no choice. When the practice began of shipping men, women, and children to America for the slave market, Africa was a continent of sharp contrasts. The civilization of ancient Egypt, developed along the Nile River in the northeast, differed fundamentally from the equally ancient cultures of the sub-Sahara savanna. Eventually many northern African countries adopted the Islamic culture from the Near East. The Muslims, members of the Islamic faith, believed in Allah as the one God, in the rituals and customs prescribed by the Koran, and in the obligation to make at least one pilgrimage to the holy city of Mecca. They combined strands of many civilizations to create a rich culture which flourished in the early medieval period. Islamic architecture, art, literature, laws, and other cultural achievements spread from the Near East through North Africa to Spain.

As the Muslims gradually penetrated the African desert they found empires such as Mali, where they established the city of Timbuktu. An important stop on major trade routes where merchants from many kingdoms bought and exchanged products such as gold, cloth, and slaves, this city had become a cultural center by the fifteenth century. Timbuktu was later captured by the Songhai and by the seventeenth century its importance had declined.

Mali and Songhai were two of the many sub-Saharan countries from which slaves were exported to America. The first slaves are thought to have come from the mouth of the Niger River, but the extent of their origin actually ranged from the Gambia to present-day Angola, just south of the Congo River. Studying available documents, including ships' manifests, Herskovits suggests that "the regions that figure most prominently are 'Guinea,' which means the west coast of Africa from the Ivory Coast to western Nigeria, Calabar, which represents the Niger Delta region, Angola, or the area about the lower Congo, and the Gambia."[21]

In fifteenth-century Africa, slavery as a condition of life was not unknown. Captives from war were made slaves, but as such were subjected neither to the condition of being property to be bought and sold nor to the hard labor associated later with slavery in the southern part of the United States. Men, women, boys, and girls to be sold as slaves were usually obtained from African chiefs and merchants, who quickly saw the economic advantages in such trade. Persons who had committed crimes for which the punishment was banishment were sold into slavery. Prisoners of war who might have been condemned as slaves added to the supply, but those who "comprised by far the greatest number were those captured by marauding bands of robbers who, with the connivance of native rulers, carried on these raids to satisfy the demands of the European dealers."[22]

The area from which most Africans were taken to be brought to the United States was quite large, but certain generalizations may be made about life in West Africa during this period. Although some cities and towns existed south of the Sahara most Africans lived in self-sufficient villages organized along kinship lines. Because most of these peoples did not have a written language, our knowledge of their culture is gleaned from accounts of travelers, oral history, and artifacts. Kinship patterns prescribed many facets of daily life, with groups comprised of "kin" or tribal relationships living together, under a king and several chiefs. As the symbolic head of state, kings were expected to exhibit strength and power and were considered sacred. Authority was divided and laws enforced according to time-honored customs and actual power delegated along hierarchical lines. Legal practices varied from courts in the Bantu states to "meetings" in other societies where "disputes are settled by meetings that can be profitably compared with the old New England town meetings."[23]

African families were polygynous, and the marriages carefully planned to the satisfaction of both families. Perhaps the greatest impact on the children was that they realized that they shared their father with a number of other children, but that they shared their mother with only her own children. Each family had its own compound with an individual house for each adult male, married or unmarried. Each wife lived with her children in a single house. Family roles were carefully delineated so that the families could develop harmoniously. Children became aware at an early age of the dual responsibility and obligations to their families and the many kinship ties involved.

African families lived in dwellings built of available materials adapted to the climate, structures which frequently were of mud walls with thatched roofs. While the men cleared the dense forests and prepared the ground for planting, the women tended the crops and harvested them. The men also fished and hunted for food and skins of animals such as the leopard and lion. After a successful hunt a prize skin or special portion of an animal might be presented to the chief or king. The men were skilled in woodworking, making benches, bowls, and many other household items.

The women tended the small children and also carded, spun, and wove cloth. Surplus crops and crafts were traded at markets occupying a consecrated area with its own shrine. The markets played a social as well as economic role. Not only were goods traded at the market but news was exchanged, family and business affairs arranged, and entertainers and dancers performed, creating a fairlike atmosphere. A traveler described a market of Mosi "on account of the many strangers who visit, ready-cooked pudding, tiggera, and sour milk are offered for sale throughout the whole day. Besides salt, cotton strips, dyed cloth, Kola nuts, corn and asses, some copper manufactured chiefly into large drinking-vessels is also brought into the market."[24]

Markets were held every four or eight days, thus becoming a unit by which time could be reckoned. For Africans a day began at dawn and ended at dark. Time was told by natural sundials such as shadows from a sacred pole. Their lives revolved around the agricultural year with ceremonies for planting, harvesting, and other important parts of the growth process.

Religion and ceremony were interwoven throughout the everyday life of the Africans. Most groups recognized the role of a supreme creator and believed in the importance of ancestors, who were highly revered and sometimes deified. Rituals marking birth, puberty, marriage, death, and other occasions were carefully observed in order to ensure a happy and prosperous life. Rituals also played an important part in sowing and harvesting crops, avoiding natural disasters, and recovering from illness. Rhythmic movements which we would term dance characterized many of the rituals.

Sportlike Activities

Evidence of sportlike activities suggests that Africans did not set aside time for sport or play as we often do today. The children learned and practiced the skills they would need as adults. They ran, swam, wrestled, fished, and hunted.

Through the autobiography of Olaudah Equiano published in 1789, we have a glimpse of boyhood in an African tribe before slavery. "I was trained up from my earliest years in the art of war; my daily exercise was shooting and throwing javelins; . . .[and later, as a slave in Africa] my young master and I, with other boys, sported with our darts and bows and arrows, as I had been used to do at home."[25]

African boats consisted of hollowed-out trees so huge that two hundred people could be accommodated. Other smaller boats were more like today's canoes, but were used for transportation rather than for "sport." Mungo Park recounts a fishing expedition which depended on the swimming expertise of the fisherman:

> . . . the fisherman paddled the canoe to the bank, and desired me to jump out. Having tied the canoe to a stake, he stripped off his clothes, and dived for such a length of time, that I thought he had actually drowned himself, and was surprised to see his wife behave with so much indifference upon the occasion; but my fears

were over when he raised up his head astern of the canoe, and called for a rope. With this rope he dived a second time, and then got into the canoe, and ordered the boy to assist him in pulling. At length they brought up a large basket, about ten feet in diameter, containing two fine fish (after returning the basket into the water) immediately carried ashore, and hid in the grass. We then went a little further down, and took up another basket, in which was one fish.[26]

Accounts of travelers describe activities which we would call sport. When Hugh Clapperton arrived in Kano he found jugglers and the Hausa boxers, whom he paid two thousand whydah to fight in an exhibition. About twenty men engaged in the boxing, which was preceded by drummers and a ceremonial show of strength and bravado. The boxers' fists were then bound with cloth and the first pair brought into the ring. The fighters boxed only men whom they did not know. If friends were paired to fight, "they laid their left breasts together twice, and exclaimed, 'We are lions;' 'We are friends.' "[27] When the fighting began, it was a free-for-all technique with blows from the heels as well as the hands. After about six pairs of fighters, Clapperton paid the boxers and the exhibition terminated.

Another traveler described horse racing, which was part of the celebration of the "Bebun Salah" in Kaiama.

> The Arab saddle and stirrup were in common use; and the whole group presented an imposing appearance.

> The signal for starting was made, and the impatient animals sprung forward and set off at a full gallop. The riders brandished their spears, the little boys flourished their cows' tails, the buffoons performed their antics, muskets were discharged, and the chief himself, mounted on the finest horse on the ground, watched the progress of the race, while tears of delight were starting from his eyes. The sun shone gloriously on the tobes of green, white, yellow, blue, and crimson, as they fluttered in the breeze; and with the fanciful caps, the glittering spears, the jingling of the horses' bells, the animated looks and warlike bearing of their riders, presented one of the most extraordinary and pleasing sights that we have ever witnessed. The race was well contested, and terminated only by the horses being fatigued and out of breath; but though every one was emulous to outstrip his companion, honour and fame were the only reward of the competitors.[28]

In Abomey, women served alongside the men including the armed forces. Sir Richard Burton noted that young girls were used as the parade corps and were "cleanly made, without much muscle; they are hard dancers, indefatigable singers, and . . . their faces are anything but ferocious—they are rather mild and unassuming in appearance."[29] The young archers acted as the parade corps and were armed with the Dahoman bow and light poisoned arrows. According to this account they also hunted elephants.

Dance, an integral part of African ritual and ceremony, expressed emotions from joy and thankfulness for a good harvest to mourning at the funeral of a family member. Africans danced to celebrate birth, marriage, recovery from an illness, as well as to ensure a successful hunt or rain for a good crop. The occasion of the dance dictated the movements of the body. Quiet, shuffling movements depicted mourning, while leaping and kicking might express the power of the tribal king. Vigorous movements requiring athletic ability characterized many African dances. Olaudah Equiano described his nation as one of "dancers, musicians, and poets."[30]

From Africa to America

For three hundred and fifty years ships from many European countries—Portugal, Spain, England, France, Sweden, the Netherlands, and Denmark—brought West Africans to both South and North America to be sold as property. It is estimated that at least one-sixth of the Africans who left on slave ships perished during the dreaded "Middle Passage," as the voyage across the ocean was called. In an attempt to keep them healthy, some ship captains insisted that the Africans exercise. "We often at sea in the evenings would let the slaves come up into the sun to air themselves, and make them jump and dance for an hour or two to our bagpipes, harp, and fiddle, by which exercise to preserve them in health; but notwithstanding all our endeavour, 'twas my hard fortune to have great sickness and mortality among them."[31] While many kings apparently used the slave trade for their own gains, others did not. In 1526 King Affonso of Congo wrote to the King of Portugal. "Merchants are taking every day our natives, sons of the land and the sons of our noblemen and vassals and our relatives, because the thieves and men of bad conscience grab them. . . . So great, Sir, is the corruption and licentiousness that our country is being completely depopulated."[32] Such abuses continued. As late as 1795 King Naimbanna wrote to a leader in the British antislavery movement that "There are three distant relations of mine now in the West Indies, carried away by one Capt. Cox, captain of a Danish ship. Their names are Corpro, Banna and Morbour. These were taken out of my river Sierra Leona. I know not how to get them back."[33]

The first Africans who came to colonial America landed at Jamestown, Virginia, in 1619, not as slaves but as indentured servants. Within two decades the custom of selling West Africans as property was established and the first laws relating to owning slaves were passed in Massachusetts in 1641 and Virginia in 1661. The staple crops grown in the south required a large labor force, a demand which could be satisfied neither by the small independent white farmers nor by the native Americans, who were rapidly decreasing in numbers and whose cultural mores did not include the necessary agricultural technology. Also, the native Indians appeared to have less resistance to certain bacterial diseases than the blacks from West Africa. Many slave ships stopped at islands in the West Indies for a period of adjustment of the Africans to the new life on which they were embarking. Eventually, they were brought to the mainland and sold, most of them in the southern states. By 1790 almost seven hundred thousand Africans had been brought to the North American colonies, all but fifty thousand to the southern plantations.

The black heritage of American sport began in a somewhat different fashion from that of the Europeans or native Americans. Until the middle of the nineteenth century a few blacks boxed, rowed, or were jockeys in interplantation contests organized by their owners, but most devised their own fun and relaxation on the plantations of the South. Following the Civil War, little integration in sport took place, resulting in separate sports for blacks and for whites. Not until the twentieth century was the impact of black athletes on American sport felt nationally; today, black athletes are an integral part of all forms of contemporary sport—professional, amateur, educational, and recreational.

The American Colonists

In 1565 St. Augustine, Florida, became the first permanent settlement in what is now the United States. The next two permanent colonies, Jamestown in the south and Plymouth in the north, provide us with evidence of colonial life in this country. They were founded for very different purposes. In 1607 enterprising Englishmen with the hope of quick fortunes—merchants, nobles, clergy, and adventurers—formed the Virginia Company and sent 120 colonists to Jamestown in "Virginia." During the first years the settlers, many of whom had agreed to seven years labor to pay for the voyage to America, lacked the knowledge and stamina to survive in the strange and hostile environment. Often ill, hungry, and poorly housed, the Jamestown colonists survived through the efforts of men such as Captain John Smith and Governor Thomas Dale. Dale imposed severe penalties on those who did not do their share of work; after several years of tight control and the welcome discovery of the profitable weed called tobacco, the colony prospered. In time the Virginia colony began to resemble the political, social, and religious life of England.

Intent on founding their own religious community based on Puritan beliefs, the Pilgrims landed in Massachusetts in 1620 to establish a government in which the church and state would be one. Like the Virginians, they suffered severe disease and hardship in the early years. These persevering settlers governed themselves, worked hard in the service of God, and prospered. Work and piety were the watchwords in the new colony. Ten years after the Pilgrims landed at Plymouth another group of Puritans settled the Massachusetts Bay Colony, and also strictly adhered to Puritan doctrines. The colonists, guided by men like John Winthrop, established their government and society to serve God first and then to serve men. Like the settlers at Plymouth they embodied the ethics of hard work, sobriety, and piety.

After the founding of the Virginia and Massachusetts colonies the first great wave of settlers came to this country in the seventeenth century from English towns, villages, and the countryside. While a growing number of English lived in small cities—only six towns in England had as many as eight to twelve thousand people—or in dirty, crowded London with its two hundred thousand people—most of the settlers came from villages and small towns. Despite the dangers of an ocean voyage in a tiny vessel, they came to America in search of a better life. In England they faced epidemics, depressions, fuel shortages, enclosure of their grazing lands, forced billeting, or religious coercion. In the new country they confronted hardships and new dangers, but also the possibility of a better life for everyone.

During the early seventeenth century the Dutch West India Company established settlements at Albany, New York, and New York City, and by the end of the century tiny villages and isolated homesteads dotted the eastern seaboard. Nevins and Commager remind us that:

> No real social distinction can be drawn between the settlers of Massachusetts and those of Virginia. The people who made both commonwealths great were drawn from the same large middle-class stratum. . . . The great majority of the emigrants to both Massachusetts and Virginia before 1660 were yeomen, mechanics, shopkeepers, and clerks of modest means; while many in all parts of America were indentured servants, who paid for their passage by a stated term of labor. Their real wealth lay in their sturdy integrity, self-reliance, and energy.[34]

From these new Americans, patterns of sport would evolve which reflected origins and backgrounds in the European countries, and also the new governments, laws, and daily lives. With settlements established on the seaboard, restless colonists, adventurers, and some newcomers pushed west to explore the vast wilderness.

The settlers learned to adapt some of their European ways to those of the native Americans, both to survive in the new land and to enjoy its many benefits. Hunting and fishing were not pastimes but a means of obtaining food, and the colonists quickly copied Indian methods. Buckskins and moccasins became practical dress for many Americans, as they learned to move quietly and stealthily through the forests while stalking game. They also learned about new foods such as corn and the best methods for farming and harvesting.

The colonists, alike in coming to a new land, were not alike in their modes of life. Different customs developed in different parts of the new world in accordance with the geography, climate, and the purposes of the new settlements. Games and pastimes followed the diverse pattern of the colonies and were different in New England, New York, Pennsylvania, the South, and the western frontier.

Sport and Pastimes of New England

In the Massachusetts Bay Colony the leaders developed their own church based on their Calvinist beliefs.

> The congregations of the Massachusetts Bay recognized no authority other than God and his word revealed in the Scriptures. The true church was composed only of God's elected saints. Membership in the church therefore depended upon proof of election. Proof consisted of the convincing testimony before the whole congregation by each aspirant to church membership that he or she had experienced a personal conversion and conviction of salvation. . . . Church membership was consequently an exclusive privilege of a minority—the Puritan elite—for even in that religious age only a minority of the population received the blessed assurance of salvation.[35]

For years the struggle to survive and the austere Puritan beliefs regulated almost every aspect of the colonists' lives. Puritan characteristics of industriousness, frugality, and sobriety led to economic success. Idleness was considered undesirable and possibly harmful. The laws of Massachusetts endorsed this belief. In 1633, a court of the Colony of Massachusetts Bay ordered all men to "worke the whole day alloweing convenient tyme for foode & rest" and "that noe person howsehoulder or other, shall spend his time idely or unprofitably under paine of such punishment as the Court shall think meete to inflicte. . ."[36] On the Sabbath, church attendance was compulsory and amusements forbidden, and on all other days, men were expected to work a full day, leaving little or no time for pastimes.

In early New England there were few violations of the many regulations against sport and amusements. The records of the Court of Assistants from 1630 to 1643 list well over three hundred crimes and misdemeanors, but only two offenses for sport and amusements. John Baker was ordered whipped for fowling on the Sabbath day and Laurence Waters' wife and others were "admonished to avoyde dancing."[37] New Englanders also attempted to forbid the native Indians from play when in 1646 they stated, "Whosoever shall play at their former games shall pay 10s."[38]

By 1690 the Puritan's approximation of the ideal theocracy, in which church and state were closely linked, began to be modified by the generations born in the "new-found land," who felt remote from the Puritan troubles in faraway England. In addition, more and more immigrants not of the Puritan faith came to this country. From the Massachusetts Bay Colony, the heart of the Puritan settlements, dissident groups migrated to Rhode Island and Connecticut. Other settlers and new arrivals moved north and west, establishing homesteads and villages in New Hampshire and Vermont. Although the Puritan characteristics of industry and thriftiness were essential to the new settlements, a general decline in religious influence occurred in both the old and new settlements.

However, in the middle of the eighteenth century a strong evangelical movement known as the Great Awakening exhorted people to return to the "straight and narrow path," denounced frivolity and secular amusements, and reinforced the Puritan ethic of hard work, sobriety, and piety.

Within this context New England life gradually accommodated "recreations," childhood games, diversions like sleigh-riding, and even contests such as horse racing. Ministers condoned fishing as a recreation which was both necessary and pleasant. Other "approved" reasons for pastimes and games included physical health and renewal of the soul to return to more productive work. Play was thought to strengthen children, and even adult men could recreate and return to their labors refreshed. In 1739 Armstrong reminded New Englanders:

> When the Body has long wearied with Labour, or the Mind weakened with Devotion, it's requisite to give them ease; then the use of innocent and moderate Pleasures and Recreations is both useful and necessary, to Soul and Body; it enlivens Nature, recruits our Spirits, and renders us more able to set about serious Business and Employment. For to intermix no Gratifications, nor Diversions with our more Serious Affairs, makes the Mind unactive, dull, and useless.[39]

The colonists valued education, and as early as 1647, just twenty years after the founding of the Massachusetts Bay Colony, every town of fifty householders was required to teach reading and writing. Even earlier, in 1635, the Boston Latin School was established, and a year after that Harvard College opened. Other colonies followed Massachusetts' lead, and soon public school education was accepted throughout New England. Few schools concerned themselves with anything but the rudiments of a classical education. Occasionally exercise programs were provided to improve the students' health.

Children's games were justified not only by a concern for health, but also by moral lessons which could be taught by means of games. Even the title of a popular little book discloses the current view of child rearing: *The Little Pretty Pocket Book, Intended for the Instruction and Amusement of Little Master Tommy and Pretty Miss Polly*. Published in 1762, it joins games with moral teachings.

Hop-Scotch

> First make with chalk and oblong Square,
> With wide Partitions here and there;
> Then to the first a Tile convey;
> Hop in—then kick the Tile away.

Rule of Life

> Strive with good sense to stock your Mind,
> And to that Sense be virtue joined.

Marbles

Knuckle down to your Taw.
Aim well, shoot away:
Keep out of the Ring
And you'll soon learn to play.

Moral

Time rolls like a Marble,
And awes every State:
Then improve each Moment,
Before 'tis too late.[40]

Such practical admonitions undoubtedly helped warrant children's play at a time when they were perceived as little adults and generally expected to behave accordingly. With or without the moral lesson, however, the children of the new nation played, like those before them and like their descendants, games such as "I Spy" or "Hide and Seek," "Button Button," "Blindman's Buff," "Prisoner's Base," "Hide the Thimble," "Town Ball," and "One O'Cat, Two O'Cat."

To meet their religious needs the American settlers erected small clapboard churches, and to meet their social needs they built taverns. The tavern has been called "the most remarkable social center that America has ever produced."[41] Taverns sprang up all over the colonies—just about a day's ride from each other, so that travelers could make their way comfortably from Canada to the south and from the east to the western frontier.

During the seventeenth and eighteenth centuries the taverns were used for social occasions, entertainment, and as a place for diversion. Travelers arrived with news of other settlements or even perhaps of European countries; newspapers sometimes could be found at the tavern, and studied; discussions of important local or regional matters took place. Bowling, billiards, cockfighting, and animal baiting were popular pastimes. Travelers passing through might pause in the village if there were good fishing nearby, or they might enter local contests of prowess or match their shooting skills against the local villagers. During the cold months ice skating on New England's frozen ponds was a favorite winter pastime.

Dinners, weddings, and festivals were organized to celebrate special occasions, and these frequently included social dancing. The ballroom with its fireplace and small stage or enclosure for musicians usually had benches along each wall. The walls were often decorated with stenciled colored flowers. One tale suggests that young women who were not invited to dance and left sitting on the bench came to be called "wall flowers."

Figure 2.9   A barn raising, example of a work bee. Courtesy of the Enoch Pratt Free Library, Baltimore, Maryland.

Training Days or Muster Days, Lecture Days, Election Days, and "bees" provided occasions for civic or worthwhile functions accompanied by contests, games, frolics, and balls. Beginning in 1639 the men organized defense units for the towns, assembling on Training Days or Muster Days for artillery practice. The protection of the settlements was serious business, but as the settlements became more established and the dangers from Indians lessened, amusements, social events, and athletic contests followed the serious business of training.

> Women and children alike looked forward to these days as a holiday, which offered a welcome break in the monotony of New England life. The Puritan tradition prevailed, however, for only an innocent diversion was anticipated. The exercises were always preceded by prayers and the singing of psalms. . . . At the turn of the century it acquired a more pronounced social complexion and became more and more a day of festivity and merriment. . . . Games, gingerbread, and grog made their appearance. . . .[42]

At a 1704 Training Day the winner of the "Olympiak Games . . . has some yards of Red Ribbin presented him [which] being tied to his hatband . . . he is Led Away in Triumph.[43]

Lecture Days provided the earnest Puritans with opportunities for midweek addresses on religious topics as well as a break in the work week. The thrifty New Englanders might bring extra produce with them to barter or sell. As Lecture Days grew, amusements and pastimes came to be part of the gathering. Election Day was another time when people assembled to perform a civic duty and remained to make the most of a social occasion.

The "bee" is an American term thought by some to allude to the social or communal character of the bee's work, and by others to have no connection with the insect. In many parts of colonial America a bee brought people together for a combination of cooperative work and play. Barns were raised, corn husked, apples prepared for cider, sauce, or drying, wood sawed, and quilts quilted. In the early spring "sugaring-off" provided occasions for testing the year's new maple syrup. To make the work time pass quickly there might be impromptu contests, but after the work there would be more contests, wrestling, and usually dancing.

Laws governing daily activities continued to be a part of New England life. From 1657 to 1786 in Boston regulations were passed banning football, sledding, gaming for money, stage plays and theatrical productions, and all Sunday pastimes. In the 1670s Plymouth Colony and Rhode Island fined horse racers five shillings. Forty years later, in 1715, an advertisement for a horse race appeared in a Boston paper. It is not known if the race actually took place. As immigrants from other religions and countries continued to settle in New England and mingled with the colonists, the Puritan attitude toward pastimes and sport changed. By the middle of the eighteenth century, the towns had grown, individuals had prospered, and New Englanders had found recreation and enjoyment in many ways. Struna points out that "The settlers sported because they were human. They required refreshment, relaxation, training, diversion, and competition. In this sense, sport broadened their quality of humanness. Yet, the case for sport lacks this ultimate simplicity. As the concept itself and the colonial participation acquired new and expanded roles, sport revealed much of the actual complexity of society."[44] Although the Puritan ethic of hard work and sobriety persisted, material comforts and leisure resulting from economic success permitted some pastimes and amusements. However, pastimes, rather than organized sport, were the order of the day.

Sport and Pastimes of New York

Social life in early New Amsterdam differed greatly from Puritan Boston. Good food, good drink, and gambling were all part of the lives of the emerging upper class or European gentry who had emigrated to New Amsterdam. The religious festivals celebrated in Holland and in other parts of Europe from which settlers came continued to be observed, although the customs, processions, and special foods were sometimes adapted to the new homeland.

Figure 2.10   Prize in 1668 horse race. Courtesy of Yale University Art Gallery, Mabel Brady Garvan Collection.

In 1664 the English took over the small settlement of some sixteen hundred people and it became New York. Colonel Richard Nicolls, the English governor, organized the first known formal horse race in this country a year later. Named after its English counterpart, Newmarket, the first course was situated where Garden City now stands. Typical of the times, Nicolls justified his action by noting that the races, held each spring and fall, were not for enjoyment, but to improve the breed of horse. A silver porringer was offered as a trophy in 1668. The first known admission fee for a sporting event occurred in 1736 when Francis Child advertised that each person would pay six "pense" to enter the field where the horse race was held.[45]

During the eighteenth century English horses were imported to improve the American horse. Rivalries soon arose between the English and American horses as reported in the following notice from May 16, 1768:

> The Hundred Pounds purse at Upper Marlborough, has been won by Dr. Hamilton's English horse Figure, beating the, hitherto, terrific Salem. As many incidents occur in a four mile heat, and we have no particulars of the sport, it is but justice to the gallant American that the public should suspend its decisive opinion until the champions have met at Philadelphia, next October; when the vanquished may recover, or the victor be confirmed in the triumphant post which, to the astonishment of thousands, he has so successfully contended for. Figure was got by a beautiful horse of that name, the property of the Duke of Hamilton; ran five times in England and won one plate; he also started two years ago against five horses at Annapolis and

beat them in four fine heats. Salem, a grandson of Godolphin Arabian, and got by Governor Sharp's valiant Othello, has run about nine times, and till this event proved in every dispute unconquerable. The gentlemen of Philadelphia have raised a purse of £ 100 and two of £ 50 each, to be run for over their course in the Fall. The particulars adapted to the late increase of fine horses in the Northern Colonies will be advertised very soon.[46]

This account confirms that horses were brought from other colonies to race in New York. Intercolony rivalry ensued, preceding the hotly contested inter-sectional contests of the early nineteenth century. Horse racing in New York provided the first inkling of organized sport in North America. A special place, a race course, was set aside for the contest; races were regulated; prizes were offered; spectators encouraged to attend; admission fees charged; and events advertised. The popular races were greatly enjoyed by the audience.

Colonial New Yorkers took pleasure in bowling, golf, battledore, tennis or fives, and cricket. "Games of 'short ball,' 'long ball,' balls driven through gates or wickets, balls thrown against a stake, balls struck by the gloved or ungloved hand, racket, stick, club, or mallet, subject to various rules and known under various names . . . were favorite pastimes with the New Netherlanders."[47] These ball games, the foundation of our modern sport, were reminiscent of the European heritage of the colonists. Also reflecting their European origin was their love for blood or animal sports. "Clubbing the Cat" meant literally that contestants threw a club at a cat suspended in a barrel from a rope. The thrower who caused the cat to leave the barrel, either by breaking a barrel stave or the rope from which it was hung, won the event. In another such game, "Pulling the Goose," the players, while riding horseback past a suspended goose, attempted to catch it. Sometimes the goose was suspended over water and the players grabbed for the goose while standing in a boat. The risk of the player falling into the water added excitement to the occasion.

In town, shooting matches were advertised, with prizes offered such as a gold watch or a house and lot. Out on Long Island some of the gentry main-tained their own game preserves and deer parks, reminiscent of those in England. Fines were charged if anyone other than the host's guests killed a deer in the private parks.

Both gentlemen and ladies were invited to take advantage of the bathing-house near North River, perhaps wearing a cork jacket proclaimed for its use-fulness in saving people from drowning. Other New Yorkers found "Their di-versions in the Winter . . . Riding Sleys about three or four Miles out of Town, where they have Houses of entertainment at a place called the Bowery."[48] Dancing was a popular pastime for both ladies and gentlemen. Mr. Hulet, a dancing master who opened his public dancing school in New York in 1770, taught the minuet, country dancing, and arranged "a private class for those gentlemen who had not learned the Hornpipe."[49]

Sport and Pastimes of Pennsylvania

The Quakers, an individualistic, peace-loving Puritan sect founded in seventeenth-century England, sought to escape imprisonment and persecution by emigrating to the New World. One of their leaders, wealthy and influential William Penn, persuaded the Duke of York to bestow some of the southern portion of his enormous grant of land in the new country upon Penn. With a 1681 charter he began to urge Quakers from England and Europe to travel to a fairer land, the province of Pennsylvania, for religious liberty and a good life. Before arriving in the New World to assume leadership in his new colony, he devised a code of laws under which the Society of Friends would live in the new land free of religious persecution. These laws, enacted by the Pennsylvania Assembly in 1682, regulated strict Sabbath behavior, and banned many pastimes and amusements. According to Jable:

> Penn placed two provisions in *The Great Laws* which regulated what he considered licentious activities. The first measure banned "rude and riotous sports." Anyone introducing prizes, stage-plays, masques, revels, bullbaits, or cockfights into the colony was subject to a fine of twenty shillings or ten days imprisonment at hard labor. . . . The second measure dealt with lesser evils. Those convicted of playing cards, dice, or lotteries received a fine of five shillings or a five-day sentence in the house of correction.[50]

By the end of the century the Society of Friends, or Quakers, were influenced by other groups who settled in Pennsylvania, and by the prosperity they enjoyed in the new country. A revision of *The Great Laws of 1682* continued to forbid Sunday activities such as stage plays, cockfights, and lotteries, but permitted "innocent diversions" such as ice skating, swimming, hunting, and fishing. As a growing number of wealthy, elite Philadelphians moved to the suburbs, and the city became a conglomeration of nationalities and religions, amusements formerly frowned upon became more and more acceptable. Dancing schools opened; bowling, billiards, bullbaiting, and cockfighting were engaged in openly, and intercolony horse races were popular.

One famous Philadelphian, Benjamin Franklin, promoted the importance of both education and physical activity. In his *Proposals for the Education of Youth* he suggested "that the boarding Scholars diet together, plainly, temperately, and frugally. That to keep them in Health, and to strengthen and render active their Bodies, they be frequently exercis'd in Running, Leaping, Wrestling, and Swimming, etc."[51]

Franklin called swimming "necessary and life-preserving," and pointed out in *The Art of Swimming Rendered Easy,* "The only obstacle to improvement . . . is fear: and it is by overcoming this timidity, that you can expect to become a master of the preceding acquirements. . . . The exercise of swimming is one of the most healthy and agreeable in the world."[52] The book includes sections on: How to Begin to Swim, Swimming Backwards, Diving, Swimming Like a Dog, To Tread the Water, To Swim Holding Up One Leg, and To Swim on the Belly Holding both Hands Still.

For most people of the colonial period amusements and diversions were informal, and frequently associated with social events. As the citizens realized they had common interests they formed groups to engage in favorite pastimes and to enjoy themselves. One of the early clubs, the Schuylkill Fishing Company, was formed in 1732 and permitted its members to fish and hunt "in the romantic solitudes of the river Schuylkill," thus proving that work and play "may be handmaidens under proper regulations and restrictions."[53] During colonial times jockey clubs were formed in part to regulate horse racing. The first of these was organized in 1766 for two purposes: to improve the breed and to enjoy "the pleasures of the turf." Members, all gentlemen, came from New York, Maryland, and New Jersey, as well as from Pennsylvania. The Gloucester Fox Hunting Club was founded in 1766 by eighteen gentlemen to maintain a kennel of fox hounds which were used in hunting two days a week. The Troop of the Light Horse of the City of Philadelphia, another social group, organized in the mideighteenth century and enjoyed horseback riding. At times, the social activities of these sport clubs appear to have been more important than the sport, but they provided opportunity for sport in an elite social setting. Although today we accept sport clubs as commonplace, these early groups or sport clubs established long before the American Revolution can be considered the beginnings of organized sport in the United States. Therefore, they play a unique role in the history of sport.

Sport and Pastimes of the South

If anywhere in colonial America sport was a function of class, it was in Maryland, Virginia, and the South. Many of these immigrants, unlike their New England counterparts, had not left England to establish a different type of society, and thus they continued the customs of their families, schools, government, and the Anglican Church. By the late eighteenth century large estates, the availability of slaves, and the English system of government made English life and customs possible.

Horse racing was the most popular sport and very much a social occasion, not only in Maryland and Virginia, but all over the South. Quarter-racing developed before course or track racing. At first these short quarter-mile races were contested on the town streets but for the safety of the pedestrians, they were later moved to straight narrow "race paths" near the edge of the town. Each path was wide enough for two horses and was about a quarter of a mile or five hundred yards long. Richmond in Henrico County, Virginia, became the center of horse racing. Quarter-racing attracted crowds—artisans, maids, ladies, slaves, hunters, people from all walks of life—ready for an outing:

> It was an occasion for merrymaking, revelry and "celebration," often of an up-roarious kind. Both sides of the race-path were crowded with excited and enthu-siastic spectators; feeling ran high and betting likewise, the stake for which the match was run being sometimes everything that an owner possessed, while upon the out-come everything belonging to the favorite's backers depended. At the starting end of the path, booths were set up for the sale of eatables, drinkables and gewgaws; peddlers and venders hawked their wares about; itinerant healers and magicians put up improvised platforms from which to proclaim the wonders that they worked; fortune-tellers plied their trade and "freaks" exhibited themselves and their de-formities. It was like a one-day fair, to which the entire countryside turned out.[54]

Quarter horses were bred for high speed over short distances. Toward the end of the seventeenth century when more fields had been cleared and were avail-able for racing, interest in course racing increased.

About 1730 Bulle Rock, a stallion, was imported to Virginia for breeding purposes. After Colonel Tasker of Belair, Maryland, brought over the brood mare Salima, fine racers were produced for the increasingly popular sport. About this time a number of hard-working, thrifty Scottish and Irish immi-grants arrived in the upper South and within a generation the more prosperous newcomers became enthusiastic about horse racing. At Williamsburg, Vir-ginia, races were held on the mile-long track each spring and fall. More cos-mopolitan than Williamsburg, Annapolis offered four days of contests during Racing Week accompanied by numerous social occasions.

Just as it had in New York, horse racing in the South gradually became more organized. In the early days it was customary to have only one event so that the onlookers could return home before dark. As general economic and social conditions changed, however, so did the race courses. Railings enclosed the final stretch; judges and jockey club members had special stands; there were stands for the public for which admission fees were charged; and some-times free temporary stands were erected. Because the rules and the enforce-ment of the rules varied from judge to judge, records from this period are doubtful. Many gentlemen rode their own horses to the races while other family members were driven out in their carriages. After the races dinner was served in a nearby fashionable clubhouse followed, perhaps, by a ball.

By the mideighteenth century Charleston was the center of Carolinian so-ciety. A third of its almost seven thousand inhabitants were white and only a few of those were in the upper social group of clergymen, lawyers, doctors, and wealthy merchants. These city residents and their families were joined for the winter social season by plantation families who maintained town houses for the malaria and winter season, making Charleston society one of the most glittering in colonial America. "Plays, balls and concerts enlivened the winter seasons, while the summers offered such diversions as horse races, cock fights, and outdoor musical programs at the Orange Gardens. Then there were the gentlemen's clubs that met regularly at the local taverns."[55]

A growing class consciousness among the wealthy encouraged young southern gentlemen to attain certain social and athletic skills. They were expected to excel in dancing, fencing, riding, and conversation. Dancing teachers often traveled from plantation to plantation to reach their pupils. In addition to dancing, the master sometimes taught fencing.

In contrast most of the Africans in the South were slaves and led a hard life of drudgery. They did not have command of their own persons and could be sold as a commodity. Many suffered physical punishment as part of their daily lives. Some of the southern blacks became fighters or boxers and were set to fight against other slaves, to provide sport and betting opportunities for their white owners. Others formed crews and raced for the pleasure and betting opportunities of whites. Sundays, holidays, and, perhaps, late summer evenings were the only time slaves could count as their own. Plantations in Virginia celebrated about sixty holidays each year when the slaves had some liberties. "They could not leave the plantation without their owner's written permission, but their time was their own and they could use it as they saw fit. Many took up the white man's religion and attended church or even held their own meetings for worship. Others arranged cockfights, and all took part in music and dancing."[56] In Carolina on Sundays they pitched pennies and played pawpaw and huzzle-cap. The slaves looked forward to Christmas as a time allowing them to stop work for about ten days or "until the yule log burned out. During the holidays visiting, singing and dancing took place. Cabin floors were cleared and participants danced the Juba, a lively dance of African origin. This was accompanied by vigorous shouts, handclapping for rhythm, and a fiddle for melody."[57]

Sport and Pastimes of the Frontier

To imagine a Charleston ball with minuets and silk gowns and then to visualize a frontier hoedown with a single fiddle and cotton workclothes help us contrast the living conditions, work, and amusements of the seacoast towns and the frontier. An itinerant Anglican preacher in the Carolina backcountry found industrious but rough settlers who made a social occasion of the minister's visit, when he "had but a small Congregation the Principal People generally riding abroad ev'ry Sunday for Recreation." He was shocked at "The open profanation of the Lords Day in this Province. . . . Among the low Class, it is abus'd by Hunting fishing fowling, and racing—By the Women in frolicing and Wantoness. By others in Drinking Bouts and Card Playing—Even in and about Charlestown, the Taverns have more Visitants than the Churches."[58]

This description might be applicable to many of the pioneers who pushed west from the eastern settlements to Kentucky, Indiana, Ohio, and Illinois. Just as it did in the East, the tavern served as the local center for sociability and entertainment. Frontier families also made social occasions of the barn raisings, corn huskings, and at times turned the inevitable ploughing into ploughing matches. Even capture by Indians sometimes resulted in contests. Daniel Boone recounts a shooting match that occurred when he was a captive. "I often went a hunting with them, and frequently gained their applause for my activity at our shooting-matches. I was careful not to exceed many of them in shooting; for no people are more envious than they in this sport. I could observe, in their countenances and gestures, the greatest expressions of joy when they exceeded me; and, when the reverse happened, of envy."[59]

During the more than 150 years of colonization, the future country, the United States of America, had begun to take shape. The eastern seaboard was well settled. Adventurers and explorers had pushed beyond the westernmost farms to what would be Kentucky, Ohio, and Illinois. The southwestern borders of the country were dotted with Spanish settlements as far west as California. Santa Fe was established in 1609 and missions and outposts extended up the California coast to Monterey Bay. The colonies of the eastern seaboard, however were far more advanced than the Spanish territories. Whether in Puritan New England, on the plantations in the South, or in New York, the colonists learned to live with people from a variety of backgrounds and religious beliefs and to govern themselves. On occasion, representatives of the colonies met to discuss their common concerns or to act for their common benefit. The idea of "America" was becoming a reality.

Commentary

North American Indians have made unique contributions to American sport, but these were not discernible during the colonial period. Long after colonial days, Americans adopted the Indian game of lacrosse. By that time it had changed from a tribal ritual to a nineteenth-century sport. Americans have also changed the Indian's means of transportation—the canoe and the kayak—to pleasure and sport craft.

During the period of colonization from 1607 to 1776 most settlers came to this country to escape constraints, as did the Puritans, or to better their economic condition, as did the Virginians and many other colonists. The Africans came unwillingly, not to better their condition but because they were sold as slaves. As immigrants from European countries arrived they formed their own communities, but gradually became part of the new society and, like future generations of immigrants, melded their ethnic traditions with those of the new country. They slowly became active in the political system, found employment in old or new industries, and became "American," rather than European.

The colonists first fought for survival in the strange and often harsh land, but as settlements became more secure and life somewhat less difficult they found time for a variety of pastimes, diversions, and some sport. This chapter examined life in colonial times and the conditions that led to the beginnings of American sport and physical education, although physical education as we think of it today did not exist at that time. These conditions are linked to the basic themes of this text.

The first theme, the concept of improving the quality of life, has been present in this country since colonial days. In the course of the almost two hundred years of colonization, the European settlers assumed the responsibility for governing and educating themselves. It must be noted, however, that the lives of most native Americans and those of the African slaves were not improved.

The second and third themes, the diversity on which the American culture is based and the perceived values that govern daily living, are closely related in this period. The settlers from different countries brought with them their religious beliefs, their daily customs, and their pastimes. The purpose of each settlement influenced the way of life and the attitude toward sport and amusement in that colony. In spite of the diversity of their backgrounds, the idea of America and of being an "American" had formed by the eve of the Revolution. This climate led to "American" sports by the end of the nineteenth century. The third theme of this book emphasizes the influence of daily values on sport. The values which governed the lives of the colonists differed according to the part of the country in which the colony was established as well as the reasons for which it was founded. The New England economy depended on the sea and its products while the southern economy relied on tobacco. In New England Puritan beliefs guided the behavior of the people; in Pennsylvania, Quaker principles directed the people's lives; in New York, Dutch customs prevailed; and in Maryland and Virginia, English traditions were followed.

Early New England's strict laws forbidding all amusements on Sunday and condoning only "necessary" pastimes such as fishing, reflected the Puritan work ethic. In the course of this period, the New Englanders justified hunting and fishing and other "innocent and moderate Pleasures and Recreation." While the Puritan work ethic is often interpreted as disapproving sport and amusements, careful study of primary evidence suggests that *proper* amusements for children, purposeful work combined with diversions, and true recreation such as fishing were acceptable. The Quakers in Pennsylvania controlled sport and recreation much like the Puritans. In New York the people engaged in traditional Dutch pastimes while, in the South, the gentry enjoyed a social life centering on horse racing, balls, and other sociable outings.

The fourth theme, patterns of social organization, is apparent in this period. Consistent with their gender role expectations, men took part in activities such as Muster Day drills, horse racing, tavern sports, and work bees. Women held their own quilting bees, attended some horse races, and provided food and took part in the merriment at Muster Days and work bees. Also, social classes differed greatly in their pastimes—from the horse racing of the gentry to the occasional frolic that slaves were allowed.

Although the fifth theme, the intermixing of technology and urbanization, did not become a major influence in the development of sport until later, some evidence exists of preparation of sport areas such as tracks for horse races during the colonial period.

By the eve of the American Revolution Dr. Samuel Johnson, in his *Dictionary of the English Language,* defined sport as "play, diversion, game, frolick and tumultuous merriment," and thus portrayed the activities of the American colonists. However, these diversions became the basis for today's sport.

Of the colonial games brought over from Europe, stool-ball and rounders evolved into baseball; golf, handball, and bowling survived; and Americans are still avid fans of the turf sports. One of the favorite pastimes of men and women, except the pious New Englanders, was dancing—whether in a city mansion, a southern plantation, a tavern ballroom, or at the conclusion of a work bee. The bee provided an occasion for pastimes and some sportlike activities. The neighbors gathered first to work industriously, then to play games and challenge one another in contests and dance. Horse racing, one of the most popular forms of entertainment in the South, began with quarter racing and developed into course racing with specially built tracks, judges, stands for the public, and admission fees.

Very little sport as it is defined in today's terms existed in colonial America. In their analysis of sport VanderZwaag and Sheehan cite "Three primary characteristics . . . the playlike nature of sport, its association with games, and its physical . . . quality." They point out that "A secondary characteristic is unique: its dependence on facilities and equipment."[60] Most pastimes and amusements of the period—from children's games to informal ball games—were casual and did not depend on facilities and equipment. Horse racing, representing pride of ownership and the desire of man to excel, relied on a stated distance for the race rather than on a sophisticated track. The pastimes of the period were informal with little attention to more than the immediate goal of completing a task such as a barn raising followed by a relaxing frolic. Some pastimes, such as fishing and hunting to provide food and racing horses to improve the breed, were considered utilitarian.

The evidence of sport, pastimes, and amusements of this period must be placed in the perspective of the times. As the settlers established the colonies, they came to be identified as "Americans," especially in the political arena.

Overall, the colonists were more concerned about making a living and the oppressive taxes imposed on them by the English Parliament than about how they spent their leisure time. When they banded together to protest the taxes and other restrictive measures, they formed the Continental Congress, which first met in 1774. Among the resolutions passed was one which "discouraged every species of extravagance and dissipation, especially all horse racing and all kinds of gaming, cock-fighting, exhibitions of shows, plays and other expensive diversions and entertainments."[61] While this resolution reveals the attitudes of the leaders of the country on the eve of the American Revolution, others from all walks of life accepted proper pastimes as a part of life and diversions from their regular duties in life. These new Americans had survived the rigors of colonialization and embraced self-government as a way of life. Colonial life included modest pastimes and social amusements which later developed into sport in the United States.

Suggestions for Further Reading

1. Brailsford, Dennis. *Sport and Society, Elizabeth to Anne.* Toronto: University of Toronto Press, 1969.
2. Culin, Stewart. *Games of the North American Indians.* New York: Dover, 1975.
3. Jable, J. Thomas. "Pennsylvania's Early Blue Laws: A Quaker Experiment in the Suppression of Sport and Amusements, 1682–1740." *Journal of Sport History* 1, No. 2 (November 1974):107–121.
4. Struna, Nancy L. "The Declaration of Sports Reconsidered." *Canadian Journal of History of Sport* 14 (December 1983):44–68.
5. Struna, Nancy L. "Sport and Societal Values: Massachusetts Bay." *Quest* 27 (Winter 1977):38–46.
6. Strutt, Joseph. *The Sports and Pastimes of the People of England.* London: William Tegg, 1867.

Notes

1. Hugh Honour, *The European Vision of America* (Kent, Ohio: The Kent State University Press, 1975), 2.
2. A. Barlowe, "Captain Arthur Barlowe's Narrative of the First Voyage to Virginia: 1584," in *Virginia Reader,* ed. F. C. Rosenberger (New York: E. P. Dutton & Company, 1948), 33.
3. Stewart Culin, *Games of the North American Indians* (New York: Dover, 1975), 587.
4. Cited in Samuel Eliot Morison, *The Great Explorers* (New York: Oxford University Press, 1978), 287.
5. Stewart Culin, *Games of the North American Indians* (New York: Dover, 1975), 32–33.
6. *The Journal of Nicholas Cresswell, 1774–1777* (New York: Lincoln MacVeagh, 1924), 109.

7. Stewart Culin, *Games of the North American Indians* (New York: Dover, 1975), 586–87.

8. Stephan F. deBorhegyi, "America's Ballgame," *Natural History* 69, No. 1 (January 1960):53.

9. Charles E. Bennett, *Three Voyages of Renê Laudonnière* (Gainesville: The University Presses of Florida, 1975), 11.

10. J. LeMoyne, cited in Herbert Manchester, *Four Centuries of Sport in America, 1490–1890* (New York: The Derrydale Press, 1931), 9.

11. William S. Davis, *Life on a Mediaeval Barony* (New York: Harper & Brothers, 1923), 62.

12. William Shakespeare, *King Henry the Fifth,* act 1, sc. 2, lines 258–287.

13. G.M. Trevelyan, *A Shortened History of England* (New York: Penguin, 1942), 315.

14. Joseph Strutt, *The Sports and Pastimes of the People of England* (London: William Tegg, 1867), 97.

15. John Stow, *A Survey of London,* reprinted from 1603 (Oxford: Clarendon Press, 1908), 92–93.

16. Joseph Strutt, *The Sports and Pastimes of the People of England* (London: William Tegg, 1867), 277.

17. Ibid., 257.

18. Edward Chamberlayne, *Angliae Notitiae,* 1669, cited in Carl Bridenbaugh, *Vexed and Troubled Englishmen, 1590–1642* (New York: Oxford University Press, 1968), 154–55.

19. Keeping the "Lord's Day" holy is called *Sabbatarianism.* The term derives from *Sabbath,* Saturday, the seventh day, and the principle comes from the Fourth Commandment. During the Reformation, Sunday rather than Saturday came to be observed.

20. L. A. Govett, *The King's Book of Sports* (London: Elliot Stock, 1890), 38–39.

21. Melville J. Herskovits, *The Myth of the Negro Past* (Boston: Beacon Press, 1958), 47.

22. Ibid., 107.

23. E. Jefferson Murphy, *History of African Civilization* (New York: Thomas Y. Crowell Co., 1972), 150.

24. Heinrich Barth, *Travels and Discoveries in North and Central Africa* (London: Frank Cass & Co., 1965), 204.

25. "The Life of Olaudah Equiano or Gustavus Vasa, the African," Boston, 1837, in *The Negro in American History,* ed. M. J. Adler (Encyclopaedia Britannica Educational Corporation, 1969), 382.

26. *Mungo Park's Travels in Africa* (New York: Dutton, 1907), 161.

27. Margery Perham and J. Simmons, *African Discovery* (London: Faber and Faber, 1957), 95.

28. Ibid., 116–17.

29. E. Jefferson Murphy, *History of African Civilization* (New York: Thomas Y. Crowell Co., 1972), 167.

30. E. Olaudah, *The Interesting Narrative of Olaudah Equiano, or Gustavus Vasa, the African* (2 vols, London, 1789), in *Africa Remembered,* ed. P. Curtin (Madison: The University of Wisconsin, 1967), 69.

31. Thomas Phillips, "A Journal of a Voyage to Africa and Barbadoes," in *A Collection of Voyages and Travels,* vol. 6, ed. Churchill (London: 1732), 230.

32. Basil Davidson, *The African Past* (London: Longmans, 1964), 191.

33. Ibid., 228.

34. Allan Nevins and Henry Steele Commager, *A Pocket History of the United States* (New York: Washington Square Press, 1966), 12.
35. Louis B. Wright, *The Atlantic Frontier* (New York: Alfred A. Knopf, 1947), 117.
36. *Records of the Court of Assistants of the Colony of the Massachusetts Bay, 1630–1644,* vol. II (Boston: County of Suffolk, 1904), 37.
37. Ibid., 9, 75.
38. Edward H. Spicer, *A Short History of the Indians of the United States* (New York: Van Nostrand Reinhold Co., 1969), 175.
39. J. Armstrong, *A Discourse Uttered in Part at Annauskeeg Falls in the Fishing Season, 1739* (Boston: S. Kneeland and T. Green in Queen Street, 1743), 1.
40. Cited in Margery A. Bulger, "Ali Ali in Free . . . The Games Children Played in Colonial America," *Early American Life* (August 1975): 48–49, 82.
41. Ruth E. Painter, "Tavern Amusements in Eighteenth Century America," *The Leisure Class in America,* ed. Leon Stein (New York: Arno Press, 1975), 92.
42. H. Telfer Mook, "Training Day in New England," *New England Quarterly* (December 1938):690.
43. *The Journal of Madam Knight,* ed. of 1825 (New York: Peter Smith, 1935), 37.
44. Nancy L. Struna, "Sport and Societal Values: Massachusetts Bay," *Quest* 27 (Winter 1977):45.
45. John Hervey, *Racing in America, 1665–1865,* vol. 1 (New York: The Jockey Club, 1944), 34.
46. Cited in Esther Singleton, *Social New York Under the Georges, 1714–1776* (New York: D. Appleton, 1902), 268.
47. Esther Singleton, *Dutch New York* (New York: Benjamin Blom, 1968), 290.
48. *The Journal of Madam Knight,* ed. of 1825 (New York: Peter Smith, 1935), 55.
49. Shirley Wynne, "From Ballet to Ballroom: Dance in the Revolutionary Era," *Dance Scope* 10, no. 1 (1975/76):72.
50. Thomas Jable, "Pennsylvania's Early Blue Laws: A Quaker Experiment in the Suppression of Sport and Amusements, 1682–1740," *Journal of Sport History* 1, no. 2 (November 1974):109.
51. Benjamin Franklin, *Proposals for the Education of Youth in Pennsylvania, 1749* (Ann Arbor: William L. Clements Library, 1927), 10.
52. Benjamin Franklin, *The Art of Swimming Rendered Easy, Dr. Franklin's Advice to Bathers* (Glasgow: Printed for the book sellers [184–?]), 4.
53. W. Milnor, *Historical Memoir of the Schuylkill Fishing Company* (Philadelphia: Judah Dobson, 1830), 2.
54. John Hervey, *Racing in America, 1665–1865,* vol. 1 (New York: The Jockey Club, 1944), 22.
55. F. P. Bowes, *The Culture of Early Charleston* (Chapel Hill: The University of North Carolina Press, 1942), 9.
56. Edmund S. Morgan, *Virginians at Home: Family Life in the Eighteenth Century* (Williamsburg, VA: The Colonial Williamsburg Foundation, 1952), 67.
57. June A. Kennard, "Maryland Colonials at Play: Their Sports and Games," *Research Quarterly* 41, no. 3 (1970):395.
58. Charles Woodmason, *The Carolina Backcountry on the Eve of the Revolution,* ed. R. J. Hooker (Chapel Hill: University of North Carolina, 1953), 47.
59. Daniel Boone, "The ADVENTURES of Col. Daniel Boon; containing a NARRATIVE of the WARS of Kentucke, 1798," in *The Discovery, Settlement and Present State of Kentucke,* ed. John Filson (New York: Corinth Books, 1962), 65.
60. Harold J. VanderZwaag and Thomas J. Sheehan, *Introduction to Sport Studies* (Dubuque, IA: Wm. C. Brown Publishers, 1978), 18.
61. *Journals of Congress,* vol. 1 (Philadelphia: Folwell's Press, 1800), 33.

Time Line

HISTORY

1776–1783
War of Independence
1778
First American dictionary, Webster's
1787
Northwest Ordinance
1789
United States of America
1803
Louisiana Purchase
1804–6
Lewis and Clark Expedition
1812
War of 1812

1821
First public high school, Massachusetts

1823
Monroe Doctrine promulgated

1825
Opening of Erie Canal

1833
Oberlin College, first coeducational college, founded
1836
Battle of Alamo in Texas
1837
Morse invented the telegraph
1840
Twenty-eight hundred miles of railway tracks in country

SPORT AND PHYSICAL EDUCATION

1788
Race horse, Messenger, imported
1802
Opening of National Race Course near Washington, D.C.
1806
American "Yankey" trots mile in 2:59
1810
Tom Molyneux defeated by Tom Cribb
1814
Georgetown University students played handball
1816
First American yacht, *Cleopatra's Barge,* built
1823
Round Hill School founded
Union Race Course, Long Island,
Sir Henry defeated by American Eclipse
1825
First track for trotting opens on Long Island
1831
Beecher's *A Course of Calisthenics for Young Ladies* published

1837
Mount Holyoke Seminary opened; required exercise

3 Pastimes, Sport, and the Beginnings of Physical Education in a Developing Country, 1776–1840

Overview

In 1823 tens of thousands of racing fans, northerners and southerners alike, jammed the roads leading to the Long Island race course to see the famous horse American Eclipse race Sir Henry of Virginia. The United States was still a young country, but that traffic jam on Long Island attested to the existence of many affluent Americans, especially in eastern towns and on southern plantations, individuals who were able and willing to enjoy the luxuries of the nineteenth-century leisure class. Yet during the same 1820s, only a few hundred miles away on the Illinois frontier, a cornhusking bee might attract a dozen scattered pioneering families to their major social event of the winter: "[The corn] is gathered in October and November, when they only take off the ears; but as the ears are covered with a large husk, they carry them as they are to the corn-crib, and then all the neighbours collect together to help husk it, and put it into the corn-crib . . . plenty of whiskey is generally found at one of the frolics . . . and they generally conclude with a dance."[1]

At about the same time, but with a very different cast of mind, aimed at improvement not enjoyment, educators Joseph Cogswell and George Bancroft opened Round Hill School in Northampton, Massachusetts, with plans to "appropriate regularly a portion of each day to healthful sports and gymnastic exercises."[2] They reflected the growing concern of Americans both for education and for exercise, especially for sedentary city dwellers, in order to maintain good health. These three vignettes characterize the diversity of pastimes, sport, and the beginnings of physical education in the United States from 1776 to 1840.

After the peace treaty ending the Revolutionary War was signed in 1783, each colony slowly shaped itself into a state with a separate constitution. Diversity of interests and differing opinions among the colonies marked the struggle to forge a new nation, as argumentative pamphlets appeared during the Constitutional Convention and the ensuing ratification struggle. Finally, in 1790 the last of the original thirteen colonies ratified the Constitution, a unique document in its time.

The authors of the Constitution represented the "new" Americans—prosperous lawyers and tradesmen in their early forties. Our basic federal documents created the basis for a new government and the political atmosphere in which we live today. The Declaration of Independence and the Constitution, including the Bill of Rights, represent the people's belief in their ability to govern themselves through their elected representatives. The Declaration of Independence speaks of certain "inalienable rights" with which mankind is endowed, among them "life, liberty, and the pursuit of happiness." The Preamble to the Constitution declares the importance of "Justice," "Domestic Tranquility," and "the general Welfare." The Bill of Rights consists of the first ten amendments, designed to protect persons and property against abuses of governmental power. These concepts have greatly influenced sport and physical education throughout the history of this country.

The first decades of the new nation were occupied with establishing and stabilizing the country. By 1803 four states were admitted to the Union, making a total of seventeen, and the Louisiana Purchase greatly increased the country's territory. Torn between ties to Europe and the need to be independent, in 1812 the young nation found itself again at war. One outcome of the war was an increasing nationalism, prosperity, and a generally "good" feeling. However, each state had its own interests and sectionalism remained a fact of life, evident in sporting events such as the horse race between Eclipse and Sir Henry. In 1823 the Monroe Doctrine set forth the basis for future foreign policy. Later, under Andrew Jackson, the policy of *laissez-faire* encouraged prosperity for agricultural and commercial interests.

In the early decades of this period, almost all of the United States was rural and relatively undeveloped. Most of the population east of the Alleghenies were rural folk who lived on small farms or in very small towns. In 1800 only thirty-three towns in the country numbered more than twenty-five hundred people. Even in 1840 only a hundred additional towns had populations exceeding twenty-five hundred, and only five cities—Boston, New York, Philadelphia, Baltimore, and Charleston—were commercial and social centers. By then twenty-six states belonged to the Union.

With the influx of some twelve million immigrants, chiefly Irish, German, and African, the established families became the "Old American Families," reinforcing and widening distances between social groups. Social classes among white Americans were comparatively fluid, but sharp distinctions were made between the Boston Brahmins and newly arrived Catholic Irish in New England, between the Astor's wealthy group and European immigrants in New York, and in the South, among plantation owners, poor sharecroppers, and slaves. In the rural and frontier areas, where land was readily available and where hard work, good weather, and luck could make even a new immigrant a prosperous farmer, social distinctions were frowned upon.

"Progress" swept the country along, as Americans with their practical and inventive minds built canals, steamboats, and railroads to carry both goods and people across the vast distances. Carriages became more elaborate and efficient but required better roads. Public roads were often little more than trails. Privately built "turnpikes" provided better roadbeds and faster transportation. After the Erie Canal's opening in 1825 increased the flow of both goods and people, other canals opened as far west as Indiana and Illinois. Robert Fulton's steamboat changed the slow river traffic to a faster paced means of transportation in 1807. Soon riverboats, especially on the Mississippi, provided a means of getting up and down the central part of the country. In 1830 the first steam locomotive appeared and, by 1840, the railroad. Following the Civil War the railroad played an important part in the development of baseball and other sports. Eli Whitney invented the cotton "gin" in 1793, and in the 1830s agriculture changed, as new technological advances like Cyrus McCormick's reaper and John Deere's plow changed farming. Cheap energy near a stream attracted many spinning and weaving industries to small towns in New England.

The new country also had its poets, painters, novelists, and educators, who contributed to the formation of American culture. Social roles became more defined in the early part of the nineteenth century, but they tended to be more ideal than real. Men were seen as builders of trade and business in the new country and women as creators of homes. The cult of "true womanhood" assigned to women the traits of piety, purity, submissiveness, and domesticity. These ideals influenced American thought and the history of women's sport for the next hundred years and more.

The religious climate of the country was set by the First Amendment of the new Constitution, guaranteeing freedom of religion. However, the Puritan work ethic and Sunday Blue Laws continued to pervade the fabric of life and thought of New Englanders, who then carried these beliefs with them as they moved westward into New York or down the Ohio River. Although interest in church activities decreased for many people just after the Revolution, a Second Awakening, similar to the Great Awakening of the previous century, swept through Protestant groups such as Methodists and Baptists, with emotional revivals and camp meetings. The number of Roman Catholics increased during this period, but did not change the powerful influence of Protestantism over the lives of most people.

By the 1820s and 1830s America's social reform movement began to take shape. A small group of New Englanders, Ralph Waldo Emerson, Henry David Thoreau, Bronson Alcott, Margaret Fuller, and others, based their beliefs on the philosophy of transcendentalism that extolled "self-reliance" in all political, religious, and other matters. Later perceived by some as do-gooders who wished to impose methods of social control on others, these early reformers sincerely believed that the United States could become a model nation and that every facet of life could be improved.

For example, education, while considered necessary, was not available to everyone. Some towns provided education for boys, but few provided it for girls. Earlier, Benjamin Franklin had pleaded for improved education. Later, Horace Mann and Henry Barnard carried on the battle for better public education and Mary Lyon pioneered women's education. Health as a desirable condition in life was also a concern of the reformers. Set against the meager medical and scientific knowledge of the period—before the need for surgical cleanliness and sanitation was understood, before anesthesia, before bacteriology, and when "consumption" and other diseases were common—the zeal of American reformers to improve people's health seems remarkable. Without understanding the physiological basis, connections were made between exercise and movement and general fitness of the body. These connections led to the first attempts at physical education in this country.

With their homes and farms established and a little more leisure for their personal interests, an increasing number of early nineteenth-century Americans found time for amusements and sport. Benjamin Franklin, the successful printer, could pursue science, government, education, and swimming. In 1743 he founded the American Philosophical Society to promote the fine arts and general knowledge in the new country. Abigail Adams discussed with her husband, John, and her friend Thomas Jefferson, her advocacy of increased rights for women and of free public education for all children of Massachusetts, regardless of sex or wealth. In the South, Washington, Jefferson, Richard Henry Lee, and other wealthy planters delved into philosophical studies, politics, education, and also enjoyed a good hunt.

Sport and pastimes from the end of the Revolution to 1840 were affected by the energy and growth of the country, its diverse social groups, and the different lives of the wealthy in the settled regions of the East and in the frontier families east and just west of the Mississippi River. This chapter will trace the beginnings of professional sport, the pastimes which preceded amateur sport in the United States, and the beginnings of physical education in schools.

Beginnings of Professional Sport

Horse racing, boxing, cockfighting, pedestrianism, and rowing attracted men from all walks of life. Although the boxing ring and cock pit were male domains, women frequented the fashionable race days at Annapolis, Maryland, and Williamsburg, Virginia. Women occasionally joined the socially elite hunting parties, but men and boys ordinarily assumed the responsibility for hunting game to supply the family table.

Horse Racing
Before and immediately following the Revolutionary War, Alexandria and Williamsburg, Virginia, and Annapolis, Maryland, were racing centers, attracting the leading citizens of the area. During the war, horses belonging to

Tories were confiscated and numerous American horses pressed into war service. Following the war, in 1788, New York banned horse racing on Sunday, and two years later, North Carolina outlawed it altogether. In New York many "upright" citizens objected to the rabble and less desirable people who frequented the races. Betts reports, "By 1795 a 'Society for Aiding and Assisting the Magistrates in the suppression of Vice and Immorality on the Lord's Day' was formed in New York."[3] The New York state legislature banned horse racing in 1802 and later Pennsylvania and New Jersey followed suit. Virginia did not stop horse racing, but placed a seven dollar limit on bets on sporting events such as cockfighting and horse racing.[4] The famed Annapolis race week did not survive the war and, while some racing continued at Annapolis, it never equalled the glamour of the prewar period.

However, with the exception of North Carolina, horse racing remained the most popular sport in the South, expanding south and west to Kentucky, Alabama, and Louisiana. Presidents and national figures enthusiastically promoted horse racing. Citing Andrew Jackson, Henry Clay, Daniel Webster, and John C. Calhoun, Hervey remarks, "It may fairly be said that at no time in the history of the United States since it emerged from the Colonial period was racing so generally identified with and promoted by our greatest national figures."[5]

Racing remained in the control of the gentry, who raced their horses ostensibly to improve the breed and develop speed and stamina—important qualities in horses which were used for daily transportation. They took pride in owning the fastest horses and in contesting and besting their friends. Wagering was common, but there was no hint of commercialism in this gentlemen's sport. Although the races were sponsored by and contested among the wealthier classes, all sorts of people attended. During the races betting was often heavy, and occasionally small fortunes were won or lost. Jockeys and trainers were drawn predominantly from the ranks of both free and slave black men, particularly in the South. This pattern continued throughout the nineteenth century.

In the late eighteenth century, interest in improving the American horse brought several outstanding English horses to the United States. Two horses, the filly Mambrina, and Messenger, both sired by the famous Mambrino, were purchased in the 1780s for breeding purposes. A third, Diomed, was acquired in 1798 by Colonel Hoomes in Virginia. Thus before 1800 excellent blood lines had been established for the future of horse racing in this country. Both American Eclipse, who raced in the 1823 match against Sir Henry, and Hambletonian, famous sire of many trotters, were descendants of Messenger. However, the American horse, Justin Morgan of Randolph, Vermont, became a legend in his own time, and established the popular line, the Morgan horse. By the end of this period American breeders developed a line distinct from the English thoroughbred.

Figure 3.1   Maryland Jockey Club, Pimlico, 1802. Courtesy of the Enoch Pratt Free Library, Baltimore, Maryland.

The opening of the National Race Course at Washington, D.C., in 1802 made it possible for the nation's political leaders to leave the affairs of state occasionally and venture out from the new capital to attend the races. The first permanent course was opened in Maryland in 1820 about three miles from Baltimore. In 1821 public racing was legalized in Queens County, New York, and at the Union Course on Long Island. It was there in 1823 that the famous encounter occurred between American Eclipse and Sir Henry of Virginia. The first of several North-South horse races, perhaps symbolizing the growing sectionalism in the country, it captured the imagination of thousands of Americans. On the day of the race, the roads leading to the Union Park were clogged with people, probably over sixty thousand. American Eclipse came home the victor in two out of three races in the first sport event in the United States to attract such a large crowd.

> There was never contest more exciting. Sectional feeling and heavy pecuniary stakes were both involved. The length of time before it was decided, the change of riders, the varying fortunes, all intensified the interest. I have seen the great Derby races; but they finish almost as soon as they begin, and were tame enough in comparison to this. Here for nearly two hours there was no abatement in the strain. I was unconscious of everything else, and found, when the race was concluded, that the sun had actually blistered my cheek without my perceiving it. The victors were, of course, exultant, and Purdy, mounted on Eclipse, was led up to the judges' stand, the band playing "See the Conquering Hero Comes."[6]

The popular interest in the race presumably reflected sectional loyalties as well as the congeniality of a social gathering, the identification with a winner, and the possibility of gain through wagering.

When the weekly *Spirit of the Times* appeared, local races and also matches from as far away as Tennessee and Kentucky were advertised. In one issue in the 1830s races were announced for Harper's Ferry, Baltimore, Gloucester, Nashville, Lawrenceville, and Columbia, with purses varying from one hundred to five hundred dollars. Fine ladies and gentlemen, legislators, clergymen, and tradesmen frequented the races. At times courts did not hold sessions and schools excused their pupils for the events. Many slaves enjoyed a holiday on race day.

Horse racing moved west with the earliest permanent settlers. Newcomers to Kentucky, Tennessee, and Illinois came largely from the southern and border states of Maryland, Virginia, and South Carolina, and brought with them their fondness for racing. Tracks were opened in Nashville, Tennessee, and in Lexington and Louisville, Kentucky, which had the first circular track west of the Alleghenies. In Kentucky the breeding of horses became a major pursuit, and the formation of jockey clubs also helped to get racing under way. Rural farmers and frontiersmen could not often get to the permanent race tracks in the cities, but they enthusiastically followed the local races held during county fairs and festivals.

After 1823 intersectional contests continued but did not command as much attention as the Eclipse-Henry race. The early 1830s saw the peak of horse racing with better tracks, more training stables, and regular reporting. Thoroughbred racing represented sport not only for the gentry, a tradition that had existed since the early days of the southern colonies, but also for other classes who could join as spectators and bettors. The common folk could also identify with the pride of community or with sectionalism in the 1820s and 1830s.

Even before the recession of 1837, however, thoroughbred racing had begun to lose its popularity. In the new nation, the place of the common man changed as did his views of sport. Rather than looking up to the gentry to set the values of American life, the common man looked to his neighbors and himself. The pervasive influence of the agrarian life in America decreased as the growth of towns, manufacturing, and commercial ventures increased. As Struna notes, "The ideals of the public and the reality of the sport had changed. . . . Prosperity, heightened regional identity, and even manufacturing prompted, or perhaps were initiated by, acquisitiveness, less fervent nationalism, and mass action and thinking."[7] The common man turned to harness racing, another form of horse racing in which the middle class could participate with enjoyment, and which might be considered more democratic.

Trotting horses were used for daily transportation and pulling lightweight wagons or carriages. The use of trotting horses to pull their carriages and wagons and the improved streets of cities such as New York and Philadelphia led men to challenge one another.

The desire to be first or, perhaps, not to be last, resulted in races on the city streets, and later on courses designed for racing. Akers suggests that trotting was deemed a worthy venture, "On the grounds of public necessity. . . . Without tests of speed and endurance in the white hot crucible of competition, how—it was asked—could breeders determine which stock was the best?"[8] New York became the center where more formal trotting contests developed. The sport moved steadily toward organization in the modern sense of the word. Using the same justification as jockey clubs in thoroughbred racing—to improve the breed—the New York Trotting Club formed in 1825. A track was built specifically for trotting, purses or prizes for races were offered, and stables with professional trainers established. Other tracks followed at Harlem, New York; Hoboken, New Jersey; and Philadelphia, Pennsylvania.

As thoroughbred racing declined in the 1830s, harness racing increased and soon became the most popular sport in the country. Adelman explains its popularity: "Harness racing surged to the forefront of the turf world and athletics in general because it captured the flow of the American experience more than any other sport of its day . . . While the nature of the horse played a critical role, of equal significance was the fact that those who governed trotting . . . internalized the values of modern society."[9] By the middle decades of the nineteenth century harness racing more nearly met the needs of mainstream America than thoroughbred racing. For middle- and upper-middle class men, trotting was an extension of their daily activities. It also provided the opportunity to engage in a friendly wager, and to prove or try to prove that their horse and equipment were just a little better than their neighbors'. When the sport organized for formal racing and prizes, they could wager on their favorite entry. Harness racing could be characterized as utilitarian, participatory, and democratic—all acceptable American traits. After all, the trotting horse itself was thoroughly American.

Boxing

In the late eighteenth and early nineteenth centuries, a few financially and socially elite men in both the South and North took up the art of boxing. Many young men of the southern gentry were familiar with the sport, since they had attended college in England where it was popular. In this country, slave owners encouraged the best fighters among their slaves to train extensively and then arranged for them to fight slave boxers from neighboring plantations. The black boxers also fought among themselves for their own entertainment. When the owners planned the fight, there was often heavy betting, and occasionally boxing superiority led to the freedom of the slave.

One successful slave boxer in Virginia, Tom Molyneux, was granted freedom by his owner because of his expertise as a boxer. He wandered north to New York City where he boxed with longshoremen, noted for their strength and roughness. In 1809 he traveled to England and found the American-born black boxer, Bill Richmond, who coached him and helped arrange matches against some of England's best fighters, against whom Molyneux won. He was then matched with the famous British champion, Tom Cribb, for the unofficial world championship. They met in 1810 under the London Prize Ring Rules and fought forty-four grueling rounds.[10] The December 19, 1810 *Times* of London reported, "The battle lasted fifty-five minutes, in which 44 rounds took place, and it was all hard fighting. Both the combatants were dreadfully beaten; and they were almost deprived of sight. . . . The *Black* gave in rather from weakness than want of courage. He is certainly one of the most promising pugilists that has appeared." A year later Molyneux was defeated by Cribb in eleven rounds.

The first American to win boxing recognition was Bill Richmond, Molyneux's mentor. Born on Staten Island, he went to England as a boy. After he established a reputation as a fine fighter, he became a valet to Lord Camelford, a devotee of horse racing, cockfighting, and boxing. Richmond fought a number of highly publicized matches between 1800 and 1818, one of which, with Cribb, he lost by a decision.

Figure 3.2   Tom Molyneux, early United States boxer.

Neither an art nor a science, boxing for these early professional fighters was a test of their ability to withstand physical punishment. Bare-knuckled and physically strong men pummeled one another, sometimes for several hours, until one of them dropped. There were few rules and many matches degenerated into kicking, biting, and gouging free-for-alls, which occasionally ended in the death of one or the other participant. In this country both boxing and wrestling matches were sometimes staged at local taverns. Scorned by many Americans, professional boxing in these years frequently attracted the rougher element in the cities and as a result was banned in local communities and in some states. However, some attempts were made to make the sport respectable. Promoters advertised boxing as "athletic exercise," while others offered lessons to "gentlemen."

Cockfighting

In city and town, village and rural farm or plantation all over America during this period, cockfighting was one of the more popular sports for men. Although it was not universally approved, many wealthy gentlemen who enjoyed the

Figure 3.3   Cockfighting, a sport of the early nineteenth century. Courtesy of the Enoch Pratt Free Library, Baltimore, Maryland.

pastime bred and maintained fighting cocks. Its general popularity carried it past its role as an early colonial tavern sport, unlike animal baiting which lost favor during the nineteenth century. Cockfighting eventually became almost exclusively associated with the lower classes. Massachusetts, presaging later sentiments against cruelty to animals, banned cockfighting in 1836.

Pedestrianism

Beginning in the 1820s and reaching a peak in the 1840s and 1850s pedestrianism, or walking races, became a craze that attracted many persons in towns, villages, and at fairs. "Walkers" or pedestrians, moving from town to town, would challenge the best walker of a community to a race, from a quarter of a mile to ten, twenty, or thirty miles. Frequently preceded by an advance man who would promote the contest and arrange the betting, some "peds" attracted crowds of twenty-five thousand. Although most races, particularly those over long distances, were conducted on roads, many owners of private race tracks sponsored and promoted pedestrian races. Pedestrianism remained popular until the early 1880s when amateur track and field events began to replace walking races.

Rowing

Just as the professional sport of "pedestrianism" preceded amateur track and field events, professional rowing preceded amateur rowing or "crew," as we know it today. Along the Gulf Coast crews of black slaves raced for their plantation owners. By 1811 longshoremen as well as English and American seamen competed in light barges on the Hudson River in New York. On February 18, 1832, the *Spirit of the Times* reported a race between nine boats near Philadelphia. Each boat was manned by a single rower and raced a five-mile course for a prize of twenty dollars "or a new boat of the same value." Rowing was also popular among middle-class young men who began to form their own amateur boat clubs in the 1820s and 1830s in cities such as Savannah, Poughkeepsie, Philadelphia, New Orleans, Mobile, Biloxi, and Detroit. The founding of these clubs and their later introduction onto college campuses established rowing, especially crew, as an upper-middle-class pastime and sport.

Horse racing, boxing, cockfighting, pedestrianism, and rowing were the precursors of modern professional sport. Harness racing, with its specially built tracks, promoters, fees, and records, was the first sport to become modernized. These early sports were engaged in for different reasons according to social class. The gentry of the early decades owned and raced famous thoroughbreds and, later, trotters. In the South they might own slaves who rowed, boxed, and perhaps trained cocks for the benefit and pleasure of their masters. The gentry engaged in sport for their own pleasure and honor, not for commercial reasons. When middle-class men attended many of the sporting events they participated as backers and bettors, not as owners. Women attended horse racing and pedestrianism events, but probably would not be found at boxing matches, rowing events, and cockfights.

One element identified with the preprofessional sports of the period was the "sporting fraternity," whom Rader describes as workingmen who had not or would not adjust readily to the new economic pattern of regular working hours, hard work, and industriousness. Among them were many bachelors and other men who found a refuge from marriage and domesticity in billiard parlors and saloons.[11] They attended and waged bets on sporting events. Many of these sports such as cockfighting never reached the respectability of mainstream American sport. Others, such as pedestrianism and professional rowing, faded from the sport scene. Still others, such as horse racing, were periodically subjected to reform in order to gain respectable status.

Pastimes and Other Amusements

The diversity of physical activity in this period is illustrated by its origins and geographical extent. Sports from other countries, such as cricket from England, were popular for some time in certain localities, but were not adopted as "American." Gymnastics from Germany, later widely influential and popular, was first introduced into this country in the 1820s. In the settled coastal states and in the frontier areas west of the Alleghenies, men hunted and fished, both to provide food and to enjoy themselves. The wealthier groups, especially in the South, followed the English example of formal fox hunting. On the ocean or lakes wealthy families enjoyed piloting their increasingly luxurious pleasure crafts, not yet called yachts. All over the country children played traditional games and invented others.

In the South the life of slaves varied from owner to owner. Some treated their slaves humanely while others dealt with them harshly and at times cruelly. Visitors from European countries sometimes described the life of the slaves on the plantations where they were guests. From these accounts we learn that it was fairly typical to celebrate a number of holidays and to grant time for the slaves to have their own celebrations or "frolics." On such occasions slaves boxed, wrestled, ran races, and played ball. Frolics usually ended with dancing. Not infrequently, either with or without permission, slaves managed to visit the slaves of nearby plantations.[12] On some plantations slaves were free after they finished their assigned tasks for the day. Bennet H. Barrow of Louisiana noted in his journal, "negroes holliday part of the day," "Finished hoeing corn second time by dinner yesterday. Holliday afterwards," and "negros Holliday since dinner."[13]

Sport and pastimes in the frontier regions of early nineteenth-century America were strongly affected by the geographic and psychological circumstances of the settlers. West of the Alleghenies most of the population was rural, dwelling on small farms and in towns of no more than a few hundred.

Figure 3.4   The old plantation. Slaves were occasionally granted times for celebrations or "frolics." Courtesy of Abby Aldrich Rockefeller Art Center, Williamsburg, Virginia.

The first families in each new region were required to be self-sufficient and to manufacture, build, grow, or do without items which might be easily purchased by people living in a city, or even in an eastern rural area. The periodic dangers posed by hostile Indians and natural calamities sharpened the settlers' sense of survival. Most families were still extremely isolated, depending for their food upon the game and fish nearby as well as upon the produce from their own farm and garden. The tavern and inn in the rural areas served several functions. "For villagers and townspeople and many farmers, . . . the inn was indispensable as a social center. It was the theater, the ballroom, the youth center, the restaurant, the bowling alley, the billiard parlor, the saloon, and the sports arena, all in one."[14]

Hunting and Fishing
Hunting, fishing, and other outdoor pursuits differed greatly, from the large estates in the East to the forests, lakes, and rivers on the frontier. The formal fox hunt was a popular sport among gentry in the South. George Washington, for example, was proud of his pack of hounds—Pilot, Music, Countess, and Truelove—and pursued the fox as frequently as he could. Jefferson, too, greatly enjoyed a chase across the rolling Virginia countryside. Elaborate riding outfits for the hunt consisting of waistcoat and buckskin breeches were usually imported from England. The southern states of Maryland, Virginia, and the Carolinas were all well known for their fox hunting, because of the open fields,

the climate, and the leisured way of life among the southern plantation owners. Even in New England some fox hunting went on throughout the eighteenth and nineteenth centuries.

To the west, from the rugged hill country of eastern Tennessee, Kentucky, and Pennsylvania, through the forests of the Ohio Valley, to the very edge of the sprawling Great Plains in western Illinois, the variety and quantity of fish and wild game staggered the imagination. The very earliest reports of this angler's and hunter's paradise were carried east by explorers, hunters, and other adventurers in the early eighteenth century. Only the British government and the hazardous journey through and over the mountains prevented large numbers of colonists from establishing themselves there prior to the Revolution. Thus, it remained for a century the almost private preserve of the French hunter-trapper-trader and the few hardy frontiersmen from Virginia and the Carolinas who shared the game and the land with the Indians. The succeeding waves of pioneers depended heavily upon fishing and hunting. They pursued fowl such as geese, quail, partridge, grouse, and woodcock, as well as animals ranging from deer and bear to squirrels and rabbits.

Hunting quickly became a recreational as well as an economic pursuit in frontier life. Basically a solitary activity, under some frontier conditions it became more social through organized group efforts like the "ring hunt": "An army of men and boys from near-by settlements would form a vast encircling line of huntsmen around an area of perhaps forty square miles. Gradually they would close in the circle, driving ahead of them all the game they could scare up. When at last the ring was so small that the harried animals began to try to break through, the signal of a huntsman's horn would start a wholesale slaughter. Guns would be used as long as this was reasonably safe, and then clubs, pitchforks, any available weapon."[15] Such hunts often resulted in the slaughter of scores of bear, deer, squirrels, and large and small game birds. While perhaps not sport by today's standards, the hunt provided a winter's supply of meat to be salted away in many household cellars. More closely related to competitive sport were the contests between teams of squirrel hunters, who could bring in hundreds and sometimes thousands of animals in one day.

Such organized hunts were, of course, not everyday events. Most hunting was done individually or in small groups. Even here, however, the hunt was usually bound to be successful because of the amount of available game and the unerring accuracy of the hunters. One example of this accuracy was the practice of "barking off squirrels." The naturalist John James Audubon recounts the demonstration provided by Daniel Boone near Frankfort, Kentucky:

We walked out together, and followed the rocky margins of the Kentucky River, until we reached a piece of flat land thickly covered with black walnuts, oaks, and hickories. As the general mast was a good one that year, Squirrels were seen gamboling on every tree around us. My companion, a stout, hale, and athletic man, dressed in a homespun hunting shirt, bare-legged and moccasined, carried a long and heavy rifle, which, as he was loading it, he said had proved efficient in all his former undertakings, and which he hoped would not fail on this occasion, as he felt proud to show me his skill. The gun was wiped, the powder measured, the ball patched with six-hundred-thread linen, and the charge sent home with a hickory rod. We moved not a step from the place, for the Squirrels were so numerous that it was unnecessary to go after them. Boone pointed to one of these animals which had observed us, and was crouched on a branch about fifty paces distant, and bade me mark well the spot where the ball should hit. He raised his piece gradually, until the *bead* (that being the name given by the Kentuckians to the *sight*) of the barrel was brought to a line with the spot which he intended to hit. The whiplike report resounded through the woods and along the hills, in repeated echoes. Judge of my surprise when I perceived that the ball had hit the piece of the bark immediately beneath the Squirrel, and it shivered it into splinters, the concussion produced by which had killed the animal, and sent it whirling through the air, as if it had been blown up by the explosion of a powder magazine. Boone kept up his firing, and, before many hours had elapsed, we had procured as many Squirrels as we wished. . .[16]

According to Audubon, such skill was not confined to marksmen of the caliber of Boone, as he witnessed the same feat by many others during the years he lived in Kentucky. He considered such skill very plausible, since "every one in the state is accustomed to handle the rifle from the time when he is first able to shoulder it until near the close of his career."[17]

The shooting match similarly served to sharpen skills essential to the frontier while, at the same time, the competition allowed the independent, proud, and self-assured rifleman an opportunity to match ability with and demonstrate prowess to his neighbors. The prodigious shooting skills of the frontiersmen were widely known, partly as a result of the various Indian wars as well as from the accounts of travelers witnessing shooting matches where the contests consisted of snuffing out a candle at fifty yards and driving a nail at eighty yards. The prizes themselves varied in value. Frequently a prize for winning a shooting match was a jug of whisky or a turkey. In prosperous periods the most popular prize was a portion of beef, which was divided among the top several contestants, the choicest portions going to the best marksman.

The popularity of the shooting matches can be illustrated by the fact that these were often the central attractions around which other contests were organized. Athletic events, consisting of throwing, running and jumping contests, were frequently held in conjunction with shooting matches or horse races, or following a court session or some other assemblage. The contests, generally for men and boys, were sometimes planned and sometimes spontaneous. Footraces at distances from fifty yards to a mile or more, jumping for distance, and the throwing of quoits were the most frequent events. The rough and tumble free-for-all fighting popular in the rural areas was also part of the life of the frontiersmen. Utilizing various tactics of hitting, kicking, biting, and gouging,

Figure 3.5   Wrestling on the frontier, which included the practice of "gouging."

the participants gave and received permanent injuries. The not uncommon sight of a man with one empty eye socket or an incomplete ear or lip severed by the teeth was mute evidence of past brawling.

Hunting, fishing, and other outdoor pursuits served several functions in early American society. In the East the formal hunt was a pleasurable pastime. For many fishing was also a pastime, but for others it served as a means of providing food. On the frontier hunting and fishing were necessary, but, as so often happens, man's desire to compete and to be the best led to contests and shooting matches.

Boating and Yachting

Many American cities of this period were located on rivers or lakes or on the Atlantic Ocean, and consequently boating and yachting were important sport activities. According to yachting historians, America's first vessel that might truly be designated a yacht was *Cleopatra's Barge.* It was built in 1816 in Salem, Massachusetts, by Retire Becket for one of the town's wealthiest citizens, George Crowninshield. As its name implies, the luxurious *Barge* had no purpose but pleasure. It was the forerunner of a class of ship that became more and more a status symbol of upper-class society. Yacht racing began in 1836, when Robert B. Forbes' *Sylph* and Commodore John C. Stevens' *Wave* raced off the Massachusetts coast. Organized yacht racing soon developed, with the founding of yacht clubs in a number of major cities.

Figure 3.6   The first pleasure craft, built at Salem, Massachusetts, 1816.
Courtesy of the Peabody Museum of Salem, Massachusetts.

Sport Clubs

During the course of this period, the sport *club* became firmly established.
Since Americans organized clubs for many purposes, it was only natural for
them to eventually form *sport* clubs. In his observations on America, de Tocqueville noted the propensity for joining together for common interests:

> Americans of all ages, all conditions, and of all dispositions constantly form asso-
> ciations. They have not only commercial and manufacturing companies, in which
> all take part, but associations of a thousand other kinds, religious, moral, serious,
> futile, general or restricted, enormous or diminutive. The Americans make associ-
> ations to give entertainments. . . ."[18]

Today persons with a common sport interest form a club which flourishes, grows
in membership, and spawns other clubs; or else it disbands when people are
no longer interested. The early sport clubs differed from the contemporary
variety in two self-limiting ways: most clubs limited their membership to a
given number of the socially elite, and they did not try to foster other sport
clubs.

In the early decades of the nineteenth century, cricket, archery, rowing, and
fishing attracted enthusiasts who formed sport clubs. By the 1790s there were
cricket clubs in Boston and New York, although Philadelphia, with an influx
of English woolen workers, soon emerged as the center for American cricket.

Cricket was also played in Kentucky and Tennessee in the 1790s, but except in the large cities it was not particularly popular. Cricket's measured bowling, its slow pace, the breaks for tea, and the long matches evidently did not adapt itself to the faster pace of American life. A men's archery club, limiting its membership to twenty-five and calling itself the United Bowmen, was formed in Philadelphia in 1828. The Cincinnati Angling Club was also limited to twenty-five members who enjoyed good fellowship as well as the "delightful and healthy amusement of angling."

Implicit within "amateur" sport is the notion of joining together and organizing; and sport clubs of this period exhibited these tendencies. Rowing clubs were an early example of amateurs banding together for the enjoyment of the sport and for sociability. Later in the century, in the 1880s, track and field or athletic clubs founded the Amateur Athletic Union, a major force in the history of amateur sport in the United States.

Bees and Other Social Occasions

Many necessary tasks were turned into social occasions when neighbors joined forces, with a challenge or contest as part of the work. With a history extending to the earliest colonial settlements, husking and quilting bees, plowing matches, as well as cabin and barn raisings were part of life on the frontier. These practical, work-oriented activities met some of the social, competitive, and economic needs of the pioneers. Chopping bees in the Illinois territory just after 1800 were held for the practical purpose of clearing land for planting or building. However, in bringing together a number of families, the normally slow, back-breaking task took on elements of play as the men chatted, joked, and contested their relative skills at chopping; the women conversed, enjoying what might be infrequent adult female companionship while the children played with one another. Further emphasizing the competitive aspect of the activity, prizes were frequently given to the person felling the most trees, husking the most ears of corn, or for whatever contest was held.[19]

Many social gatherings besides bees, including weddings, holidays, and sleigh rides, provided occasions for country dancing. The cotillion and the quadrille were dances for eight dancers in a square formation. The country dances and the reels were performed with one line of dancers facing another. The unique characteristic of the country dance was that it allowed a number of people to dance together without concern for rank. The term "ball" was applied to any formal social occasion at which dancing was the chief part of the evening's entertainment. An assembly was a gathering sponsored by a group of people who provided dancing on a regular basis for themselves and their guests. There were also some public assemblies—some sponsored by dancing masters—open to anyone who could afford the price of a ticket.[20]

Figure 3.7   Dancing in 1798. Courtesy of the Enoch Pratt Free Library, Baltimore, Maryland.

The growing popularity of dancing was not without controversy. The Calvinist clergy, for example, frequently preached and wrote against what, to them, was a sinful pastime. Others, too, denounced dance, pointing out that "dancing was calculated to eradicate solid thought. . . . In fact, versatility of mind, hatred for study, or sober reflection, are the inseparable companions of dancing schools, and the miseries resulting from them are virtually incalculable."[21] The supporters of dance were equally vocal. "Amelia," a correspondent to the Philadelphia *Minerva,* stated: "Whatever cautious cynics, in the delirium of their spleen, may allege to the contrary, dancing is incontestably an elegant and amiable accomplishment; it confers grace and dignity of carriage upon the female sex . . . it invigorates the constitution, enlivens the role of the cheek, and in its results operates as silent eloquence upon the hearts of men. Nature gives us limbs, and art teaches us to use them."[22] Fashionable dances of the day included the minuet, courante, galliard, rigadoon, gavotte, and cotillion.

Dance as a social activity was not the exclusive province of the white citizens; the African slaves also danced. The slaves, separated even from those who might have been shipped with them from their African village or country, lost many of their customs. Dance, however, was transplanted and transformed among the slaves. They danced for their own enjoyment and for their masters' entertainment. They danced the buck and wing, cakewalk, and the buzzard lope. The water dance and juba were challenge or competitive dances, and then there were the jigs, cotillions, quadrilles, and reels. The slaves took every opportunity available to them to dance, and the Saturday night dance was a regular occurrence in some places.[23]

On Sundays and holidays the slave children joined in family activities. At other times slave children looked after smaller children and, when permitted or when they had time, engaged in many childish games of their own making. It was not unusual for slave and white children to play together, but the white children usually took the part of the leaders.[24] In general, children continued to play the traditional games of childhood. There are records of games from England, and it is presumed that, as children from other parts of Europe arrived in America, some of their games found their way to the village common or nearby field. *The Boy's and Girl's Book of Sports,* published in 1839, included games such as tag, jump rope, instructions for leapfrog, and blind man's buff. It also gave complete directions and a diagram for playing "base, or goal ball":

Base, or Goal Ball.—In Base, the players divide themselves into two equal parties, and chance decides which shall have the first innings. Four stones or stakes are placed from twelve to twenty yards asunder, as *a, b, c, d,* in the margin; another
  C   is put at *e.* One of the party, who is out, places himself at *c.* He tosses
B   D the ball to *a,* in front of whom one of the *in- party* places himself,
  E   who strikes the ball, if possible with his bat. If the ball, when struck, be
  A   caught by any of the players of the opposite side, who are scattered
about the field, he is out, and another takes his place. If none of these accidents take place, on striking the ball he drops the bat, and runs towards *b,* or, if he can, to *c, d,* or even to *a,* again. If, however the boy who stands at *c,* or any of the out-players who may happen to have the ball, strike him with it in his progress from *a* to *b, b* to *c, c* to *d, d* to *a,* he is out. Supposing he can only get to *b,* one of his partners takes the bat, and strikes at the ball in turn. If the first player only get to *c,* or *d,* the second runs to *b,* only, or *c,* as the case may be, and a third player begins; as they get home, that is, to *a,* they play at the ball by turns, until they all get out. Then, of course, the out players take their places.[25]

Mary Livermore, a widely known lecturer, remembered children playing on the Boston Common Saturday afternoons: "it was gay and vocal with little girls, attired in sunbonnets and aprons, 'keeping house,' and 'playing school,' 'hide and seek,' and 'playing tag,' and sometimes, it must be confessed, making 'mud pies.' " She also remembered Puritan Sundays in the 1820s:

The Sundays of my childhood were not enjoyable days, they were observed with such unnecessary rigor . . . we children were prepared for the morning Sunday-school at nine o'clock. . . . The Sunday-school ended at half-past ten, when we adjourned from the vestry to the church. . . . When the church service was over we hurried home to the cold dinner. . . . At two o'clock we hurried back to the second session of the Sunday-school, then again to afternoon service in the church, and after that came an interminable prayer-meeting. . . . This prayer-meeting lasted until dark in the winter and until very nearly supper-time in summer.[26]

Families and neighborhood groups enjoyed games and pastimes. In the traditionally Dutch areas of New York and Pennsylvania burghers and farmers enthusiastically bowled and played skittles. Bowling on the green was particularly popular. Few were the taverns in New York that did not maintain a green for bowling or a wooden or stone platform for playing at king-pin or skittles. Some citizens would be found playing "kolf," which, it is thought, contained elements of the modern games of golf and hockey. The Dutch residents also were fond of kaetzen, a game possessing the rudiments of handball, in which the horsehair-filled ball was bounced against a nearby post, tree, or wall. Women played the game with a racket. In the winter, families of New York, Pennsylvania, and New England enjoyed ice skating, sledding, and other winter pastimes.

An examination of the pastimes and amusements of the first decades of the United States reveals a wide assortment serving a variety of purposes. Field sports such as hunting and communal gatherings such as bees were utilitarian and, at the same time, satisfied the need for recreation and enjoyment. The square and country dancing which often followed bees was informal, like life in the rural areas and small towns. In contrast, balls of the upper class were formal, like the social graces practiced by the upper classes. The middle class found summer pleasure in a pleasant boat ride while the wealthy found similar enjoyment in yachting. Children played games, as did some of the adults who found pleasure in cricket, "kolf," and bowling. Base or goal ball was still considered a children's game, but by 1845, its successor changed sport in America. Unquestionably, as the new nation grew, the variety of sport and pastimes increased to reflect the diversity of its people.

Social Reform and the Early Fitness Movement

The sense of bettering or reforming conditions of life had been an American belief since colonial times. As discussed earlier in this chapter, reformers focused on a myriad of problems: prison conditions, alcoholism, the treatment of the insane, hospital conditions, and children's illnesses. During this period reformers' concern about people's health and fitness led to physical education in the schools. Reformers worried about the health of men living in towns and cities because of the comparative lack of physical activity in their daily lives. They compared city life of the period, which might entail a ten-hour stint in a factory within walking distance of a room in a boarding house, to the physically demanding chores on a farm: managing a horse-drawn plow, spading a large garden, forking the hay, milking the cows, cleaning the barn. The reformers noticed that young men in cities often lacked the vigor of farm workers.

Accordingly, they promoted the habit of exercising in a gymnasium, which for a time became popular. Dr. John C. Warren, Professor of Anatomy and

Physiology at Harvard University, together with several prominent Bostonians, promoted a gymnasium for Boston residents in 1826. Boston's Board of Aldermen provided the land and Dr. Charles Follen, a Harvard instructor in German, taught gymnastics. A year earlier Follen had introduced German gymnastics to Harvard students. As a student in Germany he had studied with Friedrich Ludwig Jahn, German patriot and *Turnvater,* who had devised a system of exercise known as German gymnastics.

In eastern cities private gymnasiums opened in the late 1820s. Intended primarily for men, they proved popular for a few years, but within a decade the "fad" of regular gymnastic exercise in a city gymnasium had waned.

The health and fitness of girls and women presented special problems. It was generally accepted that women were weaker than men in their emotional, mental, and physiological makeup and that education for girls and women beyond the elementary level was unnecessary. Indeed, because of their "peculiar" organization, study and exercise might harm them. Social conventions influenced middle- and upper-class women, who consequently shunned vigorous exercise, physical labor, and healthful outdoor activity, while wearing modish apparel, which restricted circulation and free movement of the body. Several reformers, some of them women, spoke out for the education of women, a change to looser and more healthful fashions, and exercise. Park notes:

> Men and women of a diversity of interests and persuasions spoke out . . . for greater attention to such things as: calisthenics; playful games; exercise; less confining clothing; active recreations; instruction in physiology and anatomy; more healthful school and home environments; more physical activity in girls' seminaries.[27]

Friedrich Ludwig Jahn, 1778–1852, was born in Prussia, the son of a small-town pastor, and studied to be a teacher. After two years in the Prussian army fighting Napoleonic France, he taught in schools influenced by Pestalozzi's theories that knowledge comes from bodily activities and sensations.

Jahn's lifework began inconspicuously—leading his students on half-holidays of outdoor play, which soon developed into more organized games, simple exercises like running and jumping, and work on homemade gymnastic apparatus. As teacher/leader Jahn combined these physical activities with his passionate interest in German history and folktales, his ability in storytelling, his own energy and interest, and his skill in leadership—creating the *Turner* movement, which combined German culture and gymnastics. (*Turner,* a German word, was his choice over *gymnastics,* derived from Greek). It began as a few dozen boys eager for games, exercise, national history, and a chance to defend the *Vaterland,* but within a few years many groups of Turners emerged all over Prussia. Jahn received government recognition; then with political complications resulting from the Congress of Vienna in 1815, Prussian nationalism became suspect and the *Turner* movement was first discouraged and then forbidden. As Germany progressed toward unification, Jahn was once again in favor, and in 1842 gymnastics was formally recognized as part of education for boys. Jahn died in 1852; the memorial later built over his grave was a gymnasium. *Turnvater* Jahn was influential not only through example, but also through a book, *Die Deutsche Turnkunst,* published in 1816.

Among others, Frances Wright, Emma Willard, Mary Lyon, and Catharine Beecher proposed reforms for girls and women. Beecher, with the same pertinacity as her famous clergyman father and brother and her sister Harriet Beecher Stowe, author of *Uncle Tom's Cabin,* lectured and wrote on the physical needs of women, most notably in the 1831 publication of *A Course of Calisthenics for Young Ladies.* She founded two seminaries for women that emphasized daily exercise. Beecher, however, did not propose to alter the course of women's lives. She believed that women should be wives, mothers, and homemakers and that women's education should be directed toward those purposes. While Beecher founded several schools, all short-lived, she is, perhaps, best known for her writings on exercise and education.

Beginnings of Physical Education

In the first fifty years of nationhood American schools, academies, and colleges subscribed primarily to a conservative, rigid curriculum geared to classical languages and theological studies, which therefore, consciously or unconsciously, accepted and created the future roles of their students in American society. By and large, the curriculum ignored the health and physical activities of the students. A few educators, however, envisioned a broader concept of education which included responsibility for the health, vigor, and recreation of those in their charge. Joseph Cogswell, George Bancroft, Catharine Beecher, and Mary Lyon established schools with carefully planned exercise programs. Beecher and Dr. William A. Alcott, among others, also promoted physical education through their writings. "Alcott stressed physical activity for females and encouraged the use of physical education for shaping the character of all children. . . . He also emphasized structured exercise for elementary grades such as running, swimming, wrestling, walking, skating, coasting, ball playing, and games of physical enrichment."[28]

The advocates of school physical activities, few though they were, were unanimous in their conviction regarding the healthful benefits of exercise and sport. The New Haven Gymnasium and the New Haven Classical and Commercial School provided swimming lessons three times a week in Long Island Sound during summer terms. At the Greenfield Hill Academy in Connecticut, Timothy Dwight scheduled morning and afternoon recess periods. The boys were encouraged to take part in vigorous exercise including wrestling, leaping, and running so that they might "find a nervous frame and vigorous mind."[29]

At the Round Hill School in Northampton, Massachusetts, established in 1823, physical education was made an integral part of the curriculum. The founders, Joseph Cogswell and George Bancroft, patterned their new school

Figure 3.8 Illustration from F. L. Jahn, *Treatise on Gymnastics,* Northampton, Massachusetts, 1828. Translated by Beck while teaching at Round Hill School. Courtesy of the Amherst College Library.

after the philosophy of European educators Fellenberg and Pestalozzi. In addition to providing a progressive, liberal education in the classics, they announced that they "would also encourage activity of body, as the means of promoting firmness of constitution and vigour of mind, and shall appropriate regularly a portion of each day to healthful sports and gymnastic exercises."[30]

From the beginning they sought to fulfill this pledge by providing three play periods each day. A German immigrant, Dr. Charles Beck, who had been an active *Turner* in his homeland and was thoroughly versed in Jahn's gymnastics, was appointed to the faculty in January, 1825. Beck was given the title of Instructor in Latin and Gymnastics, thereby becoming, perhaps, the first instructor of physical education employed in an American school. In addition to gymnastics, Beck and the other instructors provided lessons in swimming, ice skating, wrestling, dancing, and other games and sports. John Forbes recalled his Round Hill days. "It was the pleasant and friendly relations of Mr. Cogswell and his masters with the boys, and the gymnastics and out-of-doors education, which made Round Hill peculiar. The boys were taught to ride,

Figure 3.9   Sketch of the Round Hill School, Northampton, Massachusetts. Courtesy of the *Daily Hampshire Gazette,* Northampton, Massachusetts.

had skating and swimming in their seasons, and wrestling, baseball and football; and, during the summer, excursions on the 'ride and tie' plan, of sometimes over a hundred miles and back, were undertaken, accompanied by Mr. Cogswell, who was himself a great walker."[31]

It is now apparent that Round Hill School, although forced to close its doors in 1834 due to financial difficulties, was one of the most significant institutions in American sport and physical education prior to 1860. It was the first American school to provide regular instruction in sport and exercise and to introduce German gymnastics. While at Round Hill, Beck translated Jahn's famous *Die Deutsche Turnkunst,* which was published in Northampton in 1828 as the *Treatise on Gymnastics.* (See Fig. 3.8)

Georgetown University, founded in Virginia in 1789, appears to be one of the earliest institutions of higher education to concern itself with recreation and sport for students. Stories are told of a fencing master in 1798, and regulations for the times and places for swimming in the Potomac River. The 1814 *Prospectus* of the college announced that "the garden and court where the students recreate, are very airy and spacious" and that "cleanliness, exercise, and whatever contributes to health, are attended to with particular care."[32] The boys, the youngest to be admitted being eight, began their day at 5:00 A.M. in the summer and 5:30 A.M. in the winter. They then had a full day of prayer, classes, study halls, and three short periods of recreation, as well as one long period of an hour and a half for recreation after the noon-day dinner. One student remembered that the study hall was locked during the

Figure 3.10   Georgetown University handball court, 1814. Courtesy of the University Archives, Georgetown University Library.

first hour of the period, but that the precaution was not really necessary. In 1814 a backboard for a handball-type game was erected with more courts added during the next decades. In addition to handball, the students enjoyed fencing and boxing. In 1831 the university announced that dancing would be taught for an additional fee. In contrast to other early colleges, especially in New England, which observed Sundays in the strict Puritan manner, Georgetown students were permitted to play ball on Sunday. One student wrote to a friend: "the Catholics think it no harm to play Ball, Draughts or play the Fiddle and dance of a Sunday, this will no doubt seem strange to you, it was so to me although I do not pretend to much sanctity, but say nothing of this in your letters home. I have never mentioned it as I know it would only make prejudices stronger, and I know it would make my mother uneasy."[33]

Other colleges of the period—Harvard, Yale, William and Mary, Liberty Hall (now Washington and Lee), Princeton, and St. John's College—appear to have concerned themselves with the intellectual and moral life of the students rather than with their physical well-being and use of leisure time. In fact, there probably was very little leisure time. The days were long and, in some schools, daily living quite demanding. Dartmouth College students, for example, were responsible for purchasing and cutting wood for the stoves in their rooms. Also, many had part-time jobs to help defray their college expenses.

The college officers expected good deportment and frequently passed regulations such as the one from St. John's in 1833 which "sternly prohibited [the students] from frequenting taverns, billiard or ball rooms."[34]

Student diaries from various colleges reveal that they were serious about their studies, their religious and moral lives, and their families. They found pleasure in the simple tasks of everyday living. Samuel Oliver wrote of his brother Edward, a student at Dartmouth, "he is sixteen years old today, wherefore I have given him sixteen slaps on his back he is going to celebrate it by making some molasses candy this evening."[35]

However, many students found some time for games and sportlike activities. Student letters and diaries from Dartmouth tell of almost daily football contests on the common, as well as ice skating, sleighing, and swinging.

June 15: . . . After school I went down to Mr. Chadwick's to swing. They have got the highest swing I ever saw. It is probably near 40 feet. It is fine sport to be swung in such a swing.

December 4, 1835: Took my skates, went down to the river and enjoyed the noble, invigorating sport of skating for three or four hours. The ice was in fine order, . . .[36]

Students of the period, younger than today's students, played games such as town ball, rounders, and one o'cat. In spite of periodic bans, football, which was more like soccer than present-day football, was a popular activity. The young men also rowed, wrestled, ice skated, danced, swam, played quoits, boxed, and fenced. While some school administrators sought to prohibit such activity, particularly the more violent football games, others encouraged faculty members to join their students occasionally in such play, in order to present a proper example and to prevent rowdiness.[37]

Between 1825 and 1830 a few colleges provided an outdoor or indoor space for gymnastic apparatus, but the only faculty supervision was that provided on a volunteer basis by interested individuals. Such "gymnasiums" of the period were located at Harvard, Yale, Brown University, Amherst College, and Williams College.

The seminaries and academies for girls of this period ranged from "finishing schools" teaching embroidery and manners, to schools working toward high academic standards. In 1786, for example, Mrs. Smith of Annapolis, Maryland, announced the opening of a boarding school for young ladies who would be instructed in embroidery, netting, and drawing. Also included in the announcement was a statement about giving "great attention" to the young ladies' health.

Through the efforts of Emma Hart Willard, the Troy Female Seminary, which later became Russell Sage College, was founded in 1821 in upper New York State and became known for its traditional academic offerings. Willard's sister, Almira Hart Lincoln Phelps, conducted the day-to-day program of physical education, which included calisthenics, dancing, riding, and walking. Dancing, designed to improve "grace of motion" and provide healthy exercise, was to be practiced only in the right atmosphere, that is, not in public. The girls were also encouraged to keep a journal in which they made observations about their own health, which would then determine the kind of exercise, food, and general living most suited to their particular constitutions.

Some schools approved mild exercise, such as walking, swimming, and horseback riding—sidesaddle, of course. Participation in games and sports was generally limited to mild contests of battledore and badminton, which might promote health through gentle exercise. Bowling contests were held on warm days during the exercise periods at Miss Pierce's Litchfield Academy in Connecticut. In 1829, at the Greenfield High School for Young Ladies in Massachusetts, the teachers and students were urged to join together in such games as battledore.

In 1825 at the Female Monitorial School in Boston, William Bentley Fowle introduced a program of formal exercises based on German gymnastics, employing exercise, marching, running, jumping, and weight lifting. The program was eventually modified and reduced to dancing because of concern by many parents that the exercises were too similar to those practiced by men. Catharine Beecher, who had called public attention to the health needs of women, founded the Hartford Female Seminary in Connecticut in 1824. In its few years of existence students there followed perhaps the most vigorous and sustained program of exercise available to women in the 1820s. They devoted thirty minutes each half day to Beecher's system of light exercises, which she called calisthenics. Accompanied by music and sometimes performed with light weights, the program was designed to exercise all the muscles harmoniously. She also encouraged the girls to ride horseback and play other games and sports. From 1833 to 1837, she directed the Western Female Institute in Cincinnati, Ohio, where she employed her educational theories.

Mount Holyoke Seminary in South Hadley, Massachusetts, founded in 1837 by the formidable Mary Lyon, with many of the same texts and expectations as nearby Amherst College for men, required its students to be sixteen years of age or older and "of mature character," and able to undertake its rigorous academic curriculum. Lyon's own perception of the role of her institution is explicit in a long letter to Catharine Beecher: "I have not been alone in considering it of great importance to establish a permanent seminary in New England for educating female teachers, with accommodations, apparatus, & somewhat like those for the other sex. Honorably to do this, from twenty to forty thousand dollars must be raised; and such a sum, raised for such an object, would form almost an era in female education."[38] Three kinds of exercise were required. Lyon justified the first of these, an hour of domestic duties, such as baking bread or making beds, as a means of saving money, enabling students to live in dormitories rather than boarding in private homes, and relieving them "from another source of depressing dependence—a dependence on the will of hired domestics." She emphasized that the work was also to promote the health of the students "by its furnishing them with a little daily exercise of the best kind."[39] An hour of domestic work, vigorous though it may have been in 1837, was only the beginning of Lyon's struggle to improve female health: "The value of health to a lady is inestimable . . . much has been said on this subject, but enough has not been *done,* in our systems of education, to promote the health of young ladies." The second kind of exercise was to walk a mile every day or to exercise in the open air an hour a day. Finally, exercise meant calisthenics. The 1839 catalogue states: "All the members of the school attend regularly to composition, reading, and calisthenics." At 8:30 every evening, each student was on one of the four stairwells in the building, following a teacher's directions and example for twenty minutes of calisthenic exercises. "One girl wanted to be excused from Calisthenics because she wanted more time to read and pray, but Miss Lyon told her exercise was a religious duty."[40]

While the need for exercise or physical education was a topic for a number of articles and speeches, relatively few programs came into being. Round Hill School closed due to financial reasons. In some of the colleges where a gymnasium had been established, the interest faded after the novelty had worn off. In 1830, speaking of the decline of gymnasiums, Warren noted, "The exercises were pursued with ardor, so long as their novelty lasted; but owing to not understanding their importance, or some defect in the institutions which adopted them, they have gradually been neglected and forgotten, at least in our vicinity."[41]

Many women's seminaries focused on "accomplishments" such as embroidery rather than on academic subjects and exercises for fitness. When Mary Lyon opened Mount Holyoke Seminary it was a major departure from women's education of the period. It is notable that she considered physical activity—domestic service, walking, and formal exercises—essential to her plan. Because Lyon incorporated exercise as basic to education, the exercise program did not fade like those at some of the men's colleges and universities.

Commentary

This chapter presented pastimes, sport, and the beginnings of physical education in the first sixty years of the United States of America. The basic themes of this book are more evident as the country became more established. In its first sixty years of independence the new nation grew rapidly but remained largely rural. Central to the new country was the growing identification as "American" and a feeling of a unique mission for the republic. The Declaration of Independence, the Constitution of the United States, and the Bill of Rights did not speak directly of sport and physical education. However, these documents created an environment of hope and freedom that has contributed to the development of many aspects of American culture. This environment offers the common man freedom and the opportunity for what has come to be called "the American dream." One aspect of the American dream is the opportunity to work to provide for oneself and one's family and, after that, to have some free time and money to be used as the individual pleases. Today, we take for granted the advantage of education, including physical education, and leisure, including sport. During the first decades of this country very few people were well educated and, with the exception of the upper-middle and upper classes, very few had much leisure time. However, the expectations and dreams existed and came nearer to reality in later periods.

Most Americans, including the twelve million immigrants who arrived during this period, continued to live in rural America or small towns. Social values and gender expectations for men did not change. While most women patterned their lives after the tenets of "true womanhood," a few followed the exercise programs promoted by Lyon and Beecher. Although ethnic groups influenced sport only casually, three young German men, Lieber, Beck, and Follen, are credited with introducing German gymnastics to this country. After the 1820s, the interest in gymnastics subsided, but by the end of the century, it would battle with Swedish gymnastics for a place in the country's schools.

Regardless of the varied backgrounds of the immigrants, conditions in the United States reinforced the basic characteristics of hard work, sobriety, and piety. The Puritan work ethic endured to control social and Sunday customs although the degree of control varied from town to town and state to state. The pastimes and amusements changed slowly from the colonial days, but the seeds of today's professional sport were sown during this time.

Most activities could properly be termed pastimes and began to be associated with social status. The middle class found pleasure in watching contemporary sport events, perhaps cheering their favorite ped or wagering on a horse at a local fair. Some games such as cricket were played but did not become "American." Children played traditional games, tag and base ball for instance. On the frontier life remained rugged, lonely, and tough, but barn raisings, bees, and other social occasions provided some respite for the lonely families.

Pastimes for the wealthy included boating or yachting. Prominent social families frequented the race season in fashionable Virginia or Maryland, rode to the hounds, and joined sport clubs. Many of these clubs combined the sport activity with social occasions.

Most blacks remained slaves with only a few hours to call their own on Sundays and holidays. However, some, like Tom Molyneux, gained their freedom because of boxing prowess. Early professional sports such as boxing and cockfighting attracted men from all walks of life—gentlemen, workers, gamblers, and the "sporting fraternity."

The beginnings of modern sport can be found in horse racing, cockfighting, pedestrianism, and rowing contests of the period. Other pastimes continued to be casual and did not meet VanderZwaag and Sheehan's criterion of dependency on facilities and equipment.[42] However, horse racing, cockfighting, and pedestrianism most nearly met these standards. Boxing regulations were codified later in the period.

Both horse racing and cockfighting depended on pride of ownership and wagering the merits of one animal against another. Horse racing became an early expression of a sport reflecting political ideology. With the country still recovering from the 1820 controversy over Missouri's admission to the Union as a slave state, sectional loyalties were played out in the race between Eclipse and Sir Henry. Some people lamented the use of sport to determine sectional victories, while others expressed relief that, after all, it was only sport.[43] By the end of the period the more democratic trotting races had surpassed thoroughbred horse racing in popularity.

Whether the contest pitted animal against animal, or man against man as in boxing, pedestrianism, or rowing, the winners expected and received monetary prizes. The later nineteenth-century ideal of "amateur" which was defined as playing *only* for the love of sport had not yet been accepted, and the boxers, peds, and rowers competed for prizes. Although the concept of team, the center of today's pro sport, had not yet evolved, informal ball games took place. The most consistent sport organization could be found in the many sport clubs of the period.

Education was deemed essential for the citizenry, but usually focused on the three "R's." Reformers and reform movements also became important in the early days of the nation, and certain educational reformers experimented with games and physical activities in education. Cogswell and Bancroft at Round Hill School, Beecher at the Hartford Female Seminary, and Lyon at Mount Holyoke College initiated seminal programs that led to the unique combination of sport and education in the United States.

The early decades of this century reflected the young country's diversity of ethnic groups, the struggle to retain sectional identity while also struggling to become a nation, and the vigorous challenge of the frontier. The seeds of later developments in United States sport could be found in the horse racing and rowing contests, the clubs formed for sport and sociability, the communal gatherings and bees, the pastimes enjoyed by children, men, and women, and the programs of simple exercises and games in a few educational institutions. In the next period a simple ball game would change the future of American sport.

Suggestions for Further Reading

1. Adelman, Melvin L. "The First Modern Sport in America: Harness Racing in New York City, 1825–1870." *Journal of Sport History* 8, no. 1 (Spring 1981):5–32.
2. Audubon, John James. "Kentucky Riflery" in *The Realm of Sport,* ed. Herbert Warren Wind. New York: Simon and Schuster, 1966.
3. Bennett, Bruce L. "The Making of Round Hill School." *Quest* 4 (April 1965):53–64.
4. Park, Roberta J. " 'Embodied Selves': The Rise and Development of Concern for Physical Education, Active Games and Recreation for American Women, 1776–1865." *Journal of Sport History* 5, no. 2 (Summer 1978):5–41.
5. Struna, Nancy L. "The North–South Races: American Thoroughbred Racing in Transition, 1823–1850." *Journal of Sport History* 8, no. 2 (Summer 1981):28–57.

Notes

1. John Woods, "Two Years' Residence in the Settlement on the English Prairie, in the Illinois Country, United States" in *Early Western Travels, 1748–1846,* vol. X, ed. R. G. Thwaites (Cleveland, Ohio: The Arthur H. Clark Company, 1904), 300.
2. Joseph C. Cogswell and George Bancroft, *Prospectus of a School to be Established at Round Hill, Northampton, Massachusetts* (Cambridge, Massachusetts, 1823), 17.
3. John R. Betts, *America's Sporting Heritage: 1850–1950* (Reading, MA: Addison-Wesley, 1974), 10.
4. John Hervey, *Racing in America, 1665–1865,* vol. 1 (New York: The Jockey Club, 1944), 74.
5. Ibid., 2:91.
6. Ibid., 1:91.
7. Nancy L. Struna, "The North-South Races: American Thoroughbred Racing in Transition, 1823–1850," *Journal of Sport History* 8, no. 2 (Summer 1981):52.
8. Dwight Akers, *Drivers Up: The Story of American Harness Racing* (New York: G.P. Putnam's, 1938), 29.
9. Melvin L. Adelman, *A Sporting Time* (Urbana: University of Illinois, 1986), 62.
10. The London Prize Ring Rules, not officially promulgated until 1838 by the British Pugilists Protective Association, stipulated that no gloves were to be used; wrestling holds were allowed; a round ended when one or both contestants were knocked down; and at the end of each round, thirty seconds of rest followed. Failure of either man to meet his opponent in the center of the ring resulted in disqualification.
11. Benjamin G. Rader, *American Sports: From the Age of Folk Games to the Age of Spectators* (Englewood Cliffs, NJ: Prentice-Hall, 1983), 30–35.
12. D. Wiggins, "Good Time On the Old Plantation: Popular Recreations of the Black Slave in Antebellum South, 1810–1860," *Journal of Sport History* 4, no. 3 (Fall 1977):260–84.
13. Edwin Adams Davis, *Plantation Life in the Florida Parishes of Louisiana, 1836–1846* (New York: Columbia University, 1943), 50, 51.

14. Paton Yoder, *Taverns and Travelers* (Bloomington: Indiana University, 1969), 122.
15. Foster Rhea Dulles, *America Learns to Play* (New York: D. Appleton-Century Company, 1940), 71.
16. John James Audubon, "Kentucky Sports," from the "Missouri River Journals (1843)," in *Audubon and His Journals,* vol. II, ed. Maria R. Audubon (New York: Charles Scribner's Sons, 1897), 460–61.
17. Ibid., 461.
18. Alexis de Tocqueville, *Democracy in America,* vol. II (New York: Alfred A. Knopf, 1945), 114.
19. Phyllis J. Hill, "A Cultural History of Frontier Sport in Illinois 1673–1820" (Ph.D. diss., University of Illinois, 1966), 82.
20. Joy Van Cleef, "Rural Felicity: Social Dance in 18th Century Connecticut," *Dance Perspectives* 65 (Spring 1976):12.
21. Philadelphia *Minerva,* Dec. 10, 1796, cited in Joseph E. Marks, *America Learns to Dance* (New York: Exposition Press, 1957), 33.
22. Ibid.
23. Lynne Fauley Emery, *Black Dance in the United States from 1619 to 1970* (Palo Alto, California: National Press Books, 1972), 80–178.
24. David K. Wiggins, "The Play of Slave Children in the Plantation Communities of the Old South, 1820–1860," *Journal of Sport History* 7, no. 2 (Summer 1980):21–39.
25. *Boy's and Girl's Book of Sports* (Providence: Geo. P. Daniels, 1839), 19.
26. Mary A. Livermore, *The Story of My Life* (Hartford, CT: A. D. Worthington, 1899), 37, 53–55.
27. Roberta J. Park, " 'Embodied Selves': The Rise and Development of Concern for Physical Education, Active Games and Recreation for American Women, 1776–1865," *Journal of Sport History* 5, no. 2 (Summer 1978):31, 32.
28. Paul R. Mills, "William Andrus Alcott, M.D. Pioneer Reformer in Physical Education, 1798–1859," *76th Proceedings,* National College Physical Education Association for Men (January 6–9, 1973):32,31.
29. Roxanne M. Albertson, "Sports and Games in New England Schools and Academies 1780–1860" (Paper presented at the North American Society for Sport History, Boston, Massachusetts, April 16–19, 1975), 2.
30. Joseph C. Cogswell and George Bancroft, *Prospectus of a School to be Established at Round Hill, Northampton, Massachusetts* (Cambridge, Massachusetts, 1823), 17.
31. S. F. Hughes, *Letters and Recollections of John Murray Forbes* (Boston: Houghton Mifflin, 1899), 44.
32. *Georgetown College,* 1814, p. 2. Georgetown University Library.
33. Student letter, August 27, 1836. Georgetown University Library.
34. T. F. Tilghman, "An Early Victorian College St. John's, 1830–1860," *Maryland Historical Society* 44, no. 4 (December 1949):254.
35. Samuel Oliver, *Journal,* Hanover, N.H., Nov. 25, 1835. Dartmouth College Archives.
36. Cyrus Parker Bradley, *Diary,* 1832. Dartmouth College Archives.
37. Roxanne M. Albertson, "Sports and Games in New England Schools and Academies 1780–1860" (Paper presented at the North American Society for Sport History, Boston, Massachusetts, April 16–19, 1975), 4–5.

38. Edward Hitchcock, *The Power of Christian Benevolence Illustrated in the Life and Labor of Mary Lyon* (Northampton: Hopkins, Bridgman, and Company, 1852), 226.

39. Ibid., 297.

40. Mary Lyon Memorabilia, p. 61. Mount Holyoke History Room, Mount Holyoke College, South Hadley, Massachusetts.

41. Quoted in Fred Eugene Leonard and R. Tait McKenzie, *A Guide to the History of Physical Education* (Philadelphia: Lea & Febiger, 1923), 250.

42. Harold J. VanderZwaag and Thomas J. Sheehan, *Introduction to Sport Studies* (Dubuque, IA: Wm. C. Brown Publishers, 1978), 18.

43. Duncan MacLeod, "Racing to War," *Southern Exposure* 7 (Fall 1979):7–10.

Time Line

HISTORY

1840
Ten-hour work day for federal
employees
1844
First telegraph in regular operation
1845
Texas agreed to annexation
1846
Sewing machine invented
1848
Revolutions in France, Germany,
Austria, Italy; subsequent immigration
Seneca Falls women's rights convention
1849
California gold rush
1852
First permanent labor union
1859
Darwin's *Origin of Species* published
1861
Abraham Lincoln became president
1861–65
Civil War
1865
Lincoln assassinated
1867
Marx's *Das Kapital* published

1869
Transcontinental railroad service begun
Knights of Labor organized

1876
Bell invented telephone
1881
Tuskegee Institute founded

SPORT AND PHYSICAL EDUCATION

1843
First collegiate rowing club, Yale

1845
Modern baseball game established

1852
First intercollegiate sport contest,
rowing, Harvard vs. Yale

1861
First college men's physical education
program, Amherst College

1866
First state physical education legislation,
California
1868
New York Athletic Club founded
1869
First professional baseball team,
Cincinnati Red Stockings
1874
Tennis introduced into country
1876
National League of Professional Base
Ball Clubs founded
Intercollegiate Association of Amateur
Athletes of America founded

4

From Games to Sport, and from Exercise to Physical Education, 1840–1885

Overview

When in 1845 Alexander Cartwright and a group of his friends changed the children's game of rounders into the adult male sport of baseball, they took the first steps toward today's organized team sports. They designed a playing field with standard dimensions, specified the equipment to be used, stated the number of players on a team, assigned them responsibilities or positions, and listed the conditions and rules under which the game would be played. As a result baseball was on its way to becoming an organized sport. Thirty-one years later the National League of Professional Base Ball Clubs was formed. This change from casual, informal play to organized sport epitomizes many changes, not only in sports in the city and countryside and university, but also in the business, social, and cultural life of the United States from 1840 to 1885.

In a very different sector of society, Matthew Vassar made plans for his new college for women, and followed Mary Lyon's plan for required exercise. In 1861 Amherst College appointed the first "Professor of Hygiene and Physical Education." Thus, by the middle of this period, educational institutions acknowledged responsibility for their students' health. Colleges for men faced unexpected problems with the beginnings of intercollegiate challenges among the students. These issues—the conceptualization of a game as an adult sport, exercise for women in higher education, and intercollegiate contests—represent the variety of developments of sport and physical education from 1840 to 1885.

At the middle of the nineteenth century, the United States had coastlines on two major oceans and more than three thousand miles of land between them. The country varied from two-hundred-year-old cities and towns in the East to the frontier which constantly pressed westward. The new nation grew from seventeen million people in 1840 to over fifty million in 1880, and became more urban. Discoveries and inventions led to ever-larger mills and factories manufacturing a variety of products from steel to clothespins. In place of horse-drawn wagons and canal barges, trains sped the manufactured goods over the growing network of railroads. People, as well as freight, traveled more and more by train and less and less in boats, carriages, and on horseback. Information and news, formerly transmitted by mail or by word of mouth, could be sent almost instantaneously over the telegraph wires.

From 1861 to 1865 the North and South engaged in a terrible Civil War, which exacted appalling costs in men and material from both sides. The nation survived but with deep wounds in both the North and South. The Emancipation Proclamation abolishing slavery was issued in 1863, and in 1868 the country ratified the Fourteenth Amendment, guaranteeing equal protection under the law to all citizens, regardless of race. A ragged trail of successes, accommodations, and failures has followed in the century since that ratification; but sport and physical education historians tend to focus on the civil rights legislation affecting equal access to these activities.

Advances in science and technology led to an increasingly secular life, although some aspects of Puritanism remained firmly embedded in American thought, such as the work ethic and Sunday as a day of rest. This was a period of growing social and economic extremes, when some people made fortunes, but in contrast millions of immigrants, hoping for a better life, barely made a subsistence living. American society included wealthy gentlemen educated in Europe; middle-class tradespeople and hardworking shopkeepers; farmers working endless hours; staunchly independent frontier families; and factory workers clustered in ever-increasing numbers in mills and tenements. The plight of the working class already had created conditions which demanded attention and change. The founding of the Knights of Labor in 1869 foreshadowed the necessity and importance of organizing workers to seek better conditions in the workplace.

The greatly expanded numbers of industrial laborers worked for twelve to sixteen hours a day, six days a week. These men and women had escaped from backbreaking work on farms or from dreary lives in villages to become factory workers in the growing towns and cities, where working hours, though long, were specified; and after work their time was their own. Their new wages also provided some money to buy manufactured sport goods—balls, bats, roller skates, perhaps even a bicycle. These incentives to pleasurable activity gave vitality to city life, which was physically less demanding but often viewed as impersonal and dull.

Peasants from European farms also emigrated to this country, joining the work force or, particularly in the Midwest, establishing their own farms. Political dissenters from Germany, middle-class Scandinavians, and many others from all over Europe came to the United States, all of them hoping for a brighter future for themselves and their families. With them came their games, gymnastics, and pastimes, which they adapted to their new homeland. German Turners initiated the American Turner Societies; the Scotsmen staged Caledonian Games; and the English imported their "athletics," called track and field in this country.

Life and thought in the United States changed rapidly during this period. In the 1840s New England produced Hawthorne's *A Scarlet Letter* and Emerson's essay on "Self-reliance," including that traditional touchstone of American thought: "Trust thyself; every heart vibrates to that iron string." These authors, differing from each other, differed still more from Henry James, the novelist of cultivated sensibilities, who by the end of the period had published *Daisy Miller*. Another change of thought occurred as Americans, who started by perceiving forests and wilderness as hostile, dangerous, or else as a source of game, began to take pride in the great natural objects discovered on the continent—waterfalls, forests, and especially mountains. They also responded to paintings of these landscapes, by the Hudson River School as well as by others. By 1885 painters and photographers vied to climb to Yosemite country in California in order to convey the "sublime" landscape of America to their countrymen.

Reform movements touched many aspects of American life in the nineteenth century. Young men were exhorted to follow the precepts of "muscular Christianity," while young women were taught to seek the tenets of "true womanhood," piety, purity, domesticity, and submissiveness. In 1848 the first women's rights meeting convened in Seneca Falls, New York, where it proposed a document, patterned after the Declaration of Independence, that would redress inequalities suffered by women and would reexamine their gender role expectations. Confident of the new country's mission to improve humankind, social reformers like Catharine Beecher, Horace Mann, William Ellery Channing, and Ralph Waldo Emerson sought to better life by attacking diverse problems in education, prison conditions, women's rights, and family life. One of those reforms was directed at the increasingly poor health of the people, particularly in the cities. Gymnasiums opened, and philanthropic organizations such as the YMCA, YWCA, and settlement houses organized exercise programs. Not so much interested in their health as in interschool rivalry, young men in the colleges engaged in a series of sport challenges which led to intercollegiate athletics. In the colleges, especially the women's colleges, physical exercise programs were instituted to improve the health of the students.

By 1860 most states had free public elementary education, but attendance was not compulsory. In 1862 the Morrill Act created one college in each state which was designated to teach agriculture and mechanical arts or engineering. Several major women's colleges came into being after the Civil War. However, in spite of the progress in education, in 1870 only 1.2 percent of the eligible population attended high school.

This chapter will examine the effects of science and technology on games and sport; the beginnings of organized professional and amateur sport; social reforms designed to improve the citizens' health; and finally, exercise and sport in educational institutions for men and women.

Technology and Sport

Scientific discoveries and technological developments in the midnineteenth century led to numerous inventions and discoveries that combined to change the daily lives of many Americans and incidentally to transform American pastimes and games. For example, the invention of the bicycle and roller skates made possible the development of new activities. Advanced technology led to architectural innovations that provided improved facilities in athletic clubs and college gymnasiums. Engineering advances were reflected in the design of yachts in the *America's* Cup races. It is impossible to list every invention and technological improvement that affected sport, but some examples will illustrate the phenomena in terms of facilities, transportation, communication, and improved sport equipment.

The discovery of electricity's use and the development of the incandescent bulb in 1879 made a major impact on urban social life. For some time gaslights had been used in armories and arenas such as New York's Madison Square Garden. Although boxers, pedestrians, bicycle racers, and spectators had grown somewhat accustomed to the mixture of gaslight fumes and tobacco smoke, they welcomed the electric bulbs which were installed in the Garden in 1882. By 1885 the Garden was completely electrified. Another early club to install electricity was the New York Athletic Club. At the end of the decade clubs, arenas, and armories from Boston to San Francisco could be lit up after dark. The first hotel to use electricity was the Prospect House, Blue Mountain Lake, New York. Altogether, the electric light bulb changed sport from an activity largely carried on in daylight hours out of doors to an enterprise possible by day and night, inside and out.

Rail travel was at first unreliable, and sometimes this disrupted sport events. By the late 1850s, improved rail service could be used for reliable transportation to race courses throughout the country, choice fishing sites for a vacation, resort hotels, and for baseball teams traveling during the summer. The Cincinnati Red Stockings' tour from Maine to California in 1869 was a "first," using local rail lines, steam ships, and a large regional rail line, the Union Pacific Railroad. The rise and success of professional "major league" baseball in the 1870s and 1880s depended on adequate rail transportation. By 1870 collegiate teams, too, traveled by train. Harvard's 1870 baseball team, on a single trip, played amateur and professional teams in New Haven, Troy, Utica, Syracuse, Oswego (Canada), Buffalo, Cleveland, Cincinnati, Louisville, Chicago, Milwaukee, Indianapolis, Washington, Baltimore, Philadelphia, New York, and Brooklyn.

Perhaps equally important was the impact of improved communication on sport. While the speed of news transmission increased with the coming of the steam riverboats and the rail system, it often took weeks before the results of an important fight or race could be known throughout the country. However, with Morse's system of telegraphy in 1844, suddenly the news was received instantaneously over the "magic wires."

The burgeoning newspaper industry immediately saw the advantages of telegraphy and by 1846, James Gordon Bennett's *New York Herald* and Horace Greeley's *New York Tribune* made use of these new inventions. In 1849 citizens in the eastern half of the country received telegraphic accounts of the Hyer-Sullivan fight held at Rock Point, Maryland. During the next decade the wires reported prize fights, horse races, trotting contests, and yachting events. In reporting professional baseball in the 1870s and 1880s, the telegraph became practically indispensable in providing the cities with news of the home team. In 1866 Cyrus Field organized the laying of the transatlantic cable, which enabled the American public to receive results of European sporting events quickly.

While sport news did not yet occupy a prominent place in the daily newspapers and in weekly and monthly journals, major events were nevertheless reported. A milestone in early sport journalism came in 1831 when William Trotter Porter published the weekly *Spirit of the Times,* the leading periodical devoted to sport in the midnineteenth century. Second only to Porter's *Spirit* was the *National Police Gazette,* founded by George Wilkes in 1845, which became the leading pugilistic journal in America. Also, a sports "extra" was published in Amherst, Massachusetts, in 1859, after Amherst College won the first intercollegiate baseball game, beating Williams College 73 to 32.

By the 1880s the telegraph revolution of the newspaper industry, the increasing use of journalists, and growing interest in sport combined to create the sports page. While some publishers were reluctant to include the topic of sport in their papers, others were not; and by the turn of the century the sports page occupied a permanent place in the daily and Sunday newspapers. Weekly and monthly magazines and journals were frequently ahead of the newspapers in exploiting the growing public interest in sport. Before the development and popularity of the daily tabloid magazine, editors not faced with strict deadlines were able to give thoughtful accounts and interpretations of important sport events.

Hundreds of inventions led to changes in existing pastimes and games, thus contributing to the growing acceptance of sport in the daily lives of many Americans. Elias Howe's sewing machine produced playing uniforms and equipment. In the 1830s the vulcanization of rubber by Charles Goodyear led to improved elasticity and resiliency of rubber balls in the 1840s, and of golf and tennis balls later in the century. Engineering principles employed in the manufacture of bicycles, from the early "bone-shakers" to the safety bicycle, later found application in automotive and other industries.[1] As manufacturing developed, machinery and improved techniques made possible the production of balls, bats, and other sport equipment which met specific standards of size, weight, and shape. This was especially significant in the rapid growth of baseball; indeed, virtually every sport was affected by new technology. For the first time all the competitors—in archery and rowing, and later in tennis, croquet, and golf—had standardized equipment. Mass production also made sport equipment less expensive and more available to the average American.

The changes brought about by science and technology altered the lives of most Americans. Wealthy men, women, and children lived luxuriously, enjoying the new inventions such as electricity, bicycles, faster yachts, and the most fashionable resorts such as Saratoga Springs, New York. The middle classes improved their daily lives, with some new tools for the farm, new fittings for the shop, and a few luxuries for the home. In 1872 Montgomery Ward opened the country's first mail order house and offered previously unheard-of merchandise to rural families.

The most drastic changes took place in the lives of city workers. The physically demanding but varied daily chores on farms or in blacksmith shops changed to routine, repetitive tasks on inanimate machines. People in cities became more dependent on others. They purchased foods instead of growing them; they lived in buildings and houses built by others; and they became increasingly dependent on city services provided by workers unknown to them.

These conditions inaugurated a more secularized society in which social institutions gradually replaced the independent, self-sufficient household. New attitudes and values developed regarding work time and free time. Work time belonged to the employer, and free time, what little there was, belonged to the worker. One way in which more and more men used their free time was sport. Sport provided social groups with which to identify. Membership on baseball teams and in sport clubs of various kinds afforded opportunities for allegiance and camaraderie in a recreational setting. This sense of community and belonging was important in the crowded, sometimes hostile anonymity of the city.

Professional Sports of the Period

Horse racing, boxing, pedestrianism, and cockfighting remained favorites of the men during this period. While men supported pugilism and cockfighting, both men and women enjoyed the races. Essentially these sports were based upon a clearly visible competition between one man fighting with another or one animal fighting with another, perhaps to the death; or upon competition among horses or men for speed—to see which horse or man was the fastest. Such time-honored types of contest had been carried on for centuries, but times were changing. The idea of paying to watch one group of men compete against another group in a game of baseball, using balls, bats, and bases, seemed remote in 1840. Yet in the 1869 season over two hundred thousand persons throughout the country turned out to see the Cincinnati Red Stockings play baseball, which was to become the American national pastime.

Baseball

Early forms of baseball, variously called base ball, goal ball, or rounders, had been played regularly by boys and young men in North America since the colonial period. Although there is some evidence that groups of men occasionally played baseball, it was usually considered a game for children or youths. Richter mentions that baseball was played by collegians in 1825.[2] It was clearly unusual, then, for a group of doctors, attorneys, bank tellers, Wall Street brokers, clerks, and small store owners to gather two afternoons a week in a mid-Manhattan meadow to play a game of ball. These men organized the Knickerbocker Club in New York City in 1842, and three years later adopted a clearly written set of rules which became the basis for the modern game of baseball.

While the precise circumstances are unclear, it is generally agreed that Alexander Joy Cartwright, a twenty-five-year-old bank employee, volunteer fireman, and charter member of the Knickerbocker Base Ball Club, played a leading role in developing a plan so well thought out that the game's basic form has remained unchanged to the present. The new rules established the design of the field, and the placement and number of players, together with a system of outs and innings. The distance between bases, set at ninety feet, was precisely calculated, since a few feet more or less would result in an uneven advantage for either the fielder or the runner. The placement of the infielders at first, second, and third bases, and a fourth player at shortstop, provided adequate coverage of the diamond; and the provision of three outfielders struck a balance between good defensive play and a reasonable chance for the batter to hit safely. The positions of the two roving short fielders and one of the two catchers previously required were abolished, so that a pitcher rounded out a team to nine players. The center of the playing field was set in a ninety-foot square, and the batter was moved from a special box and placed at the fourth or "home" base. Outs could be made by balls thrown to the bases, rather than balls thrown at the runners. The rule of "three hands out, all out" increased the pace of the game, as it was no longer necessary to retire the entire team to end an inning. At first, the game ended when one team scored twenty-one runs or "aces," but later changed to the nine-inning game. Players and public alike soon realized that these changes removed the game from the category of a children's pastime. "Base-ball, . . . is no longer a boy's game. It requires men to play the game now up to the standard comprehended by the rules in question, and men, moreover, with heads, as well as active limbs and bodies."[3] Hitting, pitching, and fielding skills, as well as individual and team strategies, became important. So appealing was the game that within a few years it dominated the American sport scene and was promoted as the "national" game.

The construction of a suburban railroad through the meadow where the Knickerbocker Club played forced the club to relocate in 1846 at the Elysian Fields across the Hudson River in Hoboken, New Jersey. The next spring it began its first full season as an organized club, playing an occasional match against a "pick-up" team composed of former Knickerbockers who declined to travel frequently to Hoboken for games.

Over the next several years the Knickerbockers continued to play regularly and added new members. Other groups played sporadically in New York, but it was not until 1851 that one of the new clubs felt strong enough to challenge the Knickerbockers. In 1854 two Brooklyn clubs were formed, and the following year three more clubs. During these early years of baseball "clubs," membership was limited by a blackball system and only "gentlemen" were admitted. The game itself was played for enjoyment, for camaraderie, and for exercise. Members were fined for swearing, disputing the umpire's decision, and appearing inebriated at a game. The casual attitude toward winning, the insistence upon good manners when playing, the presence of the formally attired umpire, and the traditional postgame party at a favorite hostelry were characteristic of the "gentlemen's" game of baseball.

The Knickerbocker's game used the "New York Rules," which were generally adopted, but in New England, the "Massachusetts Rules" (see p. 138) prevailed until the 1860s. The "Massachusetts" game was played on a square field measuring sixty feet between bases; three-foot high stakes marked bases; teams had ten to twenty players; balls were thrown at runners for outs; and one out, all out. Meanwhile, Philadelphians still played the old game of town ball.

In the 1850s the rapid expansion of the New York game to all classes and to many parts of the country was a sport phenomenon. In spite of the exclusive membership of the Knickerbockers, the game itself belonged to no one, and with balls, bats, and flat meadows readily available, working men, older men, boys, schoolboys, and college men found the game easily adaptable to their everyday lives. Perhaps the first working-class team appeared in New York in the middle 1850s. Captain Frank Pigeon of the Eckfords of Brooklyn wrote: "A year ago last August a small number of young men . . . were accustomed to meet for the purpose of enjoying the game. Being shipwrights and mechanics, we could not make it convenient to practice more than once a week."[4] Pigeon carefully detailed the account of their first match on September 27, 1856, which the Eckfords won.

Teams began forming all over the New York City area—the Mutuals, firemen of the Mutual Hook and Ladder Company No. 1; the Manhattans, a group of New York policemen; the Phantoms, barkeepers; the Pocahontas, employees of a dairy; an unnamed group of clergymen; and the Pastime Club, composed of Long Island workmen. As many as fifty clubs played in and around the metropolitan area, and an additional sixty "junior" teams were formed to serve as feeders to the senior clubs. Players rose to practice early in the morning before going to work, and many vacant lots were turned into ball fields. In the summer of 1858 a series of three contests was played between two Brooklyn and New York City all-star teams. The first of the series, held at the Fashion Race Course on Long Island, attracted over fifteen hundred people, who came by steamboat and railroad and paid fifty cents admission to watch these men struggle to win a bat and ball game.

Prior to the Civil War the game spread across the country, usually introduced by professional or business men. The Buffalo Baseball Club, with city aldermen serving as captains, began games in the late 1850s, and the Franklin Club of Detroit organized in 1857. Several members of the New York Eagles migrated to California in 1859 and soon founded the Pacific Coast Eagles. Likewise, former Knickerbockers William and James Shepard introduced San Francisco to the game in 1861.[5] In New Orleans, the city's first team, the Louisiana Baseball Club, began playing intraclub games in the summer of 1859. By the end of the year, there were seven teams in the city, mostly from the middle and upper classes, and baseball began to displace cricket in popularity.[6] Even after the war this pattern continued. In 1866, Cincinnati's first organized club was founded by a group of Harvard and Yale law graduates, while in Cedar Rapids, Iowa, most of the players were business men and community leaders.

As the baseball craze spread over the country and to all classes, it became a game which no longer was played with the social amenities thought by the Knickerbockers to be essential. Players now emphasized winning, blocked base paths, "rode" opposing players, picked fights, and contested decisions of the umpire—who was, in any case, only an unpaid member of the host club, picked by the visiting team. Unhappy with this turn of events, the older clubs found their influence on the development of the game slipping away. Reluctantly, the Knickerbockers called a meeting in 1858 to discuss the standardization of rules. Twenty-two New York area clubs attended and as a result of the meeting, the National Association of Base Ball Players was established. In succeeding years invitations were sent to clubs throughout the country. Fifty groups attended the convention of 1860 and, while membership dropped during the Civil War, it soared immediately afterward. By 1868, almost 350 clubs attended the National Association meetings.

The Civil War introduced the game to thousands of soldiers from all over the country, who played in army camps and in prison camps on both sides. For example, on Christmas Day, 1862, at Hilton Head, South Carolina, a team from the 165th New York Volunteer Infantry played a team from other Union regiments before about forty thousand soldiers.[7] The game's tremendous growth in the decade following the war soon gave baseball the appearance of an egalitarian game where everyone, young and old, rich and poor, measured each other only by playing ability. However, certain Americans were excluded from midnineteenth century organized baseball; in 1867 the National Association of Base Ball Players approved a ban on black players seeking membership. At its convention that year, the Association's Nominating Committee proposed that teams with one or more black players not be admitted to the Association. Their position was based on the belief that some members of the National Association might object to black players and that by excluding them all, no incidents would be created and no one would be "hurt." For the next eighty years the same attitude controlled organized professional baseball, and most black players were restricted to segregated barnstorming teams or "colored" leagues. Occasionally a light-skinned black player was passed off as white, Indian, or Caribbean by a team anxious to capitalize on the individual's playing ability. In essence, this ruling and attitude mirrored American society of the period.

As interest in baseball grew, communities and clubs began to compete for the outstanding players of the period. Despite the strictly amateur, no-compensation policy of the National Association of Base Ball Players, key players *were* hired for important games or recruited from other clubs for a season. The issue of amateurism and professionalism was polarized in 1869 when the young but prominent club, the Cincinnati Red Stockings, under the leadership of the dynamic manager/centerfielder Harry Wright, openly became a professional base ball club and *hired* the best players they could find. Further, they undertook an unprecedented tour through the Middle West, the East, and then the Far West, and did not lose a single game.

> From a record kept by Harry Wright. . . . Out of 57 games played the Red Stockings won 56 and tied 1. In these games they scored a total of 2,395 runs to 574 for their adversaries. The nature of the batting done is shown in a total of 169 home runs, or an average of nearly three to a game. The number of miles traveled by rail and boat was 11,877, without a serious accident of any kind. Over 200,000 people witnessed the games.[8]

Professional players won more games than the amateur players of the National Association, and other cities followed the Cincinnati Red Stockings' lead. That fall the National Association changed its position on the prohibition of professional players in match games. At its annual meeting in December, 1869, the rules were revised to recognize professionals as a class of players distinct from amateurs:

> Section 7. All players who play base-ball for money, or who shall at any time receive compensation for their services as players, shall be considered *professional* players; and all others shall be regarded as *amateur* players.[9]

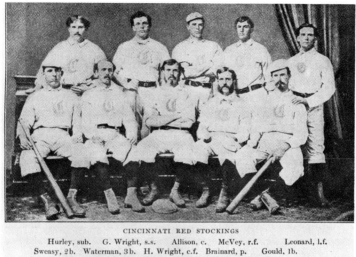

CINCINNATI RED STOCKINGS
Hurley, sub.   G. Wright, s.s.   Allison, c.   McVey, r.f.   Leonard, l.f.
Sweasy, 2b.   Waterman, 3b.   H. Wright, c.f.   Brainard, p.   Gould, 1b.

Figure 4.1 1869 Cincinnati Red Stockings. Courtesy Spalding Archives, Chicopee, Massachusetts.

Difficulties within the National Association followed and at the 1870 annual meeting there was a serious dispute between the amateur players and the professional players. The amateurs, composed of seven colleges and ten clubs, withdrew to form their own association, but within a year this group disbanded.

The National Association of Professional Base Ball Players, organized in 1871 to replace the National Association of Base Ball Players, originally consisted of about ten teams. During the period of the amateur-professional controversy the Association grew to eleven clubs, but dropped to eight in 1874. The affairs of the association were loosely organized, with games frequently being called off and some scheduled games not played at all. Attendance dropped; and although thirteen clubs joined in 1875, continuing abuses, particularly uncontrolled gambling, made the season a disastrous one. There were also disputes among the teams because of widespread contract-breaking.

These events led to the dissolution of the National Association and the formation of the National League of Professional Base Ball Clubs in February, 1876, under a constitution constructed by W. A. Hulbert and A. G. Spalding. Rather than being an association of players, the new organization was a league of clubs.

The function of Base Ball *Clubs* in the future would be to manage Base Ball *Teams*. Clubs would form leagues, secure grounds, erect grandstands, lease and own property, make schedules, fix dates, pay salaries, assess fines, discipline players, make contracts, control the sport in all its relations to the public, and thus, relieving the players of all care and responsibility for the legitimate functions of management, require of them the very best performance of which they were capable, in the entertainment of the public, for which service they were to receive commensurate pay.[10]

The new league, governed by a board of five directors, opened the 1876 season with clubs in Philadelphia, Boston, Chicago, Cincinnati, Hartford, Louisville, New York, and St. Louis. To apply for membership cities had to have a population of at least seventy-five thousand. The clubs issued contracts to players which forbade contract-breaking, which in turn discouraged clubs from "raiding" other clubs for players. Other rules forbade gambling and liquor on the club grounds, and Sunday games.

The early years of organized professional baseball reflected something of the energetic, turbulent times. Not unlike the 1980s, controversies over players' rights and salaries continued to mark professional baseball throughout this period. The newly formed National League of Professional Base Ball Clubs used many practices common to big business trusts of the period to establish control of the sport. The club owners controlled player contracts and blacklisted players who moved to other clubs between or during seasons. In 1879 came the reserve rule, which provided that each club could "reserve" five men for the following season. The entire system was periodically challenged by independent players who risked blacklisting in order to play for higher salaries in leagues not affiliated with the National League. Minor leagues served as a source of players for the major teams in an embryonic "farm system" and were granted League alliance status by the National League.

The most successful of the early rivals to the National League was the American Association of Base Ball Clubs, founded in 1882 by six clubs: Cincinnati, St. Louis, Louisville, Pittsburgh, Baltimore, and Philadelphia. Promoting their games through twenty-five cent rather than fifty cent admissions, and through Sunday games and the selling of liquor at games, neither of which was allowed in the National League, the American Association owners were able to achieve modest success which continued through 1891.

The American Association launched a new round of "trade wars," mutual blacklisting, and the first court suits involving players. One club could still "buy" another club's best players, even in the middle of a season. To bring some semblance of order to the situation, in 1883 the National League, the American Association, and the Northwestern League adopted a Tripartite Agreement—afterwards the National Agreement—"for the purpose of checking the prevailing system of player-piracy and many double-contract transactions."[11] The agreement was a comprehensive document codifying club relationships, especially the reserve system, which bound a player to the same team for his entire career unless traded, sold, or released; thus ending for a while the wild bidding for players. In another aspect of the game, the same season of 1883 saw the end of the "out on first foul bound catch," so that baseball became a fly-catch game.

Figure 4.2   Black jockeys, dominant in this period. Courtesy of the Library of Congress.

Another rival league, the Union Association, was formed in 1884 by a group of players opposed to the reserve system and financed by wealthy businessmen wishing to associate with the game. Due to mismanagement and the strength of the already established leagues, the Association lasted only one season. Thus, the National League, with its development of the National Agreement and its ability to stabilize professional baseball, created a business model that would be followed by other professional team sports in the future.

Horse Racing
During the middle decades of the nineteenth century wealthy northern industrialists, southern planters, and western businessmen supported thoroughbred race horse stables. Black antebellum slaves and postbellum freedmen were the top jockeys, trainers, and handlers. Racing devotees journeyed by horseback, carriage, and train to see thoroughbred horses race. Unreliable trains sometimes disrupted the events and caused near riots, such as the disturbance at New York's Union Course in 1842. The Long Island Rail Road oversold the available space and five thousand racing fans jammed the trains, which were then late arriving at the track. The enraged passengers rioted, overturned the cars, and demolished other railroad property. However, many of these "fans" may have been more interested in picking up some ready money in bets than in watching thoroughbred performance. By the mid-1840s, thoroughbred racing in the North, and particularly in New York, declined due to the economic depression of 1837, its continued association with gambling, and the increased interest in trotting.

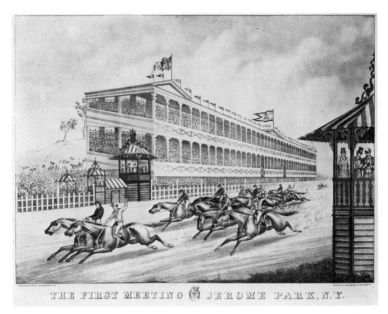

Figure 4.3   First horse race at Jerome Park. Courtesy of the Library of Congress.

In the decades before the Civil War gamblers dominated many of the tracks, making them unsuited to ladies and upper-class society. The Civil War, along with its other destruction, destroyed many southern stables, and temporarily halted horse racing. Following the war, however, racing once again began to achieve respectability as interested businessmen and social leaders came to its support. During the 1860s enterprising sportsmen moved horse racing from crowded city race courses to the country locales of the summer resort, creating the beginning of the socially elite "racing crowd." Several businessmen, including William R. Travers, chose Saratoga Springs in upstate New York for their new venture. Travers, August Belmont, and Leonard W. Jerome formed the American Jockey Club, which operated Jerome Park, closer to New York City, as an elegant track suitable for all members of the family.

The men who founded the American Jockey Club were interested in improving the breed, and they carefully controlled postwar horse racing. When other tracks followed their prescribed standards of betting and behavior, many courses frequented by rowdy gamblers closed. As the best stables often obtained horses from Kentucky's bluegrass country around Lexington, it became renowned as the home of the thoroughbred. The building of Louisville's Churchill Downs and the first running of the Kentucky Derby in May of 1875—won by Aristides, son of Leamington—increased the importance of Kentucky in the racing world. By 1885 thoroughbred racing in the United States had become prosperous and had regained some of its popularity.

Interest in trotting soared during the 1840s as the popularity of thoroughbred racing temporarily declined. It was popular in the northeast urban regions, particularly in and around New York City. The trotter was more associated with the common man than was the thoroughbred: "In contrast to the aristocratic and foreign thoroughbred, the trotter was perceived as the democratic, utilitarian, and, by logical extension, American horse."[12] In the 1840s and 1850s most owners of trotters were, in fact, of the middle class in contrast with the thoroughbred owners, who overwhelmingly tended to be from the upper class. By 1853, harness racing, with a number of trotting tracks newly constructed, was America's leading spectator sport, and over the next several years it became a staple of the rural county fairs.

By the 1860s affluent sportsmen such as Cornelius Vanderbilt and Robert Bonner, the New York publisher, were attracted to harness racing. While bringing a certain level of respectability and prestige to the sport, they also helped to fashion a much-needed sense of order in what had been up to this time a somewhat chaotic amusement. As the value of the horses began to inflate, so did the importance of more scientific and businesslike breeding practices. Likewise, there was recognition of the need for improved administration and communication within the industry. In 1870, the National Trotting Association was founded. The following year the first turf register devoted exclusively to the trotting horse was established. In 1875, *Wallace's Monthly Magazine* was founded as the first sports journal devoted exclusively to trotting and one year later the National Association of Trotting Horse Breeders was formed.[13]

By the mid-1880s, both thoroughbred and harness racing were prosperous sports in the United States. Both had their advocates and both continued to face critics who opposed them because of the gambling that was so much a part of the industry. Nevertheless, the four and one-half decades between 1840 and 1885 brought order and a modest maturity to these popular commercial amusements that sustained them during the reform era that followed.

There is evidence to support the contention that Mexican *vaqueros* (cowboys) developed many of the horsemanship skills now associated with the rodeo. The most skillful "became known as *charros,* widely recognized by their ostentatious attire and skills in roping and riding."[14] These contests became favorite attractions at fairs, festivals, roundups, auctions, and brandings throughout Mexico. "They moved north with the cattle ranches and were well established from Texas to California when the first Anglo settlers arrived. Many of the early Anglo-Texans and Californians joined in the festivities and sometimes entered the contests."[15]

In the 1840s, John Coffee Hays is credited with arranging horsemanship and marksmanship contests to train his Texas Rangers to defend the Republic of Texas against Indians, who were skillful and successful in shooting from galloping horses. Hays later established a peacetime competition among the

Texas Rangers, the Comanche, and the Mexicans. Events included trick riding and bronco-busting, now accepted as rodeo events.[16] The contests remained relatively spontaneous and unorganized, however, until the last decade of the nineteenth century when some western communities began to sponsor rodeo contests regularly.

Boxing
Whereas the race tracks were suitable for both men and women, and harness racing at county fairs and other tracks attracted family attendance, boxing matches were entertainment for "men only." The matches attracted the tradesmen, laborers, and factory hands of the growing working class of the country. These men could identify with the midnineteenth century rough, brawny fighters who used bare knuckles and relied on brute strength to gain victory.

The winner of the Tom Hyer-James "Yankee" Sullivan fight in 1849 was Hyer, who had been the leading American heavyweight fighter for eight years. Hyer retired, and Sullivan continued to fight until 1853, when he lost to John

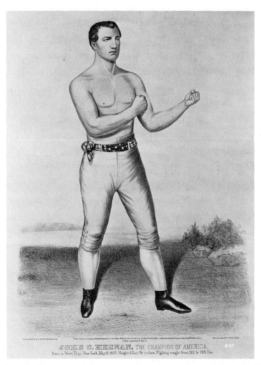

Figure 4.4   John C. Heenan, heavyweight champion of the period. Courtesy of the Library of Congress.

Morrisey. Morrisey, who trained for his fights, retired undefeated five years after his victory over Sullivan. A third champion, John C. Heenan, assumed Morrisey's title and kept it during the next few years.

Following the Civil War, respectable upper-class society discouraged the brutal sport and successfully influenced authorities to outlaw it in many parts of the country. However, boxers sometimes fought covertly in barns, warehouses, and at sea.

Boxing improved and became more acceptable after adopting the Marquis of Queensberry's code, which included three-minute rounds, a count of ten for time to rise from the floor after being knocked down, and outlawing of certain blows. Not until the 1880s and the early 1890s was the new code generally adopted in the United States. Beginning in 1881 John L. Sullivan and his eventual conqueror, James J. Corbett, fought under the Queensberry rules; by virtue of their skill and personal magnetism boxing became increasingly respectable.

Rowing

Competitive rowing during this period began with as many professionals as amateurs, but by the end of the period was almost completely amateur. One famous internationally known rower, Canadian Edward Hanlon, was considered by some as the finest North American sculler. The Ward brothers' four-oared crew reigned supreme from 1858 to 1871. While there were also races for six and eight-oared shells, most contests were for single or double sculls, and single scullers such as John Biglin, Josh and Ellis Ward, James Hamill, James Ten Eyck, Charles Courtney, and W. B. Curtis were famous throughout the east. Professional rowers competed for prizes ranging from ten dollars to one thousand dollars while bettors wagered heavily on the outcomes of races.

Perhaps the most important event in amateur rowing was the banding together of several Philadelphia clubs in 1858 to form the Schuylkill Navy. It soon became one of the most influential rowing organizations in the country. In 1872 it was instrumental in founding the National Association of Amateur Oarsmen, primarily to preserve amateur rowing for gentlemen and to guard against any form of professionalism. The Association sponsored annual regattas for national championships in several events and classes of boats. Under Commodore James M. Ferguson, the Schuylkill Navy initiated and hosted a Grand International Regatta, held under the auspices of the United States Centennial Commission, during Philadelphia's impressive Centennial Exhibition of 1876. Leading boat clubs from English cities and universities competed with American boat clubs. Amateur events occupied the first five days and professional races the last three days. The regatta was considered a highlight of the exhibition, which attracted millions of visitors who came from all the states on newly built railroads.[17]

Rowing was popular in New Orleans both before and after the Civil War. When rowing resumed in that city in 1872, it quickly became a favorite in all socioeconomic classes. While the first postwar clubs were composed of, and limited to, middle- and upper-class "young gentlemen of polish and attainments," there soon followed a profusion of clubs for men of all ranks—cotton press employees, laborers from the metal foundries, and the city's firemen. However, by the early 1890s most of the middle- and lower-class men had shifted their allegiance to other sports such as baseball and soon the southern rowing clubs were again almost exclusively the province of the upper class. Many clubs, in fact, began to offer fewer races and to expand into social organizations "dedicated to preserving the sport as a pastime for gentlemen and to providing the amenities of an exclusive club."[18]

This pattern in the South appeared to be true in other cities in which rowing was popular. The working class shifted their enthusiasm in sport from rowing to professional baseball. When professional rowing declined, some of the rowers became volunteer or paid coaches for crews in colleges and universities where rowing had become popular.

Between 1840 and 1885 the foundation was laid for professional sport in the United States. The concept of professionalism in a team sport such as baseball was accepted and the framework for league organization was established. Likewise, horse racing moved into the modern era through organization and standardization. Boxing, on the other hand, lacked the same level of order and failed to attract a significant portion of the upper-class business community. It remained therefore, outside middle-class respectability. Nevertheless, professional sport, on the whole, had gained a firm foothold on the American consciousness.

Beginnings of Organized Amateur Sport

The historian Samuel Eliot Morison calls this period an era of "joiners." He suggests that a "desire for distinction in a country of growing uniformity, and a human craving for fellowship drew the Americans into . . . fraternal orders."[19] In 1848 scientists formed the American Association for the Advancement of Science, farmers established the National Grange in 1867, and philanthropists organized the American National Red Cross in 1881. Organizations were formed by the rich and poor, by the old settlers and by the newly arrived, by the Sons and Daughters of the American Revolution and by the Ancient Order of Hibernians. Sport enthusiasts devoted to yachting or rowing or archery or track and field also started informal clubs which later became national sport associations.

Ethnic associations in many cities played a significant role in nineteenth-century United States, as they continue to do in many places today. The Scottish Caledonian clubs and the German Turner societies preserved the homeland's sports and gymnastics, as well as national customs and the native language. In major cities the private athletic clubs, formed on English models, sponsored gymnastic and track and field competitions.

Track and Field Athletics
The Scottish community initiated the Caledonian Games, which organized, promoted, and stimulated the growth of track and field athletics in the United States. Athletic games had long been an established institution in Scotland, and after several informal annual gatherings in this country to compete in their traditional games, a group of Boston Scotsmen organized the first Caledonian Club in America in the spring of 1853. A social and cultural club for men, the Caledonians held their first official games later that year. In New York a Caledonian Club was founded in 1856 and held its first games the following year. Philadelphia followed suit in 1858 and Newark three years later.

The first games of the New York club included throwing the heavy hammer, throwing the light hammer, putting the light stone, putting the heavy stone, tossing the caber, wheelbarrow race (blindfolded), sack race, standing high jump, running long jump, running high leap, short race, and broadsword dance.[20] The games, which in some cases offered cash prizes, quickly became highly organized and popular affairs which drew large crowds. For the second games in 1858, the New York Caledonian Club advertised the games and levied a twenty-five cent admission fee. The practice was successful and the succeeding years saw increased publicity and crowds of twenty-five thousand attending the games.

Further enthusiasm for track and field sports in New York was evidenced in the early autumn of 1868, when the New York Athletic Club was founded. The founders, William B. Curtis, already a noted weightlifter, and two friends, John C. Babcock and Henry E. Buermeyer, were influenced by the popularity of such sports in New York, and also by the traditional English pursuit of track and field athletics. The club's first indoor meet was held in 1868 at the Empire Skating Rink. A more extensive outdoor meet was held the following spring on a turf track near Central Park. Two years later land was secured north of the Harlem River at Mott Haven, where the club constructed the first cinder track in the United States. The New York Athletic Club began sponsoring annual spring meets, open to male amateur athletes from all parts of the country.

Beginning with the first meet, Caledonian Club athletes were prominent and successful participants in the New York Athletic Club meets. However, the Caledonian Clubs' major efforts concentrated on the annual Caledonian

Games, which became an important source of funds for many clubs following the Civil War. The Caledonian Games continued as a significant force in American track and field until about 1880 when the city athletic clubs with their strong amateur traditions became more influential.[21]

By 1879 the New York City region contained approximately a hundred athletic clubs, and other cities across the country boasted equivalent numbers. Prominent were the American, Manhattan, and Pastime Clubs, all in New York; the Chicago Athletic Club and the Olympic Club of San Francisco, the Detroit Athletic Club and the Indianapolis Athletic Club. There were also clubs in Boston, New Orleans, Cincinnati, Philadelphia, Providence, Pittsburgh, Cleveland, St. Louis, and Baltimore. The vast majority of these clubs were for men only. One of the few exceptions was the Ladies Athletic Club on Staten Island in the late 1870s, where tennis, archery, croquet, and darts were played. Until the 1880s the athletic clubs were usually composed of amateur athletes interested in pursuing a regular program of exercise and participating in track and field athletics. As the clubs became popular and their members wealthier, sumptuous facilities, financial stability, and limited membership characterized more and more athletic clubs, and a greater emphasis was placed on social as well as athletic prominence.[22]

The athletic clubs, to preserve the concept of amateurism and regulate competition, formed the National Association of Amateur Athletes of America (NAAAA) in 1879. For the next several years the NAAAA sponsored national championships and attempted to settle the many disputes about eligibility, professionalism, and other issues. However, controversies continued.

Believing that the NAAAA could no longer govern track and field competition effectively, in 1888 fifteen athletic clubs, under the leadership of the New York Athletic Club and a Philadelphia club, joined together to form the Amateur Athletic Union (AAU) of the United States. NAAAA continued to function, but with frequent controversies with the AAU. For example, the AAU Board of Governors passed a resolution that barred amateur athletes from competing in any open games in the United States not governed by the AAU, the penalty to be exclusion from all games under the rules of the AAU. Further, they prohibited AAU athletes from entering the Penn Relays, administered by the Intercollegiate Association of Amateur Athletes of America (ICAAAA), which belonged to the NAAAA. Finally the ICAAAA withdrew from the NAAAA and the AAU approved the Penn Relays for their athletes. It was clear that the Amateur Athletic Union had gained control of the track and field athletics in this country.

Yachting

When John Cox Stevens, a prominent New Yorker and an avid yachtsman, called together eight likeminded friends for an organizational meeting aboard his new yacht, *Gimcrack,* on July 30, 1844, they founded the New York Yacht Club. The nine men designated themselves the original members, selected Stevens as the first commodore, appointed a five-man committee to draft club rules and regulations, and planned a club cruise to Newport, Rhode Island, to begin in three days.[23] Other clubs had been organized during this same period but, with the exception of the exclusive Southern Yacht Club in New Orleans, had not been successful. The Civil War interrupted the sport of yachting, but soon after the war clubs sprang up in Detroit, San Francisco, Oyster Bay, Chicago, and Larchmont. The Southern Yacht Club also reorganized, and by 1878 New Orleans once again enjoyed regular racing. Most of the yachting enthusiasts came from the growing number of wealthy Americans who could afford the cost of a yacht and its maintenance and who also had the leisure time in which to sail.

The New York Yacht Club, just one year after its founding, held a formal race on July 17, 1845, "over a course that carried the fleet down through New York's Narrows, around a buoy in the Lower Bay, and back."[24] The cash prize of $225, the total of the entrance fees, was won by William Edgar with his *Cygnet.* The club's fame and tradition became firmly established in 1851 when the yacht *America,* commissioned by a syndicate headed by Stevens, responded to an invitation sent by England's Royal Yacht Squadron, and entered and won an international race around the Isle of Wight. The victorious yacht was awarded the Royal Yacht Squadron Cup and became the first American craft to win an international race. With this prize, the Royal Yacht Squadron cup, the New York Yacht Club launched the historic *America's* Cup series in 1870.

In New Orleans society before the Civil War, the Southern Yacht Club, founded in 1847, was, like many jockey clubs, "both an exclusive social organization and a regulatory group."[25] Regattas were open to members of yachting clubs and invited guests, and a day's racing often ended, as did a day of horse racing, with a dinner and a ball. The club's membership included planters, wealthy businessmen, and other socially elite residents of the Gulf Coast from New Orleans to Pensacola. Pass Christian became the southern summer resort for many of the wealthy, but those who could not be away from New Orleans enjoyed regattas on Lake Pontchartrain. With the exception of the rivers, bays, and sounds around New York City, summer sailing and yachting flourished primarily at resorts such as Newport, Pass Christian, Lake Pontchartrain, and in the Midwest on Lakes Michigan, Huron, and Erie. The charter members of most clubs were practical amateur sailors, who managed their own expensive craft. With the growing fame and prestige of the yachting clubs and victories in certain races, some wealthy men with no sailing knowledge began to join the clubs to gain social status. Some even purchased yachts and hired professional seamen to sail them so that they could be identified with the sport of yachting. Meanwhile, on rivers and lakes across the country small sailboats, skiffs, sloops, and rowboats served their owners for transportation, fishing, and pleasure. "Just messing about in boats" continued to be an enjoyable pastime for many.

Tennis

The development of the modern game of lawn tennis introduced a new sport for men and women. By the late nineteenth century there were at least three distinct court games—badminton, court tennis, and rackets—being played in Europe, primarily by the upper classes. Major Walter C. Wingfield, a British cavalry officer, is usually credited with moving the game of court tennis outdoors onto the well-manicured lawns of English estates in late 1873 with a game he patented under the name of Sphairistike. In February, 1874, a young American society girl, Mary E. Outerbridge of Staten Island, New York, while enjoying a winter vacation in Bermuda, observed several British army officers playing Sphairistike. After playing the game herself, she purchased a set of equipment and later that spring introduced it to the United States at the Staten Island Cricket and Base Ball Club.

The game of tennis also began to appear in other sections of the country. After witnessing a contest during a trip to Europe in 1874, James Dwight, now called the "father" of American tennis, procured the equipment and after his return to the United States prevailed upon an uncle to allow him to mark a court on the lawn of his estate at Nahant, Massachusetts. He and his cousin Fred Sears attempted to play the game with no lines and soon became disenchanted. Several weeks later, they again brought out the equipment and gave it another try. Apparently it was more successful, as they played through an afternoon rain in rubber boots and coats.[26] Two years later these two tennis pioneers played in the earliest recorded tennis tournament in the United States, a round robin affair in Nahant. The sport's popularity increased steadily in the East as courts were set up at clubs in Brookline, Massachusetts, Newport, Rhode Island, and Philadelphia during the late seventies.

In the South, the game appears to have had an independent introduction and growth. Shortly after Major Wingfield's original rules for lawn tennis were set forth, a group of New Orleans' English residents began playing the game regularly. In 1876 they founded the New Orleans Tennis Club, the first such organization in the United States. Although the game was played by men and women in the Northeast, ladies in New Orleans were denied access to the club's courts until the mid-1880s.[27]

As was the case with baseball a generation earlier, a lack of standardization of rules and equipment hindered the development of tennis and created numerous problems during its first several years. At what was billed as the first "national" tournament, sponsored in 1880 by the Staten Island Cricket and Base Ball Club, James Dwight and his cousin Richard D. Sears refused to play in the singles matches, after determining that the balls were "lighter, smaller and softer than the regulations provided for."[28] Later in the same year Philadelphia's Young America Cricket Club traveled to the Staten Island Cricket and Base Ball Club and found the net to be six inches lower than the height to which they were accustomed.

Figure 4.5   First National Lawn Tennis Tournament, from a drawing by H. A. Ogden in *Frank Leslie's Illustrated Newspaper,* September 18, 1880.

Basically the rules being followed were those established by Wingfield—the hour-glass shaped court, fifteen point badminton scoring, wing net five feet high on the sides and slightly over three feet in the center. One could find variations, however, in almost all locales. One club used the hour-glass court while another changed it to rectangular. Other variations affected court size, net height, and scoring procedure. In 1881 the United States National Lawn Tennis Association was formed to standardize equipment, space and court size, and to sanction tournaments as well as sponsor the "national" championships. Although only Eastern clubs were represented, it was a major step toward the development of the game, which by 1900 was played by men and women across the country.

While tennis became popular with the wealthy within a relatively short period of time, a number of other pursuits vied for their attention. One of these was polo, which after its American introduction by publisher-sportsman James Gordon Bennett, Jr. in 1873, attracted players in clubs as well as on some college campuses.

Other Popular Sports
Croquet was one of several games which brought women outdoors to join men in a mild but enjoyable exercise. Imported from France and first introduced in the midnineteenth century to the upper circles of American society, croquet spread quickly downward to the middle class, while the manufacturers strove

to keep up with the demand for equipment. The game continued to be popular as a backyard pastime for several decades and seemed to be a national sport when, in 1882, the National Croquet Association was formed and the first national tournament was held in Norwich, Connecticut. By the end of the century, however, the game was no longer popular, and tournament play had become a thing of the past.

Archery, which had been popular briefly in the early part of the century, boasted more than twenty-five clubs in the East and North by 1879. In the same year the National Archery Association was organized and held its first tournament in Chicago's White Stocking Park. The meet, open to men and women, was heralded by the editors of *Harper's Weekly* as a socially acceptable event: "The contestants were ladies and gentlemen from the cultured circles of society, and while the rivalry among the shooters was keen to the last degree, an air of such refinement and courteous dignity as is not often witnessed by observers of public games characterized everyone connected with the contest."[29]

First devised in 1863 by James L. Plimpton, the four-wheeled roller skate created another form of physical activity which was fashionable for a brief period of time in the 1870s and 1880s. Although it began with the upper classes, roller-skating soon became a popular pastime for the middle classes. Wooden roller-skating rinks were built in many cities and towns, admission fees were modest, the equipment was inexpensive, and the necessary skill was easy to acquire. In addition, roller-skating, like croquet and ice-skating, was a socially acceptable recreation for men *and* women.

Of all the inventions affecting sport, one of the most dramatic was the bicycle. When the high-wheeled "ordinary" was introduced in the mid-1870s the machine had been evolving over a sixty-year period. With a front wheel measuring fifty to sixty inches in height, the machine quickly caught on with young male daredevils who were willing to risk "headers" over the high wheel for the exhilaration of a self-propelled speed and the feeling of superiority over those walking below. Bicycling grew in popularity at an astounding rate, especially considering the high cost of the instrument—$150 to $300. By 1880 the League of American Wheelmen was founded and within six years its membership had reached more than ten thousand. The organization led the way in protesting municipal ordinances that banned bicycles from public parks and main thoroughfares and in lobbying for bicycle paths and good roads. Many cyclists enjoyed Sunday club outings of several miles. Almost immediately, racing attracted large numbers of enthusiasts. As in baseball and rowing, professionalism caused problems in regulating bicycle races.

Women and girls as well as men and boys enjoyed ice-skating in the winter months in most northern communities. During the Civil War years the women of Detroit ventured onto the ice in large numbers, and several privately owned

Figure 4.6   League of American Wheelmen Meet, Washington, D.C. from a drawing in *Frank Leslie's Illustrated Newspaper,* May 24, 1884.

rinks were opened to meet the demand. In 1868 the Hook, Dupont and Company Skating Park paid Anna Jagerisky, a well-known local woman, $150 to skate for thirty consecutive hours.[30] The promotion attracted over fifteen hundred spectators. Skating parties, at which prizes were awarded for "best costumes" for women and men, further promoted skating.

Swimming had begun to achieve some popularity as a form of recreation in the first half of the century. In the larger cities men and women were strictly segregated in the few bathing houses. When sea bathing became popular, propriety was maintained through the use of bathing machines—small wooden buildings on wheels that were pulled into the water by horses or other swimmers. Bathers changed into their swimming attire in the building and entered the water also from within the structure.

After the Civil War both men and women became particularly concerned with the "appalling" condition of female health. Swimming was thought an appropriate exercise to improve health, even in the "bathing costumes" of the day, which were heavy and fully covered the body. Nevertheless, with the construction of large bath houses in the 1870s, more and more women swam. In 1877 the New York Athletic Club sponsored what was possibly the first swimming championship for men in the United States and six years later began to hold scheduled meets.

Many people enjoyed social dancing during this period, with the country dance giving way to the square dance and its more lively swing. In city ballrooms, the country dance was slowly replaced by the European importations, the waltz and polka, although some people considered them daring or even immoral.

The men and women who went west in 1849 in the California gold rush took their dances with them and also joined in the dance traditions of the local Spanish and Mexican residents, including the fandango—a specific dance or an event. "Any major event on a Spanish ranchero that featured an informal party or general ball was called a *fandango*."[31]

The rise of *organized* amateur sport as well as more informal recreational activity reflected the growing interest among the upper and middle classes in pursuing active lives beyond the working day. The organization of clubs dedicated to the pursuit of particular sports often began with wealthy men, who ultimately came to define and rule amateur sport in the United States. Nevertheless, the middle class emulated, within a more modest economic framework, this same need for joining together in pursuit of sport. This active participation, similar to the growing identification with professional baseball teams, is an example of the ability of sport to provide a sense of community.

Social Reform and Physical Fitness at Midcentury

Amid the century's developments in amateur sport, many intellectual and spiritual leaders in the country concerned themselves with the physical and moral health of the American public. While the phrase "physical fitness" was not used at that time in the way it is used today, writers, lecturers, and teachers called attention to the poor health and declining stamina of many Americans. They recommended the beneficial effects of systematic exercises, referred to as gymnastics, and also of sports.

Catharine Beecher, lecturing about the poor health of women, denounced the social conventions that limited female physical activity in the nineteenth century. Her famous brother, the Reverend Henry Ward Beecher of Brooklyn, an American advocate of the English "muscular Christianity" movement which aimed at "breadth of shoulders as well as of doctrines," encouraged vigorous outdoor recreation, arguing that churches and other Christian associations should provide opportunities for the young men of the city to bowl, play billiards, and exercise in wholesome environments.

One of the most influential voices urging the need for exercise and sport was Thomas Wentworth Higginson, liberal clergyman, author, intellectual, and former military officer. In a series of articles in the *Atlantic Monthly,* he extolled the virtues of the athletic life, and suggested a wide variety of activities from which men might choose. Field sports were lauded as bringing one into touch with nature. Skating was highly recommended, and he agreed with Henry Ward Beecher that bowling and billiards, when rescued from the sordid surroundings of the commercial establishment, were acceptable pastimes. Boxing he saw as possessing a tendency to brutalize the mind although he conceded that limited skill and knowledge in the sport might promote desirable qualities of manliness.[32] Others, too, played significant roles in the effort to arouse their fellow citizens to the need for fitness. George Windship, a noted strongman, advocated a system of training with heavy weights. Through lecture-exhibition tours and his Boston gymnasium he urged men to seek health through strength.

In opposition to Windship's use of heavy apparatus and emphasis on strength, Dr. Dioclesian Lewis developed a "new gymnastics" which incorporated numerous exercises using light wands, Indian clubs, wooden rings, and two-pound dumbbells. Lewis was a popular and dynamic lecturer, perhaps the most effective of the fitness proponents, who in his "observations of people in all sections of the country . . . was so painfully impressed by the prevalence of pale faces, undeveloped and distorted bodies, and nervous debility that he became anxious to arouse the people to active interest in physical culture, and especially to the necessity of making it a part of school training."[33] Concerned for the health of women as well as men, and convinced of the need for systematic exercise suitable for both sexes, Lewis sought to improve not only muscle strength, "but to give flexibility, agility and grace of movement."[34] Lewis' system achieved widespread popularity in the 1850s, 1860s, and 1870s, because the heavy, fixed apparatus necessary for some strength-building systems was not required and his exercises could be performed in the home, the classroom, or other restricted areas. In 1861 he founded the Normal Institute for Physical Education, a ten-week program for training men and women to teach his system. Lewis, a prolific writer, reached many people through books such as *The New Gymnastics for Men, Women and Children* and *Weak Lungs and How to Make Them Strong.*

Private and public gymnasiums opened in many medium-sized and larger cities. In the decade prior to the Civil War a gymnasium opened in Cincinnati, the Tremont Gymnasium started in Boston, and the Metropolitan Gymnasium, the latest in design, began its program in Chicago. The Metropolitan Gymnasium measured 108 × 80 feet, with walls twenty feet high and a center dome forty feet in both height and diameter. Following the war other privately owned public gymnasiums opened in cities across the nation, including Dudley A. Sargent's Hygienic Institute and School of Physical Culture in New York. Many athletic clubs also included exercise facilities in their buildings.

The social reformers of the period were, for the most part, motivated by a sincere belief in the importance of exercise for the maintenance of physical, and by extension, intellectual and spiritual well-being. Progressive educators and clergy like the Beechers and Higginson shared an intellectual idealism and curiosity that allowed them to explore and accept new ways of uplifting the human condition. Others, such as Windship and Lewis, with similarly idealistic motivations were also able to fashion a livelihood through their advocacy of exercise. Although the direct effects of their individual efforts are difficult to ascertain, it would appear that their collective efforts were significant in preparing a climate of approval for exercise and other forms of physical activity later in the century. While public acceptance, as measured by such developments as the opening of public and private gymnasiums and instruction in schools and colleges, was sporadic between 1840 and 1885, the public was nonetheless reminded of the benefits of exercise for physical and moral uplift throughout the period. Reforming zeal, combined with the growing interest in sports and games, played a role in the emerging acceptance of exercise as a worthy ideal during the last two decades of the century.

Turner Societies

The German Revolution of 1848 brought thousands of exiles to the United States, many of whom continued their German customs and programs. Among the immigrants were many German Turners, who immediately established Turner societies. The first Turnverein, as the societies were called, was founded in 1848 in Cincinnati by Friedrich Hecker. Within three years the first national turnfest, sponsored by the United Turnverein of North America (the American Turnerbund), was held in Philadelphia and by 1859, seventy-three societies with a combined membership of over five thousand had been formed. At the end of the Civil War the societies formed the North American Turnerbund, testimony both to the popularity of the movement and to the influx of German immigrants to North America in less than two decades. By 1867 there were 148 societies with 10,200 members.[35]

The Turnverein, a social center establishing a bridge between the old culture and the new, helped preserve traditional customs, language, and celebrations, while also offering English language and American citizenship classes. Central to each Turnverein, however, was the gymnastics program. Based on Friedrich Jahn's work in Germany, but modified to the new land, each society offered instruction and attempted to provide adequate gymnasium facilities for children, youth, and adults, who were all encouraged to pursue physical fitness through gymnastics. Classes were held during the day, after school, evenings, and on weekends. The Turner movement directly affected thousands of German-Americans, and aided the acceptance of physical education in the public schools of several cities with large German-American populations.

The program or system, aiming at an overall level of fitness, employed marching, free exercises with wands, gymnastic apparatus work, a graded set of games, and dance steps for girls. The activities were taught by age groups, and periodically local turnfests were held where group exhibitions could be seen. Many other Americans became impressed by the Turner or German system of gymnastics and incorporated it into their programs, usually appointing a Turner to teach the work properly.

The Young Men's Christian Association

The Young Men's Christian Association (YMCA), founded in England by George Williams and introduced to the United States in the early 1850s, sought to provide a wholesome environment for young men newly arrived in the city. Originally organized for Bible study and evangelical work, the "Y" became interested in physical activity programs in the middle 1850s. In 1856 the Brooklyn Association's Board of Managers considered the establishment of a gymnasium, but due to financial problems and the Civil War, the plans did not materialize. In 1864 at its annual convention the YMCA received a resolution which formally expressed its commitment to physical education: "Any machinery will be incomplete which has not taken into account the whole man. We must add physical recreation to all YMCAs."[36] Five years later the first two complete YMCA gymnasiums were built, in New York and San Francisco. Slowly, additional associations began to add gymnasiums and to employ physical directors.

The YMCA's in the 1870s and 1880s included in their gymnasiums many of the weight implements of Windship, the lighter equipment of Lewis and Beecher, and the new, more scientifically based apparatus of Sargent. "But the gymnasium is only a part of the physical department. . . . In 1884 twenty-three Associations reported various other forms of physical culture, including base-ball, rambling, rowing, as well as swimming clubs and bowling-alleys."[37] The specific programs followed within the gymnasium and outside of it depended upon the training and inclination of the director.

The Young Women's Christian Association

Young women who moved to the city in the middle of the century faced problems similar to those of young men. The Young Women's Christian Association (YWCA), established in England at the same time as the YMCA, also organized chapters in American cities. In 1877 the Boston branch of the Young Women's Christian Association began a class in calisthenics, which was taught by one of the residents. Athletics was offered in a nearby park in 1882, and an exercise program was conducted for the residents of the Association's Warrenton Street Home, utilizing a few chest-weights on closet doors and in the corners of hallways. At the same time a class from the Association received free instruction in a private Boston gymnasium. When the YW's new building opened in 1884, it boasted a fifth-floor gymnasium, the first to be incorporated into any American YWCA building. Classes were taught during its first year by Anna Wood of the Wellesley College gymnasium faculty. In the next few years light gymnastic classes were reported in a number of other YWCA's. The programs offered were those of the instructor; there was no official YWCA program. Some YW's offered the work of Beecher and Lewis, others offered German or Swedish gymnastics, and still others the Delsarte system.[38]

Physical Education and Sport in Colleges

The concern for health and physical fitness slowly influenced state and city school systems to initiate instruction in health and exercise. However, wide variations in belief and implementation existed from city to city and state to state—in physical exercise as in everything else. Public elementary schools were generally established by the middle of the century; in 1874 the Kalamazoo case upheld the right of local school districts to levy taxes to support public high schools.

Although German gymnastics were introduced in the Cincinnati schools as early as 1860 and in other Midwestern cities in the 1860s and 1870s, not until the following decade were such programs a regular part of the school system. At San Francisco's Rincon School, John Swett initiated a daily program of play and exercise. He led the boys on ten to fifteen-mile hikes as well as in various ball games and insisted that the girls participate in free gymnastics and work with wands. Funds for equipment were raised through boxing and gymnastic exhibitions.

In 1866 Swett, by this time the California State Superintendent of Public Instruction, was instrumental in the passage of America's first state legislation requiring physical education in the public elementary and secondary schools. The law provided that: "Instruction shall be given in all grades of schools, and in all classes, during the entire school course in . . . the laws of health; and due attention shall be given to such physical exercises for the pupils as may be conducive to health and vigor of body, as well as mind."[39] The law specified that the primary schools must allot a minimum of five minutes twice each day for free gymnastics and vocal and breathing exercises.

Physical Education and Sport in Men's Colleges

In 1861 Amherst College, under its progressive president, William A. Stearns, fully committed itself to the concept of physical education in the curriculum by appointing Dr. Edward Hitchcock, a young medical doctor and son of a former Amherst College president, as Professor of Hygiene and Physical Education. A new gymnasium was constructed and fitted out with equipment of the period. Students were required to attend exercise classes for half an hour four times a week. Each class session began with fifteen to twenty minutes of required exercise in uniform, either light gymnastics with dumbbells, or heavy gymnastics with weights for more capable and stronger students, plus formal marching, running or "double-quick" movements. The remainder of the thirty-minute period was devoted to individual, voluntary exercise such as running, tumbling, heavy lifting, or sport activity. Although the only sport facility in the original gymnasium was the bowling alley, the new Pratt Gymnasium, built in 1884, reflected the growing interest in sport by including rooms for billiards, boxing, and baseball practice. While he welcomed the increased popularity of sport and athletic activities, Dr. Hitchcock continued to stress the need for the gymnasium exercise program as a necessary foundation for health.

With a medical education and teaching experience in the areas of anatomy, physiology, and natural history, young Hitchcock began a long tenure at Amherst College and made a lasting impact on American physical education. His physical education program was a model that was transplanted to many other colleges and universities. His original responsibilities at Amherst were to serve as medical officer of the college, instruct in hygiene, and plan and supervise a systematic program of exercise and recreation. Hitchcock was primarily concerned with improving the health of the Amherst College students through hygiene and exercise programs, and again he set a pattern which was followed in other educational institutions, which also appointed medical doctors to direct their physical education programs. The Amherst program was described in an 1869 report to the Board of Trustees:

> The design is, that all the muscles of the body should be exercised in a manner to equalize best the circulation of the blood,—to expand the lungs,—to aid the stomach in the digestion of food,—to strengthen the joints, develop all parts of the body in harmony with the most efficient action of the brain. Thus not only agility and strength of the limbs are acquired, but the vital forces of the system—fed from their natural sources of nutrition, absorption and respiration—are most abundantly supplied. The true course pointed out for physical exercise . . . is, . . . bringing the system into the highest state of physical health compatible with mental exercise.[40]

In addition, Hitchcock was active in anthropometry, an area of interest to nineteenth-century physical educators. Seeking the "average college man," he maintained records on age, weight, height, chest girth, arm girth, forearm girth, lung capacity, and pull-ups on thousands of students. Measurements were taken on all incoming students and an individual program designed for each student to procure bodily symmetry and to correct imbalances and weaknesses. Subsequent readings were made each year to measure the student's progress.

In 1859, Harvard College opened a new gymnasium building and employed its first teacher of gymnastics, Abram Molineaux Hewlett. He was described as "a mulatto, of very fine physique, and of estimable character."[41] Hewlett, a gymnast, possessed a reputation as an outstanding teacher of boxing who had operated his own gymnasium in Worcester, Massachusetts, for the preceding five years. Upon his death in late 1871, he was succeeded by Frederic William Lister.

In 1879 Harvard, like Amherst, chose a medical doctor as director of its new Hemenway Gymnasium, when Dudley A. Sargent became Assistant Professor of Physical Training and Director of the Gymnasium. Sargent undertook serious studies in gymnastics, anthropometry, and physical education, which he carried on until his retirement in 1919. Although a fine athlete himself, Sargent was primarily concerned with the fitness of the nonathlete. His purpose was "to improve the physical condition of the mass of our students, and to give them as much health, strength and stamina as possible, to enable them to perform the duties that await them after leaving college."[42] To this end he, like Hitchcock, placed great emphasis upon physical examinations as the basis upon which individual programs of exercise would be built. The examination included a personal medical history, strength tests, lung capacity tests, anthropometric measurements, and an examination of the heart and lungs before and after exercising.[43] On the basis of this information Sargent prescribed a program of appropriate exercises, always taking care to specify the

Dudley Allen Sargent (1849–1924) was born in Belfast, Maine. As a boy his favorite activities were rowing in the harbor, jumping across ice-floes in a millpond, and swimming. As a teenager he practiced gymnastics incessantly and formed "Sargent's Combination," performing gymnastic stunts, singing, dancing, and giving dramatic sketches. He joined a traveling circus as an acrobat, but at eighteen decided that he wanted more out of life.

His energetic independence led him to Bowdoin College in Maine where he studied for his B.A. degree and, at the same time, acted as director of the gymnasium, earning five dollars a week. In his gymnasium program, Sargent attracted not only the strong and agile students but also the weak and nonathletic men who were his real concern. After Bowdoin he continued his education at Yale where he earned a medical degree. While there, he argued that physical exercises should be part of the required course work.

Sargent wanted to direct a gymnasium at a college but could not secure a position. He moved to New York City where he opened a private gymnasium to help people build up weak bodies and to use physical exercise as a cure for "nervous irritability." He invented various "developing machines," translating movements he remembered from working on Maine farms—reaping, mowing, sawing, and chopping—into exercises performed with the aid of machines.

In September of 1879 he became director of the gymnasium at Harvard University. A faculty appointment at last! He moved quickly to develop a program of gymnastics and physical education which was copied by many institutions of the period. Prominent in early professional associations and active in research of the period, Sargent is best remembered for his work at Harvard, the Harvard Summer School of Physical Education, and Sargent Normal School. Throughout his life, he imbued others with his enthusiasm and techniques.

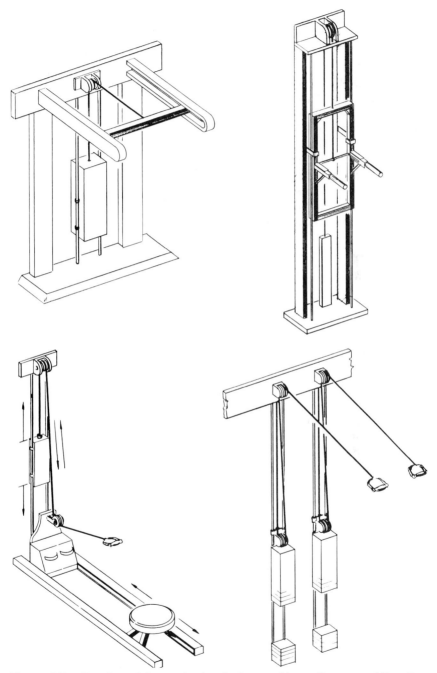

Figure 4.7   Drawing of Sargent's developing machines. Courtesy of Ron Turmelle.

amount of work and the correct adjustment of the apparatus to be used. In addition he suggested appropriate diet, sleep, bathing, and clothing. He was highly critical of the old heavy apparatus modeled after the German Turn-platz, on the grounds that most people could not use it properly. On the other hand, he criticized the Indian clubs, dumbbells, wands, and other light gym-nastic equipment as appropriate only for developing suppleness. Sargent ul-timately designed over eighty developmental machines: chest-expanders and developers, quarter-circles, leg-machines, finger-machines, high pulleys, in-clined planes, traveling parallels, and hydraulic rowing machines. He sought to design equipment that was based on scientific principles and easy to use. By 1885 it was reported that at least forty-eight institutions were using ap-paratus of Sargent's design.

At about this same time, an Englishwoman traveling in the Middle West visited some colleges with less advanced physical training:

> No suitable provision was made for physical exercise or relaxation at Oberlin Col-lege, and no gymnasium existed for either sex. During our ten days' stay we saw no sign whatever of athletic sports or exercises. . . . The utmost physical recrea-tion seemed to consist in a country walk. . . . This absence of desire for physical sports seems more or less common throughout America, and is very strange in the eyes of those accustomed to the exhibition of animal spirits in the English youth of both sexes. . . .

> I found, indeed, that at this College [Antioch] somewhat more attention was paid to physical exercise, Mr. [Horace] Mann speaking of "bathing and exercise" as the "religious rites of health," and at the time of our visit short exhibitions of "light gymnastics" (i.e., exercises of arms, &c, without machinery), took place several times a day between the recitations.[44]

Beginnings of Intercollegiate Sport

Intercollegiate sport for men in this period centered primarily on casual events in rowing, baseball, football, and track and field. It began with occasional stu-dent challenge-matches, and by the 1880s was established as a significant part of campus life.

Rowing

The history of rowing epitomized the growing public interest in sport during this time. Rowing, one of the most popular sports of the period, began at Yale in 1843 and at Harvard the following year. Rowing clubs were formed both to develop and formalize interest in the activity and to generate funds nec-essary for the purchase and maintenance of boats and other equipment. The clubs, composed of students and an occasional faculty member, also func-tioned as social organizations. Officially, however, the clubs had no affiliation

August 3, 1852. Harvard, First Place; Yale, Second Place. William J. Weeks, Yale '44, came back to college in the spring of 1843 with a four-oared White-hall boat and formed a rowing club. The next year the club purchased a six-oared racer, the *Excelsior,* and used it in races with other New Haven clubs. The first Harvard club began with a barge, *Oneida,* which the Harvard men rowed with other amateur crews on the Charles River.

The idea for a Harvard-Yale match appears to have several possible origins. According to one account, "The Yale oarsmen had their eyes on the progress at Harvard and, largely through the efforts of James M. Whiton, '53, a challenge was sent to Harvard."[45] Another story credits Mr. James N. Elkins, general superintendent of the Boston, Concord and Montreal Railroad with promoting the match to popularize the Lake Winnipesaukee area as a summer resort, which would in turn benefit the railroad as the region's major transportation system. He persuaded the two clubs to send crews to race in eight-oared barges over a two-mile course. Whatever the specific cause,

student crews from Harvard and Yale met at New Hampshire's Lake Winnipesaukee in the summer of 1852, and the event marked the inauguration of intercollegiate sport in America.

Harvard rowed the *Oneida,* and one of the crew commented that they "had not rowed much for fear of blistering their hands!" Yale had three boats, the *Halcyon, Undine,* and the *Atlanta.* Harvard won the prize, a pair of black walnut sculls mounted on silver. It was reported:

There was so much fun in the race that the crews thought they would have another go on the fifth; but that day was very stormy, and the prize was given to the Halcyon as second in the first race.[46]

Hundreds witnessed the event, including the Democratic presidential nominee, Franklin Pierce. Although a *New York Tribune* reporter commented that "intercollegiate sport would make little stir in the busy world,"[47] the event was moderately successful and hinted at the future of intercollegiate sport.

with the college or university other than the members being students. The clubs raised funds, purchased boats, constructed facilities, and scheduled matches with other clubs. The rowing clubs were, in fact, student-initiated, student-financed, student-coached, and student-administered. This model set the pattern for the beginnings of intercollegiate athletics for men in the United States.

Rowing was the first popular intercollegiate sport. By 1859, the rowing clubs at Harvard, Yale, Brown, and Trinity formed the College Union Regatta Association and in 1860 and 1861, races were rowed on Lake Quinsigamond near Worcester, Massachusetts, with Harvard winning both years. Following a disturbance at the 1860 regatta, Yale students were forced by their faculty to withdraw from all intercollegiate competition. However, in 1864 Yale challenged Harvard to another race, having obtained a professional rower to coach the team and, for the first time in the brief history of intercollegiate sport, the New Haven crew was victorious. The Harvard-Yale series continued for the next seven years.

The race with Oxford University from England against Harvard in 1869 promoted interest in collegiate rowing, and as a result crews were formed at a number of colleges. Following this, the Harvard club initiated a meeting of several New England college clubs. The conference, held on April 15, 1871, at the Massasoit House in Springfield, Massachusetts, was attended by student representatives from Massachusetts Agricultural College (University of Massachusetts), Brown University, Bowdoin College, and Harvard. As a result of the meeting the Rowing Association of American Colleges was formed.

At the Association's first regatta on July 21, 1871, Massachusetts Agricultural College defeated Brown and Harvard, an event which encouraged other small, less prestigious institutions to enter future competitions with the larger, established schools. The next year Amherst, Bowdoin, and Williams Colleges entered the regatta, as did Yale. Amherst's victory in 1872 again stimulated additional interest and six more colleges entered the 1873 meet.

After Yale's success in 1864, more clubs hired professional coaches to prepare a team for a single event or entire season until, nine years later, the Rowing Association of American Colleges passed a rule prohibiting professional coaches. By 1874 public interest in collegiate rowing had grown to the extent that as a promotional event, the Annual Association Regatta was moved to Saratoga Lake at the invitation of John Morrissey, one of the famous resort's developers. The regattas of 1874 and 1875 attracted thousands of spectators and nationwide newspaper coverage. The mid-1870s marked the height of college rowing, as baseball, football, and track and field became increasingly popular.

Baseball

Following the Civil War baseball spread rapidly across the country, among college men as well as sandlot nines and professional teams. By the mid-1870s, baseball was the most popular campus sport outside the Northeast. Amherst College played a series of games with Dartmouth College in the sixties and

---

July 1, 1859. Amherst-73, Williams-32. The Amherst College Ball Club was established in 1859, with James F. Claflin '59 as captain. A student recalled that Claflin "proposed . . . that a challenge be sent to Williams. After some preliminary negotiation a contest was arranged on July 1, on the neutral grounds of the Pittsfield Baseball Club, each team to provide its own ball. There were thirteen men on a side."[48]

The captains met to agree on the play and chose the Massachusetts Rules with the square playing field and wooden sticks for bases. It was a four-hour game, but apparently did not lag in player and spectator interest. Originally, sixty-five runs had been announced as a limit, but the final score was 73–32. There were no uniforms, gloves, masks, or chest protectors.

The news of the results reached Amherst late that night, and both the college and the town celebrated with bonfires and bell ringing. An "extra" edition of the newspaper was printed. The next afternoon the victorious team arrived in Amherst to be accorded a hero's welcome.

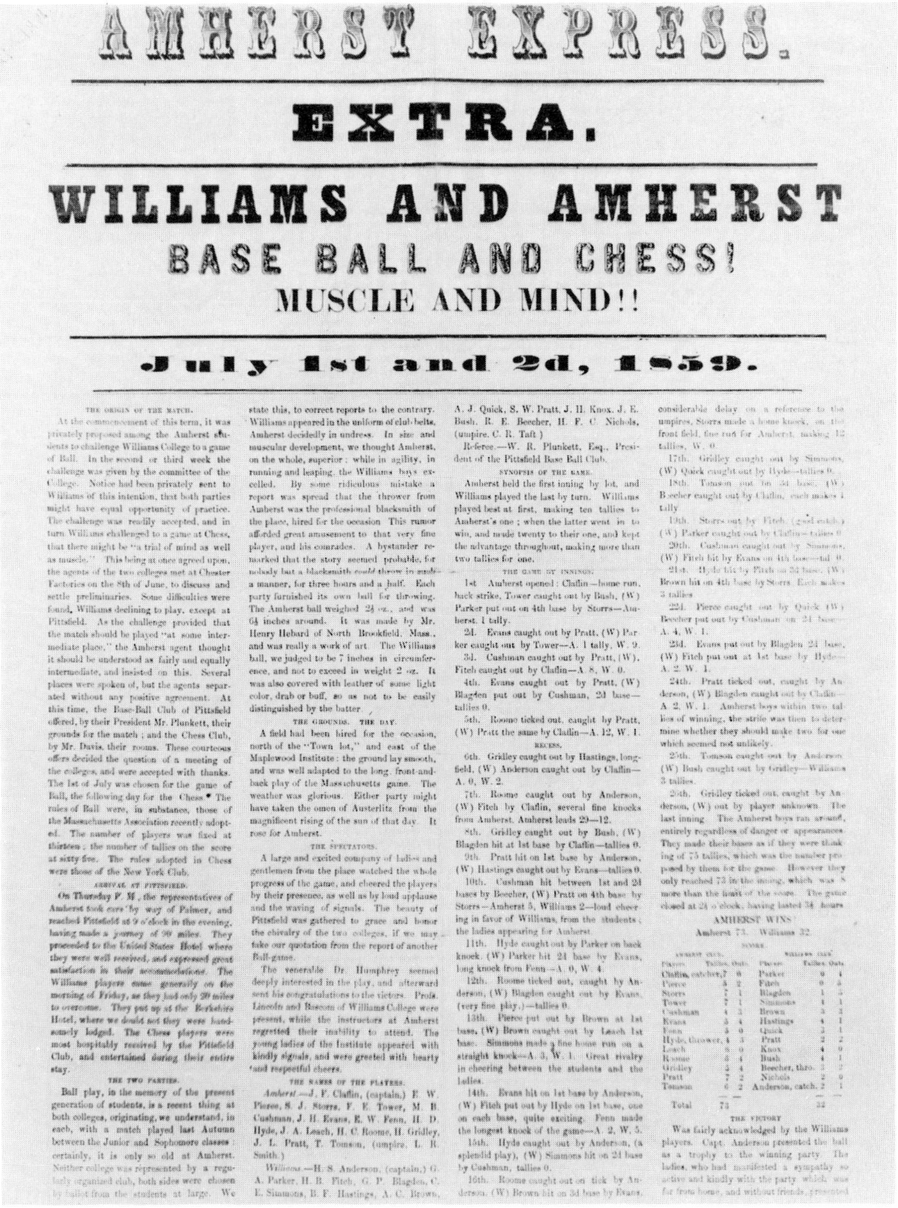

AMHERST EXPRESS.

EXTRA.

WILLIAMS AND AMHERST

BASE BALL AND CHESS!

MUSCLE AND MIND!!

July 1st and 2d, 1859.

Figure 4.8   "Extra" of newspaper issued after Amherst College won the 1859 baseball game. Courtesy of Amherst College Library.

by 1875 was playing teams as far away as Princeton. A decade later, however, baseball too achieved its greatest popularity and by the 1890s occupied second place to football at most colleges. Many colleges, including Amherst and Williams in their 1859 game, used Massachusetts Rules.

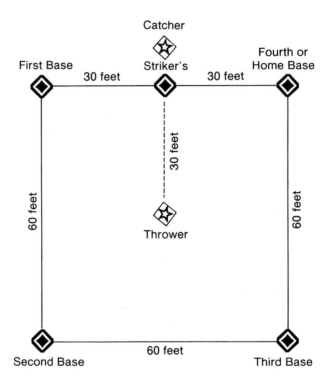

The Massachusetts Rules[49]

From *The Baseball Players Pocket Companion*
(Boston: Mayhew and Baker, 1860)

MATERIALS

The only essential materials used in playing the game beside a ball are a batstick and four wooden stakes for bases, the form and sizes of which are described in the annexed rules and regulations of the game. The ball is composed of woolen yarn and strips of India rubber wound tightly, forming a complete sphere, and covered with buck or calf skin.

THE GAME

The game is commenced by staking off a square of 60 feet for the bases, and measuring the distance of 35 feet from the thrower's to the striker's stand, as explained by diagram.

The four corners of the square are the bases. The striker's stand is the square of four feet at equal distances between the first and the fourth base. Outside of this square, and the line between the first and fourth base is the catcher's stand. In the center of the square the thrower is stationed, who delivers the ball to the striker, which, if not struck, should be caught by the catcher behind; but if struck by the batsman, he is obliged to run the bases, commencing at 1, so on to 2, 3, and 4; when arriving at 4 or the home base, he is entitled to one tally. After the first player strikes the ball and runs to the base, he is immediately succeeded by the next "in" player, who takes his turn in the order in which he is chosen. The "out" party, besides the thrower and catcher, should be stationed as follows: One player on or within a few feet from each base, who should give strict attention to the game, and be prepared to receive the ball at any time, in order to "put out" an opposite player, while passing from one base to another. One or two players should be stationed a few yards behind the catcher, to stop the ball in case the catcher should fail to do so. The other players should be stationed at different parts of the field, to pass the ball to the thrower when it has been knocked by the striker.

Football

Football on college and university campuses was both exciting and troublesome. It answered the need for a physically demanding activity which the young men found satisfying and enjoyable, but the prevalence of injuries to students, lack of administrative control of the game, and its demands on students' time created problems for administrators. In an effort to codify the rules, Princeton, Rutgers, Yale, and Columbia founded the Intercollegiate Association for Football in 1873. Harvard declined to join the group because of its style of play, in which the player could run with the ball. The following year Harvard played McGill University, using rugby rules. Interest in the rugby-type game continued, and a new Intercollegiate Football Association, formed in 1876, adopted the rugby rules. In 1879, Walter Camp, a player and coach

---

November 6, 1869. Rutgers-6, Princeton-4. For years there had been an intense rivalry between Rutgers and Princeton. Perhaps in response to the bitter 40-2 baseball defeat of 1866, or for other reasons, when W. J. Leggett '72 was elected the first college football captain, the Rutgers students challenged the men of the College of New Jersey, later Princeton University, to play a series of three football games, beginning November 6, 1869. Princeton accepted the challenge and the two captains agreed on the rules and conditions of play.

The soccer-like game was played using a round, inflated rubber ball which one player would attempt to advance toward the opponent's goal with short kicks while his teammates surrounded him to keep the opponents away. Players were not allowed to catch or carry the ball, although one could bat a ball in the air using the hands.

There were no uniforms, no padding, or other protective equipment. One account notes:

. . . a point was the sending of the ball between the goal posts at any height, there being no cross bar. Twenty-five men played on each side. They wore no uniforms. They laid aside their hats and coats and vests, reduced their clothing to serviceable limit, and joined battle.[50]

at Yale, began to place his stamp on the evolution of the game from rugby to the distinctly American form of football. A member of every rules convention from that year until his death in 1925, Camp is today considered the "father" of American football. Among his contributions to the development of the game were: 1) substitution of the scrimmage for the rugby scrum, 2) the adoption of the system of downs and yards to gain, 3) the adoption of eleven players on each team and their arrangement into positions, and 4) the allowance of tackling below the waist and the prohibition of the use of the arms in blocking.

Track and Field

Track and field athletics in colleges and universities began in 1869 when students formed the Columbia College Athletic Association and challenged other student groups. In meets that year events included the 100-yard, 150-yard, and 200-yard hurdle races, mile walk, standing long jump, high jump, and running long jump. Also in 1869, George Goldie, an outstanding Caledonian athlete, was appointed gymnasium director at Princeton University. By 1876 eleven institutions engaged in track and field athletics, and in addition in that year the Intercollegiate Association of Amateur Athletes of America (ICAAAA) was established—the oldest continuing collegiate athletic organization in the United States.

Perhaps the sudden increased interest in college track and field was partly attributable to the 1873 intercollegiate rowing regatta, when a single two-mile run was included with the rowing events. James Gordon Bennett, Jr., publisher of the *New York Herald* and a noted sport enthusiast, donated a cup to the winner of this race as well as to the rowers, and continued this sponsorship through the next several years. In 1874, five footraces were held: a one-mile run, 100 yards, three miles, seven-mile walking race, and 120-yard hurdles.[51] Several colleges, including Columbia, Cornell, Harvard, Princeton, Wesleyan, Williams, and Yale took part. Track and field gradually achieved a following and standing of its own, and the ICAAAA assumed the responsibility for hosting an annual championship meet and for regulating the sport on the college level. Caught in the controversy between the NAAAA and the newly formed AAU, the ICAAAA chose to affiliate with the AAU. By 1885 track and field took its place with football, baseball, and rowing as a main feature of the college athletic scene.

Intercollegiate athletics began as a student affair. In the early contests the students challenged the other team, the students determined the rules, and the students made arrangements for the conduct of the events. Interested sportsmen such as Bennett added incentives with cups, other prizes, and publicity. Faculty and administrative reaction to the growing popularity of intercollegiate contests in sport was mixed. Yale faculty assisted the students in the purchase of some rowing equipment, and some Harvard professors openly acclaimed Harvard's victories in certain sports. However, problems such as injuries in football caused great concern. Other faculty members persistently complained that the students in intercollegiate sport, as well as their enthusiastic fans, missed too many classes. Finally in 1882 Harvard appointed a three-man faculty committee to deal specifically with the complaint regarding the lengthy baseball schedule. Out of this grew a meeting of faculty representatives, the Intercollegiate Athletic Conference, in December, 1883, in New York City. In this first attempt by college faculty to exercise some control over intercollegiate athletics, eight resolutions were passed dealing with subjects such as the prohibition of college teams playing against professional teams; the prohibition of receiving coaching from professional athletes; limiting competition to four years for each student; requiring all games to be played on the home field of one of the competing institutions; and having a standing faculty committee supervise all contests.[52] Only three institutions—Harvard, Princeton, Cornell—ratified the resolutions and thus the problem was not solved. However, the beginnings of change in the control of intercollegiate athletics had begun, and by the turn of the century the administration and faculties of colleges and universities asserted more control over student athletics.

Physical Education and Sport in Women's Colleges

Both before and after the Civil War education for women remained either unknown or controversial, except where Mary Lyon, Catharine Beecher, and a few other dedicated women had made their mark. Opponents were sure that "feminine problems" would prevent the women from attending classes regularly and that consequently they should not be admitted to men's colleges because they would hinder the class work. Two men, Matthew Vassar and Henry Fowle Durant, disagreed with this position and set out to prove that women could engage in "higher" education equal to that of men. Both included exercise and sport in their plans.

The *Prospectus for Vassar Female College* made Matthew Vassar's thinking clear. In the college's "General Scheme of Education," Physical Education came first, "as *fundamental* to all the rest," for "Good health is essential to the successful prosecution of study, and to the vigorous development of either the mental or moral powers." In 1861 the College fully committed itself to a physical education program by planning and building the Calisthenium and planning to appoint faculty members to instruct sport and physical training. Feeling keenly the need of women to become more physically active, and eager to demonstrate that they could survive the rigors of academic life, Vassar provided a special School of Physical Training. The school, housed in the Calisthenium, contained a gymnasium 81 × 30 feet, a bowling alley 82 × 30 feet,

Figure 4.9   Mount Holyoke Seminary students in early 1860s at exercise. Courtesy of Mount Holyoke College Library, South Hadley, Massachusetts.

a music-hall 30 × 52 feet, and riding facilities with accommodations for about twenty-five horses. Vassar provided facilities for both exercise and sport for his college:

> Recreations, particularly in the open air, will not only be encouraged, but regulated and taught, and, to a certain extent, required of all the students; and the proper facilities will be furnished to render them attractive and useful. For this purpose, in-doors, the spacious and cheerful corridors of the college edifice, and, without, the beautiful college park, will afford unusual advantages. The play-grounds are ample and secluded; and the apparatus required for the Swedish Calisthenics (or Boston Light Gymnastics), and for such simple feminine sports as archery, croquet (or ladies' cricket), graces, shuttlecock, &c., will be supplied by the College.
>
> Every student will be required to provide herself with a light and easy-fitting dress, to be worn during these athletic exercises. It will be left optional with her, whether to wear it or not at other times.[53]

As plans for the college developed, Matthew Vassar heeded the advice of Sara Josepha Hale, editor of the popular *Godey's Lady's Book* and an influential proponent of women's education, and deleted the word *female* from the title. The college opened in 1865. The first annual catalogue listed a woman, Dr. Alida C. Avery, as Professor of Physiology and Hygiene and as resident physician. Also listed was Miss Delia F. Woods as Instructor in the Department of Physical Training.

The program consisted of exercises, some of which were based on Dio Lewis' work. The faculty members were evidently sensitive to the students' wishes, for in 1877 Lilian Tappan, an instructor, instituted a plan for sport in physical education. In the spring of the year she permitted the students to choose an outdoor sport in place of indoor gymnastics. This is the first indication that students were losing interest in regular gymnastic instruction and that other means might have to be found to provide instruction in regular physical activity.

VASSAR STUDENT GAME REGISTRATION[*54]
1876-77

Gymnastics
(November 13-April 13)

Number registered in gymnastics classes   270

Games
(April 23-June 2 or 27)

Ball	25
Boating	94
Croquet	108
Gardening	24
Walking	116
	367*

*Many students selected more than one game.

Henry Fowle Durant, founder of Wellesley College in 1874, followed Vassar's lead and provided for both exercise and sport. The large building on campus, College Hall, housed a gymnasium. Students were required to take exercises and to wear looser and shorter dresses than usual—about twelve inches off the floor—for exercise classes. Located on the edge of Lake Waban, Wellesley College took advantage of its setting and provided boats in which several girls could row at one time. In the winter the lake froze over, so that the students could enjoy ice skating. When Durant could not find equipment for the new game of tennis, he sent to England for rackets and nets.

About the same time, in the Middle West, when women were first admitted to the University of Wisconsin in 1873, the University fitted up a gymnasium

Figure 4.10   1876 Rowing at Wellesley College, Wellesley, Massachusetts. Courtesy of Wellesley College Archives.

in Ladies Hall. Similarly, in Boston the women of the "Society for the Collegiate Instruction of Women," later called Radcliffe College, requested Sargent at Harvard to provide gymnastic work for them. He did so and opened the Sanatory Gymnasium for them in 1881.

The place of dance in schools for women evoked sharp controversy at the beginning of the period. Society had quite diverse ideas about its propriety, although in fashionable society balls were as acceptable as was country-dancing in frontier towns. Matthew Vassar, in a 1867 report, mentions "recent writings pro and con" on the question of dancing, and he specifically mentions an essay by a minister on the "Incompatibility of Amusements with Christian Life." Vassar himself, however, urged that dance be taught in his college, "in view of its being a healthful and graceful exercise."[55] What educational institutions tended to emphasize most in dancing was its value as healthful exercise or as a means of imparting poise and a graceful carriage. Opposition to dancing on religious grounds prevented its widespread practice in the early public schools, so that dancing was more likely to be found in the seminaries. In some cases, the objections were overcome by the argument that it was "a healthful recreation and exercise, and that it prevented children from carrying on more harmful activities."[56]

During this period physical education for both men and women ordinarily consisted of exercise classes to maintain or improve the students' health. Sport programs for men and women differed greatly. Intercollegiate athletics for men began as a series of challenges or contests completely under the jurisdiction of students. Women's sport programs consisted of informal recreational sport or sport activities included as part of a physical education class. The beginnings of two very different programs, one for men and one for women, occurred in the middle of the nineteenth century.

Commentary

This chapter marks the transformation of childhood games to adult sport. This crucial development was made possible by increasing urbanization; changing notions about work time and leisure time; technological improvements in transportation, communication, and daily living; and, most specifically, shifting attitudes toward play and leisure pursuits. The chapter also highlights the acceptance of exercise programs in education and the beginnings of intercollegiate sport for men.

From 1840 to 1885 people's lives in this country varied tremendously, depending on whether they were very wealthy businessmen or slaves; marginal farmers or factory workers; well-off housewives or domestic servants. Slowly the idea of stipulating a limited number of working hours in some occupations led to time workers could call their own, although "leisure" was not yet a common concept. Gains were meager, but the "good life"—or dreams of the good life—reached an increasing number of people.

Although this period was marked by contrasts in almost every phase of life, it was also characterized by a growing feeling of identification, of "being an American." The Civil War, at a heavy price in lives and long-lasting bitterness, ended legal slavery. After the war the country ratified the Fourteenth Amendment, guaranteeing equal protection to citizens regardless of race. This amendment became the basis for civil rights legislation of the 1960s, which in turn led to greater access to sport for women, minorities, and people with handicapping conditions.

Ethnic groups directly influenced sport and the development of physical education in this period. Spanish-Americans brought the horsemanship skills of the rodeos with them from Mexico. Scottish immigrants stimulated interest in track and field athletics through the Caledonian Games. Turners promoted German gymnastics not only to improve health, but also to foster a continued interest in German culture. These and other groups contributed to the diversity of sport and exercise programs in the United States.

In spite of people's diversity, the values influencing their daily lives continued to be embedded in traditional Protestant beliefs: work was righteous; saving was essential; Sunday meant restricted activities. The 1848 Seneca Falls meeting on women's rights made little difference in the general perception of women as weaker and less intelligent than men. Social reformers turned their attention to a variety of interests affecting sport and physical education. They objected to the gambling and "undesirable elements" associated with some sports and persuaded a number of states to outlaw horse racing and discourage boxing. In sharp contrast, many social reformers campaigned for healthful exercise for men and women and higher education for women. Amherst, Harvard, and a few other institutions introduced exercise programs and departments of physical education to improve and maintain the students' health. Women's colleges such as Vassar and Wellesley, intent on proving that young women were capable of attending college and studying the same subjects as men, used both exercise and sport in their programs to assure the health of the students.

The fifth theme pursued in this work, the intermixing of technology and urbanization, is of major significance in this period. The middle decades of the nineteenth century were characterized by technological improvements in transportation, communication, manufacturing and urbanization which, together with an immense increase in population, changed towns into cities and created a climate in which games were transformed into sport.

Without the effects of urbanization, the creation of modern baseball would not have been possible and it certainly would not have developed into the first of the American "big three" in professional sports. Manufacturing made sport goods more available. Roller skates and the bicycle were invented during this period, and numerous other inventions lightened daily tasks and thus permitted more time to pursue individual interests. Some of these interests were playing baseball or bicycling or participating in other sports and some were attending sporting events such as baseball games and horse races.

The growth and consequent complexities in sport and physical education led to changes in their conceptualization and justification. Newly organized governing bodies controlled sport and gradually it became delineated into professional, amateur, recreational, and educational. In 1840 only horse racing, cockfighting, pedestrianism, and rowing could be properly termed sport. Then, in midcentury, Cartwright and his friends transformed the child's game of rounders to a sport called baseball. The new sport possessed primary and secondary characteristics of sport as VanderZwaag and Sheehan have defined them. It was playlike, associated with games, and physical in nature. When Cartwright prescribed the distances between bases and positioned the players, he altered the informal, casual atmosphere of rounders, making the game more dependent on facilities and equipment. In a very short period of time it became popular throughout the country. The United States now had its own game, designed by an American for Americans.

Other activities—some contests between persons such as tennis and croquet and some pastimes such as roller skating and bicycling—also moved toward the category of sport. Tennis, with its defined court and net separating players, as well as its dependence on facilities and equipment, met many of the criteria of sport.

The new games reflected an additional trait of sport: "As soon as sport becomes organized, part of the play dimension disappears."[57] Almost as soon as any game had a number of followers, an association was formed, filling America's craving for fellowship. Amateur sport associations standardized rules of play, promoted the sport, and sponsored national championships.

Toward the end of the nineteenth century games, exercise, sport, and dance functioned as enjoyable pastimes and diversions while providing a means of improving health. In men's colleges and in groups such as the Turners and the YMCA, sport contributed to a growing sense of community. It also furnished a livelihood for the growing number of professional sportsmen. Like other "joiners" of the period, professional baseball players organized a National Association of Base Ball Players. By 1879 each club could "reserve" five members of the team for the following year, establishing the relationship of the professional player to the team owner and leading to major controversies over players' rights a century later.

Within less than half a century, sport moved from an informal, social pastime still somewhat questioned by the Puritan tradition, to an organized component of American life. Americans found joy and satisfaction in many sports and accepted physical education as a means of improving the health and general welfare of the nation's youth.

Suggestions for Further Reading

1. Betts, John Rickards. "The Technological Revolution and the Rise of Sport, 1850–1900." *Mississippi Valley Historical Review* 40, no. 2 (September 1953):231–256.
2. Higginson, Thomas Wentworth. "Gymnastics." *Atlantic Monthly* 7 (March 1861):283–302.
3. Lewis, Guy M. "1879: The Beginning of an Era in American Sport." *72nd Proceedings,* National College Physical Education Association for Men (January 8–11, 1969):136–145.
4. Redmond, Gerald. *The Caledonian Games in Nineteenth-Century America.* Rutherford, New Jersey: Fairleigh Dickinson University Press, 1971.
5. Sargent, Dudley A. *An Autobiography,* ed. Ledyard W. Sargent. Philadelphia: Lea & Febiger, 1927.
6. Willis, Joseph D., and Wettan, Richard G. "Social Stratification in New York City Athletic Clubs, 1865–1915." *Journal of Sport History* 3, no. 1 (Spring 1976):45–63.

Notes

1. S. S. Wilson, "Bicycle Technology," *Scientific American* 228, no. 3(March 1973):81–91.
2. Frank C. Richter, *Richter's History and Records of Base Ball* (Philadelphia: Francis C. Richter, 1914), 12.
3. *DeWitt's Base-Ball Guide for 1875,* ed. Henry Chadwick (New York: Robert M. DeWitt, Publisher, 1875), 12.

4. Cited in Albert G. Spalding, *Base Ball, America's National Game* (New York: American Sports Publishing Company, 1911), 60.
5. Harold Seymour, *Baseball: The Early Years* (New York: Oxford University Press, 1959), 26.
6. Dale A. Somers, *The Rise of Sports in New Orleans, 1850–1900* (Baton Rouge: Louisiana State University Press, 1972), 50.
7. Albert G. Spalding, *Base Ball, America's National Game* (New York: American Sports Publishing Company, 1911), 96.
8. Ibid., 139.
9. *DeWitt's Base-Ball Guide for 1869*, ed. Henry Chadwick (New York: Robert M. DeWitt, Publisher, 1869), 23.
10. Albert G. Spalding, *Base Ball, America's National Game* (New York: American Sports Publishing Company, 1911), 194.
11. Frank C. Richter, *Richter's History and Records of Baseball* (Philadelphia: Francis C. Richter, 1914), 57.
12. Melvin L. Adelman, *A Sporting Time: New York City and the Rise of Modern Athletics, 1820–70* (Urbana: University of Illinois Press, 1986), 59.
13. Ibid., 69.
14. Mary Lou LeCompte, "*Charreada:* The First American Rodeo" (Paper presented at the Annual Conference of the Western History Association, October 11, 1985), 3.
15. Ibid., 5.
16. Mary L. LeCompte, "The First Rodeo in Texas," *Proceedings, 1980,* North American Society for Sport History, Banff, Alberta (May 24–28, 1980):2–3.
17. James D. McCabe, *The Illustrated History of the Centennial Exhibition* (Philadelphia: National Publishing Company, 1876), 754–55.
18. Dale A. Somers, *The Rise of Sports in New Orleans, 1850–1900* (Baton Rouge: Louisiana State University Press, 1972), 152.
19. Samuel Eliot Morison, *The Oxford History of the American People* (New York: Oxford University Press, 1965), 787.
20. *Spirit of the Times,* 2 (October 1858):69.
21. Gerald Redmond, *The Caledonian Games in Nineteenth-Century America* (Rutherford, New Jersey: Fairleigh Dickinson University Press, 1971), 42–72.
22. Joseph D. Willis and Richard G. Wettan, "Social Stratification in New York City Athletic Clubs, 1865–1915," *Journal of Sport History* 3, no. 1(Spring 1976):45–63.
23. William N. Wallace, *The Macmillan Book of Boating* (New York: Crown Publishers, Inc., 1973), 25.
24. Ibid., 27.
25. Dale A. Somers, *The Rise of Sports in New Orleans, 1850–1900* (Baton Rouge: Louisiana State University Press, 1972), 44.
26. Parke Cummings, *American Tennis: The Story of a Game and Its People* (Boston: Little, Brown and Company, 1957), 34.
27. Dale A. Somers, *The Rise of Sports in New Orleans, 1850–1900* (Baton Rouge: Louisiana State University Press, 1972), 211.
28. Parke Cummings, *American Tennis: The Story of a Game and Its People* (Boston: Little, Brown and Company, 1957), 35.
29. *Harper's Weekly* 23 (September 13, 1879):73.
30. "Remarkable Skating Feats," *Detroit Free Press,* 26 January 1868, 9.
31. Gretchen Adel Schneider, "Pigeon Wings and Polkas: The Dance of the California Miners," *Dance Perspectives* 39 (Winter 1969):23.
32. Thomas Wentworth Higginson, "Gymnastics," *Atlantic Monthly* 7 (March 1861):283–302.

33. Mary F. Eastman, *The Biography of Dio Lewis* (New York: Fowler & Wells, 1891), 70.
34. Dio Lewis, *The New Gymnastics for Men, Women and Children* (Boston: Ticknor and Fields, 1864), 9.
35. Henry Metzner, *History of the American Turners* (Rochester, N.Y.: National Council of the American Turners, 1974), 25.
36. M. L. Walters, "The Physical Education Society of the Y.M.C.A.'s of North America," *Journal of Health and Physical Education* 17 (May 1947):357.
37. Luther Gulick, "What the American Young Men's Christian Associations are Doing for the Physical Welfare of Young Men," *Annual Autumn Games* (Young Men's Christian Association of the City of New York, October 13, 1888), 20. A. G. Spalding Company Archives, Chicopee, Massachusetts.
38. Elizabeth Wilson, *Fifty Years of Association Work Among Young Women 1866–1916* (New York: National Board of the Young Women's Christian Associations, 1916), 43, 44, 99–101.
39. From Second Biennial Report—State Superintendent of Public Instruction 1866–67, Appendix E, Revised School Law, March 24, 1866, Section 55, cited in Dudley S. DeGroot, "A History of Physical Education in California (1848–1939)" (Ph.D. diss., Stanford University, 1940), 23.
40. Nathan Allen, *Physical Culture in Amherst College* (Lowell, Mass.: Stone and Huse, 1869), 16.
41. Fred E. Leonard and George B. Affleck, *A Guide to the History of Physical Education* (Philadelphia: Lea & Febiger, 1947), 269.
42. Isabel C. Barrows, ed., *Physical Training, A Full Report of the Papers and Discussion of the Conference Held in Boston in November, 1889* (Boston: George H. Ellis, 1890), 68.
43. Dudley Allen Sargent, *An Autobiography,* ed. Ledyard W. Sargent (Philadelphia: Lea & Febiger, 1927), 174.
44. Sophia J. Blake, *A Visit to Some American Schools and Colleges* (London: Macmillan and Co., 1867), 33, 138.
45. Samuel Crowther and Arthur Ruhl, *Rowing and Track Athletics* (New York: The Macmillan Co., 1905), 17.
46. Ibid., 18.
47. "Regattas on Lake Winnipisiogee," [sic] *New York Tribune,* 10 August 1852, 6.
48. Claude M. Fuess, *Amherst* (Boston: Little, Brown, 1935), 197.
49. "One Hundred Years of Baseball," *Amherst Alumni News,* October, 1958, 4.
50. William H. S. Demarest, *A History of Rutgers College* (New Brunswick: Rutgers College, 1924), 429.
51. *New York Herald,* 15 July 1874, 6.
52. Edward M. Hartwell, *Physical Training in American Colleges and Universities,* Bureau of Education Circular of Information No. 5, 1885 (Washington, D.C.: Government Printing Office, 1886), 125–28.
53. *Prospectus of the Vassar Female College* (New York: Alford, 1865).
54. Lilian Tappan, Report to the President, 1877. Vassar College Archives, Poughkeepsie, New York.
55. Matthew Vassar, "Communications," June 25, 1867, 44. Vassar College Archives, Poughkeepsie, New York.
56. Richard Kraus, *History of the Dance in Art and Education* (Englewood Cliffs, N.J.: Prentice-Hall, Inc., 1969), 125.
57. Harold J. VanderZwaag and Thomas J. Sheehan, *Introduction to Sport Studies* (Dubuque, IA: Wm. C. Brown Publishers, 1978), 19.

Time Line

5 The Organizing of Sport and Physical Education, 1885–1917

Overview

When twenty-year-old Francis Ouimet received surprised congratulations on the golf course of the Country Club in Brookline, Massachusetts, on September 20, 1913, he represented a paradox in sport. This former caddy, the son of a Brookline gardener, had just accomplished what was considered impossible; for the first time an amateur golfer from a poor family had won the United States Open Championship. He had defeated not only the best American players but also, in a stirring play-off round, had bested two English professionals for the championship.

This national golf tournament, open to both amateur and professional players, indicates a few of the many changes in sport from 1885 to 1917. A national golf association was formed and it sponsored both open and amateur championships. Today's baseball pattern of two leagues and the World Series began in 1903. By 1910 the National Collegiate Athletic Association controlled intercollegiate sport for men. The American Association for the Advancement of Physical Education held its first meeting in 1885. The increasing organization of all forms of sport and physical education was a major development of this period. The complex organization of sport and physical education reflected the complicated and paradoxical life in the United States at the turn of the century.

As a result of a massive tide of immigration, industrial expansion, and increasing technological development, United States society changed dramatically. Almost twenty million people arrived in the United States hoping for a life of plenty. Instead, they found a life filled with paradoxes. The first skyscrapers were built in the cities of the East and Midwest while new settlers on the plains were living in sod houses. Although the city poor were beginning to benefit from the social reforms advocated by religious leaders and philanthropists, many native Americans were facing extermination or eviction from their lands in the West. A few tycoons amassed enormous private wealth and corporate power in industry, mining, and railroads, while millions of workers, flocking to the crowded cities from farms and foreign lands, struggled to find jobs. Although some of the new arrivals moved west away from the large cities, most remained in overcrowded tenements, creating new social problems for the community. The labor union movement also focused attention on the plight of the working class. The Knights of Labor and the American Federation of Labor introduced the strike as an effective weapon. By 1900 labor had won its basic right to organize, to strike, and to bargain collectively.

This immense growth of industry and business was fueled by a continuing flow of inventions—electric appliances, motion pictures, the airplane, and the automobile. The new technology led to an expanded economy which in turn created occupations undreamed of fifty years earlier.

In 1900, the rapidly expanding middle and working classes in the United States reflected the changing social organization of the country. The shopkeeper, the teacher, the factory worker, the Gibson Girl secretary, the union organizer, the woman sewing in a sweat shop, the farmer, the western rancher, and the owner of a small hotel were dissimilar in many ways, but most were alike in wanting a better life and better education for their children than they themselves had experienced. In their own lives, they looked for some success and their share of the "American dream."

Sport for the very wealthy, for the middle classes, and for the workers differed greatly, however. While some differences could be clearly explained because of available space, facilities, time, equipment, and cost, the greatest difference was in the perceived function of sport in their lives. The increasing numbers of the very rich and of the upper middle class, moving in their own circles, engaged in expensive and time-consuming sports such as yachting, horse racing, polo, riding to hounds, and the "new" sports of tennis and golf. Some of these people, however, also used their money to support playgrounds and settlement houses for the city poor.

For the wealthy youth and some men and women, sport was a natural pastime. With families in summer communities in the mountains or on the shore, with riding masters, and private schools or private teachers, children learned to sail, ride, and play tennis and golf. Wealthy young men at college might enjoy intercollegiate sports, while the women at college might fiercely contest interclass championships in basketball or field hockey. Whereas the social scientist Thorstein Veblen treated sport in the "Gilded Age" as a vehicle for conspicuous consumption, the rich themselves seemed to consider their time on the links, courts, and at the track as an unquestioned part of life.

During this period sport gradually diffused from the wealthy and upper class outward to the upper-middle, the middle, and also the working class. While at one time croquet, roller skating, and bicycling had been only for the socially elite, demands for sport equipment increased production, which in turn lowered the prices and eventually put them in reach of middle-class families. The advent of public parks and urban recreation facilities increased the working persons' opportunities for sport. In 1885 facilities for the poor were generally limited to those owned by philanthropic associations, workingmen's clubs, and churches. Three decades later laborers and middle-class people were playing baseball, basketball, football, volleyball, as well as tennis and golf on publicly owned and operated courts, fields, and courses. In the cities and many towns, life revolved around the workday. The workers' new leisure permitted spending time with friends, at ethnic clubs or lodges, and at baseball games. Many men attended boxing matches even though they were not usually well advertised public events.

During these years many religious groups sharply changed their focus. The traditional mission of the church—spiritual growth and preparation for the "hereafter"—was modified to a "social gospel" which included the social and physical welfare of the people. Protestant churches initiated programs for the working class, ranging from credit unions and English classes for immigrants to child day-care centers and sport leagues for youth. Roman Catholic churches also instituted "Americanization" programs in their parishes, promoting the English language and building a network of parochial schools. Although a variety of religious beliefs existed in the United States, most of the political and cultural leaders came from the Protestant tradition, which continued to influence many aspects of life.

Even with the growing acceptance of public education in this country, only about five percent of American youth attended high school and still fewer enrolled in colleges and universities. While the curriculum continued to center on traditional subjects, some secondary and postsecondary institutions taught physical education. Intercollegiate sport for men became a rallying point on the nation's campuses. At the secondary level, interscholastic sport for boys, and to a lesser extent for girls, became a focal point for many communities throughout the nation.

Set against a changing life which was more organized than it had been in the past, sport and physical education reflected the need for associations to control and regulate new games like basketball and volleyball, as well as country clubs, school physical education, intramural programs, national tournaments, and international competition. This chapter examines the growing stability of professional sport, the increasing organization and control of amateur sport by wealthy upper-class men, the establishment of governing bodies in collegiate sport, and the development of sport in physical education.

Professional Sport

The major professional sports of this period, baseball, boxing, and thoroughbred horse racing, faced problems that threatened their survival. Baseball had internal problems, with duplicity and fraud between owners as well as between owners and players; boxing and horse racing had external problems, with many states banning the sports. Baseball and boxing had to overcome social stigma, since many players came from the lower and working classes and were considered rowdy "ne'er-do-wells." Horse racing, in spite of the social standing of many owners, was under constant attack because of gambling.

On the other hand, each sport was able to withstand these assaults because of an expanding base of popular support from the working and middle classes. With leisure time and with money to spend, the steadily growing urban population found professional sport satisfying entertainment.

Baseball

During the mid-1880s, disputes between players and owners remained the most serious threat to professional baseball. Continuing dissatisfaction with contract conditions led to a new organization, this one only for players—the Brotherhood of Ball Players. It was recognized by the National League in the fall of 1887 as an organization, "the Brotherhood agreeing to recognize the Reserve Rule upon condition that the salary of a player should not be reduced while under reservation."[1] However, the next year the League—the owners of the clubs—decided to put all baseball players into an elaborate classification scheme, with tight maximum salaries in each category; this effectively nullified their agreement with the Brotherhood. At that time the top salary was twenty-five hundred dollars. The preliminary steps had been taken for a real confrontation between owners and players. It came in the form of a Brotherhood revolt in the fall of 1889, in which most of the players of the Brotherhood, with the assistance of businessmen backers, who sympathized with the players and also desired to be part of organized major league baseball, formed the Player's National League of Base Ball Clubs. Manifestos were issued by both sides. The Brotherhood said:

> In taking this step we feel that we owe it to the public and to ourselves to explain . . . There was a time when the League stood for integrity and fair dealing. Today it stands for dollars and cents. . . . Players have been bought, sold and exchanged as though they were sheep instead of American citizens. "Reservation" became for them another name for property right in the player.[2]

Two weeks later the National League replied:

> The National League of Base Ball Clubs has no apology to make for its existence, or for its untarnished record of fourteen years. . . . It is to this organization that the player of today owes the dignity of his profession and the munificent salary he is guaranteed while playing in its ranks. . . . And the necessity for such power of preserving the circuit of a League, by approximately equalizing its playing strength, is recognized by the new League, which the seceding players have temporarily organized; for they give this "extraordinary power" of transferring players, with or without consent, and with or without club disbandment, to a central tribunal of sixteen, whose fiat is final. . . . use of such terms as "bondage," "slavery," "sold like sheep," etc., becomes meaningless and absurd.[3]

During the 1890 season the baseball organizations lost large sums of money, as they competed for the same fans in several cities. In addition, press and fans alike became tired of the bickering and name-calling, and this undoubtedly discouraged attendance. At the end of that season, with owners on both sides anxious for some kind of settlement, the Player's League dissolved, with some of its clubs merging into the National League. The following year brought the demise of the once stable American Association, and the National League again monopolized major league baseball.

The League, however, had trouble even with its monopoly. Factionalism, disloyalty, distrust, and most of all, greedy individualism on the part of the owners, together with a tyrannical attitude toward the players, arrogance toward the fans and press, and lack of firm leadership and organization, placed the National League in serious difficulty by 1900. In that year Byron Bancroft Johnson, a former newspaperman who had been the successful president of the Western League, organized the American League of Professional Baseball Clubs. After three seasons of successful operation by the new American League, the National League owners, faced with rising competitive player costs and reduced attendance, approached the American League to arrange a plan of accommodation. Thus was born a new and lasting National Agreement, recognizing two major leagues, each with eight teams plus numerous minor leagues. The reserve clause became embedded in the system. The game was controlled by a three-man National Commission consisting of the president of each major league and a third person selected by them. The 1903 season launched the new system and was climaxed by the playing of the first World Series, in which Boston beat Pittsburgh, five games to three.

By this time the game of baseball was indeed an American institution. Besides its innate excitement and widespread availability, it was promoted by skillful salesmen, one of the most prominent being Albert Goodwill Spalding. Baseball had been his life since, as a boy of 17 in Rockford, Illinois, he had discovered his powerful pitching arm. His pitching helped Boston win for several seasons; he was pitcher/manager and eventually owner of the Chicago White Stockings (later renamed the Cubs); and he helped start the National League. Although he began to devote most of his time to the flourishing sporting goods firm which carried his name, his life belonged to baseball. He regarded the game as a symbol of American democracy and sponsored foreign tours by professional "stars" to promote both baseball and the political system. In the jingoistic era of the Spanish-American War, he wanted baseball to be regarded as exclusively American. He dismissed its evolution from bat and ball games, and pressured for the appointment of a commission to study the "birth" of the game. On weak evidence, the commission in due course concluded that General Abner Doubleday, a Civil War veteran, had "invented" the game as a young man living in Cooperstown, New York. This conclusion was largely accepted at that time.

Baseball's very popularity engendered corruption. Politicians found financial and political rewards from buying into or otherwise affiliating with the local ball club. Boss Tweed and the Tammany Hall machine in New York City were notable examples of politicians in many American cities who used popular local baseball teams to promote themselves, grant favors, and mete out rewards through patronage. On the other side of the coin, owners "in" with politicians could secure special streetcar service to bring spectators to the park and favored treatment with respect to city police protection and taxes.[4]

"Organized baseball," the term used to identify the established professional major and minor leagues, flourished in the twentieth century. The new National Agreement provided stability to the leagues and helped curtail player rowdyism, especially in the American League where Ban Johnson countenanced no disrespect of umpires. Fans believed in the honesty of the players and umpires; and unprecedented interest was generated by good play, pennant races, and the annual World Series. Fans from all walks of life followed their favorites. An improved ball, somewhat livelier, enhanced the play. Stars of the period were Eddie Collins, Joe Jackson, and Ty Cobb. All these stars, and in fact, all the players in the major leagues, were white.

Attempts to include black players and to form black professional leagues were generally unsuccessful, due in part to growing racist and segregationist attitudes in the United States at that time. The first and only black players to openly play for a major league team in the nineteenth century were Moses Fleetwood Walker and his brother Welday Walker, who played briefly for the Toledo Club of the American Association in 1884. Both had played in the previous decade for Oberlin College, which earlier had been a center of the abolitionist movement.

George Stovey, a thirty-five-game winning black pitcher for Newark, was almost signed to a contract by the New York Giants in the 1880s, but objections of other major league managers forced an end to the deal.[5] Four black players appeared on the rosters of important minor league clubs in 1886. Black players continued to play on their own independent teams on an amateur and semi-professional level. In 1885, the New York Cuban Giants were formed by a group of waiters and busboys at the Argyle Hotel in Babylon, New York. A league was planned in 1887, the League of Colored Base Ball Clubs, but was never established. Another, which consisted of six white teams and two black teams, was organized two years later but collapsed within a few weeks after the start of the season.[6] Although some black players could be found on white minor league teams through the 1890s, by the turn of the century the color line was set. John McGraw, manager of the New York Giants, attempted to call a black man, Charlie Grant, an Indian, but Charles Comiskey, owner of the Chicago White Sox, objected and the pressure was so strong that even the strong-willed McGraw backed down. No black players appeared in the major leagues for almost a half century.

Boxing

Boxing, although not as widely popular as baseball, provided entertainment for many. "Gentleman Jim" Corbett, a socially refined heavyweight from San Francisco's Olympic Club, defeated John L. Sullivan in New Orleans on September 7, 1892. Corbett represented careful training and scientific boxing, in contrast to Sullivan's brute strength and aggressiveness, which was typical of the day. While outlawed in most states throughout the 1890s, the sport attracted enough supporters to continue its clandestine staging of fights in rural barns, fields, or on river barges. However, the few fighters at the top were able to arrange important bouts in more public arenas. The championship bout between Sullivan and Corbett, for instance, was held at New Orlean's Olympic Club. Carson City, Nevada, was the scene of Corbett's defeat at the hands of Bob Fitzsimmons in 1897. The latter lost the title two years later to James J. Jeffries, a burly, hardhitting former sparring partner of Corbett, in a match at the fashionable New Coney Island Sporting Club.

Despite arguments that boxing was an art and not a public display of violence, steady opposition to the sport existed in the nineties and continued until 1914. In a number of states the clergy led the antiboxing crusade and many states passed legislation prohibiting boxing. Frequent knockouts and brutality, accompanied by gambling, corroborated public criticism and the reformers' zeal to outlaw boxing.

In 1910, when Jack Johnson, black, skillful, and outspoken, defended his two-year-old world heavyweight title by defeating Jeffries, a new crisis arose. Race relations during this period were strained. The rise of extremist groups like the Ku Klux Klan was accompanied by stringent segregationist laws in the South. In other parts of the country more covert forms of racial bigotry such as discrimination in housing and employment were common.

At a time of blatant racism, Johnson flaunted his boxing superiority by demolishing a string of "white hopes," and showed his disdain for white convention by publicly escorting and marrying white women. Finally yielding to pressure from many quarters opposed to a black man as world heavyweight champion, Jeffries came out of retirement for the fight, and the white public pinned their hopes for a white champion on him. Promoted by Tex Rickard, the fight received extensive publicity. When Jeffries lost, race riots broke out in Pittsburgh, Baltimore, Dayton, and other cities across the country.

Other black boxers also established outstanding records during this period, but were generally denied the opportunity to fight in heavyweight championship matches against whites. Peter "The Black Prince" Jackson, a native of the Virgin Islands, won the black heavyweight championship by defeating American George Godfrey in 1888. Three years later, Jackson fought sixty-one rounds in five hours for a draw with soon-to-be world heavyweight champion Corbett. And yet in 1892, after challenging all comers, world heavyweight champion Sullivan declined Jackson's acceptance of the challenge with the statement, "I will not fight a Negro. I never have and I never will."[7]

Figure 5.1   Jack Johnson, world heavyweight boxing champion, 1908–1915. Wide World.

Jack Johnson (1878–1946) may have been the greatest heavyweight boxer of the century. To be born poor and black in the South, to have to struggle even to fight publicly, made his achievements more spectacular. Jack Johnson liked to be spectacular, to achieve the remarkable. At 13 he was a Galveston dockworker and later worked for Walter Lewis, an amateur boxer. For the first time Johnson thought of the ring professionally. One day he took a train which happened to go to Springfield, Illinois, where he saw some fights, entered some, and became a protegé of Johnnie Connors. He trained and fought in Chicago, then New York. On March 31, 1902, he won the world light-heavyweight championship from George Gardner in San Francisco. Finally in 1908 he knocked out Tommy Burns for the world heavyweight title. Unable to arrange such a championship fight in this country, he scheduled the bout and fought in Sydney, Australia. Perhaps his most famous victory was the fight with James J. Jeffries, who was enticed out of retirement to fight and, hopefully, defeat Johnson "for the white race." After a conviction on Mann Act charges Johnson fled from the United States and lived in Europe for several years. In 1915 he lost his championship to Jess Willard in Havana, Cuba, in 26 rounds. In 1920 Johnson returned to the United States, served the prison sentence which he had evaded and fought occasionally in exhibition fights until his late 60's. He died on June 10, 1946, as the result of an automobile accident.

Sam Langford fought successfully in several weight classifications from 1902 to 1923 but was denied the opportunity to fight for the heavyweight championship, even though Jack Johnson held the title during a major portion of his career. Other boxers such as George Dixon (1890–1903) and Joe Gans, best of the lightweights from 1902 to 1908, were successful in championship fights at the lighter weights, but many black fighters maintained that they often had to agree to lose a fight in order to be permitted a bout.[8]

Figure 5.2   Walter Hagen at the Los Angeles Open, January 12, 1929. Wide World.

Golf
Professional golf developed after the turn of the century as public links were built and more Americans began to play golf. The professional golfers were usually golf teachers at country clubs, but neither they nor the outstanding amateurs had much appeal for the general public. But Francis Ouimet's Open victory in 1913, followed a year later by Walter Hagen's championship, made golf seem more accessible to middle-class Americans.

The wealthy club members generally looked upon the professionals as hired help to assist them in learning the game. The "pros" were allowed to compete in open tournaments sponsored by the clubs in order to add interest to the contests. Nevertheless, their second class citizenship was evident by their exclusion from the clubhouses. In retrospect, however, there is little question that the professionals assisted in developing and popularizing the game through the publicity they attracted and their excellent play.

Horse Racing

Following the Civil War thoroughbred racing was revived by respected men of wealth, but only constant vigilance by track owners and operators, stable owners, reputable jockey clubs, and the law prevented racing from being controlled by professional gamblers. Millionaires such as August Belmont and his son, August, Jr., Pierre Lorillard, Leonard W. Jerome, Senator Leland Stanford, and James R. Keane combined their love of the sport, along with wealth, prestige, and managerial skills to renew racing success in the 1880s, 1890s, and the early years of the new century. Except in the economic depression in the first half of the nineties, racing prospered as all classes of people flocked to large new courses around the country. On many racing days crowds of five to ten thousand attended the New Orleans track in the winter of 1890, when the track stopped reserving special seats, sold general admission tickets at fifty cents, and allowed women to enter without charge. By 1908 the difficulty of controlling betting and charges of illegal gambling and fixed races led to a six-year suspension.

Betting at horse races was among the many targets of the social reformers of the Progressive Era of the early 1900s. Wagers were arranged between individuals or more commonly through professional "bookmakers" at the track. The reformers charged that horse racing existed only for the professional gambler and not for the improvement of the breed, as argued by the owners. With Governor Hughes' support, New York state succeeded in ending betting by 1911, but the tracks were virtually deserted in 1911 and 1912. Following popular and racing industry pressure, a modified law allowed limited betting through the parimutuel system. Only then did the fans begin to return to the tracks in large numbers. This system, developed in 1870 in Paris by Pierre Oller but unpopular in the United States until 1900, was gradually adopted throughout this country, and by the beginning of World War I thoroughbred racing was again popular.[9]

By 1917, professional sport was firmly established in the United States. Although baseball continued as the only highly organized team sport on the professional scene, other sports such as football, basketball, and ice hockey, had their embryonic independent professional teams scattered primarily through the Northeast and Midwest. In the next decade they moved from barnstorming to permanent leagues and joined baseball as a major part of the twentieth century entertainment industry. Horse racing and boxing also had their followings, as did bicycling, distance running, rowing, and billiards. Professional sport moved steadily toward its first "golden age."

Amateur Sport

In spite of the growing popularity of professional contests, the roots of sport remained at the amateur level of participatory play. From the informal, spontaneous activity of the playground, through industrial programs, to the highly organized national competitions sponsored by the Amateur Athletic Union (AAU), yacht clubs, or the golfing and tennis associations, Americans played in ever greater numbers in a constantly increasing variety of sports.

For the average American, sport participation prior to World War I was largely limited to the sports available through facilities provided by the local industry, church, municipality, or philanthropist. The YWCA and YMCA attempted to answer the needs of young single adults by providing a dormitory or safe city residence as well as a place for activities. By 1916 there were over sixty-five thousand women attending YWCA gymnasium classes, and thirty-two thousand in swimming classes.

The YMCA adapted its program to fulfill the perceived need for a moral atmosphere for young men in the cities. In 1887, by establishing a two-year course to train directors of gymnasiums, the YMCA reflected a major cultural goal of the country, self-improvement of body and spirit. Luther Gulick's statement epitomizes the view of this organization: "But the ultimate aim of every department of the Association work, including the physical department, is to lead men to Christ. So corresponding emphasis is laid upon securing gymnasium instructors who are not only thoroughly and scientifically trained, but whose supreme motive in all their work is spiritual."[10]

When some industries developed recreation programs for their employees, a new element was introduced into sport programs of the United States. Whether motivated by philanthropy or enlightened self-interest, such firms added substantially to the sport opportunities of the country. Some even capitalized on the sport craze and fielded amateur teams of talented individuals, often employed as much for their sport ability as for their business or manufacturing skills. By the start of World War I such eastern organizations as Macy's and Wanamaker's of New York, Johnson and Johnson of New Brunswick, General Electric of Schenectady, and Michelin of Milltown, New Jersey, sponsored athletic clubs. In Akron, Ohio, Goodyear Company formed teams in baseball, football, track, hockey, skating, basketball, volleyball, tennis and cricket.[11]

Similar programs were sponsored by the National Cash Register Company in Dayton, Ohio.[12] In the Chicago area George M. Pullman, founder of the Pullman Palace Car Company, created an experimental town called Pullman for the employees of his company in the early 1880s. An important part of the model community was an extensive sport and recreation program that continued until the demise of the town in 1898.[13]

Control and sponsorship of amateur sport quickly became the province of influential, wealthy men, who were themselves free to pursue even the most expensive of sports. They controlled amateur organizations such as the AAU and held prominent positions on the early committees for the modern Olympic Games. These affluent, upper-class sportsmen promoted and perpetuated their special idea of the amateur in sport as the person who played for the "love of the game" and did not taint that love by accepting money, valuable prizes, or expenses to appear in tournaments. Participating under the banner of their exclusive athletic club or country club, they paid their own expenses and expected others to do likewise. They were, in fact, the nation's arbiters and custodians of the concept of amateurism. They would remain so for the next seventy-five years.

Yachting

Yacht racing continued to be a favorite sport of the wealthy. *America's* Cup challenges in 1885, 1886, and 1887 served to stimulate more interest in that sport and by 1889, there were more than 125 yacht clubs. Yacht design improved as each Cup challenge resulted in the construction of a new defender of the title. Edward Burgess designed each of three successful American defenders in the middle eighties and greatly influenced naval architecture during the next several years. In 1893 and 1895, the Earl of Dunraven unsuccessfully challenged for the Cup against American yachts designed by Nathaniel Herreshoff. In 1899 the first of several challenges was made by Sir Thomas Lipton of the Royal Ulster Yacht Club of Belfast. The *Shamrock I*, and two years later *Shamrock II*, were defeated by the Herreshoff-built *Columbia*. Undaunted, Lipton arrived in 1903 with *Shamrock III* and promptly lost to a new defender, *Reliance*. After that there were no more challenges until 1920.

The growing interest in yachting created a demand for a smaller craft, and in 1895 the Seawanhaka Corinthian Yacht Club, of Oyster Bay, Long Island, commissioned the building of a fifteen-foot boat with two hundred square feet of sail, and offered a challenge cup for small-yacht racing. The introduction of the smaller craft broadened the socioeconomic base of the sport, but until well into the twentieth century most yachting enthusiasts were relatively wealthy.

Figure 5.3   Sailing in the 1890s.

In the Midwest, yacht racing on the Great Lakes became popular in the 1890s in cities such as Detroit, Chicago, Toledo, Duluth, and Toronto. International races for the Seawanhaka Cup and, beginning in 1896, the Canada's Cup, were events of interest; and in 1898 the first Chicago to Mackinaw race provided Great Lakes sailors with their own prestigious challenge.

The Pacific Northwest had its yachting enthusiasts of the period. In 1891 yacht races in Bellingham Bay, Washington, marked the advent of the Great Northern Railroad. E. B. Leaming, also of Bellingham Bay, boasted a yacht designed by Herreshoff. The protected waters of Puget Sound and the British influence in nearby British Columbia contributed to the popularity of yachting in the Northwest.[14]

Late in the nineteenth century, luxurious steam vessels, which began to appear in eastern yacht club basins, were used for vacations and transportation more than for racing. The development of the internal combustion engine and its adaptation to boats soon after the turn of the century led to auxiliary power for sailing vessels and power boat racing. Rich yachting enthusiasts now had a new sport and in 1904 inaugurated the Gold Cup Trophy of the American Power Boat Association.

Tennis

Throughout the eighties and nineties tennis was primarily a game for the upper classes. The national championships were held in a resplendent Newport setting during Tennis Week each year. During these decades Newport was the summer home of some of the nation's wealthy families—the Belmonts, Vanderbilts, Goelets, and Astors among others. "Summer Newporters" such as James Dwight and Dick Sears, who was national singles champion from 1881 through 1887, dominated the game. The trophies were often elaborate and expensive, sometimes paid for by entry fees of as much as twenty-five dollars. The play was strictly amateur and, as a matter of course, Dwight, Sears, and other ranking players paid their own expenses to tournaments in the United States and Europe.

In the nineties the game changed to faster, more aggressive play as many college players were all-round athletes, such as Fred Hovey, Oliver Campbell, William Larned, and Bob Wrenn, who was a Harvard football, baseball, and hockey player. All these men were national singles champions in the nineties and early 1900s. Women's singles championships began in 1887 when Ellen F. Hansell took the title. Elizabeth A. Moore was champion three times—in 1896, 1901, and 1903.

In 1900 a well-to-do young man from St. Louis, Dwight Davis, a junior at Harvard and a ranking tennis player, encouraged international play by donating the Davis Cup and establishing this prestigious competition. The first decade of the new century found many outstanding players throughout the country. A Californian, May Sutton, won the women's singles championship in 1904 at the age of sixteen and one year later became the first American to win a British national championship in any sport. The national championship tournament moved in 1915 from the exclusive resort of Newport to New York's West Side Tennis Club, a private organization, but a more accessible setting.

Tennis developed and gained popularity as more and more public courts were built. In 1909 "Comet" Maurice McLoughlin, a product of San Francisco's public courts, went east and thrilled crowds with his rocketlike serve. In 1912 he signalled the end of an era in American tennis by becoming the first national champion to come from a modest background and by learning his tennis on public courts.

At that time there was separate tennis for black players, who held their first interstate tournament in Philadelphia in 1898 through the efforts of the Rev. W. W. Walker and the Chautauqua Tennis Club. The American Tennis Association was founded in Washington, D.C., in 1916 for the purposes of "fostering and developing the game of tennis among the colored people of the United States. It encouraged the formation of clubs and the building of courts . . . and interested juniors (16–18 years) as well as boys and girls in the possibilities and advantages of this splendid game."[15] The association sponsored its first national championships in men's singles and men's doubles in Baltimore in the following year.

Figure 5.4   Longwood Cricket Club. Courtesy Spalding Archives, Chicopee, Massachusetts.

Figure 5.5   R. D. Sears. Courtesy Spalding Archives, Chicopee, Massachusetts.

Figure 5.6   The Davis Cup. Courtesy Spalding Archives, Chicopee, Massachusetts.

Figure 5.7   Belmont Cricket Club of Philadelphia, about 1885–1900. From left to right: Bertha Townsend, National Singles Champion, 1888–1889; Margaret Ballard; Louise Alderdice; Ellen Hansell, National Singles Champion, 1887. Courtesy Spalding Archives, Chicopee, Massachusetts.

and girls in the possibilities and advantages of this splendid game."[15] The association sponsored its first national championships in men's singles and men's doubles in Baltimore in the following year.

Golf

On a mild February 22 in 1888, John Reid, a Scottish immigrant living in Yonkers, New York, unveiled a set of golf clubs and balls to a small group of close friends. The party proceeded to lay out three short holes in a nearby cow pasture and Reid and John P. Upham shared the clubs to play a friendly game while the others looked on. Upon the arrival of additional equipment from Britain, the friends played through the summer and fall of that year. In November, Reid gave a dinner party attended by four of the Yonkers golfers at which time he proposed the formation of a golfing club. The group agreed upon the name, the St. Andrews Club of Yonkers, in honor of the famous club

Figure 5.8   Eleanora Sears. Wide World.

in Scotland. After several moves, in 1897 the club made a final move to Mt. Hope and constructed an eighteen-hole course.

Meanwhile other sportsmen in other cities began to play golf. The Country Club of Brookline, Massachusetts, a suburb of Boston, founded in 1882 by a group of Boston gentlemen seeking a private retreat for riding, tennis, bowling, racing, and dining, added a six-hole golf course in 1893. Ultimately enlarged to twenty-seven holes, it became one of the premier courses in the United States.

A group of Englishmen laid a nine-hole course in 1890 in the industrial center of Middlesborough, Kentucky. A few years later the country's first eighteen-hole course was built by the Chicago Country Club in Wheaton, Illinois. So rapidly did the game become popular among wealthy Chicagoans that the city had twenty-six courses by 1900.[16] The first professionally designed and constructed golf course in the United States was opened in 1891 on the eastern end of Long Island as an incorporated golf club named Shinnecock Hills.

In the summer of 1894 the Newport Golf Club hosted a men's tournament in which both amateurs and professionals competed. Twenty players took part in the thirty-six hole, two-day medal play. In December of that year the Amateur Golf Association of the United States, later renamed the United States Golf Association, was founded and announced plans for the first national championships, the Open and the Amateur, to be hosted during the same week of October, 1895, by the Newport Golf Club. The first annual women's amateur championship tournament, also held in 1895, was won by Mrs. C. S. Brown.

Blacks were generally introduced to golf as caddies but occasionally could play in the periodic caddy tournaments sponsored by many golf clubs.[17] Over the strong objections of many, but with the solid support of Theodore Haverman, president of the United States Golf Association, one black golfer, John Shippen, entered the second U.S. Open in 1896 and finished in fifth place.

Golf presents an interesting case in observing the differing role of sport among the social classes. The need for a technically developed large plot of land, expensive equipment, and maintenance fees made it a natural activity for the wealthy. The development of private country clubs, modeled after the already flourishing athletic clubs within many of the large cities, and the formation and control of the United States Golf Association, further cemented this relationship.

The game appealed to the wealthy for a number of reasons. It was challenging as a test of skill. It provided yet another opportunity for social intercourse among one's peers. It lent itself to the club format and therefore it might be available only to the "right" people. On the other hand, the attractiveness of the game could not be kept secret from the growing middle class or even from the working class. Many, like Ouimet, learned the game because they or members of their families worked at the clubs. Others in the rising middle class soon perceived the game as a status symbol as well as an enjoyable athletic pastime. For many of these persons, the ability to play the game became associated with success in the business world. Thus, like baseball, a game nurtured by the "gentle" class could not be retained for that group's exclusive enjoyment. By 1915 golf had achieved popularity with many middle-class people.

Figure 5.9   Sports of the period. Courtesy Spalding Archives, Chicopee, Massachusetts.

Bicycling

Bicycling represents another sport greatly influenced by social class. The League of American Wheelmen controlled organized bicycling and, in 1886, attempted to deal with the problem of professionalism by declaring all racers known to have connections with bicycle manufacturers to be "professionals." The League also led the drive for improved roads which, while benefitting the cyclist, served the interests of the automobile industry that followed. For the wealthy, bicycling was a favorite pastime. During the same period, delivery boys, workmen, and many others found the bicycle a practical means of transportation.

In the early years women and less agile men were restricted to the tricycle, a three-wheeled vehicle with a seat between two large rear wheels. The development of the safety cycle in 1888 with its drop bar signaled a major social and psychological breakthrough for women of the gaslight era. Women's floor length skirts made riding a bicycle difficult and dangerous. More venturesome girls and women experimented with and then adopted a shorter skirt or some form of "bloomer" costume. The new mode of dress gave women a sense of freedom which was further enhanced by the comparative speed of the bicycle. Bicycling offered young women an occasional chance to escape the watchful eye of their chaperones and to test both social and physical freedom.

By 1890 bicycle clubs were the fad in most cities and towns. Some clubs required certain social and economic qualifications for membership. For example, New York's elite Michaux Club, organized in 1895, was founded by socially prominent persons who wanted a place to ride in the winter. In the rented quarters at Bowman's Hall, the club provided morning lessons, afternoon music rides, tea in one of the club rooms, and gala evening riding parties with grand marches, bicycle dances, and formation rides.[18]

Wealthy individuals did much through their own prestige to promote cycling. John D. Rockefeller, an avid cyclist, presented bicycles to friends and associates whose health he felt was in jeopardy. Other prominent cyclists included William Rockefeller, Henry O. Havemeyer, president of the sugar trust, Chauncey Depew, president of the New York Central Railroad and United States senator, and Lillian Russell, who rode a jewel-encrusted bicycle given to her by "Diamond" Jim Brady.[19] By the late 1880s and early 1890s, the development of the safety bicycle and lower prices made cycling a more accessible sport to greater numbers of people in both the wealthy and middle classes. By the beginning of the twentieth century, the motor car, a newer, faster, noisier, riskier, and more expensive mode of transportation, largely superseded the bicycle among members of the upper class. With the declining interest of this trend-setting group and the increased availability of the automobile during the first two decades of the new century, the bicycle became relegated largely to the realm of playthings for children and youth for the next sixty years.

Hunting and Fishing

For the very rich, fox hunting continued to be a favorite pastime. The rolling Maryland and Virginia countryside remained the center for fox hunting. Hunting and fishing, as always, continued to attract participants from all levels of society, except perhaps the lower classes of the cities. Those with greater means could travel farther, and others planned hunting and fishing vacations. Rod and gun clubs increased in number throughout the country and played influential roles in state game and wildlife legislation. Such outdoor sports received added support when Theodore Roosevelt, an exponent of vigorous outdoor life, moved into the White House in 1901. "Teddy's" strong interests in the American West and big game hunting, as well as in competitive athletics, placed one more stamp of approval on sport as part of the American way of life.

Trapshooting and rifle shooting also grew in popularity between 1885 and World War I. These were particularly popular among city dwellers for whom time and space made traditional hunting impossible. Trapshooting had begun just prior to the Civil War when improvements in gun making aided shooting on the fly. In the 1860s and 1870s, better traps and the manufacture of clay pigeons made possible greater standardization for competition. Local rifle clubs sprang up around the country and stimulated interest and regional competitions. The National Rifle Association, founded in 1871, began sponsoring national rifle shooting tournaments. The National Gun Association, organized in 1885, represented a first attempt to establish national rules and regulations for trapshooting. It was soon replaced by the Interstate Association of Trapshooters in 1889 and in 1900 by the American Trapshooting Association.

Equestrian Sports

For the average Americans in small towns or on farms, horses were very much a part of their lives. They provided transportation as well as riding for pleasure. Riding academies in large cities gave the upper and middle classes opportunities for horseback riding.

Polo, first established in the East, also had followers in the West. James Gordon Bennett, Jr., the *New York Herald* publisher, instituted an occasional game in 1876 at a riding academy in New York City. The new game became popular with rich sportsmen and soon had followers and clubs in New Orleans, Los Angeles, Colorado Springs, and other cities. Polo was introduced to Texas when Bennett and his New York friends ordered a train carload of Texas ponies. LeCompte notes that "the purchase of the cow ponies sparked interest in San Antonio and polo soon became an informal favorite of local cowboys."[20] In addition, calvary officers who had learned the game at West point and were stationed in Texas, began playing regular matches with military teams and even local civilian teams, consisting of breeders, trainers and cowboys. In Midland, Texas, sometime after 1902, a women's team was formed.[21] In 1890 the Polo Association, later the United States Polo Association, was founded. America's first international match was played against Britain's Hurlingham Club at Newport in 1886. The superiority of the English players and mounts was readily apparent in the easy defeat of the Americans, but this and later matches were learning experiences for the neophytes. After another defeat in 1902, a quartet led by Harry Payne Whitney finally defeated the British at Hurlingham in 1909 and established American polo as an international sport.

By the late 1890s the rodeo began to attract participants and spectators in such cities as Denver, San Antonio, and Cheyenne. Often conducted in a festival setting, it gave the working cowboy a place to demonstrate his special skills to the world. Prescott, Arizona, is credited with hosting the first commercial rodeo in 1888 when the town advertised cash prizes for the roping and bucking events and charged an admission fee to the spectators. "Rodeo had lost its amateur status and, in a way, its claim to being a folk festival. Instead, it became a sport."[22] While rodeo events date back to the Spanish elite in sixteenth-century Mexico and many contests were held at festivals in Texas throughout the nineteenth century, it remained loosely organized until the twentieth century.[23]

Near the turn of the century, women began to participate in what is considered the oldest rodeo in existence, the Cheyenne Frontier Days. In 1899, two years after the founding of the festival, a half-mile "Ladies Cow Pony Race" was held for the prize of a forty-five dollar saddle.[24] During the next several years other women's events such as bronco riding, steer roping, trick and fancy riding, and relay racing were added. Additional opportunities for women appeared when other rodeo festivals developed in the early twentieth century, most notably the Pendleton, Oregon, "Round-up" in 1909 and the Calgary, Alberta, "Stampede" in 1912.[25]

Basketball
The need for a ball game suitable for use indoors in the winter months was apparent in the YMCA's work with young men. Luther Gulick, director of the gymnasium department of the YMCA Training School at Springfield, Massachusetts, challenged James Naismith, a young instructor in the department, to solve this problem. Naismith taught a class that had enjoyed outdoor sports in the fall, but had rebelled against the customary winter indoor activities of formal gymnastics, calisthenics, and drill. After trying indoor adaptations of soccer, football, rugby, water polo, field hockey, and even lacrosse, Naismith put together a game utilizing a soccer ball to be passed from man to man, and two goals, which were baskets suspended about ten feet in the air at either end of the court.

Figure 5.10   Dr. James Naismith.

The first game was played on December 21, 1891, with Naismith and his colleague, Amos Alonzo Stagg, captaining the two nine-man teams. The game was instantly popular with the players, and several took it back to their respective homes during the Christmas recess and introduced it to others. News of the game spread quickly through the school newsletter to "Y" physical directors, and Naismith himself travelled with a team to Albany, Troy, Schenectady, Providence, and Newport, playing basketball in each city.

Soon other colleges across the country began playing the game. After C. O. Beamis of Geneva College saw a game at Springfield, he introduced it to his classes. H. F. Kallenberg of the University of Iowa learned of the game through the newsletter. Basketball grew most rapidly, however, in the YMCA's and high schools. Gulick and Naismith believed that with their new winter sport they had solved the problem of the unruly class.

ORIGINAL RULES FOR BASKETBALL

1. The ball may be thrown in any direction with one or both hands.
2. The ball may be batted in any direction with one or both hands (never with the fist).

3. A player cannot run with the ball. The player must throw it from the spot on which he catches it; allowance to be made for a man who catches the ball when running at a good speed.
4. The ball must be held in or between the hands; the arms or body must not be used for holding it.
5. No shouldering, holding, pushing, tripping, or striking, in any way the person of an opponent shall be allowed; the first infringement of this rule by any person shall count as a foul, the second shall disqualify him until the next goal is made, or, if there was evident intent to injure the person for the whole of the game, no substitute allowed.
6. A foul is striking at the ball with the fist, violation of Rules 3, 4, and such as described in Rule 5.
7. If either side makes three consecutive fouls, it shall count a goal for the opponents. (Consecutive means without the opponents in the meantime making a foul.)
8. A goal shall be made when the ball is thrown or batted from the grounds into the basket and stays there, providing those defending the goal do not touch or disturb the goal. If the ball rests on the edge and the opponent moves the basket, it shall count as a goal.
9. When the ball goes out of bounds, it shall be thrown into the field and played by the person first touching it. In case of a dispute, the umpire shall throw it straight into the field. The thrower-in is allowed five seconds. If he holds it longer it shall go to the opponent. If any side persists in delaying the game, the umpire shall call a foul on them.
10. The umpire shall be judge of the men and shall note the fouls and notify the referee when three consecutive fouls have been made. He shall have power to disqualify men according to Rule 5.
11. The referee shall be judge of the ball and shall decide when the ball is in play, in bounds, to which side it belongs, and shall keep the time. He shall decide when a goal has been made, and keep account of the goals, with any other duties that are usually performed by a referee.
12. The time shall be two fifteen-minute halves, with five minutes rest between.
13. The side making the most goals in that time shall be declared the winners. In case of a draw, the game may, by agreement of the captains, be continued until another goal is made.[26]

The rules against running with the ball were the earliest to be relaxed. In 1893 the pivot was ruled not to be a traveling violation, and by 1896 Yale University added the dribble. By 1897 the number of players was fixed at five. At that time the colleges had one set of rules and the clubs, the Y's, and the AAU played by different rules. Agreement on rules was reached in 1915 when a Joint Basketball Committee was formed, with representatives of the National Collegiate Athletic Association (NCAA), the AAU, and the YMCA. By the outbreak of World War I basketball began to be the most popular high school sport for boys, and in the colleges, particularly in the Midwest, it was second only to football. The early barnstorming professional teams which began to appear around 1900 followed their own rules.

Figure 5.11   Early basketball at Smith College. Courtesy of the College Archives, Smith College, Northampton, Massachusetts.

Women's basketball began in the same winter that Naismith founded the game, when Senda Berenson, a physical education instructor at nearby Smith College, adapted the game for her students. Recognizing its inherent soundness and value, she changed it to conform more closely with prevailing medical, psychological and social concepts of women's physical capabilities. Other women physical educators, concerned with the roughness that they observed in the men's game, also adapted the rules. As a result, by the end of the 1890s women around the country played under many different rules. At a physical training conference held at Springfield, Massachusetts, in June, 1899, a committee was formed to develop a uniform set of rules for women. It was finally agreed that the rules would be based upon the official YMCA rules used by men but with several modifications, including the following major changes: 1) dividing the playing area into three equal zones;[27] 2) prohibiting the snatching or batting of the ball from the hands of another player; and 3) limiting the number of players to not fewer than six nor more than nine. Changes such as dividing into zones and prohibiting players assigned to one division from running into another were felt to have several advantages.

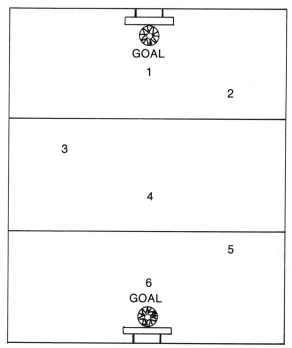

Diagram of field, showing position of six on team.

It does away almost entirely with "star" playing, hence equalizes the importance of the players, and so encourages team work. This also encourages combination plays, for when a girl knows she cannot go over the division line to follow the ball, she is more careful to play as well as possible with the girls near her when the ball comes to her territory. The larger the gymnasium the greater is the tax on individual players when the game is played without lines. It has been found that a number of girls who play without division lines have developed hypertrophy of the heart. The lines prevent the players from running all over the gymnasium, thus doing away with unnecessary running, and also giving the heart moments of rest. On the other hand, the lines do not keep the players almost stationary, as some believe. A player has the right to run anywhere she may please in her own third of the gymnasium.[28]

The prohibition of snatching or batting the ball from an opponent's hand was designed to eliminate a potential element of roughness from the game. The range in the number of players on each team allowed for the differences in the size of playing courts and also insured a minimum of two players per zone, thus protecting any one player from the exertion required to cover an entire division by herself.[29]

Volleyball

In an effort to meet the needs of his noonday businessmen's class, William Morgan, the physical director at the Holyoke, Massachusetts, YMCA developed the game of volleyball. Intended only as a light recreational activity for the group, the game soon became popular. Originally the game utilized the entire gymnasium, the rubber bladder from a basketball, and a six-foot six-inch high net. The ball was hit back and forth with the hands and an "out" was called if the ball landed out of bounds or hit the floor after more than one bounce. The game of nine innings accommodated any number of players on a team.

Morgan presented his new game, which he called *minonette,* at a YMCA sports conference at Springfield College in 1895. It was received favorably but renamed *volleyball* because of the techniques involved. The school newsletter published the rules, and within a short time the game was being played at YMCAs around the country. Soon schools and colleges incorporated the game into physical education programs, where it was played by both men and women. During World War I men in the armed services played volleyball both in the United States and Europe.

The first rule changes, made in 1900 by the Physical Directors Society of the YMCA, included the elimination of dribbling, the first bounce, and the use of innings. Twenty-one points constituted a game and the net height was raised to seven feet. Finally, balls landing on the side line were "in" and balls rebounding from the walls or other out-of-court objects were out of play. In 1912, court dimensions were established at thirty-five feet by sixty feet, a player rotation method was set, touching the net became a loss of service, two games constituted a match, and the net height was raised to seven feet six inches, and the width three feet.

Swimming and Lifesaving

The YMCA initiated the first national program to teach vast numbers of people to swim, and "during the years 1909 through 1917 about 376,000 persons were taught swimming and diving."[30] Another broad swimming program started in 1914 when Commodore Wilbert E. Longfellow of the American Red Cross initiated its Life Saving Service. The Red Cross approach emphasized teaching basic techniques to nonswimmers in a carefully developed step-by-step approach.

Beginnings of Youth Sport

Of major significance during this period was the growing acceptance of play as respectable, healthy activity. Many religious leaders and educators recommended exercise, simple play, and sport. When churches built sport facilities as a practical display of the social gospel, they gave religious sanction to "play," an action which helped to make it acceptable to those who had disapproved of "time-wasting" recreation and sport. Educators like G. Stanley Hall, Edward L. Thorndike, William James, and John Dewey praised play and sport as valuable learning tools for youth in a democracy. For some social reformers, organized sponsored play was viewed as a means of exerting social control. It was expected to "Americanize" those from diverse foreign cultures and to neutralize the meaner effects of idle life on the streets, especially for the children of working parents. Jane Addams, who worked among Chicago's poor, asserted emphatically the need for recreation, denouncing a society that did not provide adequate facilities:

> Only in the modern city have men concluded that it is no longer necessary for the municipality to provide for the insatiable desire for play. . . . and this at the very moment when the city has become distinctly industrial, and daily labor is continually more monotonous and subdivided. . . . this industrialism has gathered together multitudes of eager young creatures from all quarters of the earth as a labor supply for the countless factories and workshops, upon which the present industrial city is based. . . . This stupid experiment of organizing work and failing to organize play has, of course, brought about a fine revenge. The love of pleasure will not be denied, and when it has turned into all sorts of malignant and vicious appetites, then we, the middle aged, grow quite distracted and resort to all sorts of restrictive measures. . . . almost worse than the restrictive measures is our apparent belief that the city itself has no obligation in the matter, an assumption upon which the modern city turns over to commercialism practically all the provisions for public recreation.[31]

Doctors increasingly recommended vigorous physical activity for everyone in order to maintain health. In short, Americans now were told that exercise, sport, play, and recreation were worthwhile aspects of democratic life.

The playground movement in the United States began about this time in response to such cultural pressures. Many philanthropists, common citizens, and politicians worried about poor city children with no supervision and little fresh air or safe space to play. Streets were viewed as breeding grounds for juvenile crime. The poor and middle class were restricted in their choice of recreation and especially in their facilities for play. Particularly hard pressed for space were the children of the poor in the tenement districts of industrial centers. Often left alone all day by working parents, children roamed the streets and sought pleasure in many undesirable and unsafe centers. In addition, very young children needed clean, open spaces where fresh air and room for exercise would create a healthful atmosphere. Parks and playgrounds in crowded communities within the city could provide civilizing, healthful effects and offer the opportunity to socialize newly arrived immigrant youth.

The first efforts to organize public playgrounds originated in Boston in the 1870s and 1880s. In response to both public and private groups the city aldermen appropriated two thousand dollars to provide "playgrounds for boys

Figure 5.12   School playground, Detroit, Michigan, about 1910. Courtesy of the Detroit Historical Museum.

in the several sections of the city." Disputes over the location of these sites—either suburban or inner city—led to an impasse and not until 1887 were annual appropriations for playgrounds made by the city.[32]

The Massachusetts Emergency and Hygiene Association opened its first "sand garden" for small children in 1885. Two years later there were ten such "gardens," or what we now call playgrounds. During the first two years supervision was provided by volunteers, but soon matrons were employed in such positions. The sand gardens were so popular that in 1901 the Boston School Committee accepted the responsibility for the program, thus acknowledging the supervision of play as an appropriate function of the public schools.[33]

Although Boston pioneered this movement, other cities soon followed; and in 1890 New York's Society for Parks and Playgrounds, with the help of churches and synagogues, began a drive for playgrounds. In 1894 at Jane Addam's Hull House, the first playground in Chicago was opened. Four years later Chicago gave its first appropriation for playgrounds, one thousand dollars to the vacation school committee of local women's clubs. Further support was obtained from the Turners, who loaned apparatus for the program. At the turn of the century a group of Detroit women raised money to start a playground in a schoolyard. By 1900, a number of cities from Philadelphia to Denver had opened playgrounds.

In typical American fashion, many of the early playgrounds were initiated by philanthropists and later transferred to the local city governments. Sometimes the land for the playgrounds was donated by a wealthy benefactor and on other occasions it was set aside by the city. Usually the parks and playgrounds were located in densely populated sections of the city and planned for young children rather than older youth. The early playgrounds were often temporary and maintained only in the summers. Finally, it was customary for policemen to supervise the playgrounds, promoting the concept of child control rather than of guidance and leadership.

In 1906 the Playground Association of America was founded by Dr. Luther Gulick and Dr. Henry Curtis. The Boys' Clubs of America also began in 1906 and the Boy Scouts of America began in 1910 and the Girl Scouts in 1912. The formation of such associations, together with the increasing number of parks and playgrounds, demonstrated the growing acceptance of play in the life of children. Educators and social workers began to view sport, especially for boys, as a means of social control for the assimilation of culture and the socialization of American youth. Out of the social reforms of the nineteenth century and the changing needs of youth, a number of public, private, and government agencies established sport as a part of their programs.

Sport and Physical Education in Education

In the 1880s as the country grew in size, population, and diversity, public education for the average American became more of a reality. Public school facilities for children and youth greatly increased throughout the country between 1885 and 1917. By 1898 thirty-one state and territorial legislatures had adopted compulsory attendance laws, which increased the formal education received by the average American from four years in 1880 to six years in 1910. The national illiteracy rate was reduced from 17 percent in 1880 to 7.7 percent in 1910. On the other hand, most elementary schools limited their curriculums to reading, writing, arithmetic, and other basic subjects. In the 1890s, traditional public school education was challenged by a group of educators led by John Dewey of the University of Chicago, later of Teachers College, Columbia. Under the new influence, the curriculum expanded to include the sciences and subjects such as art, manual training, cooking, sewing, commercial skills, and physical education.

The colleges and universities changed from required courses with almost no electives to a largely elective system. In addition, the liberal arts curriculum added courses in new fields such as physics, political science, economics, sociology, music, fine arts, and advanced modern languages. Technical institutes and engineering programs also revised their curriculums; "normal," or teacher-training schools raised their standards and the number of landgrant colleges increased; and the founding of several black colleges in the South provided that region with teachers, knowledgeable farmers, and skilled craftsmen among the newly franchised citizens. Finally, graduate programs developed in many of the nation's universities.

The Development of Physical Education

In 1885 William G. Anderson convened about sixty interested persons who formed the American Association for the Advancement of Physical Education (AAAPE), which promoted physical education and provided a forum for discussing mutual problems. Physical education programs for men and women varied considerably, but the general trend over this thirty-year period was a decrease in gymnastics and an increase in sport instruction. Both the men's and women's programs had been initiated to improve health. With no formal physical education preparation available, medical doctors were appointed at institutions such as Amherst, Harvard, Yale, and Oberlin, to direct the physical education work. The background of these people greatly influenced the courses offered and the research undertaken by the faculty.

The need for teachers of physical education quickly led to programs for training teachers. In 1885 only two programs existed, one in Milwaukee and the other in Boston. Having been started by the Turners as an occasional training course in various cities, the North American Gymnastics Union (NAGU) was established in Milwaukee. By 1891 the course was two years in length and in 1903 it was extended to three years. Because the NAGU prepared its students for the Turner program, their graduates ordinarily taught in the Turnvereins or in Midwestern public schools. The NAGU emphasized German gymnastics, German, English, and other cultural subjects. The other teacher training institution of the mid-1880s was the Sargent School, opened in 1881 to train students interested in becoming teachers of physical education.

By 1890 three additional schools that also greatly influenced the development of physical education were established in this country. In 1886 William G. Anderson opened the Brooklyn Normal School to both men and women; the following year the YMCA Training School at Springfield, Massachusetts, created a department to train physical directors for the YMCA programs; and in 1889 the Boston Normal School of Gymnastics (BNSG) opened. Founded by the Boston philanthropist Mary Hemenway, BNSG modeled its curriculum after the Royal Central Institute in Stockholm and stressed Swedish gymnastics. Hemenway appointed Amy Morris Homans as the director of the school. Under Homans, the school became nationally known and, in 1909, affiliated with Wellesley College, a four-year liberal arts college. Beginning in 1917 only graduates from recognized colleges were admitted to the program.

While the curriculum and offerings of these schools differed according to their educational philosophy, they all offered anatomy and physiology, and all but NAGU taught anthropometry and sciences such as physics. An examination of the early curriculums reveals that a rigorous search was made for a curriculum that would be particularly relevant to physical education. Courses offered included physiological psychology, the relation of body and mind, mechanics of the body, and sphygmography. On the other hand, a description of one "health education" course in the 1890–91 *YMCA Training School Catalogue* reads: "Personal Purity—physiology of the reproductive organs. Effects of violation of the laws of purity; in the body, on the mind. Intellectual licentiousness, cause, effects. Hygienic treatment. Quack doctors and their methods."[34] The sports offered during this period at the various institutions also varied with the philosophy of the school: the YMCA school offered an extensive sports program; Anderson included those sports for which he had facilities; and the others offered a limited sports program.

While the Sargent School and the BNSG were originally open to women and men, both became schools for women only. They were popular, and educated many of the early women leaders. By 1904 Sargent had graduated 261 students and BNSG 312. Among the leaders graduated from Sargent were Delphine Hanna, Elizabeth Burchenal, Helen Putnam, and Lucille Eaton Hill. The graduates in BNSG's early days included Senda Berenson, Ethel Perrin, J. Anna Norris, and Blanche Trilling. In the first class graduated from Wellesley were Mabel Lee and Mary Channing Coleman. Others who were graduated in the early Wellesley years prior to World War I were Florence Lawson, Gertrude Manchester, Gertrude Baker, and Elizabeth Halsey.

Other colleges and universities soon began to offer teacher preparation programs. Beginning in 1885 at Oberlin, Dr. Delphine Hanna first prepared teachers by offering a single course to a selected group of undergraduate men. They in turn taught the physical training courses for the other men on campus because there was no director of the men's program. From this effort came three early leaders of physical education, Thomas Wood, Luther Gulick, and Fred Leonard. In 1892 Oberlin College instituted a two-year "Normal Course in Physical Training" which in 1900 became a four-year course leading to a bachelor of arts degree. During this decade George Wells Fitz, M.D., organized the first formal studies on the physiological effects of physical activity at the Physiological Laboratory in the Lawrence Scientific School at Harvard. He also taught in the department of anatomy, physiology, and physical training. "Under Fitz's direction, this department offered and awarded the first four-year degree in physical education in the United States."[35] By the turn of the century, only three other institutions had established degree programs: Stanford University, the University of California, and the University of Nebraska.

Beginning in the 1880s, early teacher training efforts also included summer school courses. In 1886, William G. Anderson and Dr. Jay Seaver began the Chautauqua Summer School for Physical Education. Sargent, with the approval of Harvard's President Eliot, instituted the Harvard Summer School of Physical Education in 1887, and attracted, over the years, hundreds of teachers who used this unique school to help improve physical education.

Between 1900 and 1917, the eastern private normal schools continued to be the most important source of qualified physical education teachers. Early in the second decade of the new century, however, four-year colleges and universities, both public and private, superseded the normal schools.[36] Graduate work was initiated and the first master's degree was awarded by Teachers College of Columbia University in 1910.

One of the major interests of the period was anthropometry. Influenced by the work of Hitchcock and Sargent, college gymnasium faculty members measured and meticulously recorded individual statistics on size, growth, strength development—all to seek the "typical" college man and woman. Between 1885 and 1900 thousands of students were charted at Harvard, Amherst, Yale, Oberlin, the University of Nebraska, Beloit College, and Wellesley. Sargent constructed life-sized statues of the "typical" college man and woman and exhibited them at the World's Columbian Exposition in Chicago in 1893. The American Association for the Advancement of Physical Education established a "Department of Anthropometry and Statistics" with Hitchcock serving as chairman. Two years later Senda Berenson of Smith College chaired a new "Committee on Vital Statistics," and in 1897 a "Committee on School Anthropometry" was formed with Henry P. Bowditch of the Harvard Medical School as its chairman. The data from the anthropometrical studies were used to prescribe specific exercises and activities to correct deficiencies and develop strength, body symmetry, and health.

Another general issue during the beginning of this era was the so-called "battle of the systems," with advocates claiming that their particular exercise "system" best produced bodily fitness in American children and youth. The Turners promoted German gymnastics, Dr. Sargent tested and prescribed individual exercises, Dr. Hitchcock used both mass exercises and individual exercises, and the BNSG promoted Swedish gymnastics. In 1889 Hemenway, a strong proponent of Swedish gymnastics, hosted the "Conference in the Interest of Physical Training" to bring the various systems to the attention of the public. The conference was held at the Massachusetts Institute of Technology on November 29 and 30, with over two thousand people attending. Papers were read by a number of outstanding physical educators, the various physical training systems were explained and debated, and the entire proceeding was presided over by William T. Harris, the United States Commissioner of Education. In spite of the controversy generated, however, the "battle of the systems" abated as play and sport became the dominant components in the changing field of physical education in the United States.

In the early 1890s various forces combined to alter the programs of college physical education. First, the growing popularity of men's intercollegiate sport introduced thousands of students to the fun and stimulation of vigorous games and athletics. The relatively dull routine of exercise programs palled in comparison to participation in sport. Second, sport developed in the curriculum as perceptive instructors like Tappan at Vassar and Naismith at Springfield recognized student interest in games and sport. Berenson of Smith College had been the first to modify the rules of basketball for women. Recognizing that Naismith probably did not envision women playing the game, she stated:

> However, directors of gymnasia for women saw at once that it was, perhaps, the game they were eagerly seeking—one that should not have the rough element of foot ball, yet should be a quick, spirited game—should cultivate strength and physical endurance, and should be interesting enough to become a part of physical training for women as foot ball and base ball are for men.[37]

A third factor affecting the shift from formal gymnastics to sport was the "new psychology" of William James, G. Stanley Hall, Edward L. Thorndike, William Kilpatrick, and John Dewey. Believing that schools, to be effective centers of learning, must be *interesting,* Dewey emphasized the role of play in the education of the child. His teaching and writing influenced generations of physical educators—and educators in general—and was perhaps the most significant factor in the growth of the play movement in physical education for young children. One of the first physical educators to support a play orientation was Thomas Dennison Wood. By 1910 Wood, head of the department of physical education at Teachers College, Columbia University, had articulated his ideas in the *Ninth Yearbook of the National Society for the Study of Education.* Known as the "new physical education," Wood's philosophy emphasized the "natural" programs of play, games, and sport for teaching intellectual awareness and moral and social behavior. Clark Hetherington, Wood's student at Stanford, exemplified this philosophy with particular energy. As professor of physical training and director of athletics at the University of Missouri from 1900 to 1910, he struggled for ethics in athletics, sport for men and for women, and for statewide recreational opportunities for the people of Missouri.

During this period the curriculum in both colleges and high schools reflected the changes in student interest and educational philosophy. These changes resulted in more games and sport in the instructional program. The growing acceptance of intercollegiate athletics for men was a subtle reinforcement of the sport and athletic programs for high school boys. More and more high school athletes became the sport stars of the college campus.

Intercollegiate Sport for Men

By 1890 intercollegiate sport for men was entrenched on most campuses in the East and in a growing number in the South, Midwest, and Far West. By far the most popular sport was football, but men also competed in baseball, track and field, basketball, rowing, and other popular sports of the period.

Most colleges across the country fielded a football team, reflecting the astonishing growth of this rough contact sport. West Point formed its first team in
1890 and by 1900 the Army-Navy game was an annual spectacle drawing
military and governmental officials as spectators. Intersectional play increased
as Midwestern teams such as Michigan, Minnesota, and Chicago challenged
the traditionally strong elevens in the East. In 1892 Stanford University and
the University of California began a rivalry that soon drew capacity crowds.
The Oakland Athletic Club, in 1895, traveled east to play teams in Chicago
and also the University of Michigan and Cornell. By the end of the century,
Thanksgiving Day games had become an annual tradition, and in 1902 New
Year's Day became another football holiday with the Rose Bowl game and the
Tournament of Roses in Pasadena, California.

While the eastern teams continued to dominate the game through the
nineties, the quality of play in other parts of the country improved as former
star players from Yale, Princeton, Harvard, and other gridiron powers were
hired to coach in the newer colleges. In 1892 President William Rainey Harper
brought former Yale and Springfield All-American Amos Alonzo Stagg to the
University of Chicago where he coached for the next forty-one years. Yale
star Mike Donahue went to Auburn University while John Heisman assumed
coaching duties at Georgia Institute of Technology. Glen "Pop" Warner left
Cornell to coach at the Carlisle Indian School, Pittsburgh, and later Stanford
University.

The first reported game between two black teams involved Biddle University (now Johnson C. Smith) and Livingstone College on Thanksgiving Day,
1892. Howard University, Lincoln University of Pennsylvania, Tuskegee and
Atlanta Universities all began play in 1894. As early as 1890 a limited number
of black players were members of predominantly white college football teams
in the North. William H. Lewis and William Tecumseh Sherman Jackson were
teammates at Amherst in 1889, 1890, and 1891 and Lewis served as team
captain in the second year. Lewis then played the 1892 and 1893 seasons at
Harvard, meriting All-American honors both years. Other black players included George A. Flippen at Nebraska, Joseph H. Lee at Harvard, George
M. Chadwell at Williams, and William Washington at Oberlin. Through the
first decade of the new century, the number of black football players at these
and similar institutions increased slightly. After graduating from Harvard Law
School in 1895, Lewis returned in 1898 to help coach the Harvard line for one
season. In 1904, Matthew Bullock, a black Dartmouth player from 1901–1903,
was hired by Massachusetts Agricultural College to coach the football team,
thus becoming the first black man to serve as a head football coach at a predominantly white college. He again filled that position in 1907 and 1908 after
an absence to attend Harvard Law School.

Figure 5.13   Fielding Yost, Glenn "Pop" Warner, Amos Alonzo Stagg, and John Heisman. Famous early football coaches. Courtesy of the University of Michigan.

The style of play in the nineties was increasingly rough and dangerous, emphasizing mass formation plays, in which players surrounded their own ball carrier and moved forward with great speed and force toward the opponent's goal. Stagg's 1891 development of the "turtleback," a solid oval of players converging on the opposing tackle, and Harvard's 1892 refinement of the "flying wedge," a kick-off maneuver in which players hung on to the clothing of the teammate ahead of them as the ball-carrier ran safely in their wake, produced countless injuries. In 1894 a group led by Yale, Harvard, Princeton, the University of Pennsylvania, and the United States Naval Academy outlawed the "flying wedge" and reduced the game's playing time from 90 to 70 minutes, but mass formation plays and violence continued. The season of 1905 saw

Figure 5.14   Men's football team at Hampton Institute. Courtesy of the Archives, Hampton University, Hampton, Virginia.

eighteen players killed and more than one hundred seriously injured. Because of the brutality, Columbia and Northwestern, among others, dropped the sport entirely and Stanford and California changed to rugby.

The forward pass helped to open the play, but mass formation plays continued. Despite changes in rules to make the game safer, football still caused many injuries. Some defended the game as a rallying point for the student body and as a character builder for the players. Further reforms by the Intercollegiate Athletic Association and stars such as Jim Thorpe of the Carlisle School and Gus Dorais of Notre Dame helped quiet critics, and college football continued to be extremely popular. By 1917, the game was played in small southwestern colleges, black colleges and white universities in the South, prairie colleges in Oklahoma, Kansas, Nebraska, and the Dakotas, as well as in the established schools of the East and the large state universities of the Midwest and Pacific Coast. Large stadiums were constructed and expansions planned as the "business" of college football became a revenue-producing enterprise.

While football drew thousands of spectators and the press, other sports had their own followers. Baseball continued to be popular with the players and track and field grew steadily. Exciting dual meets took place in the East among Harvard, Princeton, Yale, Pennsylvania, and Columbia. Track teams were

Figure 5.15   Jim Thorpe, all-around football and track and field star. Wide World.

formed at the Universities of Michigan, Chicago, Illinois, and Wisconsin in the Midwest, and at California and Stanford in the West. The University of Pennsylvania established the Penn Relays in 1894, and Drake University in Des Moines, Iowa, initiated the Drake Relays.

The time and place of the first intercollegiate basketball game are not known. There is a record of Hamline University losing to Minnesota State School of Agriculture on February 9, 1895, and of Haverford College defeating Temple University several weeks later. The first known game to use five-man squads was played between student teams from the University of Chicago and the

University of Iowa on January 16, 1896. Although some intercollegiate play continued through the late 1890s, most college teams filled their schedules with YMCA clubs and even high schools. In the East, football conference rivalries were separate from basketball leagues such as the Intercollegiate League and the New England League, which were formed in 1901. On the other hand, the Western Conference adopted basketball but it was not until about 1903 that intercollegiate conference basketball began to be stable. By the beginning of World War I, it was clear that basketball was an integral part of intercollegiate sport for men.

Of major importance to men's intercollegiate sport in this period was the trend away from volunteer student-run athletic associations to college-controlled administration. The rise of football played a significant role in this move. Its increasing popularity and financial complexity required administrative and faculty control. Hired coaches and larger stadiums represented major investments, and the colleges saw the need to appoint "athletic directors" to supervise their interests.

At the same time, conference and league affiliations brought inter-institutional stability and increased faculty control over schedules, eligibility standards, and rules of play. In 1895 faculty representatives from the Universities of Chicago, Illinois, Michigan, Minnesota, Northwestern, Purdue, and Wisconsin formed the Intercollegiate Conference of Faculty Representatives. Also known as the Western Conference and later as the Big Ten, the conference adopted resolutions aimed at controlling collegiate athletics. The growing number of such conferences resulted in increasing control over college sport.

Football injuries and fatalities, especially those in the 1905 season, raised questions about continuing the game. President Theodore Roosevelt, an avid football fan, pressured college authorities to take action. Over sixty institutions met in New York City and formed the Intercollegiate Athletic Association of the United States. In 1910 the name was changed to the National Collegiate Athletic Association (NCAA). Two years later, in 1912, the Colored Intercollegiate Athletic Association was formed to regulate football and other sports in black institutions of the South and Midwest.

The purpose of the NCAA, as stated in the second article of its constitution, was "the regulation and supervision of college athletics throughout the United States, in order that the athletic activities in the colleges and universities of the United States may be maintained on an ethical plane in keeping with the dignity and high purpose of education." Membership was open to all colleges and universities in the United States which supported programs of intercollegiate sport for men. To provide guidance to member institutions for the uniform control of intercollegiate athletics, the organization adopted the "Principles of Amateur Sport":

Each institution which is a member of this Association agrees to enact and enforce such measures as may be necessary to prevent violations of the principles of amateur sports such as:

a. Proselyting.

1. The offering of inducements to players to enter colleges or universities because of their athletic abilities and of supporting or maintaining players while students on account of their athletic abilities, either by athletic organizations, individual alumni, or otherwise, directly or indirectly.

2. The singling out of prominent athletic students of preparatory schools and endeavoring to influence them to enter a particular college or university.

b. The playing of those ineligible as amateurs.

c. The playing of those who are not *bona fide* students in good and regular standing.

d. Improper and unsportsmanlike conduct of any sort whatsoever, either on the part of the contestants, the coaches, their assistants, or the student body.[38]

The original plan, to form a governing body to regulate and control collegiate sport through stringent eligibility rules and enforcement, was quickly abandoned as impracticable. Instead, the association assumed an "educational and supportive" role for the betterment of intercollegiate sport and encouraged the formation of regional conferences to enforce eligibility and other standards. Each university or college retained control of its own athletes and its own rules.

Supplementing the "Principles of Amateur Sport" were the suggested minimum "Eligibility Rules." Although acceptance of these rules was not required for membership in the association, it was expected that individual schools would determine their own methods of preventing violations.

The NCAA conventions between 1906 and 1920 focused upon three basic issues in debates, speeches, and reports—summer baseball, faculty control, and recruitment of athletes. The issue of college athletes participating in summer baseball leagues where either they or other players were paid salaries was most vexing, for it breached the eligibility rules of the association. Members were polarized on this issue, between those who claimed a college player could not play on a professional or semiprofessional team in the summer and those who maintained that an institution could not bar a properly registered student from participating in any student program. The latter group included many who reached that conclusion after frustrating attempts to enforce a strict amateur code. The Missouri Valley Conference cancelled the entire 1911 baseball season rather than look the other way when some student-athletes denied having received pay the preceding summer. On the other hand, members of the Rocky Mountain Faculty Athletic Conference allowed their players to participate in summer baseball on minor or local teams. Eventually the issue resolved itself, through the decline of summer hotel leagues and diminishing interest in collegiate baseball in the late 1920s.

A second issue centered on faculty control of intercollegiate sport. While a number of prominent eastern and midwestern universities had moved in this direction by 1906, either through faculty appointments in physical education and/or athletics, or at least through a faculty-student athletic control board, a large number allowed most authority to rest with the student/alumni controlled athletic association, which hired coaches and ran the programs. The NCAA officially encouraged the employment of permanent faculty members with preparation comparable to that of other faculty by departments of physical education and athletics, and it discouraged hiring temporary "professional" coaches.[39] During the next decades regular faculty appointments for athletic coaches became the practice.

A third major issue of these years was that of athletic recruitment or "proselyting." The "Principles of Amateur Sport" forbade any endeavor on the part of athletic organizations, individual alumni, or university personnel to influence individuals to enter colleges or universities because of their athletic abilities, or to support or maintain student-athletes. Opposition to athletic recruitment was based upon an understanding that participation in sport was no different from participation in any other nonacademic student activity, and that influencing prospective students of athletic prominence would constitute gross overemphasis. The offering of financial or other inducements to prospective student-athletes was seen not only as a further sign of overemphasis, but even more significantly, as a step toward professionalism. This issue continues to trouble educational institutions. The public demand for winning teams, the lure of sell-out crowds to finance newly constructed stadiums, and the institutional need to attract strong alumni allegiance combined to increase the need for a steady stream of talented athletes to the campus. Holding membership in a national association which *asked* for agreement with certain principles was far easier than policing oneself in strict compliance with those principles—especially when strong suspicions existed regarding the integrity of other institutions and athletic opponents. The concept of intercollegiate sport for men as a form of public entertainment, then, was established prior to 1920. During this same era programs of collegiate sport for women developed in a different direction and for different reasons.

Collegiate Sport for Women

Competitive sports for women in this period differed from those for men in several significant ways. First, from the beginning women's programs were organized and conducted largely in Departments of Physical Education for Women in coeducational institutions or in Departments of Physical Education in women's colleges. Second, the philosophy on which the programs were planned carefully avoided the problems created by the men's programs. Women were not permitted to engage in games where injuries were numerous. Also, they excluded the public from watching their contests so that they could not be accused of fostering some of the "evils" of men's athletics. Third, the philosophy on which the women's programs were based encouraged the participation of many students rather than a few for a varsity team.

In spite of this philosophy, the women's programs continued to be criticized as too strenuous, possibly damaging to the women, and encouraging unladylike behavior. However, by carefully controlling the type of activity, by supervising all matches, and by planning types of activities which differed from the men's, women physical educators were able to provide opportunities for many women to pursue sport in acceptable surroundings and to enjoy the new games of the period. It is also true that the "acceptable surroundings" often lacked adequate space and facilities, and the new games were frequently played with makeshift equipment, as women struggled for minimal programs. Gymnastics, still the focus of most physical education programs, was questioned by Lucille Eaton Hill. In 1893 she conducted an experiment to compare the physical improvement resulting from gymnastics and rowing. Measurements taken at the beginning and end of the training period showed that rowing as well as gymnastics could strengthen muscles and increase lung capacity.[40]

Competitive sports for women were organized in a variety of ways depending upon the institution, the leadership, the facilities, and the desires of the students. There were clubs, all-college tournaments, interclass tournaments, interclass competitions, varsity programs, field days, pageants and festivals, and athletic associations.

Basketball was immediately popular and played in all parts of the country either in campus tournaments as at Oberlin, in class games, or as a varsity sport. In 1894 an English instructor at the University of Nebraska served as the manager, coach, and a player for the women's varsity basketball team. The University of Wisconsin women's team played varsity ball briefly, but found that:

> The inter-class program of competition, however, became highly organized and enthusiastically supported. After 1900 each class fielded a team in the major sports and the class winning the most tournaments throughout the year was honored at the conclusion of the sports season.[41]

When the women's basketball team at California played Miss Head's School on November 18, 1892, "it was the first women's team to officially represent the university (and the first basketball team of either sex)."[42] In 1915–16 California changed from a varsity-type program to an interclass program, but finished the season with an interclass intercollegiate competition with Stanford University, in which each school entered four teams. One type of activity that included a variety of sport and dance activities was the May Day pageant and physical education demonstration. Such festivals might include marching, mass exercise drills, demonstrations of folk dancing, and perhaps a game of some type.

A number of institutions fostered interest in sports through clubs. California organized a tennis club in 1890 and a boating club in 1901. The University of Wisconsin women had several sports clubs—a tennis club, a pedestrian club, and a bowling club. Tournaments among women students were popular and frequently satisfied the desire of women to compete. Goucher College held its first archery tournament in 1894 and awarded the winner a blue and silver hat pin. California's tennis tournament was held with nearby Mills College.

Also during this period student associations, usually called Women's Athletic Associations, developed. Although these were "student" organizations, most of them were carefully advised and directed by a woman faculty member. The first year of the Winthrop Athletic Association was successful:

> . . . already it is becoming one of the strongest and most influential organizations at Winthrop. At the close of the school session for 1913–14 we adopted a constitution and elected officers for the year 1914–15. At the beginning of this session the Athletic Association took up its work and our officers have faithfully performed their duties. For a number of years there has been need for an organization to systematize athletics and to aid in arousing an interest in all outdoor and indoor sports. The Athletic Association is meeting this long-felt need of the student body, and we prophesy for it even greater influence and more rapid growth during the coming year.[43]

In 1917 Blanche Trilling of the University of Wisconsin called a meeting of Women's Athletic Associations and assisted the participants in organizing the Athletic Conference of American College Women. The purposes of the organization can be summarized: "The efforts of the Federation are devoted to those activities which might be sponsored by the Women's Athletic Association, and which open to the student opportunity for useful recreational pursuits and the development of outdoor hobbies."[44]

As described earlier, the committee formed to standardize the rules of basketball in 1899 represented the first concerted effort to organize and control women's and girls' sports in schools and colleges in the United States. In 1905 the Committee changed its name to the National Women's Basketball Committee. The Committee set a pattern that was followed as other women's sports needed to be standardized: rules were published and suggestions made for the conduct of events, but the Committee did not regulate or sanction events. It was only by mutual understanding that the committees exerted influence. In 1917 the National Women's Basketball Committee changed to the Committee on Women's Athletics and formed committees on basketball, field hockey, track and field, and swimming.

Figure 5.16   Women's basketball about 1900 at Hampton Institute. Courtesy of the Archives, Hampton University, Hampton, Virginia.

Other Collegiate Activities for Women

Most women's physical education programs included other activities in addition to sport. Formal gymnastics or exercise programs based upon the Swedish and Sargent systems were popular among many women physical educators, depending upon which training school that person may have attended. Those using the Sargent system also utilized anthropometric measurements to design individual programs of exercise and to evaluate progress. After the turn of the century, dance activities became increasingly popular and by 1920 many women's physical education programs included dance.

The work of François Delsarte, which influenced dance in education and in theater, was originally developed to train actors and singers in expressive gesture. Although the system was limited in popularity and short-lived among physical educators, it was widely used by teachers of elocution and singing because of its emphasis on grace and poise. Melvin Gilbert's aesthetic dancing, which had a similar emphasis, was carried into the educational system by the many teachers who received their preparation in professional schools in Boston.

Among Gilbert's students who were later to become known for their contributions to dance in education were Gertrude Colby, Mary Wood Hinman, and Elizabeth Burchenal.

Experimentation in creative self-expression permeated all the arts during this time, with experimenting in dance manifested by aesthetic dance, modern dance, and Isadora Duncan's "free dance." Largely self-trained, Isadora Duncan is often credited with being the founder of American modern dance, although the term was not in use during her time and "free dance" was her own descriptive term.

Ruth St. Denis and Ted Shawn, both excellent dancers, founded a new dance company, Denishawn, that contributed significantly to American dance. In its fifteen years it exposed Americans to expressive dance, and through its school another generation of expressive dancers gained training and performing experience. The best known were Doris Humphrey, Charles Weidman, and Martha Graham.

Isadora Duncan may have been the inspiration for natural dance, but it was Gertrude Colby who was responsible for its development and practice in the public schools. For educators the value of natural dance lay in the opportunity to introduce creative activity into the physical education program. Colby had been a student of Melvin Gilbert, but when she was called upon in 1913 to evolve a rhythmic movement program for children, she found that formal dance was not suited to the goals of the new program. She based her teaching on the natural movement of children, which permitted the individual expression of the young people. Her philosophy of natural dance was based on the desire to make the children "free instruments of expression, rhythmically unified . . . enabled to express in bodily movements the ideas and emotions which come from within."[45]

Folk dance, inaugurated by Elizabeth Burchenal in 1905, is still widely used in the public schools. In order to provide suitable dances for recreational activity, she learned the dances firsthand from immigrant groups in the United States and also studied in Europe. By 1920, dance was an accepted part of many school and college physical education curriculums.

Sport and Physical Education in Schools

Following the pattern set by college men, high school boys formed their own student-directed athletic associations. By the late 1890s, however, many of the public school systems that offered physical education employed physical education teachers who could also coach interscholastic teams. Because most early physical training teachers had been prepared only for the teaching of gymnastic classes, those with sport experience were highly sought after.

Interscholastic sport first developed in cities. A Detroit High School football team existed in 1888, and in 1890 a school periodical reported that the same school's baseball team had defeated Grosse Isle, 33–3.[46] By 1892, the

Detroit High School traveled as far as Ann Arbor for baseball games. The Ann Arbor High School boasted a baseball team in 1888, although no record of games is available until 1892, when thirteen games were played, nine of which were with class teams at the University of Michigan, two with university fraternity teams and two with Ypsilanti High School. Athletic field days, consisting of various track and field events between two or more high schools, were reported in Michigan in the eighties and nineties.[47] Wisconsin appears to have been the first state to organize a high school athletic association, and by the turn of the century three other midwestern states—Michigan, Illinois, and Indiana—had similar associations. In 1903, Dr. Luther Gulick established the Public School Athletic League in New York City, and provided an outstanding model of faculty-directed athletics. However, two years later, Dr. James Huff McCurdy's national study of public school physical education concluded that most interschool competition in the United States was still student-directed. Within the next decade the growth in interest and participation brought about increased faculty control.

Throughout the country, basketball was the most popular sport for girls at the high school level. Lansing High School in Michigan played four games against Michigan Agricultural College in 1898 and Detroit's Central High School played in an intramural league from about 1900 to 1908. In New York City a Girl's Branch of the Public School Athletic League was formed by Elizabeth Burchenal in 1905, although until 1909 the program was directed by a group of prominent women in the city rather than by the school system. It should also be noted that the program excluded interschool contests. In 1909 Burchenal became "Inspector of Girl's Athletics" and the program was brought under the full control of the school system.

Great concern was raised over the issue of interscholastic sport for girls. The major criticism focused on basketball and what was perceived as an increasing emphasis on "winning at all cost." Berenson wrote in 1901: "The greatest element of evil in the spirit of athletics in this country is the idea that one must win at any cost—that defeat is an unspeakable disgrace."[48] Other objections centered on specific issues such as men coaching girls' teams, male officials, spectators of both sexes, "sensational" reporting in the press, and possible physiological harm to the health of the participants. By 1917, steps were being taken by professional educators to control and de-emphasize interscholastic sport for girls. In that year Illinois formed the first state high school athletic association for girls.

Between 1885 and 1917 wide variations existed in programs of physical education in the elementary and secondary schools of the United States. In the 1880s both the German and the Swedish systems of gymnastics were practiced in major public school systems. Carl Betz, a trained gymnastics teacher with teaching experience in a number of German-American societies in the Midwest, presented a demonstration of German gymnastics to the Kansas City

Teachers' Institute in May, 1885. In December of that same year he was appointed the first director of physical training for the Kansas City Schools. Betz was a graduate of the Normal School of the North American Gymnastic Union. From 1886 to 1892, other graduates of this school introduced similar programs in the public schools of Chicago, Davenport, St. Louis, Milwaukee, Cleveland, Sandusky, Columbus, Cincinnati, and Dayton.[49] At this time exercises were conducted in the classroom by the classroom teacher and not in a gymnasium by a physical education specialist. The classroom teacher learned the exercises from another teacher who had been designated by the school to attend classes taught by the city supervisor of physical education. For example, by 1900 there were seven specialists in Chicago supervising thirty-four schools with a total of thirty thousand children.[50]

In the public schools of Boston, Swedish gymnastics were introduced in the late 1880s under the sponsorship of philanthropist Mary Hemenway. In 1890 the Boston School Committee formally adopted the system for all of the public schools of the city, employing Dr. Edward Hartwell, formerly of Johns Hopkins University, as the director of physical training. In his annual report to the Boston School Committee in 1893, Hartwell noted 1,098 classroom teachers directed Swedish gymnastics in fifty-five grammar schools.[51]

Luther Halsey Gulick was firmly committed to games and sport as a major educational force. As superintendent of the department of physical training at the YMCA Training School in Springfield, Massachusetts, from 1889 to 1900, and as the director of physical training in the public schools of New York City from 1903 to 1908, and through his leadership in the Playground Association of America and the Camp Fire Girls, Gulick was in a position to demonstrate his belief in the value of play and sport. He particularly stressed the role of sports in the "toughening of the individual for the achievements of life."[52]

Two other physical educators illustrate the change from formal gymnastics to the "new physical education." Beginning in 1893, Jesse Bancroft served as the director of physical training of the Brooklyn Public Schools until all of the New York borough schools were consolidated in 1903. During that period she trained representatives from each school who in turn taught and monitored the classroom teachers. While Bancroft began her career devoted to systematic exercise and postural development, she was clearly ahead of her time when she soon incorporated traditional games along with gymnastics in her program. In 1903, following the consolidation of the borough schools, she served as the assistant director of physical education of the city schools of Greater New York City under the director, Luther Gulick. The two built a model program that included physical education and interscholastic sports. In 1909 she wrote *Games for the Playground, Home, School, and Gymnasium,* perhaps the most comprehensive book of games in its time.

In Detroit, Michigan, Ethel Perrin, a graduate of the Boston Normal School of Gymnastics, where she also taught Swedish gymnastics during her fourteen years as a faculty member there, served as "Supervisor of Physical Culture" for the public schools between 1909 and 1923. During that period she developed an enviable program of physical education in the elementary and secondary schools of that city. Her program emphasized games and sports as well as story plays, free standing and rhythmical exercises, and correctives. Perrin measured her success by the twenty-four elementary school gymnasiums, three hundred and fifty physical education teaching specialists and fifteen supervisors that were in place by 1920.

By 1917, several large cities had model physical education programs in the public schools. These programs, for the most part, were informal, fostering not only physical development but also intellectual awareness through games and rhythmic activities. Prior to World War I American physical education began to incorporate the "new physical education" including exercise, play, games, and dance.

Commentary

While the organizational structure of today's sport and physical education in the United States was apparent in the decades following the Civil War, it became firmly established between 1885 and 1917. The organizing of sport and physical education and the resulting effects on Americans' conceptualization and justification of sport are the overriding developments in this period. Other major changes were the invention of new sports and the introduction of playgrounds in response to the social needs of the people. Also important is the influence of social organization on sport and physical education. The other themes of this book—the expectation of the good life, the diversity of the American people, the values that influence daily living, and the intermixing of technology, industrialization, and urbanization—are interwoven within these two major themes.

Between 1885 and 1917 the United States experienced continued growth, along with industrial, technological, and social change. While the distance between the rich and poor widened, the average or middle class remained an influential sector of American society. The great number of immigrants, the increasing size of the cities, the rapid growth of industry, and the opening up of the country west of the Mississippi River altered the lives of Americans in all walks of life. Most forms of sport grew rapidly, and the distinction between professional sport and amateur sport became clearly demarcated, as did sport for whites, sport for blacks, sport for the wealthy, sport for the middle classes, sport for the poor, and sport for women.

Social stratification continued to define certain aspects of the sport world. Members of wealthy families enjoyed sports such as tennis, golf, sailing, and polo, and competed as amateurs. They strongly endorsed the traditional European view of amateurism, which permitted play only for the love of the game and not for any monetary reward. Many wealthy, influential men helped organize amateur sport associations and were active in the Amateur Athletic Union, United States Lawn Tennis Association, United States Golf Association, and the Olympic Movement. In spite of the prevailing view that women lacked physical vigor, many upper-class women enjoyed a wide range of recreational sports as well as tennis and golf.

For the middle class in this period sport functioned as entertainment, and for many it was the basis of community spirit as they rooted for home-town teams. For countless numbers of immigrants, especially men and boys, sport served as one means of joining the American mainstream. On the other hand, many ethnic groups retained their own sports. As public playgrounds and parks were built, more and more middle-class and working people, especially children, had access to American games and sport. Some reformers viewed the parks and playgrounds as a means of social control. However, public parks also served to produce champions such as Maurice McLoughlin in tennis.

By 1900 the configuration of modern American sport had emerged—team sports, ball sports, and a sport for each season: professional baseball in the spring and summer, college football in the fall, and basketball for everyone in the winter. America's Big Three of the 1980s were easily identifiable before World War I.

While attempts to bring blacks into baseball were unsuccessful, black boxer Jack Johnson became a sport champion when he defeated Jim Jeffries. Most whites did not accept Johnson's victory, and race riots broke out in several cities. In general, during this period, as in other sectors of society, black sport developed apart from white sport.

The country's proclivity for team sports stands out clearly. After years of turbulent confrontation between players and leagues, baseball established an organization that consisted of two major leagues—the National League and the American League. Each league determined a champion to compete in the "World Series" at the close of each season, a tradition that has endured for over eighty years. Two other games in which persons or teams contested other individuals or teams were devised in the 1890s and can be regarded as truly American. Although both basketball and volleyball answered the need for a winter indoor game, basketball became the more popular of the two. They began as modern sport, with a playlike quality, demand for physical skills, and dependence on facilities and equipment.

In colleges and universities men's sport revolved around college football, which remained popular, but also continued to be rough and brutal. In spite of these problems it brought recognition to institutions, and by their efforts to control the sport, the administrators shifted the responsibility for athletics from the students and alumni to faculty and athletic administrators. Larger facilities such as stadiums and gymnasiums were needed and they, too, required managing by administrators, not students. As a means of controlling intercollegiate athletics, the NCAA was formed and remains today as the principal governing body for collegiate sport.

Those who planned and organized women's sport in colleges reacted unfavorably to the conditions found in the men's program and carefully built their athletics to conform to a philosophy which facilitated the controlled development of competition, usually on the campus. As soon as sports such as basketball and field hockey were developed, the women added them to their program. At the turn of the century, control of women's collegiate sport began with the appointment of a "Committee on Women's Basketball."

Physical educators founded the American Association for the Advancement of Physical Education at the beginning of this period. Gradually, public schools and institutions of higher learning incorporated some form of gymnastics in the curriculum to promote the students' health. As sports generally increased in popularity and basketball was invented, both men's and women's physical education programs included more and more sport. Not only were games and sport obviously popular among children and high school and college youth, they were also compatible with the thinking of educational reformers. As educational philosophy changed, the curriculum reflected the thinking of these reformers. School was a real-life laboratory where the "whole" child learned to live in a democratic society. The learning of societal values could be accomplished not only through reading, writing, and arithmetic, but also through art, drama, music, and *play*. These beliefs led to a uniquely American form of physical education.

Americans' tendency to organize their lives was clearly evident in sport and physical education. In response to a number of problems, professional baseball reorganized into its present form. As amateur sport grew so did associations to govern the increasing numbers of players and tournaments, the championships, and special prizes like the Davis Cup. The first modern Olympic Games, held in 1896, foresaw the need for international sport organizations. With the NCAA in place to conduct men's intercollegiate athletics, the number of college conferences increased to regulate and supervise sport. Newly formed committees and associations approved and published rules for women's sports. Organized sport reached youth on playgrounds and with organizations such as the Boy Scouts and Girl Scouts. By the end of this period, 1885 to 1917, sport and physical education had become organized and institutionalized in American life.

Suggestions for Further Reading

1. Riess, Steven A. "The Baseball Magnate and Urban Politics in the Progressive Era: 1895–1920." *Journal of Sport History* 1, no. 1 (May 1974): 41–62.
2. Smith, Robert A. *A Social History of the Bicycle.* New York: American Heritage Press, 1972.
3. Spears, Betty. "The Emergence of Women in Sport," in *Women's Athletics: Coping with Controversy,* ed. Barbara J. Hoepner. Washington, D.C.: American Association for Health, Physical Education, and Recreation, 1974.
4. Swanson, Richard A. "The Acceptance and Influence of Play in American Protestantism." *Quest* 11 (December 1968): 58–70.
5. Hardy, Stephen. *How Boston Played.* Boston: Northeastern University Press, 1982.
6. Zuckerman, Jerome, Stull, G. Allan, and Eyler, Marvin H. "The Black Athlete in Post-Bellum 19th Century." *The Physical Educator* 29 (October 1972): 142–146.

Notes

1. Frank C. Richter, *Richter's History and Records of Base Ball* (Philadelphia: Francis C. Richter, 1914), 61.
2. Cited in Albert G. Spalding, *Base Ball, America's National Game* (New York: American Sports Publishing Company, 1911), 272.
3. Ibid., 273–76.
4. Steven A. Riess, "The Baseball Magnate and Urban Politics in the Progressive Era: 1895–1920," *Journal of Sport History* 1, no. 1 (May 1974): 41–62.
5. Jerome Zuckerman, G. Allan Stull, and Marvin H. Eyler, "The Black Athlete in Post-Bellum 19th Century," *The Physical Educator* 29 (October 1972): 145.
6. Edwin B. Henderson and the editors of *Sport Magazine, The Black Athlete— Emergence and Arrival* (New York: International Library of Negro History, 1968), 32.
7. John Durant and Edward Rice, *Come Out Fighting* (New York: Duell, Sloan and Pearce, 1946), 32.
8. Alexander J. Young, Jr., "Sam Langford, 'The Boston Tarbaby'," *Proceedings,* The Second Canadian Symposium on The History of Sport and Physical Education, Windsor, Ontario (May 1–3, 1972): 57.
9. Parimutuel is "a form of betting in which the total amount wagered, less a share for the state and management, is divided among the winning bettors in proportion to the amount wagered. In effect, the bettors themselves set the odds." *Encyclopedia International,* Vol. 14 (New York: Grolier Incorporated, 1975), 4:80.
10. Luther Gulick, "What the American Young Men's Christian Associations are doing for the Physical Welfare of Young Men," *Annual Autumn Games,* Young Men's Christian Association of the City of New York, October 13, 1888, 18, 20. A. G. Spalding Company Archives, Chicopee, Massachusetts.
11. John Rickards Betts, *America's Sporting Heritage: 1850–1950* (Reading, MA: Addison-Wesley Publishing Company, 1974), 181.
12. John R. Schleppi, " 'It Pays': John H. Patterson and Industrial Recreation at the National Cash Register Company," *Journal of Sport History* 6 (Winter 1979):20–27.

13. Wilma J. Pesavento, "Sport and Recreation in the Pullman Experiment, 1880–1900," *Journal of Sport History* 9 (Summer 1982):38–62.
14. James H. Hitchman, "Origins of Yacht Racing in British Columbia and Washington, 1870–1914," *Proceedings, 1976,* North American Society for Sport History, Eugene, Oregon (June 1976): 30–31.
15. Edwin B. Henderson, *The Negro in Sports* (Washington, D.C.: Associated Publishers, 1949), 206.
16. Will Grimsley, *Golf: Its History, People and Events* (Englewood Cliffs, N.J.: Prentice-Hall, 1966), 36.
17. Edwin B. Henderson, *The Negro in Sports* (Washington, D.C.: Associated Publishers, 1949), 223.
18. Robert A. Smith, *A Social History of the Bicycle* (New York: American Heritage Press, 1972), 116–17.
19. Ibid., 117–18.
20. John A. Lucas and Ronald A. Smith, *Saga of American Sport* (Philadelphia: Lea & Febiger, 1978), 165; Mary Lou LeCompte and William H. Beezley, "Any Sunday in April: The Rise of Sport in San Antonio and the Hispanic Borderlands," *Journal of Sport History* 13 (Summer 1986): 134.
21. Mary Lou LeCompte and William H. Beezley, "Any Sunday in April: The Rise of Sport in San Antonio and the Hispanic Borderlands," *Journal of Sport History* 13 (Summer 1986): 134.
22. James F. Hoy, "The Origins and Originality of Rodeo," in *Sports and Recreation in the West,* ed. Donald J. Mrozek (Manhattan, KS: Sunflower University Press, 1978), 24.
23. Mary Lou LeCompte and William H. Beezley, "Any Sunday in April: The Rise of Sport in San Antonio and the Hispanic Borderlands," *Journal of Sport History* 13 (Summer 1986): 139.
24. Mary L. Remley, "From Sidesaddle to Rodeo," in *Sports and Recreation in the West* ed. Donald J. Mrozek (Manhattan, KS: Sunflower University Press, 1978), 45.
25. Ibid., 50.
26. James Naismith, *Basketball, Its Origin and Development* (New York: Association Press, 1941), 53–55.
27. Senda Berenson, ed., "Official Rules," in *Basketball for Women* (New York: American Sports Publishing Co., 1903), 86.
28. Senda Berenson, "The Significance of Basket Ball for Women," in *Basketball for Women* (New York: American Sports Publishing Co., 1903), 41.
29. Ibid., 41, 43.
30. C. E. Silvia, *Lifesaving and Water Safety Instruction* (New York: Association Press, 1960), 21.
31. Jane Addams, *Spirit of Youth and the City Streets* (New York: Macmillan, 1909), 1.
32. Stephen Hardy, Chapter 4, 5 in *How Boston Played* (Boston: Northeastern University Press, 1982).
33. Clarence E. Rainwater, *The Play Movement in the United States* (Chicago: The University of Chicago Press, 1922), 22–44.
34. *YMCA Training School Catalogue, 1890–91,* Springfield, MA: 19.
35. Walter P. Kroll, *Perspectives in Physical Education* (New York: Academic Press, 1971), 194.
36. Wilbur P. Bowen, "Seven Years of Progress in Preparing Teachers of Physical Education," *American Physical Education Review* 27 (February 1922): 64.

37. Senda Berenson, "Editorial," *Basketball for Women* (New York: American Sports Publishing Co., 1903), 7.
38. *Proceedings of the Third Annual Convention of the Intercollegiate Athletic Association of the United States,* January 2, 1909, 27–28.
39. *Proceedings of the 13th Annual Convention of the National Collegiate Athletic Association,* December 27, 1918, 33.
40. Betty Spears, "The Emergence of Women in Sport," in *Women's Athletics: Coping with Controversy,* ed. Barbara J. Hoepner (Washington, D.C.: American Association for Health, Physical Education, and Recreation, 1974), 33.
41. Nancy Struna and Mary L. Remley, "Physical Education for Women at the University of Wisconsin, 1863–1913: A Half Century of Progress," *Canadian Journal of History of Sport and Physical Education* 4, no. 1 (1973): 21.
42. Roberta J. Park, "History and Structure of the Department of Physical Education at the University of California with Special Reference to Women's Sports,"1976, 5.
43. *The Tatler* (Rock Hill, So. Carolina: Winthrop College, 1915), 147; cited in Rhonda K. Fleming, "A History of the Department of Physical Education at Winthrop College," Master's thesis, University of North Carolina at Greensboro, 1973, 53–54.
44. Marguerite Schwarz, "The Athletic Federation of College Women," *Journal of Health and Physical Education* 7 (May 1936): 297.
45. Gertrude Colby, *Natural Rhythms and Dances* (New York: A. S. Barnes Company, 1922).
46. *The Argus,* October 1890, 13.
47. Lewis L. Forsythe, *Athletics in Michigan High Schools: The First Hundred Years* (New York: Prentice-Hall, Inc., 1950), 38, 49.
48. Senda Berenson, *Basket Ball for Women* (New York: American Sports Publishing Company, 1901), 20.
49. Elizabeth C. Umstead, "Elementary School Physical Education: 1885–1920" in *The History of Elementary School Physical Education: 1885–1985* (Reston, VA: National Association for Sport and Physical Education, 1985), 12.
50. Ibid.
51. Edward M. Hartwell, *Report of the Director of Physical Training* (Boston: Press of Rockwell and Churchill, 1895).
52. Luther Halsey Gulick, *Physical Education by Muscular Exercise* (Philadelphia: P. Blakiston's Son & Company, 1904), 47.

Time Line

1918
World War I ended, November 11
1919
Senate rejected joining League of
Nations
Prohibition (Amendment Eighteen)
1920
Women's Suffrage (Amendment
Nineteen)
1921
Johnson Act, restricting immigration
1923
"Teapot Dome" scandal, Harding
administration
1927
First commercial airline flight
1929
Wall Street Crash: Depression

1933
"New Deal" social legislation enacted
Prohibition repealed (Amendment
Twenty-one)

1939
World War II begins in Europe

1941
Pearl Harbor attacked; U.S. enters
WWII
1945
First atomic bomb dropped, Hiroshima
World War II ended

1919
Baseball scandal, Chicago "Black" Sox
1919–20
Man O' War won twenty out of
twenty-one races

1922
Paris track meet sponsored by FSFI
1923
White House conference on women's
athletics
1920s
Age of sport stars
1929
Carnegie investigation of men's
intercollegiate athletics
1930
Bobby Jones won Grand Slam in golf
1930s
Ren's basketball team
1931
Mabel Lee first woman president, APEA
1932
Babe Didrikson starred in 1932
Olympics
1934
Men's collegiate basketball tournament,
Madison Square Garden
1939
NCAA Men's Basketball Tournament
initiated
Little League founded
1943
All-American Girls Baseball League

6 The Growth of Sport and Physical Education During Social Change, 1917–1945

Overview

Americans were deeply shocked when eight members of the Chicago White Sox baseball team were accused of "fixing" the 1919 World Series. The public promptly called them the "Black Sox" and rejoiced when the national pastime was cleaned up and Judge Kenesaw Mountain Landis was installed as Commissioner to preside over the game. In 1923 almost 150,000 automobile racing enthusiasts watched the Memorial Day Races at Indianapolis, and more than 300,000 overall saw the World Series. In that same year, under Tex Rickard's promotion, three boxing matches drew 200,000. Superstars Babe Ruth, Bill Tilden, Helen Wills, Bobby Jones, Babe Didrikson, and many others became familiar names in millions of households. As college football grew from a casual campus sport to a major entertainment business, players such as Red Grange from the University of Illinois and the "Four Horsemen" from the University of Notre Dame were the heroes in the stadiums. Against a backdrop of cultural change and variety, the country entered an era frequently referred to as the "Golden Age of Sport."

The Armistice following World War I thrust the United States into a position of world leadership, but the country refused this role, voting against joining the League of Nations. Internal affairs absorbed the country's attention. In spite of complaints about the "iniquitous" income tax, the average American slowly accepted the increasing influence of the federal government on daily life. Indeed, overwhelming public support made possible the passage of the Eighteenth Amendment—Prohibition—prohibiting the sale of alcoholic beverages; and popular sentiment expressed in the slogan "America for Americans" fostered legislation that slowed the flow of immigrants into the country.

Inventions and technological advances led to new industries, more jobs, and higher wages. Labor unions gained power, obtained better working conditions for laborers, and the right to bargain in their behalf. Good jobs were plentiful and many Americans enjoyed shorter workdays with good pay, time-saving devices such as more efficient furnaces, electric stoves, and vacuum cleaners, and a family car.

During the 1920s, many people continued to cherish traditional beliefs in religion, manners, morals, and dress. A large majority of the people, especially in the rural areas, retained the ethic that hard work and regular savings led to success. These Americans disapproved of flappers and speakeasies and endorsed Tennessee's attempts to stop the teaching of Darwin's theory of evolution. Other Americans of the Jazz Age rejected established customs. Women voted, bobbed their hair, wore knee-length dresses, and *possibly* smoked in public. Both men and women enjoyed automobiles with rumble seats, visited speakeasies, and danced the Charleston. Church attendance among this group dwindled as Sunday became a day of rest and recreation. Many Americans adopted a middle-of-the-road approach to these swift social changes. Women might wear knee-length dresses, for instance, but might not smoke. In many families, Sunday recreation could be enjoyed, but only after attending church.

John Dewey's philosophy of "learning by doing" freed children of rote learning, and Freud's theories furnished adults with contemporary personality models. For Dewey the education of the child began by utilizing the immediate surroundings and daily experiences of the individual, and continually expanding these activities, thus permitting the child to "learn by doing." Educators further developed these ideas into acquiring citizenship and social skills that would foster the goals of democracy in the United States.

Male physical educators endorsed these trends, emphasizing that male gender role expectations such as team play, working with others, cooperation, as well as playing to win could be taught through sport. Women physical educators interpreted these theories as consistent with female gender role expectations in a modern society such as playing one's best, gaining a sense of honor, learning self-sacrifice for the sake of the team, and developing a democratic spirit. Thus, sport for men was viewed as different from sport for women, not so much in substance but in the manner in which it was conducted.

The American interpretation of Freud's views reinforced this position. He considered the male body to be normal and male characteristics to be active, aggressive, logical, and independent, consistent with rugged, masculine sport. He viewed the female body as incomplete and inferior, assigning to the female personality traits such as emotional, intuitive, passive, and dependent. While not agreeing completely with Freud, women physical educators adapted sport for women to conform to "acceptable" female traits.

Prosperity also meant that more children could be educated and could afford to stay in school longer. By 1940, almost twenty-five percent of American youth had graduated from high school. At the same time, college attendance continued to climb in both private and state-supported institutions. Physical education emerged as an accepted part of the curriculum in secondary and post-secondary institutions and in some large cities it extended into the elementary grades. Interscholastic and intercollegiate athletics, especially for men, attained unprecedented popularity.

Shortened working hours and good pay made it possible to attend professional sport events, buy sport equipment, and enjoy a wide variety of sports. The family car made beaches, golf courses, stadiums, and parks accessible. The radio brought sport events into the living room; daily newspapers devoted several pages to sport and the bulging Sunday papers an entire section; sportscasters and sports writers became part of the sport world.

After 1929 when the depression struck the United States, the government broadened its responsibility of providing for the basic needs of people. Social legislation which we now accept was considered radical at that time. Increased social consciousness was also evident when both Protestant and Catholic groups, especially in depressed urban areas where welfare programs were necessary, preached a social gospel. As increasing numbers of black people moved from the South to the northern cities in search of a better life, black churches became functioning neighborhood centers in these cities.

While many sports suffered during the depression, overall sport for the average citizen increased. In 1934, eighty thousand crowded in to see a doubleheader baseball game in St. Louis and when Santa Anita race track opened in 1937, fifty thousand Americans attended and wagered $790,000. Again, during World War II sport was affected drastically, but was never dropped or banned. All in all, between World War I and World War II, the United States became a nation in which sport was firmly woven into the fabric of its life— as entertainment, as an integral part of education, and as an accepted and worthwhile way to spend time.

This chapter looks at sport and physical education during the boom of the 1920s, the depression of the 1930s, and World War II—all periods of rapid social change. It will examine the burgeoning of professional and amateur sport, as well as the phenomenon of sport stardom. It will also show the different modes of development of men's and women's sport and physical education programs in educational institutions.

Professional Sport

Professional football and basketball were almost unheard of in the early twenties, but by 1934, a crowd of thirty-seven thousand watched the New York Giants and Detroit Lions football teams in a National Football League championship game. In basketball two strong teams developed in New York City, the white Original Celtics and the black New York Renaissance ("Rens"). By the middle thirties water shows and ice shows provided family entertainment, and other sports such as wrestling and cycling attracted sport fans with special interests. But it was the national pastime, baseball, which continued as the favorite of the sport fan.

Baseball

Perhaps the most important change in professional sport was the adoption of the commissioner form of organization, which resulted from the 1919 scandals. Allegations of a "fix" had circulated from the time of the 1919 World Series between the Chicago White Sox and the Cincinnati Reds, which was won by the Reds. Rumors continued to persist not only about the Series, but also regarding other games, and finally, in 1920, a grand jury was appointed to investigate the situation. The investigations did indeed reveal that the 1919 Series had been "fixed." The gamblers had used a go-between, Billy Maharg, who in turn finally involved eight players—Eddie Cicotte, Joe Jackson, Fred McMullin, "Swede" Risberg, Oscar (Happy) Felsch, Claude Williams, George (Buck) Weaver, and Arnold (Chick) Gandil. The men had promised to lose the series in return for a substantial amount of money in several payments, although the only payment actually made was after the White Sox lost the first game. The plan almost backfired when Kerr, *not* one of the eight players, pitched and won the third game. The eight men, called the *Black* Sox by the press and people alike, were indicted, tried, but acquitted when the confessions of Cicotte, Williams, and Jackson disappeared.

This incident, along with internal problems in the National Commission, led to the reorganization of professional baseball and the appointment of a commissioner with complete responsibility for the integrity of the sport. Judge Kenesaw Mountain Landis of the United States District Court in Chicago was named the first commissioner. In accepting the position he explained:

> It came like a flash to me, thinking of my boy, what baseball meant to him when he was young; what it means to him to-day. And I knew that is what baseball means to every kid in America. And then I realized that I could not refuse the responsibility and decided that if there were anything I could do to keep that game clean and honest, and to make it so that the kids of the United States never shall lose their ideals of the sport, it was a bit more than my duty to do it.[1]

To make good his promise to clean up baseball the eight White Sox players who had been involved in the Black Sox scandal were banned from professional baseball for life. Baseball was again the subject of a court case in 1922 when the United States Supreme Court declared that organized baseball did not constitute commerce among the states, thus upholding the reserve clause in players' contracts.

After it was reorganized under a commissioner and the disgraced players ousted, baseball continued to grow, enhanced by improved equipment, the attention of the mass media, and the emergence of the sport hero. A new ball, more tightly wound, produced more home runs and more lively play. The year the new ball was introduced, Babe Ruth's home runs increased from twenty-nine to fifty-nine. Not only did such feats please the fans, but also the increased coverage in the papers and over the radio enabled them to follow the

Figure 6.1   Byron Bancroft Johnson, Judge Kenesaw Mountain Landis, Charles Comiskey. Courtesy Spalding Archives, Chicopee, Massachusetts.

sport more closely. Men such as John Drebinger of the *New York Times,* Shirley Povich of the *Washington Post,* and Paul Gallico of the *New York Daily News* chronicled the game each summer, reported the play of the stars, and analyzed the increasing body of statistics. Although the sports page was by now a regular feature of the newspaper, the possibility of broadcasting the games over the radio made baseball owners fear that attendance in the ball parks would fall. But when sportscasters like Graham McNamee recreated the game for eager listeners, interest in the live game did not diminish but to everyone's surprise, increased.

> The popularity of radio continued to grow, and its consumer market expanded to include 250,000 auto radios by 1932. By then radio's overwhelming appeal crushed its opposition. Certainly owners welcomed the offer of networks to pay for the privilege of broadcasting games. Late in 1933, owners let bids for the exclusive rights to broadcast Series games. Landis represented baseball at the annual bargaining sessions, and in 1936 he signed a $100,000 contract for exclusive broadcasting rights.[2]

The sports writers and sportscasters had exciting games, thrilling Series, and star players to report during the two decades between the wars. While the New York Giants and New York Yankees dominated the play, teams from many parts of the country stimulated unexpected interest. Washington won its first pennant in 1924 with the President of the United States, Calvin Coolidge, joining the welcome celebration. In 1926 Rogers Hornsby led the St. Louis Cardinals to their first pennant, and in 1934 the Detroit Tigers won the American League pennant. But the thirties was the Yankees' decade, for they won five World Series.

George Herman "Babe" Ruth (1894–1948). Born in Baltimore, Ruth spent most of his boyhood at St. Mary's Industrial School for Boys. In 1914 he left St. Mary's to join a minor league team, the Baltimore Orioles. By the end of the season he had moved to a major league team, the Boston Red Sox. In 1919 he went to the Yankees where his career soared. Many of his records stood for years and some still stand today. He made money and he spent it, but he continued to play superstar ball. During his twenty seasons with baseball he made the game livelier, set records, and was a major box office attraction. The stories of his life away from the diamond were not often flattering, but in spite of them, and in spite of his rough manner and speech, his soft round face, slightly pudgy body and tapered ankles, he played baseball brilliantly, he played it joyously, and the fans loved it.

He met an elemental need of the crowd. Every hero must have his human flaw which he shares with his followers. In Ruth it was hedonism, as exaggerated in folklore and fable.

The combination of great skill on the field and a shared flaw off the field made him the most admired and theatrical man in the game.[3]

At forty years of age, his last year with the Yankees, he hit 22 home runs. The following year he moved to Boston where he did not finish the season. Ruth appeared two more times in front of his beloved fans—on Babe Ruth Day in the Yankee stadium on April 27, 1947 and again, just two months before he died, in June, 1948.

This was also the period of the sport star. From Babe Ruth's sixty home runs in 1927 to his total of 714 career homers, the Babe outshone them all. Between 1920 and 1925, Rogers Hornsby led the National League in batting and from 1921 to 1925, averaged .397, .401, .384, .424, and .403. Ty Cobb, one of the greatest hitters of all times, retired in 1928. The two Deans, Dizzy and Paul, pitched the St. Louis Cardinals to victory in the 1934 World Series. Also in 1934, Lou Gehrig set a new record for consecutive games played. Toward the end of the period new superstars such as Joe DiMaggio and Lefty Gomez appeared.

Professional baseball for black players in the 1920s was reminiscent of the early years of the game, before the National League was formed. With a strict color line in white organized baseball, scores of black teams operated throughout the Northeast, the South, and the Midwest. Often operating with minimal financial backing and plagued with contract jumping and erratic schedules, many teams had a short-lived existence.

Several team owners, led by Andrew "Rube" Foster, manager of Chicago's American Giants, recognized the advantages of a black professional league structure and in 1920 formed the National Association of Colored Professional Baseball Clubs and its major league circuit, the Negro National League (NNL), composed of teams in Midwestern cities. In late 1923 the Mutual Association of Eastern Colored Baseball Clubs, popularly known as the Eastern

Figure 6.2   George Herman "Babe" Ruth. Courtesy Spalding Archives, Chicopee, Massachusetts.

Colored League (ECL), was formed. While there were immediate conflicts over contract jumping and the raiding of NNL teams, the owners agreed to participate in a world series between the champions of the two leagues at the end of the 1924 season.

Both leagues suffered from weak structures and internal strife.[4] While the NNL had a strong, efficient, forceful leader in Rube Foster, he was often accused of dictatorial power. In the twelve years of life of the NNL, only three teams won pennants; and with this imbalance of power and with Foster's departure in 1926 the league died in 1931.

Since the Eastern Colored League lacked a single strong leader, rival owners exercised their own policies, such as cancelling scheduled league games in favor of more profitable games with nonleague teams. In 1929 the ECL, reorganized as the American Negro League, disbanded after one season.

In 1932 there was a short-lived effort to establish a new major circuit, the East-West League. In the middle of the depression, the league was unable to survive a full season. The following year, W. A. (Gus) Greenlea, a wealthy Pittsburgh numbers kingpin and tavern owner, formed a new Negro National League, composed of six Eastern and Midwestern clubs. In 1937, when the Negro American League (NAL) was established with clubs in the Midwest and South, the NNL became based in the East.[5] Unlike their predecessors, these leagues survived the depression and remained financially stable through the late thirties and forties.

The black world series was never an outstanding success, but the black All-Star game was. Like their white counterparts, the new NNL and NAL introduced an All-Star game in 1933. The following year the white All-Star game attracted 48,363 fans and the black All-Stars 30,000. The black All-Star event continued to be popular and in 1943 it was played before 51,723 fans in Chicago's Comiskey Park.[6]

Pressure to admit black professional ball players into the major leagues increased during World War II. In 1943 New York State Senator Charles E. Perry introduced a resolution in the New York Senate, pointing out the state's antidiscrimination laws. The resolution was sent to Judge Landis, who in response declared that each club could employ any players of their choice. In April of 1945 Congressman Marcantonio from New York introduced a resolution in the United States House of Representatives calling for an investigation of racial discrimination in baseball. New York City Mayor Fiorello LaGuardia appointed a committee to study the situation. Branch Rickey, president of the Brooklyn Dodgers, was a member of the committee, though he later resigned. According to the committee's report black players were excluded from professional baseball because of tradition and because of prejudice. The report further concluded that there was no rule excluding Negroes from organized baseball and no reason that Negroes and whites could not play together on a team.

Figure 6.3   Josh Gibson, all-star catcher in the Negro Leagues. Wide World.

By this time Branch Rickey had initiated plans to sign Jackie Robinson for the Montreal Royals and, later, to bring him to the Brooklyn Dodgers. Many agreed that during this period the caliber of play among the best of the black leagues was as good as, if not better than, that of the white leagues. In reply to a counter-charge that the black players preferred to play in their own league, "Dr. J. B. Martin, president of the Negro American League, said that the league had no intention of standing in the players' way 'if they had a chance to advance.' "[7] Players such as Josh Gibson, Cool Papa Bell, and John Henry

Josh Gibson (1911-1947). Josh Gibson did not live to see Jackie Robinson break the color line in white major league baseball. Born in Buena Vista, Georgia, he had moved to Pittsburgh by 1929 where he worked in a steel mill and played semipro ball with the Crawford Colored Giants. On July 25, 1930, he attended the game between the Homestead Grays and the Kansas City Monarchs during which the Grays' catcher was injured and Gibson, well known locally, was pressed into service. Gibson quit the steel mills and played black pro baseball for the next sixteen years and was considered one of the hardest hitters of all time, chalking up 89 home runs in one season. In 1931 he hit 75 homers and 61, 72, and 69 in the next three years. Playing 123 games for the Pittsburgh Crawfords, he had 441 putouts, 49 assists, and batted .379.

In 1937, along with "Satch" Paige and others Gibson was lured to San Domingo, which paid higher salaries. When Josh returned to finish the season with the Grays, he was fined a quarter of a month's salary for the escapade. Because of further salary problems he played with Vera Cruz in the Mexican League in 1940 and 1941. However, Gibson returned to the black pro teams and played many All-Star games. Josh Gibson, one of the great players in black baseball, played his last season in 1946, batting .331 and knocking in 27 home runs.

Lloyd were stars of the black leagues of the 1920s and 1930s. For them, the integration of organized baseball came too late. Others, such as Jackie Robinson, Satchel Paige and Roy Campanella, played major league baseball and demonstrated their outstanding ability.

With the integration of major league baseball in the late forties and early 1950s, the economic base of the NNL and the NAL disintegrated. The NNL folded following the 1948 season. The NAL continued playing before smaller and smaller crowds for another twelve years before its final season in 1960.

Boxing

When Tex Rickard, who had promoted the Jeffries-Johnson fight in 1910, saw Jack Dempsey fight Jess Willard, he recognized another champion. He proceeded to launch a decade of champions, earning for boxing the approval of many who had questioned the respectability of the sport. He promoted the 1921 Dempsey-Carpentier match and turned the 1926 Dempsey-Tunney fight into a two million-dollar venture. Gene Tunney, a quiet, scientific boxer, and the slugging Dempsey met again the following year in a controversial fight in Chicago. After six rounds, Dempsey caught Tunney off guard and knocked him down. A delayed, but legal count gave Tunney a few seconds more time to recover, regain his feet, and go on to win the fight. For a time interest in boxing declined until Joe Louis, the "Brown Bomber" from Detroit, began his series of victories. Having been thoroughly defeated by the German, Max Schmelling, before he captured the crown from James J. Braddock in 1937, Louis fought Schmelling again the second time. In the era of Hitler's speeches about the purity of the Aryan race, the fight had overtones of a black American fighting a white Nazi. Louis, the black American, won in only two minutes and four seconds. In 1942 Louis defeated first Max Baer and then Abe Simon, donating the first purse to the Naval Relief Fund and the second to the Army Relief Fund. Inducted into the army in February, 1942, Louis was not required to defend his title until after the war.

Horse Racing

Among the more popular "heroes" of the "Golden Age of Sport" was a two-year-old horse named Man O'War. Running only as a two- and three-year-old in 1919 and 1920, he won all but one of his twenty-one races, and lost that one to a horse appropriately named Upset. Like other sports, racing grew during the years between the two wars, and even though the sport was hard hit by the depression, it increased from 1,022 racing days in 1920 to 2,228 days in 1942. In 1937 Man O'War's son, War Admiral, won the triple crown—the Kentucky Derby, the Preakness, and the Belmont Stakes. In the same year the famous Sea Biscuit was the year's leading money winner. But the horse of the era was still Man O'War who, in 1950, was voted by the Associated Press as one of the greatest athletes of the first half of the twentieth century.

Football

The modern era of professional football began on September 17, 1920, when representatives of eleven clubs met at Ralph Hays' Hupmobile Automobile agency in Canton, Ohio. They formed the American Professional Football Association, which organized several independent teams playing in the smaller towns and cities of Pennsylvania, western New York, and Ohio.

Beginning in 1894 and 1895 with teams from Greensburg and Latrobe, Pennsylvania, professional football had existed for twenty-five years. Pickup teams of laborers and current or recent college stars played weekend games in these and other coal-mining and factory towns of Pennsylvania and eastern Ohio. The college players were often guaranteed a stipend for each game but collected the money only if any remained after the team met its expenses. Little formalized scheduling and few binding contracts existed, and it was commonplace for players to change teams each season and sometimes during the season.

In 1896 and 1897 the Allegheny Athletic Club of Pittsburgh organized successful teams with college stars such as Yale's Pudge Heffelfinger and Princeton's Langdon "Biffy" Lea. In 1902 Philadelphia challenged its western Pennsylvania rival with two teams, sponsored by the city's two major league baseball clubs. Baseball's famed Connie Mack managed the Philadelphia Athletics football team. Pittsburgh's team that same year boasted baseball star Christy Mathewson on its roster. These big city teams dominated play, attracting most of the well-known players with salaries from four hundred dollars to twelve hundred dollars for the season.

The smaller cities of the area, however, kept professional football alive until it became useful to form a professional football league. The teams in the new American Professional Football Association in 1920 included the Canton Bulldogs, Cleveland Indians, Dayton Triangles, Akron Steels, Massillon Tigers, Rochester (New York) Kodaks, Rock Island (Illinois) Independents, Muncie (Indiana), Hammond (Indiana) Professionals, Chicago Cardinals, and the Staley Athletic Club of Decatur, Illinois. They set a membership fee of one hundred dollars and agreed not to sign players with college eligibility remaining and to refrain from tampering with players signed to other member clubs. Jim Thorpe was named president of the association.

While some of the clubs succeeded financially, others did not. This, in addition to problems in scheduling, guarantees, player contracts, and the fact that Thorpe lacked administrative expertise, contributed to major changes in the league. The name was changed to the National Football League (NFL) and Joe F. Carr of Columbus became the new president. The cost of a franchise was lowered to fifty dollars, and Green Bay, Columbus, Detroit, Buffalo, and Cincinnati joined the league while Massillon, Muncie, and Hammond withdrew. The Staley Athletic Club moved from Decatur to Chicago under the ownership of young player-coach George Halas, who changed the name of the team to the Chicago Bears in 1922.

The league grew to 18 members with the addition of Toledo, Milwaukee, Minneapolis, Louisville, Hammond, Racine (Wisconsin), Evansville (Indiana), and Marion (Ohio), while Cleveland, Cincinnati, and Detroit withdrew. Franchise shifts continued over the next several years as the league struggled for stability. Just as professional baseball battled to gain respect and social acceptance in the nineteenth century, professional football fought for these same values in the twentieth century. Many college coaches discouraged their players from turning professional following graduation, since they viewed professional football as below the dignity of college players. Fielding Yost, the successful coach of the University of Michigan, openly criticized professional football even though he had played for professional teams while still a student at the University of West Virginia in the 1890s.

In 1925 two events helped to enhance the respectability and visibility of the young NFL. First, Tim Mara, a successful bookmaker, established the Giants in New York, where big-city fans could read daily newspaper accounts of the games. Second, near the end of the 1925 season, the sensational Harold "Red" Grange, following his final college game at the University of Illinois, signed a contract with the Chicago Bears. Already a household word as a result of his three-year college career, Grange was an immediate box office attraction. Furthermore, other college stars followed him into professional football.

However, the NFL's struggle for survival continued. Although by 1927, teams such as the New York Giants broke even financially, many pro teams continued at a marginal level. Under the leadership of Carr and in spite of small crowds, fiscal uncertainty, and the overwhelming popularity of professional baseball and intercollegiate football, professional football managed to survive. The NFL held its first championship play-off game in 1933 and in 1936 conducted its first draft of college players. By 1934 crowds of fifty thousand attended some of the games, and by the end of World War II professional football was firmly entrenched in the sport world.

Basketball

Professional basketball between World War I and World War II was dominated by touring teams and attempts to form leagues in New England, New York State, Pennsylvania, and various eastern cities. The most successful of the early leagues was the American Basketball League, founded in 1925 and discontinued in 1928. The National Basketball League, organized in 1938, continued into the post-World War II period before merging to form the present National Basketball Association (NBA).

The three dominant teams of the period were the Original Celtics—all white—and the New York Renaissance (Rens) and the Harlem Globetrotters, two very strong black pro teams. The Original Celtics, formed in 1914, won over ninety percent of its games during the early 1920s with Nat Holman as the star. The team played a barnstorming schedule throughout the country, competing against other professional teams, local pick-up teams, and college clubs.

Figure 6.4   Renaissance basketball team. Left to right: Clarence "Fat" Jenkins, Bill Yancey, John Holt, James "Pappy" Ricks, Eyre Saitch, "Tarzan" Cooper, "Wee Willie" Smith. Courtesy of the Naismith Memorial Basketball Hall of Fame.

The Rens were organized by Robert Douglas in 1923. In the 1925–26 season they split a six-game series with the Original Celtics. During the depression the Rens' popularity flourished, as they beat the Celtics in 1932. The Rens then won 88 games in a row, but were finally defeated by the Celts the following year. Throughout the thirties the Rens continued to win and to attract crowds. In March, 1939, the Rens accepted the invitation of the National Basketball League to play in a league tournament, which the Rens won; the victory brought them national recognition. This season was the height of their success as a team. They continued to play, but as other black teams improved, they lost some of their appeal, and in 1941 were defeated in the NBL tournament by the Harlem Globetrotters, whom Abe Saperstein had organized in 1927.

Other Professional Sport
While baseball dominated the professional sport world between the two wars, other sports reflected the increased interest in and growth of sport in general. When the New York Rangers, Detroit Cougars, and the Chicago Black Hawks were all admitted to the nine-year-old National Hockey League in 1926, professional ice hockey was assured a place in United States sports. The speed of the game, one of hockey's attractions, appealed to the fast-paced twenties. By 1942 six teams had emerged in the league—the Montreal Canadiens, Toronto Maple Leafs, Boston Bruins, New York Rangers, Detroit Red Wings, and Chicago Black Hawks. America's fascination with speed was further mirrored in bicycle racing and automobile racing, especially the Memorial Day Race at the Indianapolis Speedway.

Beginning in 1916, the Professional Golf Association of America held pro championships, but many of the better players continued to compete in the Open championships. Tennis changed from an elite amateur sport to a professional one when the theatrical Frenchwoman, Suzanne Lenglen, the American, Mary K. Browne, and four men, Vincent Richards, Harvey Snodgrass, Howard Kinsey, and Paul Peret of France successfully toured the country in 1926. The biggest indoor sport in the United States, bowling, offered prize money for men under the auspices of the American Bowling Congress and for women under the Women's International Bowling Congress. Such sports as wrestling accounted for another area of interest in sport as entertainment.

Sport spectaculars such as ice shows and aquacades were particularly popular in the middle and late thirties. Since the days of Annette Kellerman before World War I, water shows had existed, but it was Norman Ross who invented the term "synchronized swimming" for the 1933 Chicago World's Fair entertainment and initiated the elaborate aquacades of the period. Later at New York City's Jones Beach, Minneapolis, and many other cities the summer aquacade became an annual affair.

Thus, during the period between World War I and World War II professional sport increased in the number and variety of events. Before World War I most fans attended baseball, boxing, and horse racing events, but by the late 1930s the sport fan could see a tennis match, a football game, a six-day bicycle race, an aquacade, or many other sport events.

Amateur Sport

If professional sport made rapid progress between the wars, the growth of amateur sport was astonishing. Although college football was the greatest attraction, golf, tennis, swimming, field hockey, track and field, polo, rowing and other amateur sports also thrived. By 1925 the United States had attained international prominence in several sports. Five Olympic Games were held from 1920 to 1936, and in all of these the United States athletes, especially in track and swimming, turned in superior performances. In the 1920s Duke Kahanamoku and Johnny Weismuller dominated men's swimming, and in 1932 19-year-old Mildred "Babe" Didrikson appeared as a one-woman track team and won the National Women's AAU Track Meet. Sports like rowing, lacrosse, squash rackets, handball, badminton, curling, and table tennis attracted more and more enthusiasts. By the late thirties skiing, tobogganing, and other winter sports lured thousands out of doors in northern United States. Amateur sports had their sport stars just as did the professional sports, and the public responded enthusiastically to Bobby Jones, Bill Tilden, Gertrude Ederle, and Helen Wills.

Golf
Walter Hagen, Gene Sarazen, Glenna Collett, and Bobby Jones dominated the game of golf. The Walker Cup competition between the United States and British men's teams began in 1922. Robert Tyre Jones, Jr. from Atlanta, Georgia, performed the seemingly impossible task of achieving the "Grand Slam" when in 1930 he won the United States Open, the United States Amateur, the British Open, and the British Amateur. From 1922 to 1935 Glenna Collett was the consistent winner in women's golf. She entered her first major competition at seventeen and dominated the women's field for the next seventeen years, setting a record when she won her fourth national title in 1929.

Tennis
The tennis stars of the twenties and thirties were dramatic, flamboyant, and superb players. Suzanne Lenglen and Big Bill Tilden have been equaled by few players since their day. The French player, Lenglen, was theatrical on the court, and a superior player who defeated the best women players. One of the most dramatic events in her career was her default to Molla Bjurstadt Mallory in 1921. Vincent Richards teamed with Tilden that same year to take the

Robert Tyre Jones, Jr. (1902–1971).
Bobby Jones began playing golf at five and at nine won his first championship, the junior cup at the Atlanta Athletic Club. He was graduated from Georgia Institute of Technology, received a law degree from Harvard University, and was admitted to the bar. He played on five Walker Cup teams, won five United States Amateur titles, four United States Opens, three British Opens, and one British Amateur in 1930, the year he won the Grand Slam. Paul Gallico called him:

> . . . a born golfer. Everything about the game suited his body, his character, and his competitive spirit. . . . Jones played so beautifully, he was such a joy to watch in action—the

quiet elegance and smooth rhythm of his stride, the arc and pattern of the flight of his ball, that he reached the heart of even the sourest or most misanthropic old pros.[8]

Jones was described as the epitome of the amateur athlete, interpreting the rules strictly and calling strokes on himself, even those which cost him matches. After winning the Grand Slam he retired from golf competition, but continued to play and in 1934 helped plan the Masters Tournament. In 1958 he received the distinctive honor of the Freedom of the City of St. Andrews, Scotland—the second American to be so honored. The first was Benjamin Franklin.

William Tatem Tilden 2nd (1893–1953)
Big Bill Tilden, six foot one and 165 pounds, transformed the game of lawn tennis, sometimes considered not a game for the manly, to today's complex, highly skilled, hard-fought contest. He dominated first amateur and then professional tennis from the time he won the men's outdoor national singles championship in 1920 until he turned pro and retired in 1935. Theatrical in his game, controversial on and off the courts, he was a superb player noted for "power hitting, a booming cannon-ball service, cunning volley, and smashing net game."[9] Tilden's string of championships included seven American National Turf Court Championships, three Wimbledon singles titles in 1920, 1921, and 1930, one Wimbledon doubles, five United States doubles, and fifteen Davis Cup singles. He was the first American man to win the men's singles at Wimbledon. After turning pro in 1931 he continued to reign as the "King of the Courts" for the next four years, beating players such as Richards, Cochet, and Vines.

Helen Wills Moody (1906–). The daughter of a Los Angeles physician, Helen Wills played at the Berkeley Tennis Club in Berkeley, California, won the national junior girls championship at fifteen and entered her first women's nationals the following year. She was defeated in the finals by Molla Mallory but returned in 1923 to take the title. During her first years of play she continued studying and was admitted to Phi Beta Kappa. Her serious attitude and the predilections of the press gave her the nickname "Little Miss Poker Face." Her brilliant play brought her twelve Wimbledon titles, eight singles, three doubles, and one mixed doubles, seven United States singles titles, four United States doubles championships, the French singles championship, and membership on ten Wightman Cup teams. She had the distinction of winning two gold medals in the 1924 Olympic Games, the women's singles and the women's doubles, in which she teamed with Hazel Wightman. From 1922 when she won the United States women's doubles with Mrs. Marion Jessup to 1938 when she captured her eighth Wimbledon singles title, Helen Wills Moody was "Queen of the Nets."

Figure 6.5   Representatives of the first "Golden Age of Sport" in the U.S.: Bobby Jones, golf; Bill Tilden, tennis; Gertrude Ederle, distance swimming; Johnny Weismuller, swimming. Wide World.

national doubles. In 1923 the young Helen Wills won the women's national crown from Mallory and also in 1923 Hazel Hotchkiss Wightman, a top player in the United States, donated a trophy for world competition among women, that in actuality turned out to be contests between only the United States and England. After six years, Tilden was finally beaten by Henri Cochet of France. While both Tilden and Wills, later Helen Wills Moody, continued to dominate tennis on both sides of the Atlantic, other stars such as Helen Jacobs, Alice Marble, and Donald Budge made their appearance. In 1938 Budge achieved the Grand Slam in tennis. He was the first to win the British, French, American, and Australian titles in one year. A new men's star, Bobby Riggs, made his appearance in the tennis world just prior to World War II.

Swimming

Like many other sports, swimming experienced a tremendous growth both as an amateur sport and as a recreational activity. During this period competitive swimming was commanded by Duke Kahanamoku from Hawaii, Johnny Weismuller, and several women, most of whom swam under L. deB. Handley at the Women's Swimming Association (WSA) in New York. Ethelda Bleibtry, Gertrude Ederle, Helen Wainwright, Aileen Riggin, and Eleanor Holm were all WSA swimmers. In 1926, 19-year-old Gertrude Ederle amazed the world when she swam the English Channel from Cape Gris-Nes to Dover in fourteen hours and thirty-one minutes.

Gertrude Ederle (1906–). At seventeen Gertrude Ederle, daughter of a New York delicatessen owner, earned a gold medal and two bronze medals in the Paris Olympics, and held the AAU championship in the 880-yard freestyle. There appeared to be no further challenges in the swimming world for Trudy, as she was known, but in 1926 she announced that she was ready to swim the English Channel, which only five men had done—and which was considered impossible for a woman. However, the publisher of the *New York News,* Captain Patterson, sensed a good story and underwrote the venture and arranged for a coach, Thomas Burgess, who was one of the five men who had completed the difficult swim. Also he sent a woman reporter to keep the United States public informed of events, and her sister Margaret to be her companion on the trip.

After failing her first try, Ederle persevered. The second swim began as planned, but about two hours before the finish the seas became rough, and Ederle was seasick. Although her coach suggested she stop, she would not give up. When she reached shore, she was not only the first woman to swim the English Channel, she was also the record holder as her time was two hours faster than the existing men's record. Before she could capitalize on her fame, a second woman swam the Channel, making Ederle's victory not quite so impressive to the public. On her return to New York, Ederle received a "ticker tape" welcome, but not the professional contracts for which she hoped. Thirty-nine years later, she was inducted into the International Swimming Hall of Fame.

John Weismuller (1904–1984). At the age of fourteen Johnny Weismuller was spotted at a Chicago YMCA by Burt Bachrach of the Illinois Athletic Club in Chicago and persuaded to swim for the club. A year later he won his first national event. His coach utilized his natural talent and long, lean body to develop a style which revolutionized freestyle swimming. He developed a smooth relaxed style with a long arm pull and great drive, which kept him high in the water. His stroke became the model for most swimmers of the period. Overall, Weismuller set sixty-seven records, of which twenty-four were world records. He won gold medals in the 100 meters and 400 meters in both the 1924 and 1928 Olympic Games. His complete mastery of swimming and his good-natured personality helped to popularize the sport.

Field Hockey

Amateur field hockey for women developed through clubs in the major cities of the country and in localities near colleges and universities. By 1922 there was sufficient interest to form the United States Field Hockey Association. In that same year Constance M. K. Applebee of Bryn Mawr College opened her famous Pocono Hockey Camp on the grounds of Camp Tegawitha in Pennsylvania. After the children left the camp for the summer, Miss Applebee, or the "Apple" as she was affectionately called, opened the camp for one week to school girls, college and university students, teachers, and club players. At what was possibly the first sports camp, the "Apple" prodded, chided, and

Figure 6.6   Constance Applebee. Courtesy of Bryn Mawr College Archives.

goaded women and girls into improving their games and aspiring to achieve English standards of field hockey. In 1924 and again in 1933 a selected team of United States women toured European countries playing other field hockey clubs. In 1936 the United States women, in turn, welcomed teams from Australia, Wales, England, Scotland, and South Africa. After a tournament in Philadelphia, each team toured the country playing at colleges, universities, and city clubs. Outstanding United States players of the period included Anne Townsend of Philadelphia and Betty Richey, a faculty member of Vassar College, who played with the Stuyvesant Club in New York.

Track and Field
Men's track and field was dominated by university and college students such as Charlie Paddock, Glenn Cunningham, Jesse Owens, and Don Lash. In the early twenties Paddock, a University of Southern California student, starred as a sprinter. In 1923 for the first time there were three national championships, the AAU, ICAAAA, and NCAA. The crowd of thirty thousand that watched the 1924 Olympic tryouts demonstrated the increased interest in track

Figure 6.7   Jesse Owens setting one of four world records at the Big Ten Meet, May 25, 1935, Ann Arbor, Michigan. Courtesy of University of Michigan.

and field events. Sabin Carr of Yale amazed the track world when he pole-vaulted fourteen feet in the 1927 ICAAAA meet. In the thirties Glenn Cunningham of Kansas and Jesse Owens of Ohio State were among the stars. In 1935 Owens starred in both the NCAA and AAU championships and in 1936 won four gold medals in the Berlin Olympics.

In 1923 the AAU formally adopted track and field championships for women. In 1915 the Union had assumed control of women's swimming, but had not added any additional women's sports. Cautiously, in 1922 it appointed a committee to investigate the possibility of assuming control over women's track and field. This was the summer of the First Women's Olympic Games, to be held in Paris under the auspices of the Federation Sportive Féminine Internationale (FSFI), and the AAU accepted an invitation to send a team to the Paris meet. The team, coached by Dr. Harry Stewart, finished second in the meet. The following year the AAU officially announced its control over women's track and field in this country. Under the AAU, women's track grew steadily, with stars such as Babe Didrikson contributing to its increasing popularity.

Figure 6.8   Mildred "Babe" Didrikson on her way to victory in the 80-meter hurdle event at the 1932 Olympic Games.

Mildred "Babe" Didrikson Zaharias (1914–1956). Born in Port Arthur, Texas, and raised in Beaumont, Texas, Zaharias possessed the necessary traits of a champion—natural ability, the desire to win, and the perseverance to pursue a goal—but she lacked the necessary money for good coaching and the time to practice. In her junior year in high school her basketball marksmanship reached the local sports pages and captured the interest of Colonel M. J. McCombs, who was in charge of the Employers Casualty Company's women's athletic program. He arranged an office job for her and immediately put her on the company's basketball team. After basketball season, the company's athletic program included swimming, diving, track, and softball. Zaharias practiced the track events and entered the 1930 AAU nationals, winning two events. In 1932 the company sent Zaharias to the Olympic trials and national AAU meet in Chicago where she won five events, tied for a sixth and placed in two other events, thereby capturing the team title. She won national fame for her performance in the 1932 Olympics, winning two gold medals and one silver.

After the Olympics, Zaharias remained in sport, performing and playing many sports, but it was golf which eventually captured her imagination and interest. Having been disqualified as an amateur, Zaharias stopped all sport competition until she was declared an amateur again, and then between 1940 and 1950 won every major golf tournament open to her. In 1946 and 1947 she had 17 consecutive wins. In 1950 she was voted the greatest woman athlete in the first half of the present century.

Youth Sport

Organized youth sport emerged from the nineteenth-century playground movement and reflected the growing organization of society and sport. Youth groups such as the Boy Scouts, Girl Scouts, Boys Clubs, and Campfire Girls included sport in their programs. Many religious organizations also initiated social, recreational, and sport activities. In 1930 the Catholic Youth Organization was founded and immediately launched basketball and boxing tournaments. Little League baseball originated in 1939 in Williamsport, Pennsylvania, and similar youth sport programs followed.

Sport and Physical Education in Education

During the period between the two World Wars, sport, exercise, dance, and physical education became integral components of the educational system in the United States. Although programs were distinctively different for men and women, in more and more colleges and universities physical education came to be required for both men and women for graduation.

For the men, intercollegiate athletics became firmly established in the administrative structure of the institution, and sport replaced gymnastics in most physical education programs. Student sport, especially football and basketball, became important as entertainment and as a focal point for student and alumni loyalty. Many institutions provided financial aid for male student athletes, some of whom would not otherwise have been able to attend college.

The women, already teaching a variety of activities such as sport, gymnastics, body mechanics, and dance, emphasized activities in which large numbers of women could participate and effectively avoided intercollegiate programs. Most women physical educators emphasized the importance of choosing a college or university on the basis of academic offerings rather than on financial inducements through athletic programs, and they neither approved of nor permitted financial aid to women based solely on their athletic ability.

College and University Physical Education

During the 1920s and 1930s higher education expanded rapidly, as did education at all levels, and better trained teachers were in greater demand. Proponents of a child-centered curriculum and progressive education initiated the study of education as a proper field of study. The one, two and three-year "normal" schools in which many physical educators had been trained were reorganized into four-year colleges and universities or affiliated with existing four-year institutions. R. Tait McKenzie warned that graduate work in physical education would be essential. By 1917 graduate work was offered by the Normal College of the American Gymnastic Union, Wellesley College, the University of Southern California, and the University of Oregon. Zeigler reports that "Between 1926 and 1949, some fifty-four colleges and universities began Master's degree programs in physical education. . ."[10] The first Ph.D. programs in education with a major in physical education were initiated in 1924 at New York University and Teachers College, Columbia University. Five years later the Ed.D. with a concentration in physical education was offered by the University of Pittsburgh and Stanford University.

The curriculum, varying considerably from institution to institution, reflected the growing trend in physical education toward sport and social values. Dramatically increasing needs for physical education and sport teachers and responses to the changing educational philosophy led to a broad program of courses rather than a clearly defined field of study. First, the rapid growth of public education and the rapidly increasing state laws requiring physical education created a need for teachers. In 1920, 311,266 girls and boys were graduated from high school in the United States. Twenty years later the figure was 1,221,475. Second, the medical education of many early leaders in physical education was no longer seen as appropriate professional training, partly because of the growing emphasis on sport. The physical educators with a medical background were well qualified to prescribe and conduct gymnastics, but they were not prepared to teach sport or coach athletics. While the early programs, especially for men, had been largely gymnastics, by the twenties sport was the dominant component in the curriculum. For some institutions there no longer appeared to be an urgent necessity for the grounding in biological and physical sciences basic to a thorough understanding of gymnastics; rather the need was for sport teachers and coaches. Depending upon where graduate programs were conducted in each institution and on the interests and professional position of the administrator and faculty, the courses and requirements for degrees in physical education varied.

In 1931 Seward Staley pointed out that the old mind-body dualism on which the concept of physical education had been based was no longer plausible within the context of modern psychological and educational theories. He argued that the content of the physical education program was big-muscle activity and that the most appropriate title for sports in educational institutions was "sports education." He defined it as "that phase of education concerned with directing individuals in the learning of sports," and sports as "all relatively vigorous activities that individuals engage in for fun, joy, or satisfaction." He pointed out that the major portion of the class work was sports education and that the title "sports" was in agreement with the ideas of Wood, Hetherington, Williams, and Nash. Staley further noted that "sports" education would "undoubtedly produce interested, intelligent spectators at sport contests, but . . . the vital objective and outcome should be the production of participants."[11]

Physical educators in the thirties were engaged in a series of controversies, confrontations, and debates over definitions and objectives. The situation was further complicated by three outstanding and influential men, each of whom proposed a different direction for physical education. Jesse Feiring Williams defined physical education as "education *through* the physical rather than *of* the physical": under this definition, the objectives of physical education were to develop character and learn activities that could be utilized later in the student's leisure time. Charles Harold McCloy saw physical education as "the adequate training and development of the body itself," and believed in organic power, physical development, strenuous exercise, and the mastery of physical skills. Jay Bryan Nash, believing that physical education was "all the experiences children have in neuromuscular activities which are directed to the desired outcomes," taught that children should be educated for their leisure-time activities as well as for a vocation. All these dynamic men developed followings among their students and colleagues. Gerber points out that physical educators attempted the impossible task of accommodating all three positions:

> . . . physical educators adopted all three modes and believed they could effectively conduct all three types of programs simultaneously. Although there were vague ideas advanced which suggested that in the lowest grades body development and fundamental skills should be the basis of curriculum followed in the middle school years by games and team sports, and culminating in individual activities, in actual practice a little of everything was done at almost every level. . . . As a result, physical education projected itself into the anomalous situation of holding classes in accord with McCloy's suggestion, of advocating the activities urged by Nash, and of committing itself to accomplishing the social goals delineated by Williams.[12]

Figure 6.9   Jesse Feiring Williams and Jay Bryan Nash. Courtesy, Mary Roby, University of Arizona. Charles Harold McCloy. Courtesy of University of Iowa Photographic Service.

Thus, prior to World War II the study of physical education, of which sport in schools was a major component, was diffused and varied. Not every student studied the same courses and materials in every institution in every part of the country. However, there were many carefully focused programs that produced consistently excellent scholars and teachers. For master's theses in the twenties, more research was completed on the physiology of exercise and tests and measurements than in other areas of study.

The American Physical Education Association also reflected the developing interest in research, establishing the *Research Quarterly* in 1930. At that time the association also initiated the *Journal of Health and Physical Education.* A year later Mabel Lee became the first woman president of the association. That same year the association recognized a number of outstanding women and men in physical education. Ten women and thirty-eight men were honored, including Amy Morris Homans, Delphine Hanna, Elizabeth Burchenal, Ethel Perrin, Thomas D. Wood, William G. Anderson, Clark Hetherington, and James Naismith.

Increasingly, programs of intercollegiate athletics for men came to be placed within a department of physical education for men. This administrative shift was one of several factors which combined to complete a change begun prior to World War I, in which the content of the men's physical education instructional program became predominantly sport. The change was consistent with the current educational philosophy, which focused on social and citizenship goals. Organizations such as the NCAA, the National Amateur Athletic Federation, and the Playground and Recreation Association supported the new philosophy. It was thought that the objectives of men's physical education could best be met through a "sports for all" program. In response to these contentions the curriculum shifted from the goal of health through gymnastics, to character and sportsmanship through sport. Underlying the change in curriculum was the practical need for coaches rather than gymnastic teachers. According to Lewis:

> Well-intentioned administrators, assisted by a tremendous increase in the number and size of physical education programs, forced physical educators to adopt the sports program. From this point formulation of a philosophy was merely a practice in justifying the existence of programs already sanctioned by higher authority. Accommodation, then, of varsity athletics was the key factor in the transformation of the profession. The status of competitive athletics established the location of physical education in high schools and colleges; facilities, equipment, and staff secured for varsity sports determined the content of the curricula and the nature of the programs.[13]

The "sports for all" philosophy, then, was reflected in the men's program, the general physical education curriculum, and the rapid increase in the size and scope of intramural activities. The most important influence of the period, however, was the increasing popularity of intercollegiate athletics.

The women's curriculum in physical education, already strong in sport instruction, also included other activities such as body mechanics and dance. The University of Wisconsin, which inaugurated the first dance major in the country in 1926, became the intellectual center for body mechanics and dance. The work of Margaret H'Doubler, while synonymous with the development of modern dance in education, was focused upon the study of the fundamentals of human movement. H'Doubler had studied dance with Bird Larson, Porter Beegle, Alys Bentley, and at the Isadora Duncan School.[14] Upon her return to Wisconsin she set about developing a dance form which emphasized the creative nature of the dance experience based on a sound understanding of the biological nature of the body and its capacity for expressive movement. Her work became the foundation upon which American movement education in the 1960s was structured. Utilizing her undergraduate background in biology, chemistry, and physics, H'Doubler structured her courses in dance to emphasize the how and why of movement. Her 1925 book, *The Dance and Its Place in Education,* emphasizes fundamentals:

> The "course" in educational dancing will begin then with the effort to master the body as an instrument of expression. . . . These exercises are based on the natural movements of the human animal and are in themselves the systematic application of the laws of the joint-muscle mechanism. . . . They consist of a series of movements which in themselves exact fundamental coordinations, varying from the simple to the complex.[15]

In 1930 H'Doubler was joined by a former student, Ruth Glassow, who concentrated on the analysis of movement and sought to demonstrate the importance of kinesiological information to the teacher. Their work had a profound effect on women's physical education programs in the colleges and universities of the nation. Skill instruction courses for all students, not only those majoring in physical education and dance, became marked by an emphasis on the fundamentals and analysis of movement.

In the summer of 1934, the Bennington School of the Dance opened at Bennington College in Vermont. The faculty included, among others, Graham, Humphrey, Weidman, and Hanya Holm, an exponent of German modern dance. Here these artists choreographed and taught college and university teachers, who came from all parts of the country to study at Bennington and who then returned to their institutions to teach the new dance on their campuses. Many departments of physical education for women invited dancers such as Graham, Humphrey, Weidman, and Holm to perform on their campuses. Through the summer programs and the winter dance tours, early modern dance was nurtured on college campuses.

The Bennington program continued and in 1939 the school was moved to Mills College on the west coast, and then returned to Bennington where it remained through the summer of 1942. After that it was moved to Connecticut College, New London, Connecticut, where it offered summer study with leading dancers.

In women's programs during this period it was not unusual to have requirements within the physical education requirement such as swimming and, perhaps, one team sport and one individual sport. For example, at the University of Minnesota in 1927 freshmen selected sports such as field hockey, tennis, baseball, archery, track, or outdoor basketball in the spring, but in the winter the freshmen all took the same course consisting of exercise, folk dance, apparatus, and games.[16]

Figure 6.10   A summer class at Denishawn receiving instruction from Ruth St. Denis and Ted Shawn. *The Denishawn* magazine, vol. 1, no. 1 (undated—about 1923).

Intercollegiate Sport for Men

During World War I, many voices within the NCAA called for the reform of intercollegiate football. Because many young men left college to join the armed services, fewer men were left on campuses and many athletic programs were curtailed. It seemed a logical time to institute many badly needed changes. At the 1918 NCAA meeting discussions took place on proselyting, hiring practices of coaches, and improving the physical well-being of the whole student body. The convention passed the following resolutions:

1. BE IT RESOLVED, that, in the opinion of the National Collegiate Athletic Association, physical training and athletics are an essential part of education; and that in every college or university the Department of Physical Training and Athletics should be recognized as a department of collegiate instruction, directly responsible to the college or university administration.
2. THAT each college faculty should make adequate provision in the hour schedule for physical training and athletics.
3. THAT seasonal coaches, scouting (except at public intercollegiate contests), training tables, and organized training or coaching in the summer vacation are contrary to the spirit of amateur college athletics.

   In furtherance of the first resolution, seasonal coaches should, as soon as practicable, be replaced by coaches appointed for the year, or should themselves be given an appointment for a year or more.[17]

These efforts to control the game did not dampen the nation's enthusiasm for college football. Not only college students but also alumni and the general

Figure 6.11   Pioneering intramural sport at the University of Michigan.

sports fan packed the stadiums across the country, expecting dramatic contests and winning teams. By 1921, intersectional contests produced additional enthusiasm among the fans. In the East, Penn State dominated the game; in the Middle West, Iowa and Notre Dame stood out; in the South, Centre College; and in the West, California. McGeehan reported that "intercollegiate football in season draws more spectators than the national pastime."[18] The *New York Times* reported 1934 as one of the best football seasons because of "spectacular play, increased attendance, decreased fatalities, and the brilliant Minnesota eleven."[19] By 1937, twenty million people attended college football games.

The crowds required stadiums and other facilities for which the university itself might have little need. To accommodate football within the university, stadiums were financed in a variety of ways. For example, Ohio State University's first stadium was partially paid for by donors who were then assigned special seats. October 18–23, 1920, was declared Stadium Week with parades, pageants, demonstrations, and appeals for money. An "Ohio State Day," celebrated nationally on November 26, 1920, produced over $900,000, and finally, two years later, the stadium opened. From the beginning the athletic facilities of many universities developed parallel with, but not necessarily dependent upon, the institution's budget.

Such games as the Army-Navy game and the Harvard-Yale contests were sellouts and the "Galloping Ghost" and the "Four Horsemen" became familiar in ordinary households far from Illinois and Indiana. The Four Horsemen, Knute Rockne's famous backfield, helped the University of Notre Dame achieve national prominence. Under Rockne's leadership, Notre Dame from 1920 to 1930 won 96 games, lost three, and tied three. Innovations such as intersectional and post-season play increased interest in the game. During the depression Miami businessmen conceived the idea that a function similar to the Rose Bowl would attract visitors to the area and, thus, improve the economy. The first Orange Bowl game was played in 1933 between the University of Miami and Manhattan University. The New Orleans Sugar Bowl followed in 1935, again to attract visitors to the area.[20]

Gallico credits Red Grange with beginning the competition for football talent in the major football programs that resulted in the adoption of the semi-professional model:

> . . . in their frantic attempts to acquire similar attractions [to Red Grange], the universities impaled themselves front, back, and sideways on the horns of the dilemma that had been created—how to coax, lure, rent, hire, or buy football stars who would be drawing cards, while at the same time managing to keep their fingers off the swag. During this process they fractured amateur codes into so many pieces that no one has yet been able to put them together again.[21]

Whether or not undergraduate sport should be used to entertain fellow students, alumni, faculty, and the public became a controversial issue throughout the country. Usually expressed in terms of the value of athletics to the athletes themselves as opposed to the consequences of athletics as entertainment, arguments for and against men's intercollegiate athletics appeared in periodicals such as the *Atlantic Monthly, Harper's,* and *Forum.* In the November, 1926, issue of *Forum,* for example, one article favored intercollegiate athletics and one article opposed it.

In January, 1926, at the urging of the NCAA, the Association of American Colleges, the Association of Colleges and Secondary Schools of the Southern States, and the Carnegie Foundation for the Advancement of Teaching agreed to conduct a study of American intercollegiate athletics. The results of the three-year study were released in December, 1929. The report generally supported intercollegiate sport but created a tempest by citing particular colleges

Figure 6.12   Harold "Red" Grange, the University of Illinois' "Galloping Ghost."
Courtesy of University of Illinois.

and universities which allegedly engaged in questionable practices in recruiting and subsidization. More than 130 institutions were included in the
investigation, which came to the following conclusions:

1. . . . a change of values [is needed] in a field that is sodden with the commercial
   and the material and the vested interests that these forces have created. Commercialism in college athletics must be diminished and college sport must rise
   to a point where it is esteemed primarily and sincerely for the opportunities it
   affords to mature youth . . . to exercise at once the body and the mind, and to
   foster habits both of bodily health and . . . high qualities of character. . .
2. The American college must renew within itself the force that will challenge the
   best intellectual capabilities of the undergraduates.[22]

At its annual convention in 1930 the NCAA gave special attention to the
Carnegie Report. The "Report of the Committee to Study Carnegie Foundation Bulletin 23" reaffirmed the Association's commitment to faculty control, year-round coaching appointments, and the nonsubsidization and

recruitment of athletes. Its major recommendation was that each college or university use the report as a guide to examine its own practices.[23]

In spite of the attention the Carnegie Report received, its actual impact on the abuses in intercollegiate sport was negligible. A number of institutions did take steps to place intercollegiate athletics under more direct university control within institutional departments such as a department of athletics or a department of physical education. It became increasingly clear, however, that the guidelines and standards established by the NCAA were being evaded. There was growing concern over violations of the amateur code and the hypocrisy in intercollegiate sport as reported to the public by Paul Gallico in his *Farewell to Sport*, and privately by frustrated college and university presidents. In response to such pressures the NCAA revised its constitution in 1939. To be an active member institutions were required to be accredited by the regional accrediting agency and to be approved by a two-thirds majority vote by the member institutions in its district. One year later the convention added investigative and judicial procedures to the legislative functions.

Intercollegiate basketball expanded rapidly in the middle and late thirties. The elimination of the "center jump" following free throws in 1936 and after all baskets in 1937 increased the speed of the game and scoring. Following the lead of Ned Irish, other New York City sports writers began to cover metropolitan college basketball games. In 1934 Irish began promoting games between city teams as well as intersectional games in Madison Square Garden. In 1935 he began staging doubleheaders which attracted thousands and by 1940 he had established the Garden as the mecca of college basketball. The Metropolitan Basketball Writers Association founded the National Invitation Tournament (NIT) in 1938 with six teams. The NCAA followed with its own championship in 1939 but over the next decade, an invitation to the NIT was the most coveted bid by teams throughout the country. By the end of World War II intercollegiate sport for men was firmly entrenched as an integral component of American sport.

Collegiate Sport for Women

Housed in separate departments of physical education for women or in separate institutions such as Wellesley College in the East or Lindenwood College in the Midwest, women carefully developed programs which promoted the philosophy of "A sport for every girl and every girl in a sport." Women physical educators continued to build on the statements voiced by Lucille Eaton Hill in 1903, that athletics should be planned for the greatest good to the greatest number and should avoid the "evils" of men's athletics. At the 1920 meeting of the Conference of College Directors of Physical Education the group went on record as disapproving women's intercollegiate athletics for the following reasons:

1. It leads to professionalism.
2. Training of a few to the sacrifice of many.
3. It is unsocial.
4. Necessity of professional coaches.
5. Physical educators, both men and women, of our leading colleges find results undesirable.
6. Expense.
7. Unnecessary nerve fatigue.[24]

Two years later women physical educators took more direct action to control competition for women through the Committee on Women's Athletics of the American Physical Education Association, which now included committees on basketball, field hockey, track and field, and swimming. Some women physical educators served on the AAU committee to investigate track and field competition for women and objected to the AAU's acceptance of the invitation to the 1922 First Women's Olympic Games in Paris. The AAU did not hold jurisdiction over women's track and field, and there were certain aspects of the meet which the women physical educators questioned. When the AAU decided to send a team to the Paris track meet in spite of the women's opposition and named Dr. Harry Stewart to coach the team, many women physical educators strongly objected.

At this time the leaders of the National Amateur Athletic Federation, founded to promote sport for men, approached Mrs. Herbert Hoover to organize the women in the United States as part of the federation. At her suggestion a national conference was called to determine the position and program of sport and athletics for women. In April, 1923, women and men representing a variety of organizations and institutions met in Washington. The participants included Marjorie Bouvé, Boston School of Physical Education; Eline von Bories, Goucher College; Dr. William Burdick, Playground Athletic League; Rosalind Cassidy, Teachers College, Columbia University; Katherine F. Lenroot, Children's Bureau, U.S. Department of Labor; Emma Dolfinger, American Child Health Association; Commodore W. E. Longfellow, American Red Cross; and Helen McKinstry, Central School of Hygiene and Physical Education. After two days of meetings four actions were taken: (1) a Women's Division of the NAAF was established; (2) sixteen resolutions prepared by a committee chaired by Dr. J. Anna Norris were adopted; (3) a committee chaired by Blanche Trilling reported the conference; and (4) Mrs. Hoover was elected permanent chairwoman and Blanche Trilling, University of Wisconsin, named vice-chairwoman. The Women's Division began its activities with two purposes in mind, to act as a clearing-house for problems in athletics for girls and women, and to establish the standards set forth in their platform statements.

B. ORIGINAL RESOLUTIONS

As Adopted by the Conference on Athletics and Physical
Recreation for Women and Girls, April 6–7, 1923

I. *Resolved,* That it be noted that the term "athletics" as used in this Conference has often included the problems connected with all types of noncompetitive as well as competitive physical activities for girls and women.

II. Whereas, The period of childhood and youth is the period of growth in all bodily structures, and
Whereas, A satisfactory growth during this period depends upon a large amount of vigorous physical exercises, and
Whereas, The strength, endurance, efficiency, and vitality of maturity will depend in very large degree upon the amount of vigorous physical exercise in childhood and youth, and
Whereas, Normal, wholesome, happy, mental, and emotional maturity depends in large part upon joyous, natural, safeguarded big-muscle activity in childhood and in youth.
Be It Therefore Resolved,
  (a) That vigorous, active, happy, big-muscle activity be liberally provided and maintained and carefully guided for every girl and boy; and
  (b) That all governments—village, county, state, and national—establish and support adequate opportunities for a universal physical education that will assist in the preparation of our boys and girls for the duties, opportunities, and joys of citizenship and of life as a whole.

III. *Resolved,* That there be greater concentration and study on the problems and program of physical activities for the pre-pubescent as well as for the adolescent girl.

IV. *Resolved,* in order to develop these qualities which shall fit girls and women to perform their functions as citizens:
  (a) That their athletics be conducted with that end definitely in view and be protected from exploitation for the enjoyment of the spectator, the athletic reputation, or the commercial advantage of any school or other organization.
  (b) That schools and other organizations shall stress enjoyment of the sport and development of sportsmanship and minimize the emphasis which is at present laid upon individual accomplishment and the winning of championships.

V. *Resolved,* That for any given group we approve and recommend such selection and administration of athletic activities as makes participation possible for all, and strongly condemn the sacrifice of this object for intensive (even though physiologically sound) training of the few.

VI. *Resolved,*

(a) That competent women be put in immediate charge of women and girls in their athletic activities even when the administrative supervision may be under the direction of men.

(b) That we look toward the establishment of a future policy that shall place the administration as well as teaching and coaching of girls and women in the hands of carefully trained and properly qualified women.

VII. WHEREAS, A rugged national vitality and a high level of public health are the most important resources of a people,

Be It Therefore Resolved, That the teacher-training schools, the colleges, the professional schools, and the universities of the United States make curricular and administrative provision that will emphasize

1. Knowledge of the basic facts of cause and effect in hygiene that will lead to the formation of discriminating judgments in matters of health.
2. Habits of periodical examination and a demand for scientific health service.
3. Habits of vigorous developmental recreation.

To this end we recommend:

(a) That adequate instruction in physical and health education be included in the professional preparation of all elementary and secondary school teachers.

(b) That suitable instruction in physical and health education be included in the training of volunteer leaders in organized recreation programs.

(c) That definite formulation be made of the highest modern standards of professional education for teachers and supervisors of physical education and recreation, and the provision of adequate opportunity for the securing of such education.

VIII. *Resolved,* That in order to maintain and build health, thorough and repeated medical examinations are necessary.

IX. *Resolved,* That since we recognize that certain anatomical and physiological conditions may occasion temporary unfitness for vigorous athletics, therefore effective safeguards should be maintained.

X. WHEREAS, We believe that the motivation of competitors in athletic activities should be that of play for play's sake, and

WHEREAS, We believe that the awarding of valuable prizes is detrimental to this objective,

Be It Resolved, That all awards granted for athletic achievement be restricted to those things which are symbolical and which have the least possible intrinsic value.

XI. *Resolved,* That suitable costumes for universal use be adopted for the various athletic activities.

XII. WHEREAS, We believe that the type of publicity which may be given to athletics for women and girls may have a vital influence both upon the individual competitors and upon the future development of the activity,

Be It Resolved, That all publicity be of such a character as to stress the sport and not the individual or group competitors.

XIII. WHEREAS, Certain international competitions for women and girls have already been held, and

WHEREAS, We believe that the participation of American women and girls in these competitions was inopportune,

Be It Resolved, That this is the sense of this Conference that in the future such competitions, if any, be organized and controlled by the national organization set up as a result of this Conference.

XIV. *Resolved,* That committees be appointed for study and report on the following problems:
  (a) Tests for motor and organic efficiency
  (b) The formulation of a program of physical activities adapted to various groups of the population
  (c) The relation of athletics to the health of pre-pubescent and post-pubescent girls
  (d) Scientific investigation as to anatomical, physiological, and emotional limitations and possibilities of girls and women in athletics, and a careful keeping of records in order that results may be determined.
XV. *Resolved,* That the sincere and hearty thanks of the members of this Conference on Athletics and Physical Recreation be extended:
  (a) To the National Amateur Athletic Federation for its suggestion that this Conference be called; and
  (b) To Mrs. Herbert Hoover for her vision and devotion in organizing this Conference and in making possible the vitally significant achievement of coordination of the various agencies for women's athletics.
XVI. *Resolved,* That the National Amateur Athletic Federation be requested to publish these Resolutions and distribute them:
  (a) To all members of this Conference
  (b) To all present members of the National Amateur Athletic Federation
  (c) To the Associated Press and the United Press
  (d) To the American Physical Education Association, with the request that they be copied and distributed to all members at the Springfield Convention.[25]

Within two days after the Washington, D.C., conference many of the same women such as Blanche Trilling, Helen McKinstry, and Agnes Wayman traveled to Springfield, Massachusetts, to attend the annual meeting of the American Physical Education Association. As part of the APEA program the Committee on Women's Athletics received a report of the Washington conference creating a Women's Division of the NAAF. The newly created platform for women's athletics was endorsed by the CWA. Thus within a year after their objections to the United States women's participation in the Paris track meet, the women leaders in physical education had promoted their principles of athletics through the CWA and the newly formed Women's Division of the NAAF.

The women's philosophy, emphasizing a broad program of sport, medical examinations, women leaders, and protection from exploitation, was promoted by both associations through national programs. Through both the NAAF and the APEA the women collected data, wrote articles and books on athletics, broadcast over the radio, spoke to professional associations, and met with local clubs. They coined phrases pointing up their belief that in intercollegiate athletics girls would receive more "physical straining than training." Data collected from fifty colleges revealed that intercollegiate athletics for women "does not exist in the colleges of the United States except in a very limited number and percentage" and that "There is little tendency on the part of physical

Figure 6.13   Mabel Lee, Blanche Trilling, and Agnes Wayman. Courtesy American Alliance for Health, Physical Education, Recreation, and Dance.

directors to change their opinions on this subject. . . . Of those who have changed of recent years, the majority have changed from an attitude of approval to one of disapproval."[26]

Women physical educators did not disapprove of all competition in sports, but rather devised several forms of competition that they believed promoted their philosophy. The most popular were play days or sports days. The events were usually informal and the program planned for mass participation. The Triangle Day in central California, held in 1927, was typical.

TRIANGLE SPORTS DAY IN CENTRAL CALIFORNIA

A Triangle Sports Day was held at the University of California November 6, 1926, with three neighboring colleges (Mills, Leland Stanford Jr. and the University of California) taking part.

Each college had been invited to send at least 60 girls (and as many more as possible) to participate. These 180 girls were divided into squads of 30 each, 10 from each college. There were 6 carefully chosen squad leaders, 2 from each college. Each squad was given a number and a color (1. yellow, 2. red, 3. purple, 4. green, 5. blue, 6. pink).

From 9:30 to 9:40 the squads were given opportunity to select a name and compose a yell.

At 9:40 the contests began with informal games—shuttle relay and pass ball relay. Then followed 3 games of net ball (squads 1 & 3, 2 & 4, 5 & 6). Hockey was played in five minute halves with no time between halves (squads 1 & 2, 3 & 4, 5 & 6). Tennis was played on 6 courts, 4 players each, in progressive fashion. The winners of 2 out of 3 games moved to the next higher court and the losers stayed. While the tennis was going on, impromptu games of hop scotch and marbles were played. A swimming meet ended the day (1. 25 yard relay, 2. surface diving for discs, 3. medley relay race for form and speed).

Awards throughout the day were a blue ribbon for first place and red for second place with the name of the event in gold letters.

At 12:30 a luncheon was served, at which there was an interesting program of speaking.

Those who participated in this sports day bore testimony to the value of meeting new college women and to the gaining of new ideas of sportsmanship. They had great fun without the feeling of intense college rivalry.[27]

Other sports days, in which each school participated as a team, often modified the games to the occasion. Playing periods might be shortened, round robin competition employed, and novelty events interspersed with sports. The closing event was a tea or social hour that provided a time when students from the various colleges could compare their institutions or talk with each other. Other types of approved competition included swimming and archery "telegraphic" meets in which each institution held the competition on its own campus and mailed the results to the hostess institution, who determined the ratings and mailed them back to the competing colleges. The Women's Division also suggested field days and carnivals. Intramurals increased and in many colleges and universities students engaged in keen interclass competition.

Women's philosophy of sport clearly did not include the idea of women in the Olympic Games, and women physical educators actively protested the women's events in the 1928 and 1932 Games. One year after their unsuccessful petition to exclude track events for women in the 1928 Games, the Women's Division adopted two resolutions: one opposing women in the 1932 Games and one addressing itself particularly to the track and field events in 1932. It was the latter resolution which was sent in 1930 to M. Baillet-Latour, president of the International Olympic Committee, and M. J. S. Edström, president of the International Amateur Athletic Federation. Copies of the petition and letters together with a request to adopt similar resolutions were sent to the International Council of Women, Women's Pan-Pacific Conference, Sixth Pan-American Congress on the Child, a committee of Great International Associations, and the National Council of Women in the United States. The IOC deleted the 800-meter race in 1928 not because of the petitions, but for other reasons. As late as 1938 the Women's Division requested that girls under sixteen be barred from the Olympic Games.

In the United States sports included in the women's programs followed the rules established by sport committees of the CWA. In 1932 that group reorganized to become the National Section on Women's Athletics (NSWA). These sport committees, which increased to over a dozen, determined which rules would be followed, made changes in the rules, proposed ratings of officials, published the results of meets such as telegraphic meets, and published helpful articles for teachers. One of the major changes during this period, the shift in women's basketball from the three-court to two-court game, occurred in 1936.

A study of the thirties reveals four major trends in women's physical education and sport: (1) an increase in opportunities in sport for women and an increase in the numbers participating; (2) a growing use of research as a basis for planning and improving sport and athletic programs; (3) a greater acceptance in society of the concept of women in sport; and (4) a reexamination of the position limiting intercollegiate athletics. By the end of the thirties some women physical educators like Bernice Moss and Gladys Palmer had proposed competitive programs for the skilled woman athlete, and even Mabel Lee, a strong opponent of women's intercollegiate athletics, had somewhat changed her views on the subject. During the latter part of the period the women experimented with certain competitions such as the Ohio State University invitational golf tournament in 1941.[28]

One of the most influential groups of women physical educators organized officially as the National Association for Physical Education of College Women in 1924. Between 1910 and 1915 Amy Morris Homans had invited certain directors to visit Wellesley College to exchange views on current problems, and in 1915 this group became the Association of Directors of Physical Education for Women. Two years later midwestern women organized as the Middle West Society of College Directors of Physical Education for Women. In 1921 the Western Society for Physical Education of College Women was organized, and in 1922 there was a move to form a national society. The actual organizational meeting took place in 1924 when the Association of Directors of Physical Education for Women in Colleges and Universities became a reality. Membership was limited to directors or chairwomen of departments and thus any resolution or action was influential. Only after World War II was membership opened to faculty from all ranks.

Sport and Physical Education in Schools

With public education a responsibility of the state and local government, the extent, content, and development of sport and physical education differed from state to state, city to city, and town to town. In the early 1920s, following World War I, many states passed laws requiring physical education in order to improve the physical condition of children and youth. However, according to the state and the availability of facilities, many high school programs could not be implemented, while other programs, especially those in the cities, followed programs similar to the colleges and universities.

The program for boys usually included interscholastic sports, ordinarily under the jurisdiction of a state high school athletic association. In 1931 forty-seven states conducted their associations with an executive board and usually had full control of the program. The sports for which state championship contests were conducted included football, basketball, baseball, and track, with basketball tournaments most frequently held.

The picture for girls was quite different. By 1928, twenty-one states had some form of organization and twenty had none. Twelve states controlled athletics for both boys and girls and five states had an association solely for girls. In 1925 the National Association of Secondary School Principals indicated they would use their influence against interscholastic athletics for girls. In some states girls played boys' rules, while in others, they followed the rules proposed by the Women's Division of the NAAF. Seven states with special programs for girls were North Carolina, Illinois, Iowa, Nebraska, Kansas, Oklahoma, and Colorado.

In Oregon, high school physical education was planned to furnish opportunities for "normal physical development, . . . learning activities and health standards which will 'carry over' and be of use . . . in later life, and . . . for the development of leadership, responsibility, loyalty, team-play, and sportsmanship."[29] The program to meet these objectives included remedial gymnastics, gymnastics, dancing, self-testing activities, individual athletics, organized sports, and games. Across the country in Brookline, Massachusetts, the program started in kindergarten, permitting each child to develop large-muscle activities, imagination, and self-expression. The child was allowed "protected freedom" in the gymnasium to invent exercises and activities that were not imposed by an adult. The progressive school movement suggested that in the upper grades teams should be organized by the boys and girls themselves.

High school physical education in the twenties and thirties is difficult to describe in generalities. Some cities and towns had excellent programs, others mediocre to poor programs, and many had no programs at all. During the depression physical education was frequently curtailed or dropped entirely as budgets were cut. On the other hand, high school football and basketball programs helped to occupy the time of unemployed people during the depression, to entertain the public, and to provide a sense of community.

Sport and the Depression

The Great Depression, which swept the country during the thirties, altered sport in the United States, both favorably and unfavorably. Tunis disputed the generally accepted theory of the "Boom of the Twenties" and proposed that the thirties launched the real sports boom.

> Today there is a more intelligent appreciation of the values of real sport, there are more persons of average ability competing, there are more participants who are interested in the game for the game's sake, more people playing than ever before in our history. Not merely is this a greater period for athletics than the era of the super-champion, but there is every likelihood of greater times ahead.[30]

The stark reality of massive unemployment with its accompanying frustration, humiliation, and fear left millions of people with nothing to do and little money for travel or amusements. Although physical education, like art and music, was often dropped from the high school curriculum, by the end of the depression sport in all sectors of society had survived and in many cases prospered. While elite sports such as golf and tennis were the hardest hit during the depression, family sport, youth sport, and informal sport activities increased. Both men's college and professional sport responded to a number of promotional devices, but perhaps the greatest impact on sport was the time, money, and personnel expended by the federal government. By the end of the depression more than ten federal agencies had recreation or sport-related programs and services. These included the National Park Service, Forest Service, Tennessee Valley Authority, Public Works Administration, National Youth Administration, the Civilian Conservation Corps, and the Works Progress Administration.

Both the National Youth Administration (NYA) and the Civilian Conservation Corps (CCC) were planned for youth. Over 1,500,000 young adults were being added to the labor market each year with the prospect of neither full-time nor part-time employment. The youth programs endeavored to reduce the size of the labor market and at the same time provide training for future jobs. The NYA, part of the Emergency Relief Appropriation Act of 1935, supplied part-time work to high school and college students and to former students between the ages of eighteen and twenty-five. High school students worked three hours on weekdays and seven on Saturday, while college and university students could be employed eight hours a day. Employed as construction workers, they built and repaired stadiums, swimming pools, tennis courts, and other recreational facilities. Further, the fact that they were able to remain in school also allowed them time to participate in intramural and other sport programs.

The Civilian Conservation Corps, largely directed toward conservation and forest protection, opened its first camp in Luray, Virginia, in April, 1933, and by August, 1935, over 500,000 men were enrolled in the program. Men between the ages of eighteen and twenty-five whose families were on relief had preference and could enroll for no more than two years. For many, the CCC meant three meals a day, clothing, and purposeful work, and they gladly sent the required twenty-two dollars to twenty-five dollars of their thirty dollars a month pay home. As part of their planned program the men improved national and state parks, built swimming pools, and other recreation and sport facilities. Their major goals were reforestation and other conservation projects and only incidentally sport. The CCC men lived in barracks built in rows, military style, with recreational or sport facilities nearby. When camps were close enough, intercamp as well as intramural events were planned. The CCC was part of the Indian Emergency Conservation Work, and these camps also included sport. Rather than being planned in military-type rows, the Indian camps were built in the shape of a horseshoe with room for a softball diamond in the center.

The Works Progress Administration, begun in 1935, sought to employ people in the field of their expertise. The projects were of great variety but included stadiums, swimming pools, gymnasiums, and other sport facilities. In Kansas alone 344 public buildings were erected, including auditoriums, swimming pools, and gymnasiums. In New England and other northern states ski facilities were constructed, which aided skiing in becoming a popular winter activity. A number of universities added to their athletic and physical education facilities through the use of the WPA program.

Softball grew at an extraordinarily rapid pace in the thirties. By 1934 an estimated two million Americans were playing the new game under the auspices of the American Softball Association. Gerber reports that one thousand women's teams played the 1938 season in California.[31] Betts explains the phenomenon:

> Softball, more adaptable to both sexes and to all ages, less expensive to maintain and lacking little of the dash and drama of baseball, rapidly attained the position of one of America's favorite recreations. By 1940 there were some 300,000 organized clubs and the Amateur Softball Association claimed at least 3,000,000 affiliated players. Veterans of Foreign Wars posts promoted junior softball, and a "Cripple A League" of oldsters who played a simplified version reputedly had 2,500 teams in Chicago. A new support of the diamond world had been found and at the end of the Depression interest in baseball seemed as keen as ever.[32]

In addition to the promotion of softball and youth baseball during the depression years, professional baseball introduced night baseball and opened a Hall of Fame. The Babe finished his amazing career in 1935, but other players such as Lou Gehrig, Lefty Gomez, Joe DiMaggio, and Dizzy Dean became the new heroes of American fans. Although night lighting for sport had existed for several years, it was first used in major league baseball in 1935 when Cincinnati played Philadelphia. Many industries and merchants sponsored semipro teams or local teams in twilight leagues. A native of Cooperstown, N.Y., Stephen C. Clark, proposed a national baseball museum and saw his dream become a reality when the National Baseball Hall of Fame and Museum opened in Cooperstown in 1939. The first players to be enshrined in the Hall, Ty Cobb, Walter Johnson, Christie Mathewson, Babe Ruth, and Honus Wagner, were elected in 1936.

The pervasive mood of futility during the depression was somewhat lifted by the extravaganzas of water shows and ice carnivals. After Sonja Henie's final Olympic appearance in 1936 she turned professional and her tours launched a series of ice show entertainments.

As the thirties drew to a close the United States, recovering from the depression and swinging into a defense industry economy, had accepted sport for men and for many women as a positive, productive use of leisure time. During the prosperity of the twenties middle-class Americans had been introduced to the world of sport, and during the depression they had helped build their own playing fields and develop their own patterns of sport participation.

> . . . millions of urban workers—men, women, and children—were finally enjoying the organized sports that had been introduced by the fashionable world half a century and more earlier. Democracy was making good its right to play the games formerly limited to the small class that had the wealth and leisure to escape the city. No exact totals can possibly be given as to the number of active sports participants in comparison with attendance at sports spectacles in the 1930's . . . there is every reason to believe that in the 1930's the public was spending far more of its leisure . . . on amateur than on professional sports.[33]

Sport and World War II

A general European war began in 1939, and by the summer of 1940 most of Europe was controlled by German and Italian armies. The United States became the "arsenal of democracy." On December 7, 1941, when Japan attacked Pearl Harbor, the United States declared war on Germany, Italy, and Japan.

In 1940 a Selective Service bill was passed and millions of men were drafted into the army or volunteered for other branches of the armed services. To free men for active duty, women's armed services were created: WAVES (Navy), WAC (Army), SPARS (Coast Guard), and women Marines. "Including voluntary enlistments, over 15 million people served in the armed forces during the war: 10 million in the army, 4 million in the navy and coast guard, 600,000 in the marine corps. About 216,000 women served"[34] as nurses and in the women's branches.

After the passage of the Selective Service Act almost four million dollars was set aside for sport activities and equipment by the War Department. Former athletes were called into service and coached soldiers, to help develop tough, hard fighters out of young men who had been reared to believe in peace. Gene Tunney became a naval commander in charge of the physical fitness program. One-time wrestling champion Ed Don George, Art Jones of the Pittsburgh Steelers, and others instructed servicemen in sport. Football, boxing, wrestling, track, and swimming were adapted to train soldiers, rather than to provide fun and enjoyment through the sport. Major Theodore P. Bank commented:

> We Americans are all aware of the obvious physical benefits derived from participation in competitive athletics, but we sometimes forget the intangible benefits the soldier receives from competitive athletics. Sports like boxing, or other sports involving bodily contact, rapidly develop in the individual man the sense of confidence,

aggressiveness and fearlessness that is always desirable in a trained soldier. Sports like football, basketball and other team-play sports also develop the principles of coordination between groups of men that are invaluable on the battle field.[35]

The women's branches had their own fitness and sport programs.

The campuses of the nation were training centers for many special programs for all the armed forces. Civilians on campuses and in cities and towns added their efforts in planning social and sport activities for the men and women in the services. Lincoln, Nebraska, for example, converted a skating rink to an area for badminton, archery, shuffleboard, volleyball, and table tennis, as well as occasional square dancing. In Hartford, Connecticut, citizens converted a school building into a recreation area for black soldiers.

While sport moved into the background of American life, it remained a small but significant part of the war effort. Early in 1942 President Roosevelt expressed his belief that professional baseball players of service age should be expected to enlist or serve their country, but that baseball itself could provide recreation and help keep morale high. Other leaders felt that men overseas would welcome the normalcy of the baseball seasons and would like to hear how their favorite teams were performing. Professional baseball never stopped, but many players volunteered or were drafted, and former players were called back or minor league players were brought up from the farm clubs. Because of travel restrictions the teams trained in the North and made other adjustments to wartime life. Baseball became the vehicle for selling millions of dollars worth of war bonds, and the ball parks became collection points—in 1943, for example, a million pounds of scrap metal, twenty-three thousand pounds of rubber, and twelve thousand pounds of waste fat were collected at the ball parks for use in the war effort.

In case baseball could not survive the 1943 season, the Chicago Cubs owner, Philip K. Wrigley, organized the All-American Girls Baseball League to keep his park open. The women played modified softball rules that moved more and more toward major league rules, until the only difference was a five-foot shorter basepath. Players, most of them eighteen to twenty-five years of age, were supervised by a chaperone, and as further reassurance of their respectability they were not allowed to wear slacks, shorts, or jeans in public, nor could they wear their hair too short. Professional personnel administered the regularly scheduled games in Chicago and other midwestern cities such as Kalamazoo and Muskegon, Michigan; South Bend and Fort Wayne, Indiana; Peoria, Illinois; and Racine and Kenosha, Wisconsin. The women played well, were greatly admired, and the teams' standings were followed with interest by their fans. The end of the war brought a change in internal management of the league, and the advent of television contributed to the close of the league in 1954. However, for more than ten years a successful professional women's league existed. The nonprofit status, carefully supervised players, and slogans such as "Recreation for the War Worker" and "Family Entertainment" created an "All-American Girl" reputation for the league and its players.[36]

Elsewhere members of sport organizations such as yacht clubs helped instruct naval officers. The AAU promoted an extensive fitness program. Sport during the war tried to provide quality entertainment for the armed services, war workers, and the general public. Leaders encouraged physical fitness and utilized sport events to increase the sale of war bonds.

By September, 1945, World War II was over. The country was both jubilant and sorrowful—grateful that the Allies had won, saddened by the more than one hundred thousand who would not return home, and weary of the four years of high-pitched effort. As the country moved to a postwar boom, sport was part of the new decades to come.

Commentary

Between World War I and World War II life in the United States underwent many social changes that affected sport and physical education. During the 1920s more Americans than ever before enjoyed "the good life." Many possessed to some degree the two conditions necessary for sport—money beyond that required for basic needs and leisure time—and many had private transportation in the form of a bicycle or family car. Public transportation on the trolleys and trains made travel much easier and faster than in earlier days. The money Americans spent on sport equipment, toys, and other amusement-related goods almost doubled between 1921 and 1929. To attend sport events they spent thirty million dollars in 1921 and sixty-six million dollars in 1929. In the same period the number of passenger cars sold jumped from 1,905,500 to 4,455,100. Those who could not attend sport events could now listen to them on the radio.

The economic boom of the twenties partially accounted for the growing acceptance of sport in American society. In addition, changes in social behavior, such as more informal clothing, dance crazes like the Charleston, greater use of the automobile, and shorter working hours created a climate in which sport flourished. As education and conditions of employment improved and the standard of living rose, Americans discovered more and more sports available to them.

The cultural diversity of Americans was reflected in sport. The increase in public school education acted as a catalyst to what Betts called "the melting pot of the playing fields."

> After the early 1920's the flow of the foreign-born to this country declined as a result of the new immigration acts, and the problem of the immigrant in our national life soon centered on children who comprised the second or third generation. . . . Nowhere was the process of Americanization more in evidence than in sport.

. . . Families whose chief recreation had been folk dancing or the beer garden found the children enthusiastic over athletic games. Many parents failed to understand these games and called them "foolish, wasteful, ridiculous and immoral," while the child rebelled against European forms of play and resented the parent's antagonism toward American games.[37]

While the second and third generations of European immigrants blended into mainstream society, the races remained sharply separated. With the exception of a few institutions, racial groups attended different schools and colleges and competed in separate conferences. Upper-class whites belonged to country clubs for whites and upper-class blacks belonged to country clubs for blacks. There were separate amateur associations and separate tournaments in sports such as tennis and golf. Major league baseball was also segregated during this period. Black players, many of whom were excellent, played on teams that attracted large crowds. Investigations of racial prejudice in baseball began in the early 1940s and led to baseball's integration following World War II.

In spite of the many social changes, the basic values of most Americans continued to be influenced by conservative Protestant views. Men dominated most aspects of life and sport was considered good training for boys to become men. While a few top women performers in tennis and swimming were admired, most Americans expected girls and women to refrain from physically demanding or rough sports that were not considered "ladylike."

To some degree the prosperity of the twenties blurred the differences between lower-middle and middle-class, and middle-class and upper-middle-class families. More people could afford to participate in sport, to attend sport events, and to enjoy holidays that might include sport. High school sport events brought out the entire community and, in Iowa and a few other places, the town cheered the girls' basketball team as fervently as they did the boys' team.

Perhaps the most paradoxical situation of the twenties was the growth of college football, which became the most popular fall sport in the United States, and on the other hand, the controlled development of collegiate sport for women. College men stars turned student sport into public entertainment with intersectional play and postseason "Bowl" games. The semiprofessionalism and commercialism accompanying the use of student sport as public entertainment was criticized but accepted by most institutions. Women physical educators safeguarded women from such professionalism by promoting programs that encouraged the "greatest good to the greatest number" through play days and sports days. By this period sport had become the dominant component in physical education in all levels of education. Physical education for women nurtured and developed modern dance as the winter tours to the college and university campuses and the summer schools sustained the early dance companies.

Participation in all forms of sport—professional, amateur, recreational, and educational—increased greatly. Many games met all of VanderZwaag and Sheehan's criteria for modern sport, and sport itself reflected Loy's description as "a game occurrence . . . a social institution, and as a social situation or social system.[38]

Popular sport ranged from professional baseball and auto racing to bowling and ice shows. All forms of sport existed: person against person as in swimming or wrestling; persons (team) against persons (team) as in basketball; and persons against the environment as in sailing and ice skating. In some sports such as auto racing and ice shows the environment changed from natural to man-made, especially constructed for the sport or entertainment. Throughout the period both the competitors and the fans increasingly valued excellent performances.

This search for excellence reflected the country's admiration of sport heroes and heroines, who broke records, won championships consistently, and frequently displayed charismatic personalities. A significant fact about many of the nation's sport heroes and heroines was their middle and working class background—proof that sport was available to more and more Americans.

Across the nation, high school, college, and professional events became community functions. The ceremonial aspect of sport—singing the national anthem, the alma mater or the school song, and in some cases, offering a prayer for victory or a good contest—became part of the event. Sport served to bring people together to identify with the team, the town, or the city.

Overall, sport and physical activity increased during the Great Depression. During the boom of the twenties many people had become involved in sport, but during the depression more and more people engaged in sport as a means of finding satisfaction, achievement, and a sense of community denied them elsewhere. Although sport had made its greatest strides in the period prior to World War I, in the time between the wars sport became an integral part of life for all classes of Americans. However, a number of Americans did not have equal access to the full range of benefits of sport and physical education. Sport and physical education for all remained illusive until after World War II.

Suggestions for Further Reading

1. Betts, John Rickards. *America's Sporting Heritage: 1850–1950.* Reading, MA: Addison-Wesley Publishing Company, 1974.
2. Gerber, Ellen W. *Innovators and Institutions in Physical Education.* Philadelphia: Lea & Febiger, 1971.
3. Lee, Mabel. "The Case for and Against Intercollegiate Athletics for Women and the Situation Since 1923." *Research Quarterly* 2, no. 2 (May 1931): 93–127.
4. Lewis, Guy M. "Adoption of the Sport Program 1903–39: The Role of Accommodation in the Transformation of Physical Education." *Quest* 12 (May 1969): 34–46.

5. Lockhart, Aileene S., and Spears, Betty. *Chronicle of American Physical Education.* Dubuque, IA: Wm. C. Brown Publishers, 1972.
6. Zeigler, Earle F., ed. *A History of Physical Education and Sport in the United States and Canada.* Champaign, IL: Stipes Publishing Company, 1975.

Notes

1. H. S. Fullerton, "Baseball—the Business and the Sport," *American Review of Reviews* 63 (April 1921): 420.
2. David Voigt, *American Baseball,* Vol. 2 (Norman: University of Oklahoma Press, 1970), 233–34.
3. Marshall M. Smelser, "The Babe on Balance," *The American Scholar* 44 (Spring 1975): 299.
4. Robert Peterson, *Only the Ball Was White* (New York: McGraw-Hill Book Company, 1970), 88.
5. Ibid., 92, 93.
6. Ibid., 100.
7. Ocania Chalk, *Pioneers of Black Sport* (New York: Dodd, Mead, and Co., 1975), 78. More detailed information on black sport of this period can be found in this work.
8. Paul Gallico, *The Golden People* (Garden City, N.Y.: Doubleday, 1964), 279.
9. Ibid., 124.
10. Earle F. Zeigler, ed., *A History of Physical Education and Sport in the United States and Canada* (Champaign, IL: Stipes Publishing Company, 1975), 279.
11. Seward C. Staley, "The Four Year Curriculum in Physical (Sports) Education," *Research Quarterly* 2, no. 1 (March 1931): 82, 90.
12. Ellen W. Gerber, "The Ideas and Influences of McCloy, Nash, and Williams," in *The History of Physical Education and Sport,* ed. Bruce L. Bennett (Chicago: The Athletic Institute, 1972), 98–99.
13. Guy M. Lewis, "Adoption of the Sports Program, 1906–39: The Role of Accommodation in the Transformation of Physical Education," *Quest* 12 (May 1969): 42.
14. "Margaret N. H'Doubler," *Dance Encyclopedia,* ed. Anatole Chujoy and Phyllis W. Manchester (New York: Simon and Schuster, 1967), 449.
15. Margaret H'Doubler, *The Dance and Its Place In Education* (New York: Harcourt, Brace & Company, 1925), 43.
16. Helen W. Hazelton, "The University of Minnesota Plan for Freshmen Work," *Bulletin* (September 1927), Mary Hemenway Alumnae Association, Graduate Department of Hygiene and Physical Education, 7. Wellesley College Archives, Wellesley, Massachusetts.
17. *Proceedings of the 13th Annual Convention of the National Collegiate Athletic Association,* December 27, 1918, 38.
18. W. O. McGeehan, "Our Changing Sports Page," *Scribner's Magazine* 84, no. 1 (July 1928): 58.
19. "20,000,000 Saw College Games as Football Scaled New Heights," *New York Times,* 26 (December 1937): S3.
20. Fred Russell and George Leonard, *Big Bowl Football* (New York: Ronald Press, 1963), 72–75.
21. Paul Gallico, *The Golden People* (Garden City, N.Y.: Doubleday, 1964), 259.

22. H. J. Savage, *American College Athletics* (New York: The Carnegie Foundation for the Advancement of Teaching, 1929), 310.
23. *Proceedings of the 25th Annual Convention of the National Collegiate Athletic Association,* December 31, 1930, 83, 84.
24. *Bulletin* (1920–21), Mary Hemenway Alumnae Association, Department of Hygiene, 48. Wellesley College Archives, Wellesley, Massachusetts.
25. Alice A. Sefton, *The Women's Division, National Amateur Athletic Federation* (Stanford: Stanford University Press, 1941), 77–79.
26. Mabel Lee, "The Case for and Against Intercollegiate Athletics for Women and the Situation Since 1923," *Research Quarterly* 2, no. 2 (May 1931): 122–23.
27. *Bulletin* (March 1927), Mary Hemenway Alumnae Association, Graduate Department of Hygiene and Physical Education, 28–29. Wellesley College Archives, Wellesley, Massachusetts.
28. Judith Davidson, "Sport for Women in the Thirties," University of Massachusetts, 1977.
29. Gertrude B. Manchester, "Physical Education in the High School," *Bulletin* (1924–25), Mary Hemenway Alumnae Association, Graduate Department of Hygiene and Physical Education, 13. Wellesley College Archives, Wellesley, Massachusetts.
30. John R. Tunis, "Changing Trends in Sport," *Harper's Monthly Magazine* 170 (December 1934): 86.
31. Ellen W. Gerber et al., *The American Woman in Sport* (Reading, MA: Addison-Wesley Publishing Company, 1974), 117.
32. John Rickards Betts, *America's Sporting Heritage* (Reading, MA: Addison-Wesley Publishing Company, 1974), 279.
33. Foster Rhea Dulles, *America Learns to Play* (New York: D. Appleton-Century, 1940), 349.
34. Samuel Eliot Morison, *The Oxford History of the American People* (New York: Oxford University Press, 1965), 1007–8.
35. Theodore P. Bank, "Army Athletics," *Hygiea* 19 (November 1941): 876.
36. Merrie A. Fidler, "The Development and Decline of the All-American Girls Baseball League, 1943–1954," Master's thesis, University of Massachusetts, 1976.
37. John Rickards Betts, *America's Sporting Heritage* (Reading, MA: Addison-Wesley Publishing Company, 1974), 330.
38. John W. Loy, Jr., "The Nature of Sport: A Definitional Effort," *Quest* 10 (May 1968): 1.

Time Line

HISTORY

1945
United Nations founded

1947
Beginning of "cold war"
1948
State of Israel proclaimed
1950
Korean War started
1954
Supreme Court overturned *Plessy v. Ferguson;* segregated schools banned
1957
USSR orbited Sputnik; subsequent U.S. pressure for more science in schools
1963
President Kennedy assassinated
Student riots at Berkeley; then on other campuses
1965
U.S. intervention in Vietnam escalated

1969
Americans landed on moon

1974
Watergate scandal; President Nixon resigned

1979–81
Hostages held in Iran
1979–87
Terrorism spread

SPORT AND PHYSICAL EDUCATION

1946
All-American Football Conference formed
1947
Jackie Robinson joined Brooklyn Dodgers
1949
Ladies Professional Golf Association formed
National Basketball Association formed
1951
College basketball gambling scandal
1960
Wilma Rudolph won 3 gold medals in Rome Olympics

1964
Muhammad Ali won world heavyweight boxing title
1965
Houston "Astrodome" opened
1966
Professional football's first "Superbowl"
Major League Baseball Players' Association formed
1969
Diane Crump first woman jockey on major track
1971
Association for Intercollegiate Athletics for Women (AIAW) established
1972
Title IX of Educational Amendments
1973
Secretariat first horse in twenty-five years to win Triple Crown
Billie Jean King defeated Bobby Riggs in challenge match
1981
Major League baseball strike
NCAA sponsored women's intercollegiate sport
AIAW suspended operation
1982
National Football League strike

7 Sport and Physical Education for Everyone, 1945–1987

Overview

In 1946 Jackie Robinson became the first black in the twentieth century to be signed to a major league baseball club. That same year Kenny Washington went with the Los Angeles Rams of the National Football League and four years later the Boston Celtics drafted Chuck Cooper of Duquesne. In 1949 the Ladies Professional Golf Association was formed and by the mid-1980s sport fans were following the careers of top golfer Nancy Lopez and tennis professional Martina Navratilova as well as those of Tom Watson and Ivan Lendl. For the first time blacks, women, and other minorities played more than a token role in sport.

Since World War II not only have racial and gender barriers in sport been infiltrated, but civil rights legislation, the twentieth century women's movement, and a reexamination of professional players' rights have lent support and credence to the "sport for everyone" ideal. In 1980 over sixty-six percent of United States' youth had graduated from high school and over fifty percent attended an educational institution beyond high school. Most American children took part in physical education programs consisting of fitness activities and lifetime sports.

The civil rights movement of the 1950s and 1960s focused on the right of minorities to have equal access to all facets of life in the United States— education, public accommodations, the political process, and employment. The movement employed nonviolent procedures to change many segregation practices in the South. The 1954 Supreme Court *Brown v. Board of Education of Topeka* decision reversed the "separate but equal" ruling in the *Plessy v. Ferguson* case of 1896. Led by Dr. Martin Luther King, Jr., other black religious leaders, and student groups, white and black resisters held sit-in demonstrations that broke the segregation patterns in stores, theaters, and public facilities in many southern cities. In March, 1963, thousands of people marched on Washington, D. C., protesting many forms of discrimination and in 1964 a broad civil rights bill was passed under President Lyndon B. Johnson.

The civil rights movement challenged the myth that sport was the most democratic institution in society. By the sixties professional and collegiate teams were charged with maintaining race quotas, with "stacking" black players in certain team positions to restrict their numbers in a game at any given time, with inadequate academic counseling for black intercollegiate players, with discrimination in off-season employment and endorsement contracts for black professional players, and with the lack of black coaches, managers, and athletic administrators in predominantly white institutions. In addition, black athletes entered the civil rights movement, lending their name and influence to the cause. The threat of a boycott by black members of the 1968 United States Olympic team was the most dramatic of several incidents in which the athletic arena was used to publicize problems of black athletes.

The civil rights cause involved not only black athletes, but also white players who spoke out on issues that they perceived as unfair or improper. Stimulated by the writings of sport sociologists and a few players, some athletes increasingly criticized the autocratic approach to athletics at a time when they and their peers protested an undeclared war in Vietnam and other civil inequities. Professional football and baseball players contested the reserve clause in their contracts through lawsuits. The owners also took refuge in the courts as they sought immunity from antitrust laws. The use of the law court in sport became an accepted practice.

The women's movement of the 1960s and 1970s, sparked by Betty Friedan's *Feminine Mystique,* brought the continuing unequal status of women to the attention of the country. Proponents supported equal pay for equal work, women's entry into traditionally male-oriented professions such as engineering and law, and access to prestigious positions usually held by men. Following the passage of the 1964 Civil Rights Bill in which Title VII prohibited discrimination in employment practices on the basis of race, color, religion, sex, or national origin, the Equal Employment Opportunities Commission (EEOC) was established to issue standards for enforcing the law. The National Organization for Women (NOW), founded in 1966, the Women's Equity Action League (WEAL), and other women's organizations promoted equality in many facets of the work place. Title IX of the Educational Amendments of 1972 specifically addressed equal opportunities in physical education, sport, and athletics in educational institutions.

These laws and other social forces interacted to produce a climate in which women's sport in general expanded in scope, and women's professional sport in particular made rapid strides in numbers, organization, prize money, press coverage, and general acceptance. This explosion, the twentieth century women's movement, civil rights legislation, and the impact of individual athletes such as Mildred "Babe" Didrikson Zaharias and Billie Jean King, all contributed to a growing support of equality of opportunity for women in sport. Golf and tennis became the major professional sports for women, but there were also professional women bowlers, ice skaters, softball players, jockeys, basketball players, track and field performers, and football players. In the 1970s women athletes became an important and integral part of sport in every aspect: girls seeking equal chances in youth sport such as Little League; college women asking for a greater number of sports, more competition, and more support; and professional women golfers and tennis players demanding and obtaining a greater share of prize money.

In this period a great many Americans enjoyed affluence, adequate health care, opportunities for education, and employment. Many others, however, remained at the poverty level. Following the Vietnam and other conflicts in the South Pacific, Asian immigration increased markedly. America again began to meld other cultural influences into its everyday life.

While religion appeared to have less influence on the lives of average Americans after World War II, many clerics took an active role in the civil rights movement. Several groups such as Zen Buddhists and fundamentalist Christians attracted persons who sought, among other things, a meaningful reinterpretation of ethical values. Beginning in the late 1970s and continuing through the 1980s, a surge of political conservatism, Protestant fundamentalism, and a return to "basic values" was evident in religion, schools, and even television advertisements. In contrast to earlier conservative movements, this one approved rather than disapproved of sport and physical education.

Postwar technology in communication, fabrics, physiology, and transportation all affected traditional sports and created new ones. By 1960, television had become a major force in presenting sport to Americans. More than twice as many people watched a single World Series baseball game in 1975 (seventy-six million for the seventh game) than attended all the major league games played in that year (more than twenty-nine million). Transportation from continent to continent took only a few hours and made international competitions and world championships an established part of worldwide sport. In the United States teams habitually traveled by air, and intersectional events became commonplace. Sport also grew into a significant part of the economy, with hundreds of professional sport performers, thousands of student athletes, thousands of amateur sportsmen and sportswomen, hundreds of thousands of sport participants, and millions of sport fans. These performers, participants, and fans were actual or potential consumers of sport-related goods, equipment, and clothing in a multibillion dollar industry. The advertising and marketing of sport, operating sport resorts and facilities, manufacturing of sport equipment and clothes, and other sport-related enterprises became part of the sport world. A prosperous economy encouraged more participants in sport, more spectators, more television coverage, and a growing acceptance of sport and physical education as pervasive forces in American life.

Sport and physical education no longer needed to be justified. Sport expanded in all sectors—professional, amateur, recreational, and educational. After Title IX of the Educational Amendments of 1972, many physical education programs brought boys and girls together in classes for the first time.

Many school systems began physical education in the elementary grades. From the time they were small children, sport and physical education were available to most Americans. This chapter will examine the social changes and improved technology that occurred after World War II as they affected all sectors of sport and promoted physical education for everyone.

Professional Sport

Following World War II professional sport became the dominant component of the American sport scene. Alterations in rules or team strategies among the professionals influenced changes in amateur and school sport and games. Professional organizations became the models for organized sport for children and youth, and the professional athlete became the sport hero for millions of youngsters. Professional sport was promoted through advertising, books, and especially television, which became the key to financial success for entire leagues.

Many sports were opened to women during the period following World War II. Some sports, such as bowling and ice skating, had had professional women participants for years. Many ice skating professionals, such as Norwegian Sonja Henie, were former Olympic medalists. Recent skaters such as Peggy Fleming and Dorothy Hamill became stars of ice shows. But skaters of lesser billing in ice shows came from the growing number of professional women ice skaters. Professional golf for women was initiated in the late 1940s, but it was not until two decades later that sport began to provide stable careers for talented women athletes. Since the early 1970s, professional opportunities for women in tennis, basketball, softball, volleyball, horse racing, and even football have increased. However, some sports and groups, like women's professional football and basketball, faded quickly.

The growth of professional sport was largely a phenomenon of an affluent and hi-tech society. Sport on television entertained millions, super jets transported teams across the country and to other continents, manufacturers supplied athletes with the latest equipment, and computers assisted in recruiting athletes and scheduling games. Over fifty million Americans have watched the Super Bowl football game each year since 1975, and regular sports on television changed the eating habits of millions of families. In 1983 over forty-six percent of American households watched the Super Bowl. In addition, crowds turned out to watch men and women of various racial and ethnic backgrounds compete professionally in games and contests unheard of at mid-twentieth century. The development of professional sport in this period will be traced by examining changes in "the big three," baseball, football, and basketball, and looking at other popular pro sports.

These changes include the stabilization of sport governance, racial integration, the general development and promotion of the game, especially with the advent of television, and recognition of professional sport as part of the nation's entertainment industry.

Professional Team Sports

Baseball

Major league baseball, with its American and National Leagues, the World Series, and a commissioner in charge, was the first to establish a stable governance pattern. The pattern, in place by the 1920s, successfully withstood the mid-1940s threat of the short-lived Mexican League. Baseball was also the first of the major professional sports to sign a black player, Jackie Robinson, following World War II.

In 1945 Branch Rickey organized the United States Baseball League, to be comprised of black teams, including a team named the Brown Dodgers. Rickey sent scouts to find players for the Brown Dodgers, but especially to seek one man—an excellent baseball player to integrate professional baseball. The person chosen would have to be able to play with white players, to get along with them, and to be able to withstand the taunts, discrimination, and unpleasant situations that undoubtedly would occur. The scouts found Jack Roosevelt Robinson. Rickey explained his long-range plans to Robinson. First, Robinson would play with the Montreal Royals and, then, with the Brooklyn Dodgers. Above all, Robinson's job was to integrate major league baseball and he must be prepared to work toward that end.

Rickey permitted the United States Baseball League to fold and sent Robinson to Montreal. On April 11, 1947, Robinson played in his first regular season major league baseball game, paving the way for hundreds of black players in professional sport. Carefully groomed in the club's Montreal farm team for two years, Robinson made his debut without the predicted race riots and withstood the suspicions, taunts, and threats of players and fans alike. His selection as "Rookie of the Year" in 1947 and as "Most Valuable Player" for the Dodgers in 1949 insured the success of the "noble experiment." In the next few years the Dodgers signed other talented black players such as Joe Black, Don Newcombe, and Roy Campanella. The American League had its first black player in 1948 when Bill Veeck of the Cleveland Indians signed outfielder Larry Doby.

Until 1953 major league baseball was strictly an eastern and midwestern affair, with Chicago and St. Louis the most western cities in the leagues. Much to the consternation of the owners, baseball attendance dropped from 20,972,601 in 1948 to 16,616,310 in 1955. Although television had been accepted by the 1950s, the owners at first blamed it for the drop in attendance.

The Boston Braves of the National League drew only 281,278 spectators in 1952. The following year an experiment changed the structure of baseball from a few cities in the East to a nationwide network. In 1953 the Boston Braves moved to Milwaukee and had instant success with 1,826,397 in attendance. In 1954 the St. Louis Browns became the Baltimore Orioles, and in 1955 the Philadelphia Athletics were the Kansas City Athletics. The West Coast acquired major league teams in 1958 when the New York Giants moved to San Francisco and the Brooklyn Dodgers switched to Los Angeles. League expansion in 1961, 1962, and in 1969 resulted in four divisions, each league consisting of two divisions, the champions of which competed in a playoff to determine the league pennant winner. The expansion brought more cities into the national structure of the game and more demand for baseball on television. Cities with regional television markets became desirable home cities for baseball franchises, and television rights meant economic survival of major league clubs. By the 1970s both the All-Star game and the World Series were major television attractions. Widespread televising of major league games did, however, mean the doom of many minor leagues, who were unable to attract spectators and fans.

In 1962, when the Yankees gained their twenty-seventh American League pennant, another New York team, the Mets of the National League, began a losing streak that became as much a box office attraction as winning. During one losing season, 1963, they drew a million fans. They had finished last five times, and placed second to last twice in their league, when they shocked and delighted the sports world in 1969 by winning both the pennant and the World Series. Arthur Daley of the *New York Times* explained: "The Mets did far more for baseball than just bring championship banners to Shea Stadium. They gave a shot of adrenalin to the entire baseball establishment with an injection of renewed life, vitality, interest and excitement, all woefully diminished of recent years."[1]

In 1948 the sports world mourned the death of George Herman "Babe" Ruth, the man who had brought unprecedented popularity to baseball. At the time of his death many of Ruth's records remained as lasting testimony to his greatness. New stars such as Ted Williams, Stan Musial, Jackie Robinson, Willie Mays, and Micky Mantle, while perhaps lacking the theatrical qualities of the early star, nevertheless responded to changes in the game and provided new thrills and records. The New York Yankees began their string of victories which led them to five consecutive World Series championships from 1949 through 1953 and a total of ten World Series championships and fifteen American League pennants between 1947 and 1964.

By the beginning of the sixties, two of Ruth's most hallowed records—sixty home runs in one season and 714 career home runs—still stood. In 1961, Roger Maris of the New York Yankees broke the first record by one in a season that was six games longer than the Babe's 1927 year, thus creating a controversy over whether or not the record was actually broken. The second record fell on April 8, 1974, when Henry "Hank" Aaron of the Atlanta Braves hit his 715th home run.

The game itself changed in this period. In 1930, sixty-six players with four hundred or more times at bat had batting averages over .300 while in 1968 Boston's Carl Yastrzemski won the American League batting title with .301. In an effort to bolster the hitting, which had declined steadily, the American League instituted the "designated hitter" position to replace the pitcher in the batting order in 1973. As the hitting became less important, pitching came to dominate the game due to the development of relief pitchers, greater emphasis on home run hitting, larger ball parks, and more night games.[2]

The opening of the Houston Astrodome in 1965, with its artificial turf on which the ball moved faster (and players fell harder) than on natural grass, sparked a period of new stadium construction in cities with established teams as well as those with new franchises. A number of new multi-purpose stadiums installed artificial turf which was economical, easily maintained, and readily adaptable to a variety of sports and other events. The number of night games increased to draw the people unable to attend afternoon games and also to adapt to prime time on television.

In 1953, a congressional committee repeated an investigation into baseball's exemption from antitrust laws. In 1970 the Supreme Court confirmed earlier decisions that baseball was not subject to antitrust laws. Inside the baseball world, players expressed their growing concern about the conditions of their employment. One baseball historian concluded that "Many players now saw themselves as workers and seemed more interested in money and pensions."[3] In 1946, the owners averted formation of a players' union by allowing player representatives to attend meetings and help formulate more equitable contracts. The Major League Baseball Players' Association (MLBPA) evolved from these informal arrangements and gradually gained strength and recognition by the National Labor Relations Board (NLRB) as the certified representative of the players. Beginning in the late 1960s, the owners and the players accepted arbitration as a means to settle disputes, and in the 1970s the NLRB ruled that the employees of baseball, umpires as well as players, came under its jurisdiction.

MAJOR LEAGUE BASEBALL EXPANSION 1952–1987

American League

1952	1955		1961	
Boston Red Sox	Baltimore Orioles	(1954)	Baltimore	
Chicago White Sox	Boston		Boston	
Cleveland Indians	Chicago		Chicago	
Detroit Tigers	Cleveland		Cleveland	
New York Yankees	Detroit		Detroit	
Philadelphia Athletics	Kansas City Athletics	(1955)	Kansas City	
St. Louis Browns	New York		Los Angeles Angels	(1961)
Washington Senators	Washington		Minnesota Twins	(1961)
			New York	
			Washington	

National League

Boston Braves	Brooklyn		Chicago	
Brooklyn Dodgers	Chicago		Cincinnati	
Chicago Cubs	Cincinnati		Los Angeles Dodgers	(1958)
Cincinnati Reds	Milwaukee Braves	(1953)	Milwaukee	
New York Giants	Philadelphia		Philadelphia	
Philadelphia Phillies	Pittsburgh		Pittsburgh	
Pittsburgh Pirates	New York		St. Louis	
St. Louis Cardinals	St. Louis		San Francisco Giants	(1958)

(   ) Year franchise changed name or entered league.

* Divisional winners playoff for pennant in each league; winners compete in World Series, established in 1903.

MAJOR LEAGUE BASEBALL EXPANSION 1952–1987

American League

1969	1987
Eastern Division	*Eastern Division*
Baltimore	Baltimore Orioles
Boston	Boston Red Sox
Cleveland	Cleveland Indians
Detroit	Detroit Tigers
New York	Milwaukee Brewers (1970)
Washington	New York Yankees
	Toronto Blue Jays (1977)

Western Division		*Western Division*	
California Angels	(1965)	California Angels	
Chicago		Chicago White Sox	
Kansas City Royals		Kansas City Royals	
Minnesota		Minnesota Twins	
Oakland Athletics	(1968)	Oakland Athletics	
Seattle Pilots	(1968)	Seattle Mariners	(1977)
		Texas Rangers	(1972)

PLAYOFFS

American League Pennant

World Series

National League

Eastern Division		*Eastern Division*	
Chicago		Chicago Cubs	
Montreal Expos	(1962)	Montreal Expos	
New York Mets	(1962)	New York Mets	
Philadelphia		Philadelphia Phillies	
Pittsburgh		Pittsburgh Pirates	
St. Louis		St. Louis Cardinals	

Western Division	*Western Division*	
Atlanta Braves (1966)	Atlanta Braves	
Cincinnati	Cincinnati Reds	
Houston Colts / Astros (1962)	Houston Astros	
Los Angeles	Los Angeles Dodgers	
San Diego Padres (1969)	San Diego Padres	
San Francisco	San Francisco Giants	

National League Pennant

In 1969 some players boycotted the opening of spring training because of a dispute over owner contributions to the pension fund. Three years later major league players staged a thirteen-day strike, again over the issue of the pension fund, and delayed the opening of the season ten days, causing the cancellation of eighty-six regular season games. In 1973, the owners agreed that a player with ten years of major league experience, the last five with the same club, could not be traded without his consent. Over the years several players tested the tight control of the players by the owners. After the principle of arbitration had been accepted by baseball, Andy Messersmith of the Los Angeles Dodgers and Dave McNally of the Montreal Expos, both of whom had played a year without signing a contract, contested the proposed renewal of their contracts. Arbitrator Peter Seitz agreed with the players, ruling that "the practical effect of [the case] was to allow all players currently under contract to play out their option year and become free agents."[4]

In 1976 a collective bargaining agreement was reached between management and the Players' Association. During the next several years bidding for free agent players caused salaries to increase greatly. By 1981 the average player's salary had reached $150,000, with some players signing contracts for over a million dollars per year. During 1980 and 1981, the team owners, predicting fiscal chaos, sought compensation for the teams losing players through free agency. Bargaining negotiations between the owners and the Players' Association were unsuccessful and on June 12, 1981, the players went out on strike. The American public was deprived of major league baseball for fifty days. In the extremely complicated compromise settlement, the players retained the concept of being free agents; the owners who lost free agents were provided with compensation in various combinations of draft choices, players selected from a "pool," and money. The owners hoped the increases in salary would slow down. Regardless of the outcome, it was generally agreed that the summer of 1981 was not the same without a full season of major league baseball. A players' strike in August, 1985, was quickly settled after two days.

Baseball struggled with the increased popularity of football and basketball, with a greater variety of active sports and interests available to people, and with the impact of television with its wide range of program offerings about sport and many other topics. The owners also struggled with escalating salaries and players' demands. However, in the mid-1980s baseball continued to be one of the "big three" in the nation's world of sport. Teams and leagues were balanced competitively, attendance figures were solid, and television ratings good. For many, baseball was still the "national game."

Football
The growth of professional football is a modern sport phenomenon. Americans who believed that baseball was the national game were startled and disbelieving when professional football burst on the sports scene in the 1960s. By 1967, having withstood several challenges, the National Football League

(NFL), headed by a commissioner, controlled professional football. World War II decimated the young NFL, but by 1946 it recovered, and the All-American Football Conference (AAFC) formed as a rival to the older league. The AAFC signed some NFL players and drafted top college talent. In 1949, the AAFC merged with the NFL, which awarded franchises to the Cleveland Browns, the San Francisco 49ers, and the Baltimore Colts. The other teams were disbanded and the players distributed among the remaining clubs. In 1950 the NFL reorganized into two conferences, the National and the American, and also in that year held a playoff to determine a championship team.

A second rival league, the American Football League (AFL), was organized in 1960 by a number of wealthy businessmen led by Texan, Lamar Hunt. The new league raided NFL and college teams, escalating player salaries at a rate alarming to owners and fans alike. In 1966, a merger of the NFL and AFL was negotiated to begin in 1970. The name National Football League was retained and the league organized into two conferences, the American and National, each with three divisions. The next rival, the World Football League, which played only the 1974 season, was never a threat to the NFL.

In 1983 NFL control was again challenged with the organization of the United States Football League (USFL). Plans for a new league were announced in 1982 to begin in 1983, playing from March to July. The idea of spring football could not be sold to enough fans and, after three seasons, the new league proposed moving to the traditional fall season. The USFL sued the NFL in an antitrust suit, alleging that the NFL, acting as a monopoly, denied the new league access to the fall season, including lucrative television contracts. In its defense, the NFL asserted that it had neither prevented nor hindered the USFL and that the demise of the USFL was due to mismanagement. Unsuccessful in its suit, the USFL cancelled its 1986 season, leaving the NFL in undisputed control of professional football.

After thirteen years without a black player in professional football, Kenny Washington and Woody Strode broke the color line in 1946 without the publicity and fanfare given to Jackie Robinson. Both Washington and Strode, excellent college players from the University of California at Los Angeles, joined the Rams when they moved to Los Angeles. Integration was further established when the Cleveland Browns signed Marion Motley and Bill Willis. Like Robinson in baseball, these early professional football players suffered taunts and other forms of discrimination.[5]

The initiation of the free substitution rule in the early fifties allowed increased specialization by players and thus more highly skilled performances. The new rule permitted greater recognition of players such as the defensive linemen, long the unsung laborers of the game. Stars such as Joe Schmidt of the Detroit Lions, Dick Butkus of the Chicago Bears, and Joe Green of the Pittsburgh Steelers became football heroes. Offensive position stars such as Johnny Unitas, Jim Brown, Gale Sayers, Joe Namath, and O. J. Simpson

PROFESSIONAL FOOTBALL EXPANSION 1946–1987

National Football League

1946	1950	1961
Eastern Division	**American Conference**	**Eastern Conference**
Boston Yanks	Chicago Cardinals	Cleveland
Philadelphia Eagles	Cleveland Browns (1950)	Dallas Cowboys (1960)
Pittsburgh Steelers	New York Giants	New York
New York Giants	Philadelphia Eagles	Philadelphia
Washington Redskins	Pittsburgh Steelers	Pittsburgh
	Washington Redskins	St. Louis Cardinals (1960)
		Washington
Western Division	**National Conference**	**Western Conference**
Chicago Bears	Baltimore Colts (1950)	Baltimore
Chicago Cardinals	Chicago Bears	Chicago
Detroit Lions	Detroit Lions	Detroit
Green Bay Packers	Green Bay Packers	Green Bay
Los Angeles Rams	Los Angeles Rams	Los Angeles
	New York Yanks	Minnesota (1961)
	San Francisco 49ers (1950)	San Francisco

All-American Football Conference 1946–1949

Eastern Division
Brooklyn Dodgers
Buffalo Bisons
Miami Seahawks
New York Yankees

Western Division
Chicago Hornets / Rockets
Cleveland Browns
Los Angeles Dons
San Francisco 49ers

American Football League 1961–1970

Eastern Division
Boston Patriots
Buffalo Bills
Houston Oilers
New York Titans / Jets

Western Division
Dallas Texans / Kansas City Chiefs (1963)
Denver Broncos
Oakland Raiders
San Diego Chargers (1961)

(   ) Year franchise changed name or entered league.

* Six division winners plus two wild card teams in each conference compete for conference championships. Conference champions compete in Super Bowl. First Super Bowl was in 1966.

PROFESSIONAL FOOTBALL EXPANSION 1946–1987

National Football League

1970	1987	
National Conference	**National Conference**	*PLAYOFFS*
Eastern Division	*Eastern Division*	
Dallas	Dallas Cowboys	
New York	New York Giants	
Philadelphia	Philadelphia Eagles	
St. Louis	St. Louis Cardinals	
Washington	Washington Redskins	

Central Division	*Central Division*	
Chicago	Chicago Bears	
Detroit	Detroit Lions	National Conference
Green Bay	Green Bay Packers	Champion
Minnesota	Minnesota Vikings	
	Tampa Bay Buccaneers	
	(1976)	

Western Division	*Western Division*	
Atlanta Falcons (1966)	Atlanta Falcons	
Los Angeles	Los Angeles Rams	
New Orleans Saints (1967)	New Orleans Saints	
San Francisco	San Francisco 49ers	
	2 wild cards	

American Conference

Eastern Division	*Eastern Division*	Super
Baltimore	Indianapolis Colts (1984)	Bowl
Boston	Buffalo Bills	
Buffalo	Miami Dolphins	
Miami Dolphins (1966)	New England Patriots	
New York	New York Jets	

Central Division	*Central Division*	
Cincinnati Bengals (1967)	Cincinnati Bengals	
Cleveland	Cleveland Browns	
Houston	Houston Oilers	
Pittsburgh	Pittsburgh Steelers	American Conference
		Champion

Western Division	*Western Division*	
Denver	Denver Broncos	
Kansas City	Kansas City Chiefs	
Oakland	Los Angeles Raiders (1982)	
San Diego	San Diego Chargers	
	Seattle Seahawks (1976)	
	2 wild cards	

brought additional excitement to the game. More recent stars include Dan Marino, Walter Payton, and Mark Gastineau. The superb coaching of George Halas, Vince Lombardi, Tom Landry, Bill Walsh, and Don Shula gave football scientific precision, which appealed to millions of "armchair quarterbacks" across the nation. As early as 1960, many argued that the game had passed baseball as the nation's most popular sport.

The phenomenal growth and popularity of pro football was attributed largely to television. Like their peers in baseball, the football owners were at first opposed to the concept of free viewing of games on television. The NFL's policy of televising only games away from home and blacking out the home games on local television seemed to build interest and encourage ticket sales. By 1957, games were telecast into 175 cities and millions of people watched young Jim Brown of Cleveland begin his career by winning "Rookie of the Year" honors. In 1958 over twenty million watched the championship games.

In the early 1960s the National Broadcasting Company signed a contract to televise the newly formed American Football League games, infusing enough money into the league to save its faltering franchises. Throughout the decade television contracts grew more lucrative and league owners considered those revenues necessary to meet spiraling personnel and other operating expenses. The Professional Football Hall of Fame opened in 1963 in Canton, Ohio, the home of early professional football.

In the 1970s and 1980s, additional changes improved the game and the ambience surrounding it. Television continued to play a major role in football's popularity. The camera was able to pick up developing plays, and the commentators analyzed them between downs. The use of isolated camera shots and instant replays after crucial plays brought the television fans closer to major decisions in the games. As important as television was to the popularity of professional football, the game itself was well suited to telecasting. With the teams well balanced, the games were exciting to watch. Monday Night Football became a regular television feature; all the major networks aired football games; and Super Bowl Sunday became an unofficial national holiday.

In 1956 the players in the National Football League formed a Players Association that had little influence during the first years of its existence. When the rival AFL began, its players formed the American Football League Players Association (AFLPA) and, with the merger of the NFL and the AFL, the two groups joined in the National Football League Players Association (NFLPA).

In 1970 the players and owners failed to make a settlement before the season. After a short lockout and strike, a four-year contract was signed. Again in 1974, when an agreement had not been reached, the players initiated a strike, which was unsuccessful because the players were not unified.

While football did not have a reserve rule like baseball, it did operate under a practice known as the "Rozelle Rule," named for commissioner Pete Rozelle. Under this rule a player could move to a different team, provided that the new team compensated the player's old team. If an agreement could not be reached between the teams, the commissioner, in this case Rozelle, determined the appropriate compensation, effectively inhibiting the players from moving freely to a new team. After John Mackey successfully challenged the Rozelle Rule in 1976, the NFLPA moved to a stronger position, acting as a union negotiating on behalf of the players.

The 1982 season brought the longest player strike in the history of United States professional sport. Following the second game of the season the players walked out on a strike that lasted fifty-seven days. As a result of the negotiations the players achieved an increase in the minimum wage scale and post-season play, a merit bonus system, severance pay, and other improvements in players' rights. However, the settlement left the control of professional football with the owners, since the NFLPA was unable to obtain its original demand of a percentage of the gross revenue of each team or a percentage of the television revenues. Management also retained the restrictive free agent system since the NFLPA did not attempt to change it. Football players' labor matters, like baseball, were governed by a collective bargaining agreement and were under the jurisdiction of the NLRB.

In 1986 the NFL was firmly in control of the game. Football stadiums, often seating sixty or seventy thousand people, were full. Fans who were not among those in the stadium watched the games on television. Many people considered football the biggest of the 'big three" of professional sport.

Basketball

Professional basketball was the last of the "big three" to establish its present controlling organization, the National Basketball Association (NBA). Prior to World War II, professional basketball consisted of traveling teams such as the Harlem Globetrotters, local regional leagues, successful "national" tournaments, and unsuccessful short-lived "national leagues."

The Rens, the popular black prewar team, disbanded after the 1948 season when the team was persuaded to represent Dayton, Ohio, in the National Basketball League (NBL). The Globetrotters continued to play during World War II and, after the war, expanded their tours to include all of the United States. In the early 1950s the team began to visit overseas, often introducing basketball to other countries. The players were highly skilled and also extremely clever at trick shots, rapid ball handling, and clowning, which they inserted into their game to please the audience. Some sport critics likened the Globetrotters' carnival atmosphere to the minstrel shows of the South, pointing out that middle-class Americans accepted blacks as entertainers, but not as athletes. The Globetrotters recognized that sport was part of the entertainment industry and, while they thrilled the audiences with their skill, they also brought enjoyment to the fans.

PROFESSIONAL BASKETBALL 1949–1987

National Basketball Association

1949–1950*
Merger: BAA & NBL
Eastern Division
Baltimore Bullets
Boston Celtics
New York Knicks
Philadelphia Warriors
Syracuse Nationals
Washington Capitols

Central Division
Chicago Stags
Fort Wayne Pistons
Minneapolis Lakers
Rochester Royals
St. Louis Hawks

Western Division
Anderson Packers
Denver Nuggets
Indianapolis Olympians
Sheboygan Redskins
Tri-Cities Blackhawks
Waterloo Hawks

1961–1962
Eastern Division
Boston
Philadelphia
New York
Syracuse

Western Division
Cincinnati Royals   (1957)
Detroit Pistons   (1957)
Los Angeles Lakers (1960)
St. Louis

1967–1968
Eastern Division
Baltimore Bullets   (1963)
Boston
Cincinnati
Detroit
New York
Philadelphia

Western Division
Chicago Bulls
Los Angeles
St. Louis
San Diego Rockets   (1967)
San Francisco Warriors (1962)
Seattle Supersonics   (1967)

	American Basketball League 1961–1962	American Basketball Association 1967–1976
	Eastern Division Chicago Cleveland Pittsburgh Washington	*Eastern Division* Indiana Pacers Kentucky Colonels Minnesota Muskies New Jersey Americans Pittsburgh Pipers
	Western Division Hawaii Kansas City Los Angeles San Francisco	*Western Division* Anaheim Amigos Dallas Chaparrals Denver Nuggets Houston Mavericks Oakland Oaks New Orleans Buccaneers

(   ) Year franchise changed name or entered league.
* The Basketball Association of America and the National Basketball League merged to form National Basketball Association.
** Six best teams (record) in each conference compete in playoffs with division winners receiving a bye into quarterfinals; the winners in each conference compete for World Championship.

PROFESSIONAL BASKETBALL 1949–1987

National Basketball Association

1976–1977

Eastern Conference
Atlantic Division
Boston Celtics
Buffalo Braves
New York Knicks
New York Nets
Philadelphia 76ers

Central Division
Atlanta Hawks   (1968)
Cleveland Cavaliers   (1970)
Houston Rockets   (1971)
New Orleans Jazz   (1974)
San Antonio Spurs   (1973)
Washington Bullets   (1973)

1986–87

Eastern Conference
Atlantic Division
Boston Celtics
New Jersey Nets   (1978)
New York Knicks
Philadelphia 76ers
Washington Bullets

Central Division
Atlanta Hawks
Chicago Bulls
Cleveland Cavaliers
Detroit Pistons
Indiana Pacers   (1976)
Milwaukee Bucks

PLAYOFFS

Eastern
Champion

World Championship

Western Conference
Midwestern Division
Chicago Bulls
Denver Nuggets
Detroit Pistons
Indiana Pacers
Kansas City Kings
Milwaukee Bucks   (1968)

Pacific Division
Golden State Warriors (1971)
Los Angeles Lakers
Phoenix Suns   (1970)
Portland Trail Blazers (1970)
Seattle Supersonics

Western Conference
Midwest Division
Dallas Mavericks   (1980)
Denver Nuggets
Houston Rockets
Sacramento Kings   (1985)
San Antonio Spurs
Utah Jazz   (1979)

Pacific Division
Golden State Warriors
Los Angeles Lakers
Phoenix Suns
Portland Trail Blazers
Los Angeles Clippers   (1984)
Seattle Supersonics

Western
Champion

The National Basketball League survived World War II. In 1946 the Arena Manager's Association organized the Basketball Association of America (BAA) with the idea of adding more events, bringing larger audiences to their arenas, and making a good profit. Although they patterned the BAA on successful baseball practices, the new league had difficulty competing with the established NBL. After BAA league president Maurice Podoloff persuaded four NBL teams that the BAA had greater potential for crowds and profit, the two leagues negotiated a merger.

In 1949 the National Basketball League and the Basketball Association of America merged into the NBA with seventeen teams in cities such as Anderson and Indianapolis, Indiana, Syracuse and Rochester, New York, Sheboygan, Wisconsin, and Waterloo, Iowa, as well as larger cities such as St. Louis, Chicago, and New York. In 1953, professional basketball averaged only three thousand spectators per game. By 1959, the NBA drew over two million in attendance, moved most teams from small cities to major population centers, reduced itself to eight teams and operated on a fiscally sound basis. With the increasing popularity of professional basketball, not only did the NBA expand in 1961 but a rival, the American Basketball League (ABL), was founded with eight teams. The ABL folded in 1963, but four years later the American Basketball Association (ABA) started with George Mikan as commissioner. The new league attempted to be different from the NBA by instituting a three-point shot from twenty-five feet, a thirty-second shot clock, and a red, white, and blue ball. Efforts to outbid other teams, accusations of questionable practices between the leagues, and the problems of undesirable franchises led the NBA owners to oppose a merger with the ABA. However, two leagues created many problems and after lengthy negotiations a merger was arranged in 1976, completing a twenty-five year cycle of merging, expanding, rivaling, and merging. The NBA name was retained.

Integration followed a somewhat different pattern in basketball. Although two excellent black teams, the Rens and the Harlem Globetrotters, played an important role in the early growth of professional basketball, the NBA was the last of the major sport associations to be integrated. In the 1950 draft the Boston Celtics surprised the league by selecting a black college player, Charles Cooper of Duquesne, then playing with the Harlem Globetrotters. Another black, Earl Lloyd, was drafted by the Washington Capitols and Nat "Sweetwater" Clifton moved to the New York Knickerbockers from the Harlem Globetrotters.[6] In 1967 Bill Russell was named player-coach of the Boston Celtics, the second black manager in a major league sport. The first was John McLendon, a former coach of a black college, who had been hired by the Cleveland club in the short-lived American Basketball League in 1960. In 1980–81 the NBA All-Star team included eight black players and two white players.

By 1980 blacks dominated professional basketball. Some people attributed this domination to the competitiveness of black players. Julius Erving of the Philadelphia 76ers expressed his view that "what the black athlete did was to enhance the game with an expression all his own, taking the basics to another dimension. Soon the white player began to emulate these thoughts and moves and eventually the game became what it is today—a stage where a unique combination of the team concept and individual expression are presented in pure form."[7]

Although planning for the Naismith Memorial Basketball Hall of Fame began in 1936 and the first inductees were elected in 1959, the Hall of Fame did not open until 1968. Located in the city in which basketball was invented, Springfield, Massachusetts, it moved to a larger site within the city in 1985.

Like players in baseball and football, basketball players did not recognize the need for a players association until Larry Fleisher, an attorney and agent for some of the players, organized the National Basketball Players Association (NBPA) in the 1960s. Once organized, the NBPA bargained successfully. In 1964 the players delayed the start of the All Star Game for a few minutes until they were assured of certain actions by the owners.[8] Oscar Robertson headed the list of a number of players who sued the NBA to prevent restrictions on player movements. The complex settlement, finally made in 1976, favored the players and became a landmark in settling later disputes. A two-day strike at the beginning of the 1985 season led to a five-year contract. The agreement involved greater contributions by the owners to the pension fund, a simplification of the free agency system, and an increase in the minimum player salary and the players' share of the playoff revenues. The NBPA followed the pattern of the MLBPA and the NFLPA. Many disputes were settled by arbitration and the players' association acted as a union under the jurisdiction of the NLRB. The NBA retained a regional identification, with no team west of Minnesota until Denver entered the old NBL in 1948–49 and the Minneapolis Lakers moved to Los Angeles in 1960.

Like football, basketball experienced phenomenal growth beginning in the fifties and continuing into the seventies. George Mikan in the late forties, and Bill Russell and Wilt Chamberlain in the fifties and sixties, established the importance of the "big man" in basketball. Fans found the agile, aggressive giants exciting as they scored and scored and scored. Mikan, of the Minneapolis Lakers, signaled the coming of the super-tall center but the seven-foot Chamberlain demonstrated in his play the importance of the position and beginning in 1959–60 led the league in scoring for seven straight years. In 1961–62 he reached a high of 4,029 points and later became the first player to pass twenty-five thousand points in his career. Although Chamberlain took individual honors, Russell's Boston Celtics won the team titles in eight consecutive league races from 1959 to 1966. Russell is credited with renewing the importance of the defensive players. Stars of the period included Bob Cousy, John Havlicek, Jerry West, Elgin Baylor, and Oscar Robertson.

Figure 7.1 Bill Russell (6) and Wilt Chamberlain, reaching basketball heights in the 1960s. Wide World.

Both black and white players became basketball stars in the 1970s and 1980s. In 1969 the Milwaukee Bucks drafted black Lew Alcindor who later changed his name to Kareem Abdul-Jabbar. With Abdul-Jabbar the Bucks earned the NBA championship in 1971. He then joined the Los Angeles Lakers for the 1975–76 season where he continued his outstanding career. Ervin "Magic" Johnson of the Lakers was another important black player of the period. The Celtic's Larry Bird was named "Rookie of the Year" in 1980. He helped take the Celtics to national championships in 1981, 1984, and 1986. The Lakers won in 1982 and 1985. From 1975 to 1984 eight different teams won the NBA championship—Golden State, Boston, Portland, Washington, Seattle, Los Angeles, and Philadelphia.

As with other professional sports, television helped to popularize the game and to provide a major source of income. Important changes in the game added to its interest. The twenty-four-second shot clock, initiated in 1954, made the game faster and increased the number of possible shots for each team. The three-point distance goal was added for the 1979–80 season. With careful promotion, increasing attendance, national media coverage, and television contracts, basketball became the last of the "big three" in professional sport.

Ice Hockey

While not as popular as the "big three," ice hockey parallels their organization. Until 1967 the National Hockey League (NHL) consisted of six teams located in northeastern United States and eastern Canadian cities—Montreal, Toronto, Boston, New York, Detroit, Chicago—with Canadian players greatly outnumbering Americans. That year the NHL doubled the number of its franchises and, by 1972, had expanded to sixteen teams coast to coast. Also in 1972, the World Hockey Association (WHA) was organized with twelve teams. With artificial ice making indoor rinks possible, major league hockey, inherently a cold climate sport, could be played all over the United States. To introduce hockey to the southern cities a massive education program was undertaken, beginning with teaching young people to play the game. However, it appeared that the followers of the new franchises were generally transplanted northerners.[9] The WHA, neither very successful nor a serious threat to the NHL, disbanded in 1979 with the NHL absorbing four of its teams.

Strong youth and college hockey programs in the northern states began to feed increasing numbers of American players into the NHL. The unexpected victory of the U.S. Olympic hockey team in the 1980 Olympics demonstrated dramatically that hockey in the United States had come of age; at the same time national pride in the achievement boosted interest in the sport, especially when more than ten players from that Olympic squad were signed by NHL teams. Regular telecasts of hockey started in 1956, increased into the early

1970s, and then fell sharply as viewer interest declined. After 1975, games continued to be telecast in Canada, but only locally and on cable networks in the United States. After the New York Islanders captured the Stanley Cup for four successive years, 1980 to 1983, the Edmonton Oilers, with star Wayne Gretzky, won the cup in 1984 and 1985. The Montreal Canadiens took the 1986 championship.

Although a players' association formed in 1957, it was not effective until the league expanded in 1967. A new National Hockey League Players' Association (NHLPA) achieved recognition from the owners. In general, labor relations in ice hockey have been peaceful and negotiations have been cooperative.

Throughout the modern period many professional team sport figures have been considered American heroes and heroines and have played that role. Others have reminded the public that they are human and subject to human frailties. In several sports, including baseball, football, basketball, and ice hockey, substance abuse of drugs and alcohol and minor skirmishes with the law have occurred. Drug testing of professional athletes was the subject of collective bargaining in the 1980s and counseling was made available to players with problems of substance abuse.

Although baseball, based on a series of historic court decisions, remained outside the antitrust laws, football and basketball came under their edict. As an industry, professional sports operated as a cartel. Since 1876 when the baseball owners defined the role of clubs as managing teams, and thus players, they have been tightly in control of the sport. Baseball established the pattern of one association, a commissioner in charge, and players who are under the control of the owners. Many players found this arrangement acceptable and for years resisted the idea that they be treated as union members.

As professional sports developed with occasional rival leagues competing for players, contracts that prohibited players moving from team to team, and lucrative television deals, the players found it necessary to form players' associations that bargained on their behalf. The first agreements came in the late 1960s and, by the mid-1970s, professional team sports were firmly established under the National Labor Relations Board, with the players' associations considered "unions" and professional sports designated as part of the country's entertainment industry.

In the mid-1980s the owners still exercised great power; however, over the past two decades, through players' associations, the players have made strides toward a greater voice in league policies. While professional team sports provided a sense of community in the lives of many Americans, individual sports such as tennis and golf became increasingly popular. Two sports, horse racing and boxing, favorites since colonial times, continued to attract their own following.

Other Professional Sports

Tennis

Tennis, the conservative stronghold of the pure amateurs, changed little in patterns of competition from about 1875 to the mid-1960s. Since that time the world of tennis has undergone a drastic revolution which resulted in open championships, increased professional play, and more prize money for women. In 1947 Jack Kramer, singles champion at Wimbledon and of the United States, and Bobby Riggs toured North America and, in 1949, Pancho Gonzales toured with Kramer. The following year a combined men's and women's tour featured Kramer, Pancho Segura, Gussie Moran, and Pauline Betz Addie. In 1954 Kramer stopped playing to promote world professional tennis tours. Much to the consternation of countries competing in Davis Cup matches, he signed many top amateurs from around the world. Australia was hard hit in 1957 when Ken Rosewall signed with Kramer for fifty-five thousand dollars and Lewis Hoad agreed to a twenty-five-month $125,000 contract.

For years amateurs in tennis received expense money for tournaments but were excluded from playing against professionals. The All-England Club proposed that the Wimbledon championships be open to professional and amateur players alike. The international tennis governing body, International Lawn Tennis Federation (ILTF), rejected such proposals until 1967 when the British Lawn Tennis Association recognized no difference between amateur players and professional players. In return, the ILTF announced that each country must determine the status of its own players. In 1968 for the first time Wimbledon was an open tournament when Rod Laver and Billie Jean King were victorious. By 1970 the ILTF recognized three classes of players, amateurs recognized by their country's national association, professionals recognized by their country's national association, and professionals who played under contract.

In 1968 two organizations in this country controlled professional tennis, National Tennis League and World Championship Tennis. Texas millionaire and sportsman Lamar Hunt sponsored the latter group and in 1970 bought control of the former and combined the two groups. For women, the breakthrough came in 1970 when eight women refused to compete in the Pacific Southwest Open at Los Angeles in which the men's prize was $12,500 and the women's $1,500. Instead of playing in Los Angeles the women—Billie Jean King, Kerry Melville, Peaches Bartkowicz, Kristy Pigeon, Valerie Ziegenfuss, Rosie Casals, Nancy Gunter, and Judy Dalton—entered the first Virginia Slims tournament in Houston, Texas. The Houston Eight, as they came to be called, braved the wrath of the United States Lawn Tennis Association, but led the way to greater purses for women's tennis. In 1971 the Virginia Slims tournaments averaged $16,590 and grew to $81,818 in 1975. Also, the women, with King in the lead, pressured Wimbledon to better the women's purse.

Figure 7.2   Billie Jean King, first woman athlete to earn $100,000 in a single year. Wide World.

In 1974 a new concept, World Team Tennis, in which mixed teams based in a number of cities played five sets at an event, again changed professional tennis. The sets—women's doubles, men's doubles, women's singles, men's singles, and mixed doubles—were scored and the team that won the most games won the match. Unlike traditional tennis, spectators were encouraged to cheer, hoot and whistle for their favorites. This form of tennis was disbanded in 1979.

Throughout the period interest was sustained because of colorful players. Kramer's ability to combine playing with selling helped establish postwar professional tennis. The temperamental but brilliant play of Gonzales kept him near the top throughout the fifties, and Rosewall and Hoad added international interest to the tours. The featured American player for most of the seventies was controversial Jimmy Connors who by the age of twenty-two was ranked the top player in the world. Also near the top throughout the late sixties and early seventies was calm, steady Arthur Ashe, the only black American in the first rank of professional players. Beginning in 1976, Sweden's Bjorn Borg began an unprecedented sweep of five straight Wimbledon men's singles titles and displaced Connors as the undisputed best male player in the world. In 1979 and 1980, brash young John McEnroe won the United States national singles crown and became the primary challenger to Borg. McEnroe defeated Borg at Wimbledon in 1981 but was dethroned in 1982 by Connors.

Billie Jean King, the first woman tennis player to win more than $100,000, crusaded for women in tennis and women in sport. Women's tennis received an unexpected boost when King played Bobby Riggs in 1973. The commercial ballyhoo surrounding this "battle between the sexes" caused some question as to whether it was spectacle or sport, but when the play began, it was clearly a serious match. King soundly defeated Riggs: "What began as a huckster's hustle in defiance of serious athleticism ended up not mocking the game of tennis but honoring it. This night King was both a shining piece of show biz and the essence of what sport is all about."[10]

Chris Evert Lloyd became the leading woman tennis professional in 1976. In a relatively short time she captured two Wimbledon crowns, two United States Opens, two French Opens, two Italian Opens, and three Virginia Slims Championships. In 1976 the next four leading women were Evonne Goolagong, Virginia Wade, Rosemary Casals, and Martina Navratilova. The growing popularity of the women's game in recent years can be demonstrated by the tournament earnings. In 1986, Navratilova led with $1,328,829 with Lloyd following with $972,782.

By 1986 professional tennis players could enter about seventy tournaments. Ivan Lendl of Czechoslovakia and Boris Becker of West Germany were the first and second ranked men with Navratilova and Lloyd the leading women players.

Golf

In 1946 Ben Hogan earned $42,556 on the pro golf tour, while in 1984, Tom Kite led the winners with a total of $375,699. This great increase reflects the growth of professional golf from the early 1940s to the 1980s. Through the efforts of promoter Fred Corcoran in the early 1940s prize money increased and professional golf expanded. Under the Professional Golfer's Association (PGA) Tournament Player's Division the number of tournaments, the course standards, and the players themselves improved the image of pro golf. The affluent fifties found more and more players who not only played more golf but also followed the professional players closely. This trend continued into the eighties.

Figure 7.3   Kathy Whitworth, professional golfer of the 1960s and 1970s. Wide World.

The professional golfers themselves contributed to the continuing success of the game with their improved performances and lower scores. In the late forties and early fifties, fiercely competitive Ben Hogan and Sam Snead were in top form, and at the end of the fifties and early sixties Arnold Palmer's aggressive, daring style of play led the professional game. In 1962, young Jack Nicklaus' superb strength, accuracy, and concentration defeated Palmer. By 1963, both Palmer and Nicklaus earned more than $100,000 in prize money. In 1980 forty-four players earned more than $100,000 and the leading money-winner was Tom Watson with $530,808. Curtis Strange with $542,321 was the top winner in 1985. Golfers' careers lengthened, resulting in more interest in the men's Masters Tournaments. In 1986 Nicklaus won his sixth Masters title at age forty-six.

The first opportunities for women to earn money in golf were through the endorsements of golf equipment and apparel. Babe Didrikson Zaharias reported "I signed up with the Wilson Sporting Goods Company, to be on their advisory staff and have them market Babe Zaharias golf equipment. . . . I also signed with the Serbin dress manufacturers, who made a golf dress that I designed."[11] During World War II, in 1943, an amateur golfer, Betty Hicks, a physical education teacher, Ellen Griffin, and a golf professional, Hope Seignious, organized the Women's Professional Golf Association to promote golf for women, including professional golf. An early supporter of the association and active from the beginning was Zaharias. Immediately after the war these women initiated the United States Women's Open Championship, but the association was uncertain of its future and was reorganized in 1949 as the Ladies Professional Golf Players Association, and a year later incorporated under its present name, the Ladies Professional Golf Association (LPGA).

As the Women's Professional Golf Association, the group sponsored the U.S. Women's Open from 1946 to 1953 when the United States Golf Association assumed responsibility for the Open. In the first Open, Patty Berg beat Betty Jameson; Zaharias won the championship in 1948 and 1950; and Louise Suggs repeated the double victory in 1949 and 1952. The LPGA tour grew slowly and, even with Fred Corcoran appointed to conduct the tournaments, the prizes were small and the situation difficult. By 1950 the tour included just nine tournaments. From 1953 to 1975, the players conducted their own affairs, but in 1975 appointed a commissioner to administer the LPGA.

The LPGA experienced a spurt of growth in the fifties and has continued to expand. Both the number of events and the prize money increased from twenty-six events and a purse of $140,447 in 1956 to thirty-three events and a purse of three million dollars in 1977. Individual earnings also increased from Mickey Wright's high of $20,000 in 1962 and Kathy Whitworth's $65,064 in 1972 to Nancy Lopez' $416,472 in 1985. As with other sports, television exposure increased the attendance at tournaments and, in turn, the number of golfers.

Horse Racing

The "sport of kings" generated excitement in 1946 when Assault won the Triple Crown, and two years later Citation repeated the feat. Not until 1973 did another horse, Secretariat, again take the Triple Crown. Surprisingly, within five years two more horses won the crown when Seattle Slew (1977) and Affirmed (1978) were each victorious in the Kentucky Derby, the Preakness Stakes, and the Belmont Stakes.

One of the outstanding jockeys of the period was Willie Shoemaker, who at twenty-two rode 485 winners in 1953, a record at that time. Other top jockeys were Eddie Arcaro, who retired in 1961 with 4,779 victories, and Johnny Longden, who rode 6,026 winners in a forty-year career ending in 1966. At the age of seventeen, Steve Cauthen became the first jockey in horse racing history to reach six million dollars in purse earnings in 1977. Beginning the season as a sixteen-year-old apprentice jockey, he rode 477 winning horses and was named *Sports Illustrated* "Sportsman of the Year." In 1978 he won the Triple Crown on Affirmed.

Figure 7.4　Robyn Smith, first woman jockey to ride a winning mount at a major track. Wide World.

Other jockeys who made news were Diane Crump and Robyn Smith, who pioneered a new sport career for women. Crump became the first woman to ride in a regular thoroughbred horse race at a major track on February 7, 1969, at Hialeah. The next year she became the first woman to ride in the Kentucky Derby. One of the most publicized breakthroughs for women in a professional sport, however, was Robyn Smith's hard-fought battle to obtain mounts as a jockey. Smith's first victory in 1969 paved the way for some sixty women who rode at tracks in 1974, although at that time only Smith and Mary Bacon were considered important jockeys.

In 1946 member tracks of the Thoroughbred Racing Assocation organized the Thoroughbred Racing Protective Bureau to "insure that the public is furnished an honest, clean racing spectacle, as well as to protect their patrons from undesirables," and the following year they adopted a code of racing standards.[12] State governments not only welcomed the industry's efforts to police itself but also were pleased with the revenue from parimutuel betting. Between 1940 and 1962, New York State alone collected $1,100,000,000 in taxes from this source. In 1965 in the twenty-six states allowing betting a record forty million people wagered $3,351,000,000 on thoroughbred racing.

In 1948 almost 5,500,000 attended trotting races in the United States, and the purses totaled nearly ten million dollars. By 1974, attendance had jumped to approximately twenty-seven million and the purses to over $134,000,000. Harness racing had joined other sports in the business of entertainment. Considering all forms of horse racing—thoroughbred, harness, quarter horse, and races at fairs—enthusiasm for horse racing has leveled since 1975. Due to the increased costs of the sport, by the mid-1980s there was a growing trend away from individual ownership of horses and toward syndicated ownership.

Boxing

During World War II the world heavyweight title remained in the hands of Joe Louis, who as a member of the United States Army conducted exhibitions for troops around the world. In 1946 he defeated Billie Conn and after holding the title for thirteen years, retired in 1949. In 1950, in an attempted comeback to pay income tax debts, he was defeated by Ezzard Charles and was forced to retire. A succession of heavyweight titleholders followed: Charles (1949–51), Jersey Joe Wolcott (1951–52), Rocky Marciano (1952–55), and Floyd Patterson (1956–59, 1960–62). The leading middleweight was the brilliant stylist, "Sugar" Ray Robinson.

During the fifties boxing suffered from overexposure on television, and many small clubs where young boxers honed their skills were forced to close. Rumors of fixed fights led to a United States Senate Committee to study organized crime. Later, on March 8, 1957, a federal court decided that boxing promoter J. D. Norris, the International Boxing Club, and Madison Square Garden were in violation of the Sherman Antitrust Act. After that, public interest in boxing dropped until colorful Cassius Clay wrested the title from Sonny Liston in 1964. Given to boasting, impromptu poetry, and an entertaining style in the ring, Clay was the most controversial fighter since Jack Johnson. Immediately following his title victory Clay announced himself as a member of the Black Muslim sect and changed his name to Muhammad Ali. After successfully defending his title several times in 1965 and 1966, he refused to be drafted for military service in 1967 because he had become a Muslim minister. He was the object of great controversy and the World Boxing Association stripped him of his title. Uncertainty prevailed about the title holder even after the World Boxing Association held an elimination tournament with little-known Jimmy Ellis emerging victorious. But Joe Frazier, who had been recognized as champion in six states, refused to enter the WBA tourney. Early in 1970 Frazier defeated Ellis and the matter appeared settled. However, Ali, in the midst of legal battles over his draft status, declared that he remained the champion. Finally, in 1973 he was allowed to return to the ring and on October 30, 1974, he defeated George Foreman, clearly establishing his right to the title. Three and one-half years later, Ali lost his title to Leon Spinks. After seven months,

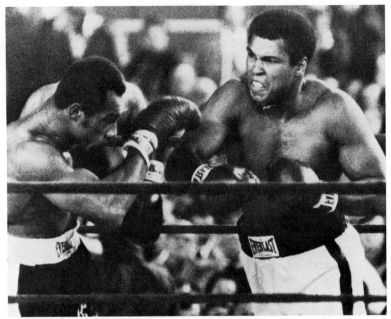

Figure 7.5   Muhammad Ali, the dominant personality in boxing in the 1960s and the 1970s. Wide World.

on September 15, 1978, Ali became the first man in heavyweight history to gain the world title a third time. Retiring from the ring shortly thereafter, he attempted another comeback on October 2, 1980. Twenty years after winning a gold medal at the 1960 Olympic Games, Ali was easily defeated with a knockout by Larry Holmes.

In the 1980s three organizations regulated boxing: the World Boxing Association in the United States, the World Boxing Council, and the International Boxing Federation. Boxing's popularity appeared to have decreased either due to the continued allegations of brutality in the ring, the public's preference for other sports, or the lack of colorful personalities.

In addition to the professional sports discussed in the preceding section, there are many others that are popular in the United States, including bowling and auto racing. Professional soccer is an example of a sport which appeared to be successful in the 1960s but has since declined in popularity. In 1967, the formation of two professional soccer leagues greatly increased interest in soccer. The new soccer leagues signed many European players, but rarely attracted crowds over twenty-thousand and lost five million dollars the first year. The next year the leagues merged to form the North American Soccer League (NASL). The league dropped to five teams and then increased to fifteen teams by 1974 and added five more in 1975. Stars such as Pele helped increase interest in the game. The NASL suspended its season in 1985 as a new form of the game, indoor soccer, struggled for existence. The World Cup, won in 1986 by West Germany, continued to draw national and international attention to soccer.

With the exception of major league baseball, football, and basketball, women participated in most professional sports by the 1980s. In 1978, the Women's Professional Basketball League was formed with teams in eight cities. A year later it changed its name to the Women's Basketball League (WBL) consisting of fourteen teams, twelve of which survived the season. The league struggled with financial problems and disbanded in 1982. Several women joined NBA clubs for brief periods, but did not remain with the teams.

By the mid-1980s professional sport reached almost every section of the United States. Stadiums, arenas, golf courses, and facilities for other sports were accepted parts of city landscapes. With transportation easily available many Americans elected to attend professional sport events. If they could not attend in person, they could watch their favorite sport on television. Championships attracted the largest audience of television viewers with over forty-eight percent of American households watching the 1985 Super Bowl and over twenty-five percent seeing the 1985 World Series. The number of households viewing any one sport event was lower toward the end of the period, but a considerable number of people continued to watch sport on television.

For football, baseball, and basketball over half of the viewers were men and about one third women. Thus, in the 1980s professional sport continued to be perceived as more appropriate for men than women although it was more acceptable for women than in midcentury. It was evident that both men and women enjoyed and found satisfaction in watching excellent athletic performances and in becoming part of a game in which the outcome is largely uncertain. Perhaps the sense of community and the identification with a team were the most important reasons for Americans' pleasure in professional sport. With mobility almost a norm for many Americans, men, women, children, and families could become attached to a team—they could become a Denver fan while living in Denver, a Seattle fan while located there, and a Boston fan if the family moved to New England. On the other hand, many children who grew up in a city with a sport franchise remained dedicated fans of that team throughout their lives.

Amateur Sport

Professional sport grew enormously after World War II, but amateur sport expanded almost beyond belief. Participation increased, the general level of performance improved, records were broken, and international competition became commonplace. The term "world-class athlete" became an accepted expression. Such people devoted many hours each day to practice and entered a regular program of events, including regional, national, and world championships. They also spent a great deal of money in order to participate in the sport of their choice. Financing the amateur was done in several ways: sometimes the athlete's family provided the money; sometimes grants-in-aid permitted college men and, after 1973, college women to continue their sport during their education; and sometimes sport organizations provided expense money for meets.

The nineteenth century "amateur"faded by the 1980s. As athletes trained more extensively for optimal performances, they found it necessary to seek livelihoods that permitted them to spend all their time on their sport. Under new rubrics of international sport federations they endorsed products, appeared in commercials, and made selected appearances. Fees for such services were placed in certain "trusts" from which the athletes could draw funds for living expenses. Such practices are treated more fully in Chapter 8, pp. 383–84.

Swimmer Don Schollander's experience was typical of the 1960s. When Schollander demonstrated unusual promise in swimming by the end of his freshman year of high school he left his family in Oregon and entered a California school to swim with the Santa Clara Swim Club.

> In Oregon I had done well just training an hour a day because everyone else was training an hour a day, too: but in California, where everyone was training three hours a day, I was in another league. At Santa Clara I began two-a-day workouts, something entirely new for me; an hour and a quarter in the morning before school, two hours after school.

> ....

> At Santa Clara we arrived at the pool at 6:30 A.M., and George Haines, striding up and down with a megaphone, would order a 500-meter warm-up swim. Five hundred meters is a third of a mile. Then we would swim another 500-meters "pulling," using only the arms. Next, 100-meter repeats, probably five. Another long swim, more repeats, breathing drills, turning drills, starting drills, one more long swim and we had worked an hour and a quarter and were through for the morning. In the afternoon we were back for more of the same. At the peak of training we were swimming about eight miles a day.[13]

Women became a significant component of amateur sport following World War II. Some of the same factors which contributed to women's greater participation in professional sport also led to an increase in amateur sport. Postwar affluence permitted time for sport, money for equipment and instruction, and a growing social acceptance of sports such as horseback riding, tennis, golf, swimming, and gymnastics. Many girls and women struggled with changing concepts of femininity in work and play. They were "finding their own images of woman at her utmost in many . . . forms of sport. And in both work and sport, their choices reflect their own definitions of the feminine image which is currently acceptable within their own social milieus."[14]

The federal government became involved in amateur sport due to the growing emphasis on international competition. During the cold war of the fifties, it became clear that Communist nations were using the amateur sport arena to promote their ideology. Since 1950 the United States State Department has sponsored "goodwill" tours including athletic competition and instruction. International amateur sport has become, then, not only the measure of a nation's amateur athletes, but also a reflection of the socio-political system and an index, however illogical, of its success in economic, political, and military spheres.

Golf

Amateur golf since World War II was conducted largely in the shadow of the professional game. While media coverage was primarily devoted to the latter, the amateur game thrived with thousands of new golfers. The National Amateur Championships sponsored by the United States Golf Association (USGA) served not only to determine the nation's best amateur players, but also to facilitate their joining the professional ranks. The Amateur Public Links Championship grew in importance as municipal, county, and state-owned courses increased. By the early 1970s entries for the regional qualifying rounds were running into the thousands. In Walker Cup play from 1947 through 1979 only once, in 1971, did the men lose to Great Britain. In approximately the same period, from 1948 through 1980, the American women won the Curtis Cup fifteen times. As in the case of the men, amateur golf tended to be the route for women to become professional golfers. Pros Louise Suggs and Babe Didrikson Zaharias were both United States Golf Association women's amateur champions before joining the Ladies Professional Golf Association in the 1940s. While the USGA women's amateur tournament had been held since 1895, the United States Women's Open began in 1946.

Tennis

Amateur tennis in the United States from 1946 to 1968 was marked by conflict, controversy, and charges of hypocrisy. Conflict over the professional versus the amateur game, with Jack Kramer frequently cast in the role of villain, rocked tennis circles. As first Kramer and then other players turned professional, the Americans managed to win only three Davis Cup championships between 1950 and 1967: in 1954, 1958, and 1963. Vic Sexias in 1954, Tony Trabert in 1955, and Arthur Ashe in the sixties were among the well-known men tennis players.

In 1947 and 1948 the United States took the Wightman Cup with Margaret Osborne duPont and Louise Brough as the leading players. In 1950 Althea Gibson was the first black in the national grass court championships. Although Maureen "Little Mo" Connally was ranked the number one woman in tennis in 1952 and 1953, Gibson continued in the championship race, winning the French crown in 1956. Also that year she undertook a Far Eastern tour arranged by the State Department, reached the finals at Forest Hills, and won the doubles at Wimbledon. In 1958 she took the United States and British championships, was named the Associated Press woman athlete of the year, and was honored by a ticker-tape parade on her return to the United States.

Beginning with Ashe's victory in the 1968 U.S. Open, a number of world-class men and women players emerged, including King, Connors and Lloyd, each of whom turned professional. More significant, perhaps, was the fact that by the mid-1970s millions of Americans had discovered the game. Indoor tennis facilities sprang up at a record pace and the demand for equipment and playing time and space was unprecedented.

Sports Organized by the Amateur Athletic Union

During most of this period the AAU controlled many amateur sports in the United States such as basketball for men and basketball for women, boxing, track and field, synchronized swimming, and wrestling. Although the AAU and NCAA signed an "Articles of Alliance" in 1946 in an effort to reconcile their differences, disputes between the two organizations continued. In the early 1950s athletes, coaches, and the NCAA charged the AAU with maintaining dictatorial attitudes regarding established policy, ignoring requests by athletes for hearings, denying foreign trips to athletes and coaches who criticized the AAU, managing AAU track meets unsatisfactorily, inadequately preparing teams for foreign competition, and failing to coordinate and process applications for national and world records.[15]

By the end of the decade the complaints intensified until, in 1960, the NCAA cancelled the "Articles of Alliance" with the AAU, refusing to honor any suspensions imposed upon college students by that organization. In 1962, NCAA-related coaches and administrators attempted to form new federations in basketball, track and field, gymnastics, baseball, and wrestling. Collegiate, military, religious, recreational, and scholastic personnel were part of the proposed organization.[16]

The struggle over sanctioning contests, particularly in track and field, continued with the athletes caught in the middle of a crossfire of boycotts and threats of suspension between the NCAA and the AAU. In order to insure an Olympic team in 1964, Attorney General Robert Kennedy mediated a temporary reconciliation in 1962, and General Douglas MacArthur another in 1963.

After the NCAA barred college men from participating in the 1965 track and field team trials in San Diego, and the men's team lost to the Soviets in an international meet, a Sports Arbitration Board was appointed by Vice President Hubert Humphrey to attempt to resolve the conflict. A reluctant and uneasy truce was made that lasted through the mid-1970s with only a few serious sanctioning disputes.

Aside from the political struggles for jurisdiction, track and field athletes achieved major gains in the first decade following World War II. At the summer Olympic Games in 1948 seventeen-year-old Bob Mathias won the decathlon. Harrison Dillard, a high hurdler from Baldwin-Wallace College, won eighty consecutive races in the sprints and hurdles during 1947 and 1948.

In the fifties, American track and field stars broke many barriers. In 1951, Bob Richards became the second man to clear fifteen feet in the pole vault. Two years later, Wes Santee of Kansas threatened the four-minute mile as he ran 4:02.4. That same year Parry O'Brien, with his revolutionary shot-put style, came within striking distance of sixty feet and Walter Davis cleared 6' 11½'' in the high jump. Of these three, only O'Brien reached his goal by putting the shot 60' 10'' in 1954. It was England's Roger Bannister who broke the four-minute barrier in 1954 at Oxford, when he ran 3:59.4. Charles Dumas finally surpassed the seven-foot barrier with a high jump of 7'½'' in 1956. A third important record was broken, also in 1956, when Glen Davis of Ohio State University ran the 440-yard intermediate hurdles in 49.9 seconds and the 400-meter intermediate hurdles in 49.5 seconds. In 1958, the first United States-Russia track and field meet was held in an effort to promote a cultural exchange between the two countries.

Technological improvements such as the fiberglass vaulting pole, which revolutionized the event, resulted in unprecedented performances in the 1960s. Instead of the fast, strong athlete of the aluminum pole days, the new vaulters required exceptional gymnastic ability. The world record in the pole vault soared from 15' 10¼'' in 1961 to 19' 8¾'' in 1986.

Other changes included foam landing pits for the vault and high jump, composition tracks, jumping and throwing pads, lighter, more comfortable running shoes and uniforms, and electronic timing devices. The softer landing pits removed much of the discomfort of landing, thus encouraging better performances. The composition tracks required less maintenance and provided more consistent surfaces for varying weather conditions.

In 1964 Jim Ryun became the first high school boy to break the four-minute mile. Two years later, with a time of 3:51.3, he became the first American in over thirty years to hold the world record in that event. Perhaps most significantly, United States distance runners achieved international status when Billy Mills and Bob Schul became the first Americans to win the Olympic 10,000- and 5,000-meter runs in 1964 and Frank Shorter captured the marathon title at Munich in 1972. Bill Rodgers became the dominant United States and world marathoner in the late 1970s and early 1980s. By the mid-1980s, however, the majority of the best male and female distance runners came from other countries.

Track and field for women in the late 1960s and the 1970s burst into popularity. During the 1950s and early 1960s the Tennessee A & I State University program produced the core of the U.S. women's international teams. The Major Daley Youth Foundation in Chicago also provided a needed organization, beginning in the late fifties, for noncollege girls and women.

The indomitable Stella Walsh continued to compete after World War II. At forty-two years of age in 1953 she won the pentathlon in the western region of the AAU. Both Walsh and Olga Fikotova Connolly competed for other countries in the Olympics, but Connolly, who competed in the discus for Czechoslovakia in 1956, married Hal Connolly, a hammer thrower, and became a star for the United States at the national and international level.

Wilma Rudolph, known as the "darling of the Rome Olympics," was a black American from Clarksville, Tennessee, who had been crippled after an illness while a young child. After two years she began to walk again and by the time she reached high school had become an all-state basketball player. Spotted by the Tennessee A & I State University coach, Ed Temple, Rudolph began running in high school and made the 1956 Olympic team. But 1960 was the year when she won three gold medals and in 1961 she received the Sullivan Award. Another outstanding black woman, Wyomia Tyus Simburg, also attended Tennessee A & I and earned one gold and one silver medal in the 1964 Olympic Games. At Mexico City, when she again won the 100-meter sprint, she supported the black athletes' protest. When the Professional International Track Association was formed Tyus Simburg ran in the only event for women, the 60-yard dash. In international track the United States women surprised the Soviet women in 1969 by winning the meet 70–67.

Perhaps the greatest change in women's track and field has been the reinstatement of longer distances, the addition of cross-country events, and the marathon. Having given up the longer distances at the time women's athletic events were added to the Olympic Games, it was over fifty years before women again ran the 1500-meter race. They were assumed to be unable to compete in the longer distances. However, as interest in women's track developed, the athletes demonstrated excellent performances at the longer distances. Training and practice showed that women had remarkable stamina. The American record in the women's 1500-meter run was lowered to 3:59.43 by Mary Decker in 1980. Top women competitors in the 1980s included Evelyn Ashford, record holder in the one-hundred-meter dash, and Jackie Joyner who broke the heptathlon record. In 1972 the Boston Marathon bowed to public pressure and officially admitted women. Marathons for women as well as for men became increasingly popular. By the early 1980s the dominant figure in women's long distance running was Decker, who set a new world record (4:21.7) for the mile run and broke several world records at various distances. Joan Benoit Samuelson, who broke the 1983 women's Boston Marathon time with 2:22.43, won the first women's Olympic marathon in 1984. The 1987 winner for women in the Boston Marathon was Rosa Mota of Portugal.

The AAU continued to promote amateur basketball for men and women. Teams frequently represented a business firm, industry, armed service or, in the case of women, a business college or other college not affiliated with the Division for Girls and Women's Sport. Championship teams in men's basketball included the Phillips Oilers, Phillips 66ers, and Capital Insulation, Los Angeles. The Wayland College team, also known as the Hutcherson Flying Queens, and the Nashville Business College team dominated women's play.

Following the war, American men reasserted themselves on the international swimming scene. At the 1948 Olympic Games they made an unprecedented sweep of the swimming events. Challenged briefly by the Australians in 1956, the American men continued to dominate throughout the 1960s and 1970s. Highlights included Don Schollander's four victories in the 1964 Olympic Games, Mark Spitz's seven gold medals at Munich in 1972, and the eleven of twelve victories by the U.S. men's team at Montreal in 1976 in the face of a strong East German team.

The United States dominated international swimming meets for women from the early 1950s to 1976. In fact, the young women, sometimes referred to as the United States "water babies," were considered a sport phenomenon. Record after record fell as thirteen- and fourteen-year-old girls became world record holders. Ann Curtis began this trend, although she was an older seventeen when she set her first records. At eighteen she was the first woman to receive the Sullivan Award. Curtis broke the minute barrier in the 100-yard freestyle for women with a time of 59.4 seconds. In the 1950s the AAU age-group swimming program paid off handsomely for the women. In the 1960s swimmers such as Chris von Saltza, Sharon Stouder, and Debbie Meyer set national and Olympic records. Meyer, who won the Sullivan Award in 1968, was the second woman swimmer to receive this honor.

Other Amateur Sports

Beginning in the 1950s United States figure skaters became world champions. Dick Button was the first American man to capture the world title, which he held from 1948 through 1952, and was also the first skater to win the Sullivan Award. Button was followed by two American brothers, Hayes Allan Jenkins, who won the title from 1953 through 1956 and David Jenkins, title holder from 1957 through 1959. Tenley Albright became the first American to win the women's world championship in 1953. She captured it again in 1955 and then another American, Carol Heiss, took the title from 1956 to 1960. In 1966 Peggy Fleming, another American, held the title from 1966 to 1968 and Tim Wood took the men's title in 1969 and 1970. Many skaters such as Peggy Fleming in 1972 and Dorothy Hamill in 1976 joined ice shows as skating stars after winning gold medals in the Olympics. The 1986 world and national figure skating champions were Brian Boitano for the men and Debi Thomas for the women. Thomas became the first black figure skater in history to win either title.

The game of field hockey reflected the growing interest in women's sport. By 1972 an estimated sixty-five thousand girls and women played in both school and club hockey. The practice of announcing all-star or nationally selected teams continued, as did the teams touring other countries. In 1963 the eighth International Federation of Women's Hockey Association's tournament was held in the United States with twenty-two countries represented. Following the tournament fourteen teams toured the United States. Field hockey for women was included in the program of the Olympic Games for the first time in 1980.

Although the United States Women's Lacrosse Association was organized in 1931, its greatest growth was after World War II. International competition began with the United States team touring the British Isles in 1935. As in field hockey, the teams were honorary and the top women players were picked for each position. The outstanding player of the period was Betty Richey of Vassar College, who was selected for twenty-one teams from 1933 to 1954.

Softball continued to grow as a sport for all. Church leagues, industrial and business leagues, and leagues sponsored by municipal departments of parks and recreation maintained programs for boys and girls and women and men of all ages. In women's softball the Raybestos Brakettes dominated play for much of the period with Joan Joyce the leading player. In 1975 Joyce joined the International Women's Professional Softball Association. Throughout the 1970s and into the 1980s, both slow-pitch and fast-pitch softball enjoyed great popularity in all regions of the country.

On November 8, 1978, President Carter signed Federal Law 95–606, "The Amateur Sports Act of 1978." The purpose of the law was "to promote and coordinate amateur athletic activities in the United States, to recognize certain rights for U.S. athletes, to provide for the resolution of disputes involving national sports organizations and/or athletes, as well as to designate the United States Olympic Committee as the central coordinating agency for all sports on the programs for the Olympic and Pan American Games."[17] The impetus for the act was the desire of Congress to put an end to the longstanding jurisdictional disputes among amateur sport governing bodies. Pursuant to this legislation the AAU's function changed from the regulation to the promotion of amateur sport. For the first time, a comprehensive structure for the administration of amateur sport in the United States was established with the force of law.

In the 1960s and 1970s many Americans turned away from sports which involved competitive events and national championships. Instead, they found their enjoyment and satisfaction in informal activities that took them out to woods, lakes, mountains, and back roads. Backpacking, mountain climbing, bicycling, and cross-country skiing grew rapidly after the mid-1960s. Outdoor pursuits were perceived by many to be truly recreational for the participants.

Figure 7.6   There was a greatly increased interest in wilderness sport in the 1960s and 1970s.

"The growing popularity of wilderness sports may thus be viewed as part of a wider search for emotional and spiritual contentment, a search which has spawned American interest in and approval of such phenomena as Transcendental Meditation, yoga, Zen, est, and a host of other 'True Ways.' "[18]

As prosperity increased following World War II, more and more Americans skiied at the many resorts which opened in New England, the northern Midwest, and western mountain regions. In 1950 the Federation Internationale de Ski held the world championships in the United States for the first time. Four years later the National Ski Association Hall of Fame opened in Ishpeming, Michigan. Although a few champions such as Andrea Mead Lawrence emerged in the early 1950s the United States was not one of the top international skiing contenders. The United States Ski Educational Foundation hired a professional coach to work with the National Alpine team in 1965. By the 1970s skiers such as Barbara Cochran and Billy Kidd competed successfully in international competition.

Boating became a major recreational pursuit for millions. In 1972 approximately thirty million Americans participated in some type of recreational boating activity.[19] Sailboats, canoes, power boats, kayaks, and rowboats filled the lakes, streams and inland waterways. Sailing, with thousands of small regattas, was perhaps the most popular aquatic activity, although by actual count, the fishermen undoubtedly outnumbered the sailors. World-class rowers in the United States rowed both for colleges and for private clubs. In international competition usually the eight-oared shells were college crews, while the fours, doubles, and singles were club rowers. However, in 1964, Philadelphia's famed Vesper Boat Club proved the exception by defeating Harvard and California in the Olympic trials.

In 1985 over seventy percent of Americans considered themselves sports fans and participated in sport or fitness activities.[20] In the mid-1980s Americans engaged in archery, cycling, skiing, polo, fencing, and a host of other sports, each with its association and competitions. Americans sought to extend the limits of the body by combining sports such as swimming, cycling, and running in the triathlon. The 1978 Iron Man competition sparked the new sport which formed its own association in 1982. Older Americans were not forgotten. The AAU controlled twelve senior sports while other sports, such as swimming, had their own associations. Sport for young children became a specialty.

Youth Sport
While adults were turning to sport in increasing numbers, they were also organizing youth sport into a complex network of Little League Baseball, Inc., Pop Warner Football, Biddy Basketball, Pee Wee and Midget Hockey, and AAU age-group swimming, wrestling, skiing, and track and field. All these developed and expanded during the 1940s, 1950s, 1960s, and 1970s. By 1980, it was estimated that about twenty million children between the ages of six and sixteen participated in nonschool youth sport programs across the nation.

Credit for the superiority of both men's and women's swimming in the United States was given to the AAU age-group swimming, which identified future stars as early as ten years of age. In thousands of swimming clubs throughout the country, children trained in programs comparable to those of adults of the 1920s and 1930s. The programs produced a number of record holders, many of whom were in their teens.

In centers of great hockey interest such as Detroit, Minneapolis, and Boston, hockey games among four- and five-year-olds were televised on local stations in the early 1970s. Indoor hockey arenas built by cities and private entrepreneurs scheduled both professional adult hockey and youth hockey in their programs.

From its inception in the mid-60s the American Youth Soccer Organization attracted thousands of boys and girls. Based on a philosophy of "everyone plays" and intent on keeping the competition without undue pressure, the organization was sufficiently successful to send a team to tour and play in West Germany in 1975. By the end of the decade it appeared to be the fastest growing team sport for both boys and girls.

Although the soccer organization was established for both boys and girls, and the AAU age-group swimming had always been coed, most youth sports excluded girls. In general, the attitudes reflected values common in the 1950s and 1960s regarding women and girls in sport. Many city programs did not offer girls' sports, on the assumption that they were not appropriate and that little girls did not want to play. With increased national interest in sports, however, little girls did want to play. Since the early 1970s many softball leagues, called Little Leaguerettes or Lassie Leagues, have been successful.

Carolyn King, Ypsilanti, Michigan, on the other hand, wanted to play in the national Little League for boys, and went to court to be admitted. When Little League, Inc. in New Jersey made efforts to exclude girls from the league, the court ruled that girls must be allowed to play.[21]

Youth sport was characterized as a trend "which led to changes in the American family structure and in many instances added a new dimension to the socialization of children . . . the degree to which children's sports became organized mirrored an often proclaimed American characteristic of being overly regimented, businesslike and competitive."[22]

Youth sport was controversial from the beginning. In the early 1950s critics questioned the physical and emotional impact on youth of highly organized sports with state, national, and even world championships. Dr. Creighton Hale, president of Little League, Inc., cited his own research findings that alleged no adverse physical or emotional effects when programs were properly supervised.[23] Reports of problems such as unqualified coaches, excessively long seasons, improper medical advice, inadequate equipment, injuries, and undue pressures to adopt a "winning" philosophy continued to be leveled at Little League, but the programs remained popular.[24]

The realization of sport for everyone has increased rapidly since World War II. For young swimmers interested in world-class competition, for members of a new judo club in a small town, for families bicycling together, for fans at a high school football game, for athletes in the Special Olympics—for these and other youth, sport has become an integral component of society in the 1980s. The advent of television as a focal point in American homes seemed to reinforce the sport trend, for the more sports people watched the more they wanted to participate.

Sport and Physical Education in Education

College and University Physical Education

At midcentury, on most campuses in the United States, physical education for women and for men existed in separate departments. The curriculum and activities offered, and their administration, expressed the major philosophical differences between physical education for women and physical education for men. On the one hand, departments of physical education for women, regardless of the size or type of institution, tended to have common goals, similar programs, and similar problems. These departments shared a philosophy of appointing broadly prepared rather than highly specialized faculty:

> Few departments of physical education for women separated their three functions of teacher preparation, general physical education and extra-curricular physical recreation or sport into different staff responsibilities. The same people who ran the sport programs conducted the teacher education programs and thus indoctrinated the teachers-to-be in the national philosophy.[25]

Figure 7.7   Intramural coed activities. Courtesy of the Department of Athletics, University of Massachusetts.

The departments for men, on the other hand, demonstrated no such uniformity of purpose among institutions. In many of the large universities with major intercollegiate athletic programs there was some philosophical conflict between the faculty who primarily taught in the men's physical education teacher preparation program and those whose primary assignment was coaching. In smaller institutions or those with less ambitious athletic programs, the physical education teaching faculty and coaching staff were usually the same people.

In the decades following World War II, the men's programs emphasized traditional team and individual sports. Touch football, volleyball, basketball, softball, swimming, tennis, golf, badminton, and handball were taught in most institutions. In the East, soccer, lacrosse, and fencing were frequently offered, and by 1960 were included in many other universities across the country.

The variety and scope of courses broadened in the late sixties and early seventies as students demonstrated a marked interest in recreational sports such as backpacking, scuba diving, mountain climbing, orienteering, bicycling, and skiing. Other popular activities included the oriental martial arts, personal defense, and aerobic conditioning. Professional preparation programs generally contained a strong biological science base and an emphasis on secondary school physical education and coaching.

As the major intercollegiate programs prospered during the forties, fifties, and sixties, they often provided the funds to construct recreational facilities and to underwrite a wide range of intramural and competitive athletics for men. On other campuses student activity fees provided funds for the construction of intramural and recreation buildings for both men and women. By the

1970s many programs in large universities were removed from departments of physical education and athletics and placed under the control of offices of student services.[26] Activities offered to the students ranged from the traditional football, basketball, baseball, and track to handball, squash, coed team sports, frisbee, and bowling.

The late 1950s and early 1960s brought a resurgence of the sports club movement that had existed in the preintercollegiate days of the midnineteenth century. The enormous increase in the student population of this period played some part in the growth of sports clubs. Not only were there thousands of students interested in activities, but they were sufficiently affluent to support a club sport. Club activities ranged from formal teams in soccer, rowing, lacrosse, skiing, volleyball or other sports not included in the varsity program, to sailing, backpacking, and rock climbing. Competitive activities such as skiing, sailing, soccer, and lacrosse often included regularly scheduled contests with clubs from other institutions. The noncompetitive pursuits usually involved only the club members themselves, and their popularity reflected the contemporary societal interest in individual recreational sport.

Women's programs during this early period responded to the tenor of the times, which fostered prewar femininity. Expressive activities like modern dance, synchronized swimming, movement education, and gymnastics grew in popularity. Fitness, posture, carriage, and proper daily body mechanics were the postwar modes for optimal personal development. Team games were taught, sometimes for the cooperation thought to be inherent in team play, but they were not as popular as the growing list of other sports in which women participated. As interests expanded, so did programs: tennis, archery, many forms of aquatics, canoeing, ballet, jazz dancing, and skiing could be found across the country by the late 1950s and early 1960s.

In reaction to the war, a reexamining of democratic processes and ideals became important. Emphasis on developing and achieving the goals and objectives of physical education classes by involving students in decision-making was believed to reflect and teach the democratic process. Students were encouraged to participate in instructional classes of their own design. These procedures created a climate in which the less skilled woman could be comfortable, but, in many instances, the time spent in this group process lessened the actual time available for activity and frustrated the highly skilled woman.

The development of physical education for women in historically black colleges was somewhat slower than in many white institutions. About the time of World War II most teacher education colleges required physical education. In 1946 Xavier University in New Orleans offered a wide range of activities including field hockey, tennis, archery, handball, speedball, folk dancing, recreational activities, soccer, and track and field.[27]

In addition to the instructional program, departments of physical education for women administered club and intramural activities. There were also conferences or associations of college women interested in a specific sport such as

The Synchronized Swimming Group

of

The Women's Recreation Association

of

Brooklyn College

presents

"Alice in Waterland"

An aquatic version of Alice's Adventures

DECEMBER 1955

ANNUAL . . .

Spring Dance Concert

BY THE

WAYNE UNIVERSITY

DANCE WORKSHOP

assisted by the

STUDENT DANCE GROUP

Friday, May 23, 1952
8:30 p.m.

UNIVERSITY THEATRE

. . Program of Dances . .

1. Trio of Dances
   France . . . . traditional folk music
   Polka . . . . music by Elizabeth Walberg
   Schottische . . . . music by Elizabeth Walberg
   Student Dance Group

2. Patterns of Celebration . . . . music by Wallingford Riegger
   Dance Workshop
   assisted by John Angry and Charles King

3. Nuptial Prelude . . . . music by Maurice Ravel
   Norma Gillette

4. Silly Stuff . . . . traditional American folk songs
   (recording by Tom Glazer)
   Goodbye, Liza Jane
   What Are You Made Of?
   Toddle Diddle, Dink-Dink
   Dance Workshop

5. Pensée de Jeunesse . . . . music by Bela Bartok
   Student Dance Group

6. A Ceremony of Carols . . . . . music by Benjamin Britten
   (recording for treble voices and harp by RCA Victor Chorale,
   Robert Shaw conducting)

   Procession   Spring Carol
   Walcum Yule!   Deo Gracias
   Res Miranda   Recession

   The words of these carols are in Latin and Middle English
   suggesting a medieval source. All of them have some religious
   significance.
   Dance Workshop

INTERMISSION

7. Three Faces of Fear . . . . music by Bela Bartok
   Agitation   Apprehension   Panic
   These dances about the cumulative effects of fear first show a pervasive
   tension and restlessness, then a foreboding of impending disaster, and finally
   a reaction to catastrophe.
   Dance Workshop

8. The Old Chisholm Trail . . . . traditional American folk song
   (accompaniment—Richard Bock)
   Harriet Berg

9. Two Nocturnes . . . . music by Alex North
   Dusk . . . . Norma Carter
   Midnight . . . . Jeanette Melick

10. Feminine Rituals: The Shower
    Dance Workshop
    assisted by Thomas Andrus

11. "Ways to Say Goodnight" . . . . . . poem by Carl Sandburg
    Student Dance Group

12. Festival Dance . . . . music by Alexander Tansman
    Dance Workshop
    assisted by Arthur Chabot, Darwin Knight, Nicholas Michelakis

Choreography for most of the group dances is by the performing group, assisted by the Directors. Solo dances were
choreographed by the performers.

Figure 7.8   Programs for synchronized swimming event, Brooklyn College, and university dance concert, Wayne State University.

skiing or sailing. Students with specialized interests such as modern dance and synchronized swimming frequently were organized as a club with a member of the physical education faculty assigned as an adviser, sometimes as part of her departmental responsibilities. The programs varied but the typical dance or swim club met regularly to practice, choreograph, and produce special performances or concerts once or twice a year. The clubs were usually organized and run by students with strong faculty support. Highlights of a "typical" year in women's physical education might consist of a sports day in the fall, basketball class competition, and a field day in the spring, as well as annual concerts or shows presented by the modern dance club and synchronized swimming club. Women physical education majors often provided the leadership for department activities and by graduation were well trained in the conduct of programs for physical education of women.

Through the mid-1960s, many institutions maintained physical education course requirements for all undergraduate students. By the end of that tumultuous decade, however, a number of colleges and universities had eliminated required courses in a number of disciplines, including physical education, even while professional association meetings and faculty senates continued to debate the relative merits of required versus elective programs.

As the social climate was altered by forces such as the midtwentieth century women's movement, economic constraints in the 1980s, and federal legislation, many institutions combined departments of women and men while others reorganized. Ohio State University combined departments in 1971, the University of Nebraska in 1974, the University of Georgia in 1975, and Purdue University in 1976. In 1973 one example of reorganization was the School of Physical Education at the University of Massachusetts. The departments had been Physical Education for Women, Physical Education for Men, Leisure Studies, Exercise Science, and Athletics, but after the reorganization were Athletics, Exercise Science, Sport Studies, and Professional Preparation in Physical Education. By 1981, with the exception of single-sex institutions, most physical education and related programs were taught in departments with both men and women faculty and men and women students.

From the early physical fitness research efforts of the 1930s and 1940s to the attitudinal and behavioral studies of the fifties, the serious investigations of the many dimensions of sport and physical activity had progressed steadily. Through their writings and their courses in physical education curriculums, scholars such as Delbert Oberteuffer, Eleanor Metheny, and many others exposed two generations of students to the theoretical foundations of sport and physical activity. In 1965, two sport sociologists at the University of Wisconsin, Gerald Kenyon and John Loy, called for American scholars to join them as they moved "toward a sociology of sport."[28] Shortly thereafter Bruce Ogilvie and Thomas Tutko popularized the newly developing field of sport psychology.

Many working in these fields were physical educators with some training and more than a little interest in the questions raised through such study. A few were scholars trained exclusively in psychology, history, philosophy, or sociology with an interest in sport. Within a few years universities offered an occasional course in some aspect of the study of sport. Primarily housed in departments of physical education, these courses began to be grouped together to form majors or specializations, generally at the graduate level. Such specialization developed first at the doctoral level and then moved downward, perhaps as these new degree holders assumed college teaching positions. In 1970, the State University of New York, College at Brockport, developed an undergraduate major in sport science. The new program was described as "the study of man as he develops and participates in the social institutions that supply his varied needs and wants for competitive physio-cognitive behavior."[29] The University of Massachusetts introduced a program in sport studies three years later. Many universities followed with diversified major programs in physical education at the undergraduate and graduate levels with specializations such as sport psychology, sport sociology, sport history, sport philosophy, sport management, exercise physiology, biomechanics, and athletic training.

Growing interest in the academic study of sport brought scholars together into new associations. In the early 1960s those interested in sport sociology joined with already productive European sociologists in the Committee for Sociology of Sport of the International Council of Sport and Physical Education, within UNESCO. In 1966 the North American Society for the Psychology of Sport and Physical Activity was formed. Six years later the Philosophic Society for the Study of Sport was founded and in 1973 the North American Society for Sport History held its first convention on the campus of Ohio State University. Finally the Association for the Anthropological Study of Play was organized in 1974–75, and the North American Society for the Sociology of Sport formed in 1978. Each of these associations provided scholars with opportunities to share research and exchange views. Further, they gave visibility to the field of study and a sense of common effort to their members.

The National Association for Physical Education of College Women (NAPECW) and the National College Physical Education Association for Men (NCPEAM) joined forces in 1963 to publish *Quest,* a semiannual monograph of scholarly papers. From the beginning, *Quest* encouraged high-quality manuscripts on a wide variety of subjects, from professional preparation in physical education to sport theory. In addition, the two associations further encouraged scholarly productivity through the presentation of papers at their annual meetings. In 1974 the NCPEAM and NAPECW initiated further combined efforts, among which was the first joint meeting, at Orlando, Florida, in January, 1977. In June, 1978, at the second joint meeting held in Denver, Colorado, the two established organizations merged to become the National Association for Physical Education in Higher Education (NAPEHE).

The American Association for Health, Physical Education and Recreation, until 1937 the American Physical Education Association, provided physical educators with a broad program and a national voice. Its annual national, district, and state conventions offered programs relevant to current issues. Special task forces and workshops considered subjects such as elementary physical education, drugs and sport, desirable practices in elementary, junior and senior high school athletics, women in sport, and the interpretation of research. In 1974 AAHPER reorganized into seven associations: American Association for Leisure and Recreation; American School and Community Safety Association; Association for the Advancement of Health Education; Association for Research, Administration, Professional Councils, and Societies; National Association for Girls and Women in Sport; National Association for Sport and Physical Education; and National Dance Association. At that time the name was changed to the American Alliance for Health, Physical Education, and Recreation and in 1979 it was again changed to the American Alliance for Health, Physical Education, Recreation, and Dance (AAHPERD).

Intercollegiate Sport for Men

Following the war, the nation's colleges and universities experienced a period of unprecedented growth as thousands of servicemen took advantage of the educational benefits of the G.I. Bill of Rights. The prewar enrollment high for all institutions of higher education in the United States was 1,494,203 in 1939–40.[30] By 1946 that figure was 2,078,095 and by 1950 had reached 2,659,021.[31] With this influx, hundreds of small colleges that had found it difficult or impossible to field men's varsity athletic teams from 1942 through 1945 now restored their intercollegiate programs and welcomed a new group of talented athletes. "Big-time" programs in colleges and universities shared in student growth and in the enthusiasm of Americans to put the war behind them. The tradition of college football and basketball, well established during the first half of the century, became a major facet of the entertainment industry beginning in the late forties. In the 1946 football season four teams— Michigan, Notre Dame, Ohio State, and UCLA—played to over 500,000 spectators each. That same year, seventeen postseason bowl games drew 478,000 fans and $1,765,000. Two years later, front-ranked Michigan regularly played to eighty thousand at each of its home games. In 1949, 102,000 were on hand for the Army-Navy game, and the two teams in the midst of winning streaks—Oklahoma and Notre Dame—captured national interest and thousands of spectators. By 1955, the Big Ten Conference drew a total of 3,121,649 to its football games and since 1976, top-ranked Michigan has averaged over 100,000 spectators at home games. In 1986, a total of 36,387,905 persons attended football games at 666 four-year colleges in the United States. This was an increase of almost seventy-six thousand over the previous year.

Figure 7.9 Expanded athletic facilities at the University of Michigan. Courtesy of University of Michigan.

Football alone made major college sport a big business. However, following the postwar years, college basketball also emerged as an important business enterprise. In the East, the major attractions were the Madison Square Garden college doubleheaders and tournaments. Teams from all over the country coveted the chance to play in the Garden against the top-ranked New York City teams—City College of New York, New York University, Long Island University, St. John's University, Fordham University, and Seton Hall University. In 1947, 655,676 spectators saw the Garden's college program, which included twenty-eight doubleheaders and postseason National Invitation Tournament (NIT) games.

Outstanding basketball was played throughout the country by teams such as the University of Kentucky, Bradley University, Ohio State University, University of Utah, and Stanford University. Bill Russell of the University of San Francisco in 1955 and 1956 and 7-foot Wilt Chamberlain of Kansas in the late fifties drew more fans and by the early 1960s the NCAA Championship tournament finals were a prime-time television attraction. The success of Coach John Wooden's UCLA teams from 1964 through 1975 and the play of stars such as Cazzie Russell (Michigan), Lew Alcindor and Bill Walton (UCLA), Pete Maravich (Louisiana State), Jerry Lucas and John Havlicek (Ohio State), and Oscar Robertson (Cincinnati), built an unprecedented television audience in the 1960s and early 70s. Large universities built new basketball arenas in the sixties and seventies to accommodate ten to twenty thousand spectators. The growing popularity of the game in the 1980s encouraged some universities to construct facilities seating more than twenty thousand persons. The NCAA championship tournament field expanded to sixty-four teams in the early eighties and even the official announcement of the field was made into a television event. The value of the television contracts became evident. In 1987, teams playing in only the first round received over $265,000 while the two teams competing in the championship final earned over one million dollars each. Basketball joined football as a major source of financial support for the athletic budgets of many large and small institutions.

The spectacular growth in the popularity of college athletics was not without problems. The pressure to win in order to sell tickets to meet expenses necessary to recruit athletes produced a climate conducive to cheating, scandal, and hypocrisy. In the late 1940s the NCAA found it necessary to assume an enforcement role because of repeated reports of recruiting violations among its members. In July of 1946 a "Conference on Conferences" was held for the purpose of determining "Principles for the Conduct of Intercollegiate Athletics." As a result of this conference the NCAA adopted a "sanity code," in 1948. The main points were (1) principle of amateurism, (2) principle of institutional control and responsibility, (3) principle of sound academic standards, (4) principle governing financial aid to athletes, and (5) principles governing recruiting.[32] In 1950, seven schools were cited for noncompliance with the code, but a motion to suspend the institutions failed to receive the necessary two-thirds endorsement. In 1952, new legislation was adopted dealing with academic standards, financial aid, ethical conduct, and out-of-season practice in football and basketball.

Throughout the fifties the NCAA strengthened its enforcement powers and penalized offending institutions. Continuing reports of wrongdoing through the sixties, however, prompted the organization to further expand its enforcement arm. By 1976, eleven full-time investigators were on the staff with the responsibility of following up on every serious charge of illegal procedure by member institutions.[33] Penalties for violations ranged from a warning of suspension from postseason bowl games, championships, and television appearances to limiting the number of allowable grants-in-aid in the sport at issue, to outright dismissal from the NCAA.

The most serious crisis in college sport was one which threatened its very credibility, one which involved gambling and basketball. Because of the practice of giving "point spreads" to equalize the betting chance, certain gamblers approached individual players on favored teams to persuade them to "shave" points and keep the winning margin within the predicted range. The first reported instance of such tampering occurred in 1945 when rumors of a fixed game between Brooklyn College and the University of Akron caused a significant fluctuation in the point spread and cancellation of the game. All five Brooklyn players admitted taking bribes to throw the contest.[34]

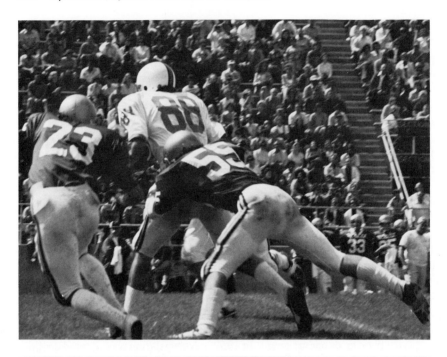

Figure 7.10   Contemporary intercollegiate sports.

A major scandal occurred in 1951 when more than thirty players from seven schools—City College of New York, Long Island University, Manhattan College, New York University, University of Kentucky, Bradley University, and University of Toledo—were found by the New York District Attorney to have conspired to fix game scores during the 1949 and 1950 seasons. The coaches of the indicted colleges claimed no knowledge of the schemes, which affected both the schools and the players. The National Basketball Association issued a lifetime ban on all of the implicated players whether or not they had been found guilty in the courts. The University of Kentucky was suspended for one year by both the NCAA and the Southeastern Conference and sat out an entire season. Long Island University, where the highly respected coach Clair Bee accepted blame for not knowing about the fixing, and for failing to instill his standards in his players, dropped intercollegiate basketball for six years. CCNY deemphasized the sport and moved out of the "big time." Manhattan College, New York University, Bradley and Toledo carried on their programs through the troubled years. Many colleges, sensing a tie between Madison Square Garden and the gamblers, ruled the Garden off limits for their basketball teams, and the golden age of New York doubleheaders was over. Basketball historian Neil Isaacs disputed the connection between New York City and gamblers by pointing out that traditionally the betting lines had been established in cities such as St. Louis, Cincinnati, Kansas City, Minneapolis, and more recently, Las Vegas.[35] The fact that "point-shaving" scandals occurred again in 1961 and 1965 involving thirty-nine players and twenty-three schools was evidence that New York City and the Garden were not the sole causes of basketball fixing.

As both college basketball and football moved through the 1970s, cries of overemphasis, winning-at-all-costs, recruitment abuses, transcript fixing, and illegal financial support continued to surface. Coaches such as Penn State's Joe Paterno and Arkansas' Frank Broyles asserted that recruiting violations in college football were at an all-time high.[36] Institutions such as Minnesota and California State University, Long Beach, were placed on probation after the coaches, under whom the offenses in the basketball programs had occurred, had left for other positions. The latter situation prompted many, including college presidents, to call for punishment of guilty coaches rather than singling out the institution or players.

During the 1979–80 academic year a new series of scandals made headlines. Basketball coaches at the University of New Mexico were dismissed for allegedly involving themselves in transcript tampering and, in efforts to meet eligibility requirements, enrolling student-athletes in nonexistent summer extension courses offered by other institutions. Similar violations resulted in five of the ten members of the prestigious Pacific Athletic Conference (Pac-10)—the University of Arizona, Arizona State University, University of Southern California, UCLA, and the University of Oregon—being placed on probation by the conference and ruled ineligible for the 1980 football championship and postseason bowl games. Once again, editorials were written and speeches were made denouncing the pressures to "win-at-all-costs," that were basically responsible for such actions on the part of coaches. At its annual convention in January, 1981, the NCAA passed further legislation designed to lessen the opportunity for athletic coaches and officials to influence the academic admissions, registration, and record-keeping processes for student-athletes:

1. Require athletes to complete a specific number of credit-hours (12) each term to remain eligible for varsity athletics;
2. Require colleges and universities to publish their standards for measuring students' academic progress;
3. Hold presidents and chancellors responsible for certifying that their athletes are academically eligible;
4. Prohibit the use by athletes of extension and credit-by-examination courses from other institutions;
5. Require athletes to get the approval of "appropriate academic officials" before they take summer courses at other colleges;
6. Require junior-college students who had a grade-point average of less than 2.0 in high school to graduate from the junior college before they would be eligible for varsity sports in a four-year institution.[37]

Responding to evidence of continuing corruption and abuses in big-time college sport, the NCAA and the influential American Council on Education (ACE) each appointed a committee to make proposals to solve these and other problems. In January, 1983, over strong objections from administrators of black colleges, the NCAA passed an ACE-sponsored proposal that established minimum academic qualifications for students to compete in Division I intercollegiate athletics during the freshman year. To be enforced beginning in August, 1986, the regulations required eligible students to have earned in high school a 2.0 (out of 4.0) average in English, mathematics, social sciences, and natural or physical sciences; the legislation also set minimum academic test scores for entering students. Other proposals approved in 1983 restricted recruiting by alumni and boosters; began the enforcement of NCAA rules in women's sports earlier than originally announced; and required institutions to include in coaches' contracts a clause notifying them that infractions of NCAA rules would be cause for dismissal.

With only slight revisions made in 1985, the minimum entrance requirements went into effect as scheduled. As predicted by black college administrators, many athletes, including blacks, were forced to either remain ineligible during their freshman year at the school that recruited them, or to enroll at a Division II or III institution or one not affiliated with the NCAA. In 1987, NCAA Division II and NAIA institutions also voted to adopt academic standards similar to those instituted by Division I.

In spite of the existing legislation, big-time intercollegiate athletics continued to be plagued by recruiting scandals and by an even more serious problem, drug abuse among athletes. In 1987, after repeated convictions for NCAA rules infractions, Southern Methodist University was given the so-called "death penalty" in its football program. Found guilty of continuing illegal payments to football players after already being on probation for a similar offense, the university was banned from competing in football during the 1987 season and was restricted to playing only seven away games and no home games during the 1988 season. Faced with the prospect of being unable to field a competitive team in 1988 since many players would have either graduated or transferred to other schools, SMU administrators decided to forego the 1988 season as well. Through such extreme measures, the NCAA sought to send a clear warning to all member institutions that repeated violators would be dealt with severely.

Of equal concern, however, was the growing specter of substance abuse in college sport. The problem encompassed so-called "performance enhancement" drugs such as anabolic steroids, favored by many football players, wrestlers and weight throwers in track and field, as well as illegal street drugs including marijuana, cocaine, and certain prescription and nonprescription medicines. The cocaine-induced death of University of Maryland basketball All-American, Len Bias, in June, 1986, in addition to several highly publicized drug scandals involving professional players during the preceding year, brought demands that intercollegiate sport take decisive steps to address the problem. Beginning in the fall of 1986, mandatory drug testing was instituted for all participants in NCAA championship events and football bowl games. While several football players were banned from participating in postseason bowl games because of evidence of steroid use, officials were cheered by the fact that testing during the men's and women's NCAA postseason basketball tournament resulted in no evidence of drug use among players. Pleased by a lower than expected rate of positive test results following the fall sports season, John L. Toner, chair of the NCAA Special Postseason Drug-Testing Committee, admitted that "Going into this (drug-testing of student-athletes), we were a little bit apprehensive as to how much positive results we'd get. We did expect a result somewhere in the eight to 10 percent range, and I'm very, very happy to report we're getting a two to three percent positive result on the basis of those 1,050 student-athletes we've tested."[38] However, in a legal challenge to the mandatory testing program mounted by a female diver at Stanford University in 1987, the court upheld the student's refusal to take part in such testing on the grounds that it was an invasion of privacy.

Perhaps the most significant event within intercollegiate sport in the 1980s was the creation of the Presidents' Commission within the NCAA in 1985. Critics charged that big-time athletics was out of the control of the institutions and that the chief executive officers on each campus would have to become more directly involved in the administration of these programs. The commission was established to provide more direct leadership by the presidents and chancellors at the national level. In its first two years of existence the Presidents' Commission exerted major influence in the passage of legislation concerning drug testing, maintenance of the academic eligibility rules passed in 1983, reduction in the number of football and basketball grants-in-aid, and the size of coaching staffs.

While big-time college football and basketball continued to dominate the news throughout the period, other sports also attracted the attention of the public. The NCAA initiated National Championship Tournaments in baseball (1947), ice hockey (1948), and skiing (1954). In addition, a College Division was established in 1956 for those institutions not wishing to pursue major programs in football and basketball. In 1973, the NCAA approved a major reorganization into three divisions based on the size of the institution and its athletic facilities, and/or the scope of its intercollegiate athletic program, and/or the financial aid provided for its student-athletes. Named Division I (major programs), Division II, and Division III, Division I was further divided in 1978 into Division I-A Football and Division I-AA Football. The smaller National Association for Intercollegiate Athletics (NAIA), founded in 1938 to conduct athletics in small colleges, increased to about five hundred member institutions in 1973. Athletic programs in junior colleges were organized under the jurisdiction of the National Junior College Athletic Association (NJCAA).

Baseball labored as a spring sport with little attention from the public or the professional leagues through most of the period in many sections of the country. Beginning in the 1960s, however, the colleges became a valuable source of experienced players. As developmental costs for the minor league system continued to rise through the mid-70s there was widespread speculation that college baseball, like basketball and football, would become the primary "feeder" to the major leagues.

Ice hockey, in areas with strong traditions in that sport, also became a self-supporting activity through sell-out crowds in modern ice arenas. College track and field and swimming programs continued to provide the basic vehicles for training world-class athletes for international competition. In 1967, the United States Collegiate Sports Council was formed by the NCAA, NAIA, AAHPER, and the NJCAA to select representative teams of men and women from the United States for participation in the World University Games.

The major problem facing intercollegiate sport during the 1970s and 1980s was financial. As the economy declined during the recession of 1974–75 and again in the early 1980s, the cost of goods and services rose and the nation's colleges and universities found operating funds diminished. Some schools dropped football, while others found themselves raising ticket prices, eliminating other sports, and limiting grants-in-aid, recruiting budgets, and travel expenses. Efforts were made to curtail costs on a national level through NCAA-enforced limits on travel squad size, on-campus visits by recruits, visits by coaches to recruits, and total grants-in-aid. Such efforts, favored by the less affluent Division I and II schools, were vigorously opposed by most of the stronger schools, who threatened to leave the NCAA and form a new governing body. In the early 1980s all major college football institutions, with the exception of those in the Big Ten and the PAC Ten, formed the College Football Association (CFA). The CFA mounted a legal challenge to the NCAA football television contract. The lawsuit filed by the University of Oklahoma and the University of Georgia was successful on restraint-of-trade grounds and individual schools or athletic conferences were then free to negotiate their own television contracts beginning in 1985. The largest and most successful programs were motivated to arrange their own television packages by the lure of more frequent appearances and larger revenues. By 1987 there was evidence that while the most successful programs reaped greater financial rewards, the vast majority of schools appeared less frequently on national and regional telecasts and gained less revenue than under the former NCAA pact. Nevertheless, in the late 1980s, although administrators voiced continuing concern over rising costs, college sport remained extremely popular.

Collegiate and Intercollegiate Sport for Women

When World War II ended, intercollegiate athletics for women did not exist in its present form. Today's program evolved from "extramurals" meaning interinstitutional competition. Programs and extramural events followed the carefully developed "Desirable Practices in Athletics" published by the National Section on Women's Athletics (formerly the CWA) in 1949.

The standards included concepts such as:

1. Provide opportunity for each player to lead according to her merit and to follow according to her willingness and ability to adapt herself to others and to a common end.
2. Provide for the selection of members of all teams so that they play against those of approximately the same ability and maturity.
3. Be taught, coached and officiated by qualified women whenever and wherever possible.
4. Include the use of official rules authorized by the National Section on Women's Athletics of the American Association for Health, Physical Education and Recreation.
5. Promote informal social events in connection with competition.
6. Limit extramural competition to a small geographic area.
7. Provide a program of competition for girls separate from that arranged for boys (eliminating such events as doubleheader games or "curtain raisers") except in those activities in which boys and girls are encouraged to play together on mixed teams.[39]

The first "experiment" in extramural tournaments was a highly successful intercollegiate golf championship initiated by Gladys Palmer at Ohio State University in 1941. Although there was some protest in the beginning, the tournament was held annually under exemplary conditions and a college woman was named national collegiate champion. Betsy Rawls, later a golf pro, was a winner of this tournament. By 1956 Ohio State felt that it could no longer continue to sponsor the golf event and sought other institutions to sponsor the tournament. By this time the increasing extramural competitions and the desire of college women for competitive opportunities began to concern women physical educators. Three associations created a tripartite committee to deal with the situation. In 1957, the Division for Girls and Women's Sport (DGWS), formerly the National Section on Women's Athletics, the National Association for Physical Education of College Women, and the Athletic and Recreation Federation of College Women, an association of students, formed the National Joint Committee on Extramural Sports for College Women. The committee planned to develop standards for the conduct of extramural events for college women and to sanction tournaments.

Also about this time individual sport enthusiasts began to form regional and national associations to provide organized competitions. By the mid-1960s New England women skiers competed in the Women's Intercollegiate Skiing Conference, women sailors in the New England Women's Intercollegiate Sailing Association, fencers in the Intercollegiate Women's Fencing Association, squash players joined and competed in the United States Women's Squash Racquets Association, and by the 1970s rowers had their own association.

The 1960s proved to be a period of rapid change in women's collegiate sport. The philosophy of the DGWS, reflecting the women physical educators of the time, impelled a revision of their "Statement of Policies and Procedures for Competition in Girls and Women's Sports." "For the college woman and high school girl who seek and need additional challenges in competition and skills, a sound, carefully planned, and well-directed program of extramural sports is recommended." DGWS further outlined standards for collegiate competition such as conducting the program in the women's physical education department, and being sure that the program did not interfere with the student's academic program. It was also made clear that "Girls and women may not participate as members of boys and men's teams."[40] They again affirmed the philosophy that student athletes should not receive financial aid for superior skill alone. Athletic scholarships were not approved, but financial aid for needy students was acceptable.

By this time a groundswell of interest in women's sport was forming. Also in 1963 the DGWS, in cooperation with the United States Olympic Development Committee, sponsored the first of five institutes to promote Olympic sports. For the first time in almost fifty years the Olympic Movement was directly promoted by women physical educators. Philosophically committed to promoting a sport for every girl rather than high-level sport for a few, many women were not prepared to coach students or teams at expert levels. The institutes planned to work with selected teachers from every state who, in turn, would return to their states and hold additional clinics to spread Olympic sports and to improve girls' and women's sport performance in general.

The structure of the National Joint Committee on Extramural Sports for College Women proved unwieldy and the administrative procedures difficult. After eight years, in 1965 the associations which started the NJCESCW agreed to disband the committee and to have DGWS assume control of women's intercollegiate athletics. To complicate the situation, the women's movement of the midsixties, to the delight of some and consternation of others, chose sport as one of the suitable arenas for equal rights struggles. The remainder of the decade of the sixties and the early seventies was fast-moving, full of radical changes for women.

National championships, involving the kind of intense competition that women physical eductors had traditionally avoided, remained another issue through the sixties and seventies. In 1964 the NCAA appointed a Special Committee on Women's Competition to act as a liaison with other sports organizations in this area. In response to NCAA actions and a number of other pressures, the board of directors of the American Association for Health, Physical Education, and Recreation, under whose auspices DGWS operated, conducted national championships for college women, beginning in 1967. In that year the DGWS formed a Commission on Intercollegiate Athletics for Women for the purpose of proposing appropriate intercollegiate athletic programs, of sponsoring national championships, and of organizing women's intercollegiate competition under one structure. The commission was terminated in 1971 and the Association for Intercollegiate Athletics for Women (AIAW) was established with Carole Oglesby as the first president. The AIAW held national championships for women from 1971 through 1981. The AIAW and the NCAA made several unsuccessful attempts to discuss the governance of women's college sport, and in 1975 the NCAA unilaterally proposed offering championships for women. Largely through the efforts of the AIAW, proposals for NCAA women's championships were defeated in 1978 and 1979. In the latter year another organization, the National Association of Intercollegiate Athletics (NAIA) also approved national championships for women, to begin in 1980–1981. In 1980 the NCAA approved women's championships for the academic year 1981–1982. The AIAW discontinued its national championships beginning in 1982–1983 and suspended operation.

The impressive expansion in women's and girls' athletics was given further impetus by an amendment to the Civil Rights Act of 1964, Title IX of the Educational Amendments of 1972, applicable to institutions receiving federal funds: "No person in the United States shall on the basis of sex be excluded from participation in, be denied the benefits of, or be subjected to discrimi-naton under any educational program or activity receiving Federal financial assistance . . ."[41]

In a release on June 3, 1975, the Secretary of Health, Education, and Welfare declared that the law affected the nation's sixteen thousand public school systems and nearly twenty-seven hundred post-secondary institutions. The effective date of the regulation was July 1, 1975, with elementary schools being allowed one year to comply with the regulations, high schools two years, and institutions of higher learning three years. Covering a wide range of topics such as admissions and treatment of students, employment, and services to students and employees, the law included several sections that dealt specifically with physical education and athletics.[42]

In these areas of policy and practice, schools and colleges were directed to open all classes to all students without distinction as to sex, with the exception of sports involving bodily contact such as wrestling, boxing, rugby, ice hockey, football, and basketball. The ruling "does not prohibit grouping of students in physical education classes and activities by ability as assessed by objective standards of individual performance developed and applied without regard to sex." In addition, "Where use of a single standard of measuring skill or progress in a physical education class has an adverse effect on members of one sex, the recipient shall use appropriate standards which do not have such effect."[43]

The greatest publicity, however, surrounded the rulings affecting interscholastic and intercollegiate athletic programs:

Section 86.37 Financial assistance.

(a) *General.* Except as provided in paragraphs (b), (c) and (d) of this section, in providing financial assistance to any of its students, a recipient shall not: (1) On the basis of sex, provide different amount or types of such assistance, limit eligibility for such assistance which is of any particular type or source, apply different criteria, or otherwise discriminate; . . .

Section 86.41 Athletics.

(a) *General.* No person shall, on the basis of sex, be excluded from participation in, be denied the benefits of, be treated differently from another person or otherwise be discriminated against in any interscholastic, intercollegiate, club or intramural athletics offered by recipient, and no recipient shall provide any such athletics separately on such basis.

(b) *Separate teams.* Notwithstanding the requirements of paragraph (a) of this section, a recipient may operate or sponsor separate teams for members of each sex where selection for such teams is based upon competitive skill or the activity involved is a contact sport. However, where a recipient operates or sponsors a team in a particular sport for members of one sex but operates or sponsors no such team for members of the other sex, and athletic opportunities for members of that sex have previously been limited, members of the excluded sex must be allowed to try-out for the team offered unless the sport involved is a contact sport. For the purpose of this part, contact sports include boxing, wrestling, rugby, ice hockey, football, basketball and other sports the purpose of [sic] major activity of which involves bodily contact.

(c) *Equal opportunity.* A recipient which operates or sponsors interscholastic, intercollegiate, club or intramural athletics shall provide equal athletic opportunity for members of both sexes. In determining whether equal opportunities are available the Director will consider, among other factors:

(i) Whether the selection of sports and levels of competition effectively accommodate the interests and abilities of members of both sexes;
(ii) The provision of equipment and supplies;
(iii) Scheduling of games and practice time;
(iv) Travel and per diem allowance;
(v) Opportunity to receive coaching and academic tutoring;
(vi) Assignment and compensation of coaches and tutors;
(vii) Provision of locker rooms, practice and competitive facilities;
(viii) Provision of medical and training facilities and services;
(ix) Provision of housing and dining facilities and services;
(x) Publicity.

Unequal aggregate expenditures for members of each sex or unequal expenditures for male and female teams if a recipient operates or sponsors separate teams will not constitute noncompliance with this section, but the Director may consider the failure to provide necessary funds for teams for one sex in assessing equality of opportunity for members of each sex.[44]

As part of the procedures, each institution underwent a self-study to evaluate the existing situations and developed plans for compliance with the law. Local, regional, and national publicity and debates raged in the months following the signing of the law. Although the legislation covered a wide range of topics, the debate and public interest centered on athletics. Nationally recognized football coaches met with the president of the United States in efforts to maintain their control over intercollegiate athletics. Leading newspapers and magazines featured discussions both for and against the proposed changes. Some immediate improvements in women's programs resulted, partly related to Title IX and partly related to the increased interest in women in sport.

The case of *Kellmayer v. the NEA, AAHPER, DGWS, AIAW, NAPECW, and the Florida Association for Physical Education of College Women, the Southern Association for Physical Education of College Women, and the Florida Commission of Intercollegiate Athletics for Women* in 1971, represented a group of students from Marymount College in Florida who had been awarded tennis scholarships and were denied the right to participate in an AIAW tournament. On the advice of attorneys the AIAW statement regarding financial aid based on women's athletic ability was deleted from their regulations. Thus, the possibilities of women to receive athletic scholarships increased, at first modestly, and then dramatically. By 1974, Arizona State

University, which had awarded twenty athletic scholarships for women the previous year, increased the number to seventy. Budgets for women's athletics jumped at the University of Georgia from fifteen thousand dollars to eighty thousand dollars and at the University of California at Los Angeles from sixty thousand dollars to one hundred eighty thousand dollars. While most women's budgets did not equal that of the men's, many were much larger by the 1980s. In 1987 several large universities such as Texas, UCLA, and many in the Big Ten Conference sponsored women's programs with budgets in excess of two million dollars. More money meant stronger programs. By 1987 the NCAA sponsored thirty-five national championship events in three divisions in sixteen sports for women, while the NAIA sponsored eight events in eight sports.

In the 1980s basketball appeared to emerge as the "showcase" spectator sport for women. Adoption of the full court game in 1971 had contributed greatly to spectator appeal. Television coverage of the final championship game exposed millions of spectators to the most highly skilled college players in the nation. In 1987 the semi-finals of the NCAA Division I Women's Basketball Championship Tournament in Austin, Texas, attracted a record 15,514 paying spectators. Moreover, the University of Texas averaged 6,639 spectators at its home games in 1986–87 to set the NCAA single season record for women's basketball.[45]

A number of women were added to the professional staff of the NCAA beginning in 1981. Likewise, women coaches and athletic administrators were placed on the numerous governing committees and the NCAA Council. On the other hand, by 1987 there was a great deal of concern expressed over the large number of men coaching women's teams and the small number of women administrators in collegiate sport.

Sport and Physical Education in Schools

Physical education for junior and senior high school boys and girls continued with a strong emphasis on games, sports, and dance. The boys' program through the 1950s generally emphasized the major team sports, although those schools with proper facilities often included such individual activities as tennis, golf, and swimming. Girls' programs tended to focus on the team sports of field hockey, basketball, volleyball, and softball, and other sports such as badminton, tennis, golf, and modern dance. This pattern was somewhat affected in the mid-1950s when the Kraus-Weber test results indicated that American children were less fit than European children. Public and official concern resulted in a temporary emphasis on physical fitness-producing activities in school programs.

In the mid-1960s there was increased interest in activities that sought to equip boys and girls with recreational sport skills, such as tennis and golf, that could be pursued throughout life. In the early 1970s these were expanded in

Figure 7.11   Physical education activities in an elementary school.

a few schools to include skiing, backpacking, canoeing, and other outdoor recreational pursuits. Further, under the influence of Title IX guidelines, coeducational participation became increasingly prevalent in many activities.

Elementary school physical education, generally confined to the major cities
through the 1950s, became a "new frontier" in the sixties as fast-growing suburban communities as well as small to medium cities developed broader curriculums. The American Association for Health, Physical Education and
Recreation encouraged the movement through publications, workshops, and
numerous sessions at national, district, and state conventions.

The concept of "movement education" became one focus of attention for
elementary physical education in the 1960s. One version was popularly attributed to the English system based upon the work of Rudolph Laban. This
system stressed the "art of movement" and encouraged children to explore
their physical environment and ways of moving within it. An American school
of thought, also called "movement education," was based on the early work
of Margaret H'Doubler and Ruth Glassow at the University of Wisconsin.
This version emphasized analyzing and understanding the "science of movement." Both stressed learning and understanding the fundamentals of body
movement through problem-solving activities related to space, time, and flow
of movement. Each school of thought had its own followers among physical
education teachers.

Recent research in the perceptual-motor development of children has brought renewed attention to fundamental movements and the importance of orderly skill acquisition. Psychologists, motor-learning specialists, and reading specialists suggested that the child's motor development was central to self-perception, motor behavior, and some aspects of social behavior. An increasing number of public schools have provided special training in this area.

Under Title IX the high schools were allowed two years to comply with the law. The high schools generally reflected the philosophy of the colleges, with one major difference—there was only one governing body for interscholastic athletics for both boys and girls. However, the philosophy of many high school physical education teachers regarding interschool athletics for girls began to change. The increased participation of girls at the high school level was more dramatic than at the college level. Statistics from the 1974 Sports Participation Survey of the National Federation of State High School Associations revealed:

> The increase in girls participating has been nothing less than phenomenal. From 1971 to 1973 it grew by over 530,000 and from 1973 to 1975 by over 480,000. Thus, there was an increase of over 1,000,000 from 1971 to 1975 in the number of girl participants. In 1973 there were 26 activities listed for girls. Participation increased in 14 of those categories and there were three new activities listed for the 1974–75 school year.[46]

In spite of the significant increase, financial support remained a problem. In 1972 New Brunswick, New Jersey, budgeted thirty-seven hundred dollars for boys' track and one thousand dollars for the girls' track team. At a small school in Pennsylvania $460 of a $19,800 sport budget was allocated to the girls' program.[47] On the other hand, Iowa had a well-developed program with over ten state championships in sports. Thus, as with the other subjects and activities in the United States high schools, the quality and quantity differed from state to state, city to city, and town to town. In the early part of this period, many segregated high schools attended by blacks lacked gymnasiums, especially if the school had a small population. In a 1950 study of over four hundred black college freshmen in three different geographical areas, Spear found:

> For the most part, students from schools of under 1,000 reported a lack and/or inadequacy of facilities and outdoor areas in comparison with those of over 1,000. . . . Gymnasiums, locker rooms, and shower facilities were lacking in a majority of the segregated schools represented, and while some schools which lacked gymnasiums made other arrangements for indoor physical education, a large number did not.
>
> . . . Girls from segregated schools were, in large part (60.5 per cent), dissatisfied with physical education activities available in preparatory schools. Tennis and swimming were the most desired activities and basketball, softball, and volleyball the most popular available sports.[48]

Iowa's girls' basketball was both a phenomenon and a source of state pride. In March, 1977, *Time* magazine reported:

> Tournament week is an official holiday for many schools, and the players, their chaperones and supporters checked into hotel rooms that had been booked for a year. They commandeered entire floors, lugging hair curlers, stereo tape decks and stuffed mascots. One coach brought along a toaster to ensure breakfast for his flock. Between forays to Frankel's clothing store to gawk at the array of trophies—including the 3-ft.-high bronze totem for the winning team—the girls decorated hallways with flowers and telegrams sent by fans back home.[49]

However, it should be noted that the Iowa girls played "two-court" basketball, with the players limited to action in half the court. The DGWS, in recognition of the increasing stamina of women and the changing times, had changed its rules in 1971 to the five-player, full-court game. By 1980 all areas of the country played the full-court game.

The boys' programs continued to grow in popularity throughout the period. By 1976 the National Federation of State High School Associations reported over four million boys from all fifty states competing on interscholastic teams in thirty-one sports. Over one million competed in football and almost 700,000 in basketball but other activities ranged from pentathlon (seventy-five) to outdoor track and field (644,813).[50]

The greatest controversy during the 1940s and 1950s raged over elementary and junior high school athletics. For the most part, few interscholastic programs in the public schools were maintained for children under the sixth grade. Many school systems declined to allow contact sports below the seventh grade, and others restricted all junior high school athletic programs to intramural status.

The civil rights movement brought an end to many segregated school systems and high school athletic associations throughout the South. Many small southern towns consolidated into one integrated high school and faced the problem of integrating the faculty as well as the student body. In numerous instances charges were made that the white head coaches retained their positions while the black coaches were relegated to assistant roles or dismissed.

In other parts of the country segregation based on housing patterns was more difficult to overcome. By the mid-1970s, city school systems were becoming increasingly black while suburban areas remained predominantly white. Racial conflicts among spectators at interscholastic sport contests involving the two types of schools were not uncommon. At the collegiate level the 1950s brought larger numbers of black student-athletes to predominantly white campuses in most parts of the country. It was not until the 1970s, however, that numbers of blacks were recruited by large southern universities. To counteract this trend and to attract a national black following, a few institutions

Figure 7.12   Coach Eddie Robinson with Grambling State University football team at Houston's Astrodome. Courtesy of Grambling State University.

such as Grambling State University began scheduling games on neutral sites in major cities around the country. In spite of the stronger competition, however, Grambling's famous head football coach and athletic director, Eddie Robinson, was willing to view the situation from a larger perspective:

> In places like Runston [a nearby town], it used to be that blacks went to their games and whites to theirs . . . now the kids are mixed on the teams and everybody goes together.
>
> I look at the crowd going in together, sitting together, eating hot dogs together. It's football and athletics that's really got them together. If that means I maybe lose a boy, is that more important than the schools being together—and that black kids may come out with a better degree?[51]

In the late 1970s and early 1980s, the growth of interscholastic sport combined with a corresponding decrease in state tax allotments, and with inflation, placed severe financial constraints on local school districts. As a result, programs throughout the country were forced to eliminate junior varsity teams in some sports and rely increasingly on outside support by parent and community "booster" clubs. Many began to fear that the effects of such funding practices would place undue emphasis on developing winning teams for the sole purpose of enhancing gate receipts and assuring continued community support. Furthermore, the increased demand for coaches to direct boys' and girls' teams led some states to eliminate the requirement of teacher certification for part-time, nonteaching coaches. By 1981, renewed interest was generated within the National Association for Sport and Physical Education and the National Association for Girls and Women in Sport as well as other education associations to combat the so-called "rent-a-coach" problem. State education agencies and colleges and universities were encouraged to develop certification standards and training programs for the person interested in coaching a sport but not in teaching physical education.[52]

Sport and physical education in the schools and colleges of the United States became more inclusive and accessible in the four decades following World War II. Physical education at all grade levels became more common. Competitive interscholastic and intercollegiate sport programs for the highly skilled were extended to include girls and women. The racial integration of public schools and colleges increased opportunities for all youth to test themselves against the best of their peers in sport as well as other spheres. At the same time, school and college sport experienced problems associated with overemphasis. These included compromised academic standards, recruitment scandals, drug abuse, and financial cost containment. By the mid-1980s intercollegiate sport was in the midst of the most exhaustive public self-examination in its history.

Commentary

This historical narrative has traced the developments and changes which have led to today's sport and physical education in the United States. Major themes have been employed to explain how simple pastimes and concerns about people's health have been transformed into highly organized sport and physical education. These themes intertwine through the years, some having more influence than others in different periods.

The first theme looks at the good life of the "American dream" which includes health and sport. While this dream has not been universally attained, it has become part of our heritage. The second theme, the effects of the cultural diversity of America on sport, is evident throughout our history. While the customs of over fifty different countries have contributed to our culture, and ethnic sport still persists in some communities, American sport and physical education have their own distinct configuration and practices. Basketball and volleyball were invented in America. The United States' educational system is unique in its approach to physical education, sport, and interinstitutional athletics.

The perceived values that govern daily living, the third theme in this book, were altered to a degree by the social movements of the 1960s; however, many survived unchanged. A heritage from the early colonies is the ethic of hard work leading to achievement and success. In spite of the acceptance of increased governmental intervention in our lives, many Americans remain traditional in their views of family life and appropriate roles for men and women. Sport continues to be considered essential for boys. Due to the social movements of the 1960s, it may be considered more essential for girls in the 1980s than it has in the past. Physical education and the right to fitness are now an accepted part of American education.

The next theme, social organization, has affected the development of sport and physical education in this country. In the early decades the gentry pursued their own pastimes—horse racing, fox hunting, and other gentlemanly sports. The common folk and slaves might gather to watch the gentry race their horses. The common men hunted, and fished, and had their shooting matches, and everyone—men, women, and children—took part in bees. In their little spare time the slaves made their own pastimes on the plantations.

In the 1840s middle-class men turned baseball into an institutionalized sport that rapidly diffused to all classes and changed the concept of sport in America. Collegiate sport began in the 1850s with student challenges and professional team sport began in the 1860s with the Cincinnati Red Stockings. The few privileged men and women who attended college were introduced to some of the early exercise and physical education programs. Basketball was invented on a college campus, but quickly spread through the YMCAs and other colleges. Basketball and bicycling brought about important changes in sport for women.

As sport expanded and became organized into amateur associations, upper-class men controlled most of the organizations. During the prosperity of the 1920s and the depression of the 1930s sport participation, in general, increased, but was largely segregated by race. Sport for women did not grow as much as sport for men. Many schools added physical education to their curriculum but dropped these programs during the depression.

The intermixing of technology and urbanization, the fifth theme, has greatly affected sport and physical education since the early decades of the nineteenth century. Urbanization, mass production and such inventions and discoveries as the railroad, electricity, the wireless, and vulcanization of rubber made possible the organization and modernization of sport. Improvements in transportation and communication permitted teams to travel more easily and the public to be informed about sport events. This was especially true after World War II with the advent of manmade fibers and materials, intercontinental air travel, television, and computers.

The final theme, the conceptualization of sport and physical education, has evolved gradually from horse racing in colonial days and reformers' concerns about health in the nineteenth century to today's complex and intertwining programs of sport and physical education. The first theme and the last theme, the expectation of the good life and the conceptualization of sport and physical education, are highlighted in this chapter.

The period from 1945 to 1987 was generally affluent and brought the "good life" within the reach of many Americans. With money to spend on nonessentials and more opportunity to pursue leisure time interests, people turned to sport and the active life in greater and greater numbers. While professional and college sport programs set new attendance records, sport-minded families and persons exerted pressure to expand such facilities as parks, courts, diamonds, hiking trails, bicycle paths, and ski slopes. Recreational sports attracted millions of players. In spite of critics who saw nothing but a "nation of spectators," more and more Americans became active participants in recreational sport. By 1976 many national parks, such as California's popular Yosemite Park, were forced to limit access because of overwhelming crowds of visitors. Sales of recreational camping vehicles, trail bikes, and other off-road vehicles such as snowmobiles and water craft soared. With sport the major component of physical education, sport and physical activity had, indeed, become pervasive forces in American society.

Television acquainted millions of people with unfamiliar sports and also showed more and more of the familiar games. The response was an increase in sport participation as well as an increase in the time television stations devoted to sport and sport-related themes. Television revenue financed professional sport and created a demand for sport, while at the same time, producers changed some aspects of sport to meet the requirements of television viewing and programming.

The civil rights movement included desegregating professional sport and efforts to correct injustices in amateur and school and college athletics. Although the percentage of black players increased in baseball, football, and basketball, only in the latter were significant gains made in placing blacks in managerial and executive positions. Professional sport was viewed as a part of the entertainment industry and, to protect their rights, professional players organized players' associations. The women's movement focused attention on sport, and by 1980 a few professional sportswomen earned over one hundred thousand dollars in golf and tennis each year. In the schools and colleges, aided by federal legislation, girls and women competed on interschool and intercollegiate teams in a variety of sports.

As a form of cultural expression, sport in the 1980s could be classified as professional, amateur, educational, and recreational. It included a spectrum of games from the big three—football, baseball, and basketball—to the triathlon, and contributed to many facets of American life. In addition to entertaining thousands of fans and millions of television viewers, pro sport provided a sense of community to the many people who identified with a major pro team. Others not only identified with the team but derived internal satisfaction and fulfillment from the rituals, ceremonies, and symbols which accompany sport events. Many also identified with players whose athletic excellence they admired or whose successes they cherished as an unattainable personal goal, transcending their ordinary life. Professional athletes who excelled in their game usually reflected years of practice and a commitment to develop their talents.

While sport served as their major means of livelihood, for many professional sportspersons the game also provided satisfaction and pleasure. Amateur athletes and student-athletes who competed at the national and international levels also made a commitment to sport in terms of personal dedication, time, and resources. Amateur sport such as college football and basketball and Olympic teams served much the same function in the United States as did professional sport. Many student-athletes and amateurs used sport as an apprenticeship to a career in professional sport.

Our contemporary society meets the conditions that permit sport to become a pervasive influence. In our generally affluent society, more people than ever before have money to spend on sport and choose to use some of their time to participate in sport and fitness activities or to watch sport events. In a manner which is very different from the early years of this country, sport and physical education have become accepted and approved cultural activities. Further, sport and physical education provide means of challenging one's self or setting personal goals: a ten-year old girl in Little League, a forty-year old "yuppie" jogging, or a seventy-year old man in a master's swimming meet. Through youth, high school, college, adult, and senior programs, sport provides a sense of community and an opportunity to share common values and experiences.

Sport and physical education in the 1980s were seen as part of the "good life," that has been pursued by Americans in various ways for two hundred years. Clearly Americans have elected to spend a great portion of their leisure time and money on these activities. Whether they seek enjoyment, wellness, challenge, status, or fellowship, a great many Americans associate sport and physical education with personal fulfillment and "the pursuit of happiness."

Suggestions for Further Reading

1. Berryman, Jack W. "From the Cradle to the Playing Field: America's Emphasis on Highly Organized Competitive Sports for Pre-adolescent Boys." *Journal of Sport History* 2, no. 2 (Fall 1975):112–31.
2. Gilbert, Bill, and Williamson, Nancy. "Sport is Unfair to Women." *Sports Illustrated* 38, no. 21 (May 28, 1973):88–92, 94–98.
3. ———. "Are You Being Two-Faced?" *Sports Illustrated* 38, no. 22 (June 4, 1973):44–48, 50, 53, 54.
4. ———. "Programmed to Be Losers." *Sports Illustrated* 38, no. 23 (June 11, 1973):60–62, 65, 66, 68, 73.
5. Olsen, Jack. *The Black Athlete: A Shameful Story.* New York: Time-Life Books, 1968.
6. Rader, Benjamin G. *In Its Own Image: How Television Has Transformed Sports.* New York: The Free Press, 1984.
7. Wilson, Wayne. "Social Discontent and the Growth of Wilderness Sport in America: 1965–1974." *Quest* 27 (Winter 1977):54–60.

Notes

1. Arthur Daley, "Sports of the Times," *New York Times,* 21 December 1969, sec. 5, 2.
2. Associated Press Sports Staff, *A Century of Major American Sports* (Maplewood, N.J.: Hammond Inc., 1975), 59.
3. David Q. Voigt, *American Baseball,* vol. II (Norman: University of Oklahoma Press, 1970), 289.
4. *Professional Sports and the Law* (Washington, D.C.: United States Government Printing Office, 1976), 13.
5. Edna and Art Rust, Jr., *Art Rust's Illustrated History of the Black Athlete* (Garden City, N.Y.: Doubleday, 1985), 242.
6. Ibid., 310, 311.
7. Ibid., 328.
8. "NBA Players Threatened Strike in Dispute Over Pension Plan," *New York Times,* 15 January 1964. Cited in Robert C. Berry, William B. Gould IV, and Paul D. Staudohar, *Labor Relations in Professional Sports* (Dover, MA: Auburn House, 1986), 158.
9. Roy Blount, Jr., "Losersville U.S.A.," *Sports Illustrated* 46 (March 21, 1977):85.
10. Curry Kirkpatrick, "There She Is: Ms. America," *Sports Illustrated* 39 (October 1, 1973):32.
11. Babe Didrikson Zaharias, *This Life I've Led* (New York: A. S. Barnes & Co., 1955), 180–81.
12. Frank G. Menke, *The Encyclopedia of Sports,* 5th ed. (New York: A. S. Barnes and Company, 1975), 594.
13. Don Schollander and Duke Savage, *Deep Water* (New York: Crown Publishers, Inc., 1971), 13–14.
14. Eleanor Metheny, *Movement and Meaning* (New York: McGraw-Hill Book Company, 1968), 77.
15. Eric Danoff, "The Struggle for Control of Amateur Track and Field in the United States—Part 1," *The Canadian Journal of History of Sport and Physical Education* 6, no. 1 (May 1975):58–59.
16. Arnold Flath, "A History of Relations between the N.C.A.A. and the A.A.U., 1905–1968," in *A History of Physical Education and Sport in the United States and Canada,* ed. Earle F. Zeigler (Champaign, IL: Stipes Publishing Company, 1975), 211.
17. C. Robert Paul, Jr. and R. Michael Moran, eds., *The Olympic Games* (Colorado Springs: United States Olympic Committee, March, 1979), 11.
18. Wayne Wilson, "Social Discontent and the Growth of Wilderness Sport in America: 1965–1974," *Quest* 27 (Winter 1977):56.
19. *Statistical Abstract of the United States, 1976,* U.S. Department of Commerce, 217.
20. *The World Almanac and Book of Facts* (New York: Scripps Howard, 1986), 859.
21. Jan Felshin, "The Social View," in *The American Woman in Sport* by Ellen W. Gerber, Jan Felshin, Pearl Berlin, and Waneen Wyrick (Reading, MA: Addison-Wesley Publishing Company, 1974), 217, 218.
22. Jack W. Berryman, "From the Cradle to the Playing Field: America's Emphasis on Highly Organized Competitive Sports for Pre-adolescent Boys," *Journal of Sport History* 2, no. 2 (Fall 1975):131.

23. Creighton J. Hale, "What Research Says About Athletics for Pre-High School Age Children," *Journal of Health, Physical Education, and Recreation* 30 (December 1959):19.
24. Terry Orlick and Cal Botterill, *Every Kid Can Win* (Chicago: Nelson-Hall, 1975); Chapter 4 in James A. Michener, *Sports in America* (New York: Random House, 1976).
25. Ellen W. Gerber, "The Controlled Development of Collegiate Sport for Women, 1923–1936," *Journal of Sport History* 2, no. 1 (Spring 1975):9.
26. Harry R. Ostrander, "Financing Intramural Programs," in *Intramural Administration: Theory and Practice,* ed. James A. Peterson (Englewood Cliffs, N.J.: Prentice-Hall, Inc., 1976), 261, 262.
27. Ruth E. Spear, "A Study of the Needs and Provisions in Physical Education of Women Students in Selected Negro Colleges," Master's thesis, Smith College, 1950, 19.
28. Gerald Kenyon and John Loy, "Toward A Sociology of Sport," *Journal of Health, Physical Education, and Recreation* 36 (May 1965):24–25, 68–69.
29. Clark V. Whited, "Sport Science, The Modern Disciplinary Concept of Physical Education," *74th Proceedings,* National College Physical Education Association for Men (December 27–30, 1970):227.
30. U.S. Office of Education, *Biennial Survey of Education in the United States, 1944–46,* 8.
31. U.S. Office of Education, *Annual Report of the Federal Security Agency, 1947,* 205; Garland G. Parker, *The Enrollment Explosion* (New York: School & Society Books, 1971), 40.
32. *U.S.A. 1776–1976, NCAA 1906–1976* (Shawnee Mission, KS: National Collegiate Athletic Association, 1976), 17.
33. Larry Van Dyne, "College Sports Enforcement Squad," *The Chronicle of Higher Education,* 7 March 1977, 1, 14.
34. Neil D. Isaacs, *All the Moves* (Philadelphia: J. B. Lippincott Company, 1975), 104.
35. Ibid., 106.
36. Richard Starnes, "An Unprecedented Economic and Ethical Crisis Grips Big-Time Intercollegiate Sports," *The Chronicle of Higher Education,* 24 September 1973, 1, 6.
37. Lorenzo Middleton, "NCAA Toughens Rules, Says Athletes Must Complete 12 Credits Each Term," *The Chronicle of Higher Education,* 19 January 1981, 1, 6.
38. "A Change of Attitude Has Taken Place," *The NCAA News,* 14 January 1987, 1.
39. National Section on Women's Athletics, "Desirable Practices in Athletics" (Washington, D.C.: American Association for Health, Physical Education, and Recreation, 1949).
40. Division for Girls and Women's Sports, "Statement of Policies for Competition in Girls and Women's Sports," *Journal of Health, Physical Education, and Recreation* 34 (September 1963):31–32.
41. U.S. Department of Health, Education, and Welfare, *HEW Fact Sheet,* June, 1975, 1.
42. *Federal Register,* 40, no. 108 (June 4, 1975):24141.
43. Ibid.
44. Ibid., 24141–24143.

45. "Women's Play-off Paid Attendance a Record 15,514," *The NCAA News,* 8 January 1987, 16.
46. Memorandum, C. B. Fagan to College and University Athletic Directors, Commissioners of Conferences, and League Directors, National Federation of State High School Associations, November 13, 1974, 2.
47. Bill Gilbert and Nancy Williamson, "Sport is Unfair to Women," *Sports Illustrated* 38 (May 28, 1973):90–91.
48. Ruth E. Spear, "A Study of the Needs and Provisions in Physical Education of Women Students in Selected Negro Colleges," Master's thesis, Smith College, 1950, 137–39.
49. "Hooping it Up Big in the Cornbelt," *Time* 109 (March 28, 1977):85.
50. "1976 Sports Participation Survey," The National Federation of State High School Associations.
51. Larry Van Dyne, "The South's Black Colleges Lose a Football Monopoly," *The Chronicle of Higher Education,* 15 November 1976, 8.
52. "Alliance Addresses Major Dilemma: Coaching Certification," *Alliance Update* (March 1981), 1, 5; and Matthew G. Maetozo, "Athletic Coaching: Its Future in a Changing Society," *Journal of Physical Education and Recreation* 52 (March 1981):40–43.

Time Line

The Cycle of the Modern Olympic Games

Olympiad	Date	City	Olympic Winter Games
I	1896	Athens	
II	1900	Paris	
III	1904	St. Louis	
IV	1908	London	
V	1912	Stockholm	
VI	1916	not celebrated	
VII	1920	Antwerp	
VIII	1924	Paris	Chamonix, France
IX	1928	Amsterdam	St. Moritz
X	1932	Los Angeles	Lake Placid
XI	1936	Berlin	Garmisch-Partenkirchen
XII	1940	not celebrated	
XIII	1944	not celebrated	
XIV	1948	London	St. Moritz
XV	1952	Helsinki	Oslo
XVI	1956	Melbourne	Cortina d'Ampezzo, Italy
XVII	1960	Rome	Squaw Valley
XVIII	1964	Tokyo	Innsbruck, Austria
XIX	1968	Mexico City	Grenoble, France
XX	1972	Munich	Sapporo, Japan
XXI	1976	Montreal	Innsbruck
XXII	1980	Moscow	Lake Placid
XXIII	1984	Los Angeles	Sarajevo, Yugoslavia
XXIV	1988	Seoul, Korea	Calgary, Canada

8 The Olympic Games, Ancient and Modern

Overview

The most influential organization in international sport today is probably the International Olympic Committee (IOC). The IOC is responsible for the conduct of the modern Olympic Games, the most prestigious competition for world-class athletes. Olympic competition affects almost every aspect of today's sport, from age-group AAU swimming to the promotion of field hockey for men. The modern Olympic Games, instituted in 1896, are a revival of an ancient festival that according to tradition began in 776 B.C.

In order to appreciate the place of the Olympic Games in the history of sport and to understand the modern Olympic Games, this chapter will examine both the ancient Olympic Games and the modern Olympic Games.

The Ancient Games

For over twelve hundred years the ancient Games took place at Olympia, a large sanctuary on the Alpheus River in the northwest part of the Peloponnesus, the peninsula which forms the southern half of Greece. Other athletic competitions were held elsewhere in the Greek world. The Greek citizens appear to have been the first people who made sport and athletics an integral part of their daily lives. Evidence of their sport and physical activities is found in the myths that were handed down by word of mouth from generation to generation, in the literature of the period, and in the ruins and artifacts that have been discovered by archaeologists. To comprehend the influence of the ancient Greek Olympic Games on the modern Olympics we will study ancient Greece; sport traditions found in poems by Homer; the role of athletics in two contrasting city-states, Sparta and Athens; major games or festivals, the most important of which was the Olympic Games; and the changes that occurred in sport and athletics during the period of the festivals, from about 800 B.C. to 400 A.D.

Greece, 800 B.C. to 400 A.D.

Brilliant sunshine, a warm climate, rugged mountains, sparkling azure seas, and hundreds of islands dotting those seas—all evoke some idea of Greece. The first Greeks are thought to have been wanderers from the north and east who settled in the sheltered valleys between the mountains. Others found their way to the islands and then to the mainland where they established settlements near the sea. Some continued east across the islands in the Aegean and founded colonies along the western shores of Asia Minor. Prior to the ninth century B.C. Greek, or Hellenic people as they were known, lived as far northeast as Troy, as far south as the islands of Thera, Rhodes, and Crete, and as far northwest as Elis.

In the early days the family or clan controlled Greek life. Clans claimed descent from a common male ancestor and were bound together by religious rituals, burial practices, family ties, and military dependence. The beginnings of Greek sport and concepts of "an athlete" are attributed to rituals developed within the clans. Footraces besought the gods for good crops; games and contests honored the dead at funeral ceremonies; and both footraces and chariot races were used to establish the prowess of the clan's leader. Winners of contests brought honor to their families through their victories and, slowly, the tradition of the elite, male athlete developed as men used sport to prove their *"aretē,"* their total excellence—physical, mental, and moral. While winning was not everything, it *was* important. Hardy underscores the Greeks' emphasis on "success and achievement. A noble attempt did not prove nobility; success did. Greek society had no praise for the loser, regardless of how valiantly he struggled; success, not intention, made the man."[1]

These families with their strong ties, ritualistic customs, and traditions of success formed the aristocracy of the emerging city-states. For hundreds of years the city-states were frequently at war with one another and gradually formed leagues for their mutual protection. According to one legend, an effort to establish peace among the city-states resulted in the first Olympic Games. By 550 B.C. the four major athletic festivals as well as many minor ones had been initiated; games, gymnasiums, and stadiums had become part of daily life in Greece. In 490 B.C. the Persians invaded Greece but, after a long war, were defeated. The Greeks, in turn, invaded and colonized parts of Asia Minor, southern Italy, and northern Egypt. They built their towns much like those in the homeland and lived much as they did in Greece, taking with them their love of athletics and their games. Indeed, gymnasiums have been found as far from mainland Greece as Jerusalem, Italy, and Egypt.

Among the Greek city-states Sparta and Athens engaged in a continuous rivalry ending in the Peloponnesian War in which Sparta defeated Athens. Frequent conflicts among other Greek city-states further weakened Greece, until, by 190 B.C., she fell to the powerful Roman armies from the west. During the next two centuries conflicts within Greece and invasions from without brought to a halt Greek influence on civilization. However, year after year, at festival after festival, national and international interest in the games persisted. As the Christian influence increased, attempts were made to discontinue the games. Finally, in 393 A.D. Theodosius I officially abolished the Olympic Games. Even after this edict, athletic festivals continued, but gradually diminished in importance until the Games faded out of existence.

Perhaps the wonder of our sport heritage from Greece is that sport was a part of the culture that has shaped much of our Western thought. Greek philosophers, mathematicians, poets, architects, sculptors, and playwrights have made major contributions to our world. We still admire the beauty of the Parthenon on the Athenian Acropolis, we still read the poetry of Homer and Sappho, we still study the philosophy of Plato and Aristotle, and we still watch the dramas of Aeschylus, Sophocles, Euripides, and Aristophanes. In addition, our democratic form of government is patterned after Greek concepts of civil control. In a brief period of cultural ascendancy these people of Hellenic origin laid many of the foundations of Western civilization, including sport.

To the Greeks their gods were totally anthropomorphous beings, differing from men only in their extraordinary power and their exemption from death. From the top of Mount Olympus, where the deities lived, Zeus ruled the universe, Poseidon the sea, and Hades the underworld. Hera was the sister-wife of Zeus. Other major gods and goddesses included Apollo, Ares, Dionysius, Hephaestus, Hermes, Aphrodite, Artemis, and Demeter. There were also children of mortal women by Zeus or some other god. Rituals honoring the gods and asking for their help were performed at birth, marriage, death, opening sessions of government, athletic festivals, and many other functions. The Greeks bargained with the gods and goddesses in prayer, thanked them with sacrifices for special favors such as winning a contest, and blamed them for defeat. The Greeks also believed that the gods, jealous of their special prerogatives, condemned the sin of pride or *hubris* in men and women who forgot they were mortal.

Greek society was not a classless society. *Citizens,* the only class with voting privileges, conducted the affairs of the city-state. *Resident foreigners,* some of whom had been established in the city for years, were active in the business affairs of the city, but not the civic affairs. The third class in Greek society was the *slaves* and, even among the slaves, a hierarchy existed. It is estimated that half the slaves worked in the fields and industries while the other half were in domestic service. If the domestic slave was talented, his life was much like that of a family member, except for individual rights such as voting and participating openly in the affairs of the city.

Not only did men control the government and business of the city-state, but they also were the masters of the family. Home life was directed by the man and carried out by the woman. The woman's place, especially in Athens, was in the women's quarters of the Greek home. For women, *aretē* meant modesty, chastity, obedience, and remaining inconspicuous.

Figure 8.1 Map of ancient Greece. From Robert C. Lamm, Neal M. Cross, and Rudy H. Turk, *The Search for Personal Freedom,* Vol. I, 7 / e. Copyright © 1984 Wm. C. Brown Publishers, Dubuque, Iowa. All Rights Reserved. Reprinted by permission.

The woman's subordinate position explains, in part, the bisexuality of many Greek citizens. Upperclass Greek men frequently had a family and, at the same time, engaged in a sexual relationship with a youth from another upperclass family. Such relationships were accepted and expected. Ordinarily, an older man became the role-model for a young man, thus sponsoring him into the society of the adult Greek world. Several reasons have been proffered in explanation of this custom, one being that the gymnasium, which literally means "the place where men exercise naked," prized the male body and created an atmosphere which fostered homosexuality.

This brief sketch of Greek history and culture may serve as an introduction to the study of Greek sport and athletics.

The First Written Accounts of Athletics

Homer's epic poems, the *Iliad* and the *Odyssey,* contain the first descriptions of sport and organized athletics. Contemporary scholars assign the assembling of the *Iliad* to the late eighth or early seventh century B.C. and the *Odyssey* somewhat later.

Throughout Greek history these two poems have been memorized by Greek children as the foundations of Greek education. The poems demonstrate the moral and ethical conduct valued by the ancient Greeks; Homer's heroes and heroines displayed that special brand of nobility and excellence called *aretē.* In these two Greek classics, references to athletics, games, sport, and dance are interwoven, making it clear that these activities were part of daily Greek life in the epic period and that the language of sport was understood by the Greeks.

The *Iliad* describes a few weeks in the tenth year of the Trojan War, while the *Odyssey* recounts the return journey of Odysseus after the war. In the *Iliad* there is a detailed description of games held to honor Patroclus, who was killed in battle. While memorial games are part of today's sport world, in the ancient days the games were held as part of funeral ceremonies. The Trojan War started when Paris, a prince of Troy who was visiting Sparta, abducted Helen, the wife of King Menelaus. Menelaus' older brother, Agamemnon, King of Mycenae, led an army in a thousand ships from Greece to Troy to force her return. The siege of Troy proved difficult. The gods constantly intervened on both sides, and the war dragged on for ten years. In the final year, the period covered by the *Iliad,* Agamemnon quarreled with his best fighting man, Achilles, who withdrew from the fight, taking his men with him. The Trojans then gained the upper hand until Patroclus, Achilles' best friend, persuaded Achilles to let him return to the battle. When Patroclus was killed, Achilles reentered the war to avenge his death and, with the help of the gods, turned back the Trojans. The funeral that Achilles conducted in honor of Patroclus involved building an enormous funeral pyre on which he placed the offering for the dead: honey, oil, horses, hunting dogs, and twelve young Trojans slain in reprisal for Patroclus. After the burning of the pyre, elaborate games were held in his honor.

These games are the first literary account of athletics. Homer tells the story this way:

Akhilleus held the troops upon the spot
and seated them, forming a wide arena.
Prizes out of the ships, caldrons and tripods,
horses and mules and oxen he supplied,
and softly belted girls, and hoary iron.
First for charioteers he set the prizes:
a girl adept at gentle handicraft
to be taken by the winner, and a tripod
holding twenty-six quarts, with handle-rings.
For the runner-up he offered a six-year-old
unbroken mare, big with a mule foal.
For third prize a fine caldron of four gallons,
never scorched, bright as on casting day,
and for the fourth two measured bars of gold;
for fifth, a new two-handled bowl.[2]

Throughout the description of the games, contemporary sport concepts appear. Achilles administered the games, selected the contestants, awarded the prizes, and settled disputes. In announcing the first race, the chariot race, Achilles withdrew his own horses in honor of Patroclus pointing out:

Now where they stand they droop their heads for him,
their manes brushing the ground, and grieve at heart.[3]

Five contestants entered the chariot race. Nestor's son, Antilochus, was one of the contestants and, not unlike a father of today advising his son at a sporting event, Nestor offered this advice:

these are slow horses, and they may turn in
a second-rate performance. The other teams
are faster. But the charioteers
know no more racing strategy than you do.
Work out a plan of action in your mind,
dear son, don't let the prize slip through your fingers.[4]

He concluded with careful instructions for rounding the turning-post:

> As you drive near it,
> hug it with cart and horses; you yourself
> in the chariot basket lean a bit to the left
> and at the same time lash your right-hand horse
> and shout to him, and let his rein out. . . .
>
> If on the turn you overtake and pass,
> there's not a chance of someone catching you—[5]

The son did not win the race, and, indeed, came in second only as the result of such careless driving that he was accused of committing a foul. During the race the contestants alleged that the gods interfered, resulting in disagreement over the awarding of the prizes. Achilles settled all arguments and announced the next event, boxing.

He invited any two men to enter the event. Huge and powerful Epeius entered and for a while it appeared as if there might not be another contestant, but finally Euryalos accepted the challenge. Epeius won the match and, after the final blow, "gallantly . . . gave him a hand and pulled him up."[6] The boxing was followed by the wrestling event in which Ajax and Odysseus wrestled until Achilles interfered, saying:

> No more of this bone-cracking bout.
> The victory goes to both. Take equal prizes.
> Off with you, so the rest here can compete.[7]

The prizes for the next event, the footrace, included a bowl which had belonged to Patroclus and which Achilles gave as a prize in memory of his companion. Antilochus, Ajax, and Odysseus entered the race. Near the end of the race Ajax led, followed by Odysseus, who prayed to the goddess Athena to help *him* be the victor. His prayers were answered as Athena caused Ajax to slip and fall. When Ajax complained that the gods must have interfered, the crowd laughed. Other events at the funeral included a close combat fight in armor, finally pronounced a draw; a throwing contest similar to putting the shot; and an archery competition in which the target was a tethered wild pigeon. The funeral games in honor of Patroclus ended with a spear throw. Homer completes the account of the games as the contestants and spectators leave. Achilles is alone with his grief:

> The funeral games were over. Men dispersed
> and turned their thoughts to supper in their quarters,
> then to the boon of slumber. But Akhilleus
> thought of his friend, and sleep that quiets all things
> would not take hold of him. He tossed and turned
> remembering with pain Patroklos' courage. . . .
> With memory his eyes grew wet.[8]

The *Odyssey,* the tale of the journey of Odysseus returning from Troy to his home, included a variety of adventures among which are many references to sport. After a banquet on the island of Phaeacia, games and contests were held in honor of Odysseus. After several contests, footraces, wrestling, discus, and boxing among the Phaeacians, Odysseus was invited to compete, but declined. The Phaeacians taunted him, saying "As I see it . . . you never learned a sport, and have no skill in any of the contests of fighting men."[9] Odysseus answered the challenge by selecting a discus stone, heavier than those thrown by the Phaeacians, and tossing it farther than any of his hosts. Throughout both the *Odyssey* and the *Iliad* Homer's descriptions of sport are detailed and vivid.

Only a few of Homer's more pertinent references to sport and athletics have been included here, but, from these, we can identify many sport traditions, customs, and behaviors with which we are familiar. Although we do not hold games as part of funeral ceremonies, we commemorate individuals with annual sporting events. Just as now, spectators and contestants argued among themselves. A father advised his son on strategies for winning. In the games honoring Patroclus, Achilles was the organizer, the referee, and the umpire, indicating the need for officials to administer athletic events. Several situations emphasized fair play and sportsmanship. In the wrestling event the winner gave the loser a hand and pulled him up, and Achilles stopped the wrestling match before the contestants were badly hurt. Another example of sport behavior associated with sportsmanship is the ability to accept defeat. When Ajax complained about losing the footrace, the crowd laughed at him as if to tell him he should not complain. After the chariot race, Antilochus, the second-place winner, challenged the decision and Achilles ruled in his favor.

The athletes in Homer's classics displayed many of the sport behaviors we see today. Concepts of accepting decisions, fair play and good sportsmanship, and many others are illustrated in the funeral games for Patroclus. At the same time we also see some of the less desirable sport behaviors. The athletes argued among themselves and the spectators gave opinions and behaved much the way our spectators behave today. These and many other passages from Homer demonstrate that our heritage of sport from Greece is over twenty-five hundred years old and consists of well-developed concepts and traditions.

Contrasting Views of Sport

Sparta and Athens were the two most important city-states in ancient Greece, less than two hundred miles apart but with vastly different governments, educational systems, and views of sport. Sparta reflected the use of sport and athletics by the government to further the purposes of the state. Her men sought to bring her glory both on the battlefield and in the stadium, while her women strived for perfect babies for the state. In Athens, while all citizens were expected to be loyal to the city and ready to fight, it was the total excellence of the individual man which was prized. Sport and athletics contributed to physical excellence, which was one aspect of male *aretē*.

These two major city-states, Sparta and Athens, spoke the same language, claimed the same heritage, worshipped the same gods, but although both took fierce pride in being Greek, they were at opposite extremes in their political and cultural lives. Hale contrasts the two city-states: "Athens produced in statecraft a Solon, a Themistocles, a Pericles; in drama an Aeschylus, a Sophocles, a Euripides, an Aristophanes; in sculpture a Phidias, a Praxiteles; in architecture a Mnesicles, one of the builders of its new Acropolis; in history a Thucydides; in philosophy a Socrates, a Plato; whereas Sparta in its prime produced soldiers."[10] Both city-states have contributed to our heritage in sport and athletics. Both Sparta and Athens provided education that emphasized skills required in combat, and also led to optimum physical condition. Sparta is to be remembered as the first society that required a regimen of exercise for both boys and girls. In Athens moral and physical excellence, *aretē,* was the goal for men. Its concepts of excellence and all-out performance are still prized in sport. Specialized facilities such as gymnasiums, stadiums, and other athletic facilities were very much a part of the life of Greek citizens just as special athletic facilities are accepted and expected today.

Greek Athletic Festivals

For over twelve hundred years athletic festivals were an important part of Greek life, and they have left a significant legacy to modern sport. Archaeological findings at sites such as Olympia, Delphi, and Epidaurus reveal stadiums, starting devices, palaestras, statues bearing inscriptions about athletic contests, and lists of Olympic victors' names. During the period when the athletic festivals flourished and were at their height, the four major games were the Olympic, Pythian, Isthmian, and Nemean. They were Panhellenic in nature, meaning that contestants from all over Greece could compete. In the four-year cycle of an Olympiad, the Olympic Games and the Isthmian Games were held in the first year. The following year, the second year of the Olympiad, the Nemean Games were celebrated; in the third year the Pythian and Isthmian Games were held; and in the fourth, the Nemean Games.

While the Olympic Games were the most prestigious, next in importance were the Pythian Games which were held in Delphi, the sacred site of the oracle of Apollo and, according to Greek legend, the center of the world. Located northeast of Athens along the Gulf of Corinth, Delphi's mountainous setting accommodated a theater, temples, treasuries housing valuable displays from cities, and above the sanctuary, a stadium. One legend relates that the

Figure 8.2 Trophies won at Panathenaic and other games. Courtesy of the Metropolitan Museum of Art, Rogers Fund, 1959.

first Pythian Games celebrated Apollo's victory over the serpent Python, while another suggests that the Pythian competitions in music and literary works had been conducted for many centuries and that only later were the Games instituted. The prizes awarded to the victors of the Pythian Games were wreaths of laurel.

The Isthmian Games honored Poseidon, the god of the sea, and celebrated not only athletic events, but also musical and literary competitions. The traditional prize wreaths were made of pine in recognition of the site of the Games, near Corinth in a pine grove sacred to Poseidon. The Nemean Games, held in alternate years between the Olympic and Pythian Games, honored Zeus and awarded the victors wreaths of wild celery.

Summary of the Major Panhellenic Festivals

Festival	Site	Began	In Honor of	Prize	Year of Olympiad
Olympic	Olympia	776 B.C.	Zeus	Olive wreath	First
Pythian	Delphi	582 B.C.	Apollo	Laurel wreath	Third
Isthmian	Corinth	582 B.C.	Poseidon	Pine wreath	First and third
Nemean	Nemea	573 B.C.	Zeus	Celery wreath	Second and fourth

Origin and Description of Olympic Games

Although the traditional date for the beginning of the Olympic Games is usually considered to be 776 B.C. the actual origins are lost in antiquity. Olympia, which was never a village or town, is a remote area about ten miles from the mouth of the Alpheus River in the district of Elis. The first temple at Olympia, dedicated to Hera, the wife of Zeus, was erected about the tenth or eleventh century B.C. The date lends credence to the tales of the worship of the Mother-Goddess or Earth-Mother before the Greek gods came to live on Mount Olympus. Prior to 1000 B.C. there were, on occasion, athletic festivals at Olympia, first to honor the goddess Hera, and, later, the god Zeus. In the two centuries prior to 776 B.C., before the first records of the Games were kept, almost nothing is known about the games, and the shrines at Olympia appear to have been neglected.

Firsthand accounts of the early Olympic Games have never been discovered; thus our first literary introduction to the Games is the choral poetry of Pindar, a fifth-century B.C. poet, who composed odes or "hymns" celebrating victors in the festivals. Although Pindar does not describe the athletic events in detail, his odes impart a sense of the beauty of the ceremonies. The odes convey the importance of the victor and the glory accorded him both at the festival and in his home city-state. For Pindar, the Olympic Games were the most glorious of all:

> But if, my soul, you yearn
> to celebrate great games,
> look no further
> for another star
> shining through the deserted ether
> brighter than the sun, or for a contest
> mightier than Olympia—[11]

Pindar's second Olympian ode attributes the origin of the Olympic Games to Heracles who "founded the Olympian Games." The third Olympian ode describes how the judge:

> raises his unerring hand
> over a man's head
> and places on his hair the silver-gray
> adornment of olive

which Heracles had brought from the Danube to be the most "beautiful trophy of contests at Olympia."[12] Pindar relates another legendary version of their origin, in which Pelops won his bride in a chariot race and commemorated his victory with a shrine and games at Olympia. Later writers also mention Pelops and Heracles as founders of the games, and Phlegon, writing in the second century A.D., recounts this interesting story. Three men, Lycurgus of Sparta, Iphitus of Elis, and Cleisthenes of Pisa, conceived the idea of holding games to promote political harmony among the city-states of Greece. They traveled to Delphi and consulted the oracle there. She directed them to declare a truce among the cities which would take part in the games. A messenger carried this edict throughout Greece. Some Peloponnesians who did not support the holding of the games "were visited by disease and a blight on their crops which caused them distress."[13] The people sent their leaders back to Delphi where the priestess proclaimed that the disease and blight were the results of Zeus' anger because the people failed to celebrate the Olympic Games as promised. The citizens were not satisfied and consulted the oracle themselves. They were told:

> O inhabitants of Peloponnesus . . . go to the altar.
> Sacrifice and hearken to whatever the priests . . . enjoin.[14]

As a result of the ruling of the oracle, the priests of Elis administered the Games at Olympia. The Delphic oracle was consulted about the Olympic Games another time. When asked whether or not wreaths should be placed on the victors, she affirmed the use of wreaths and directed that the wreaths be made from wild olive trees.

Although Phlegon's version is but one of several concerning the beginning of the Olympic Games, it accounts for some actual customs of the Games. A truce was actually declared during the year of the festival so that the competitors could travel to Olympia and participate in the games without fearing attack; the games were conducted by men from Elis; and the official prize awarded was the olive wreath. The Games were characterized by a religious quality, having been dedicated to Zeus and ordained by a sacred oracle from Delphi.

During their first two centuries the Olympic Games were local in character. Most athletes were from Sparta or Athens and, traditionally, free-born citizens of Greek ancestry. The athletes, officials, and spectators were all men. The only woman permitted to watch was the priestess of Demeter, who presided over the Games from a seat of honor. Actually, authorities differ on this point. One account suggests that unmarried girls viewed the Games, while another reports that women who were in Olympia on the days of the events were thrown over the cliffs of nearby Mount Typaeum.

As the games became more important and the number of events increased, Olympia changed from a remote wooded glen where temples to Hera and Zeus stood and where occasional games were held in their honor, to a crowded complex of temples, athletic facilities, buildings, and statues. Within the Altis, the name of the sacred area housing the temples, the largest and most important one was dedicated to Zeus and contained his statue, seven times life size, made by Phidias of gold and silver. Zeus' temple was surrounded by Hera's temple, other smaller ones, commemorative statues, and treasuries, which were small buildings erected by the city-states to hold offerings honoring their local victors. Outside the Altis were the athletic facilities, the stadium to the east and the hippodrome to the south. Beside the path leading to the stadium stood a number of Zanes or statues calling attention to athletes who violated the regulations of the games. The offending athletes were barred from future Games and paid a fine which was used to erect the Zanes, which in turn served to remind the competitors of the shame and punishment they would receive if they broke any rules.

The stadium, a flat area for running, was enclosed by the Hill of Cronos and other embankments which accommodated some forty thousand spectators. The gymnasium and palaestra were west of the Altis. The gymnasium was typical of the period, a large area surrounded by two porticos which were used as practice tracks. The porticos were roofed to permit the athletes to practice in the shade. The palaestra or wrestling area was adjacent to the gymnasium; nearby baths completed the athletic complex.

A month before the Games, the athletes arrived to be tested, observed, and supervised by the Hellanodikai, the administrative committee of the Games. As the first day of the festival approached, more and more people arrived. Male members of the athletes' families, historians, philosophers, poets, painters, sculptors, and others interested in athletics came from near and far. Distinguished visitors were housed in the Leonidaion; but most citizens traveled with servants bearing tents, clothing, food, and utensils and created a temporary household for their stay at Olympia. The atmosphere was that of a fair; food, souvenirs, and amusements were peddled. Gardiner describes the occasion:

Meanwhile, visitors of all classes and from every part were flocking to Olympia. The whole Greek world was represented, from Marseilles to the Black Sea, from Thrace to Africa. There were official embassies representing the various states, richly equipped; there were spectators from every part, men of every class. Men, I say: for the only people excluded from the festival were married women, and even if unmarried women were allowed to be present, few probably availed themselves of the right except those in the neighbourhood. Apart from this Olympia was open to all without distinction, to hardy peasants and fishermen of the Peloponnese and to nobles and tyrants from the rich states of Sicily or Italy. All had the same rights. There was no accommodation for them except such as they could provide or procure for themselves; there were no reserved seats at the games, indeed there were no seats at all. The plain outside the Altis was one great fair, full of tents and booths. There you might meet every one who wished to see or to be seen, to sell or to buy: politicians and soldiers, philosophers and men of letters, poets ready to write odes in honour of victors in the games, sculptors to provide them with statues, perhaps already made, horse-dealers from Elis, pedlars of votive offerings, charms, and amulets, peasants with their wine-skins and baskets of fruit and provisions, acrobats and conjurers, who were as dear to the Greek as to the modern crowd.[15]

Figure 8.3 Model of Olympia about 150 A.D. Courtesy of the Metropolitan Museum of Art, Dodge Fund, 1930.

Sacrifices and ceremonies filled the first day. The second day began with the chariot race and the horse races, followed by the footrace, the long jump, the discus, and the javelin. The pentathlon occupied the rest of the day. Another period of sacrifice took place on the morning of the third day, then came more athletic events until the fifth day. The final day consisted of feasting, rejoicing, and paying tributes promised to the gods. While other athletic festivals differed in detail, their general program and atmosphere was similar to that of the Olympic Games.

The Athletic Events

The program of events at athletic festivals changed relatively little during the twelve-hundred-year period of the ancient games. Some changes occurred, events were added and dropped, but the program was more stable than today's sport programs. Footraces, jumping, discus, javelin throw, wrestling, boxing, and combinations of these events made up the contests during the festivals; in addition, there were chariot races and horse races. Although these events seem familiar to us, there are a number of differences between the ancient and modern performances.

Even though women did not compete in the Olympic Games, they competed in other festivals. They wore a short garment with one shoulder bare and the skirt length just above the knees. Male athletes competed in the nude, perhaps to avoid any question of mistaken identity or, according to one legend, to avoid the disaster of one lead runner who lost the race when his garment fell around his ankles.

Footraces

At Olympia the men competed in four races: the stade, one length of the stadium; the diaulos or two lengths of the stadium; a race in armor, also two stades in length; and the dolichos, a long-distance race. While the dolichos could be any distance from seven to twenty-four stades, at Olympia it appears to have been twenty. Other festivals included a middle distance event of about eight hundred meters.

The method of starting the ancient footraces has never been satisfactorily explained. Archaeologists have uncovered what are assumed to be starting devices, but no firsthand accounts of their use have been found. At Olympia, Delphi, and Epidaurus stone sills with narrow, parallel grooves are embedded in the end of the stadium. It is theorized that these are starting blocks on which the runners placed one foot on the back line and one foot on the front line, digging their toes in the grooves, starting in an upright position rather than the modern crouch. This idea is supported by figures on vases which depict racers with one foot in front of the other, knees slightly bent. A statue of a girl runner shows the back foot placed against a raised stone suggesting another method of starting.

Recent excavations at Isthmia have uncovered a more sophisticated system that permitted all runners a simultaneous start. The stone sill has no grooves, but at regular intervals there are sockets. Behind the starting sill is a pit and between the pit and the sill are brass staples. Harris explains: "Each runner had a starting gate like a railway signal. The moving arm was worked by a cord which ran from the short end of the arm through the staple and along the groove to the pit. All the cords were held by the starter standing in the pit, and when he released them, all the arms fell at the same time, thus ensuring a fair start."[16] A careful examination of the illustrations of runners suggests that the style varied according to the distance of the race. Although we know something of the techniques used by the ancient runners, we know nothing of their times or records. The victors' lists indicate only the winners and thus we cannot compare the time of the early runners with modern runners.

The Jump

The Greeks did record the length of at least two jumps which far surpass any modern ones. Phayllus of Croton is reported to have jumped fifty-five feet and Chionis of Sparta fifty-two feet. One explanation of the superior jumps is that the Greeks actually performed a hop, skip, and jump. Gardiner, however, suggests that the records are fictitious:

> Herodotus, Aristophanes, Plutarch, and Pausanias all mention him [Phayllus] but know nothing of his fabulous jump. The epigram is said to have been inscribed on his statue at Delphi. But though the base of this statue has been found there is no

Figure 8.4   Lead jumping weight. Courtesy Museum of Fine Arts, Boston, H. L. Pierce Fund.

trace on it of the epigram. Nor is there any evidence that the epigram was contemporary with the event. Indeed we cannot trace it further back than the second century A.D. But whatever its date there is no reason for taking it seriously. The sporting story is notorious: still more so is the sporting epigram; and this epigram is merely an alliterative jingle.[17]

In ancient athletics jumpers carried weights or *halteres* in each hand, at least during part of the jump. Several *halteres* have been discovered and many appear on vases and other objects. Some resemble today's telephone receivers, some are similar to dumbbells, and still others have holes for the fingers. We do not know what the precise function of the *halteres* was, but it has been suggested that they were released at some point during the jump to provide more forward impetus. Philostratus, a third century A.D. writer, declared that the weights assured a firm landing.

Throwing the Discus
A number of reasons have been proffered for the many different shapes, sizes, and weights of the discus used in ancient times. One theory suggests that the antecedent of the discus was the stone throw used in battles, and that the discus approximates a battle stone. It is generally assumed that the smaller and lighter instruments were used by boys. There appears to be more than one method of executing the throw. Perhaps the best-known sculpture of a discus thrower is that of Myron. Gardiner analyzes the sculpture:

Figure 8.5   Athlete with discus, early fifth century B.C. Courtesy of the Museum of Fine Arts, Boston, H. L. Pierce Fund.

Myron has chosen to represent a moment between the backward swing and the forward swing where there is an apparent pause. . . . The thrower, raising the diskos level with his head in both hands, has swung it vigorously downwards and backwards in his right hand, at the same time turning his whole body and his head to the right. The right leg, which is advanced, is the pivot on which the whole body turns, the left foot and left arm merely helping to preserve the balance. We may note, too, the rope-like pull of the right arm. This turn of the body round a fixed point is the essence of the swing of the diskos. The force comes not from the arm, which serves only to connect the body and the weight, but from the lift of the thighs and the swing of the body.[18]

Throwing the Javelin

The numerous representations of the javelin throw show at least one major difference between the ancient and modern event. To increase the distance of the throw, the ancient javelin thrower employed a leather thong bound to the center of the shaft and forming a loop through which one or two fingers could be inserted. It is believed that the thong imparted a spin that contributed to the steadiness of the flight and increased the distance of the throw.

Figure 8.6   Athletes practicing. Courtesy of the Museum of Fine Arts, Boston, H. L. Pierce Fund.

Wrestling

The most popular Greek sport was wrestling, which took place in a specially prepared section of the stadium called a skamma. To protect the wrestlers in their falls, the area was dug up and covered with a layer of sand. Prior to competing, the wrestler oiled his body and dusted it lightly with sand. After wrestling and before bathing, the oil and sand were scraped off with a strigil, a small instrument designed for that purpose. The match was scored on the best of three falls. Wrestling was a frequent subject in poetry and for vase paintings.

The Pentathlon

The pentathlon was introduced into the Olympic Games in 708 B.C. and combined the five events previously described: the footrace, jump, discus throw, javelin throw, and wrestling. Scholars have debated two issues regarding this ancient event: the origins, and the method of determining a winner. A legendary origin comes from Philostratus who relates that Jason created the pentathlon in order to name Peleus the best athlete among the Argonauts. Peleus was acclaimed victor after winning the wrestling, although he placed second in all the other events. According to Gardiner, "These five events were representative of the whole physical training of the Greeks, and the pentathlete was the typical product of that training. Inferior to the specialized athlete in his special events, he was superior to him in general development, in that harmonious union of strength and activity which produces perfect physical beauty."[19]

Figure 8.7   Pancration, 550-500 B.C. Courtesy of the Metropolitan Museum of Art, Rogers Fund, 1905.

Boxing

Although boxing was well known by Homer's time, it was not introduced at Olympia until 688 B.C. The Greek boxing "glove" was actually a strip of leather or thong about ten feet in length wound around the boxer's knuckles, hands, and up the forearms. Softer, padded thongs were worn for practice. Ancient boxing was not conducted in a ring, did not have rounds, and did not group fighters according to weight. The fight lasted until one man either was knocked out or admitted defeat.

Pancration

Philostratus described the pancration as the sport that is "prized the highest even though it is composed of uncompleted wrestling and uncompleted boxing. . ."[20] Today we picture the contest as an all-out fight combining boxing and wrestling, permitting kicking, but prohibiting biting and gouging. The event was strictly regulated and, as in boxing, terminated when one opponent acknowledged defeat.

Horse Racing and Chariot Racing

Harris suggests that the Greek hippodromes were agricultural lands pressed into service as a race course after the crops were harvested. "Any flat stretch, as soon as the crops were taken off and the exposed soil baked by the summer sun, would afford adequate going for horses or chariots, provided it was not crossed by watercourses or irrigation channels. The only preparation needed to convert such a stretch for racing was the removal of any large stones and the provision of two turning-posts."[21] Numerous athletic festivals throughout the Greek world included horse races. While the race-card varied, one program from Athens in the second century B.C. listed twenty-five events. In 680 B.C. four-horse chariot races were held at Olympia and, later, mule-cart races, jockey-ridden races, and races for colts added. The chariot race provided an opportunity for women to have some part in the Olympic Games. Although Cynisca of Sparta did not attend the Olympics or drive the chariot, her horses won the chariot race in 396 and 392 B.C. Other women who owned horses that won chariot races at Olympia were Belistiche, Theodota, Euryleonis, and Kasia.

Training for the Festivals

The trainers and coaches were frequently former athletes, who, after their years of victories, taught others their knowledge and expertise. Numerous paintings on Greek vases provide ample evidence of training devices and methods. Apparently a long instrument was used to prod or correct the athletes. Not until the accounts of Galen and Philostratus in the early centuries of the Christian era is there much written evidence of athletic training. Nevertheless, scholars have developed a general theory of training based on the fragments that do exist. By the fifth century B.C. the informal athletic festivals of Homer's time had changed into organized meets with coaches and trainers. Young men spent much of their time practicing for the festivals and, if competing at Olympia, reported for special training a month before the Games. Lucian, a satirical writer of the second century A.D., imagines Solon, the Athenian law giver of the sixth century B.C., trying to explain the training of Greek athletes to Anacharsis, a bewildered visitor from Scythia. Solon tells Anacharsis that they have "invented many forms of athletics and appointed teachers for each. . ." Each event had its purpose in training for all-round athletes from learning "to fall safely and get up easily, to push, grip and twist," to become "accustomed to endure hardship and to meet blows," to run "in deep sand, where it is not easy to plant one's foot solidly," and to jump obstacles "carrying lead weights as large as they can grasp."[22] Gradually the emphasis on training to do well in every event changed to specializing in one event. By the fifth century B.C. special diets were in vogue to increase the weight and strength of boxers, wrestlers, and pancrationists.

By the second century A.D. when Greece was under Roman rule, there is more information on training. We know that the average Greek man still considered physical training and the gymnasium important. Galen traced the beginnings of the athletic events and made suggestions for suitable body types for each event. Thus, coaches and trainers of the period were well aware of

Figure 8.8   Athletes practicing, fifth century B.C. Courtesy of the Metropolitan Museum of Art, Fletcher Fund, 1927.

the importance of diet, exercise, body types, and daily habits in the performance of athletic events. Lacking today's knowledge and sophisticated training devices, they utilized the information of the day and attempted to construct theories and practices that would improve performances.

Women in Athletic Festivals

Although they were barred from the Olympic Games, the women held their own festival at Olympia and, according to a few fragments of evidence, also participated in athletic events in other parts of Greece. The games at Olympia honored Hera, the sister-wife of Zeus, and are thought to represent a very early matriarchal society. The temple of the great Earth-Mother on the hill of Cronos within the Altis is one of the oldest temples at Olympia. Recent European scholars suggest that the footrace, the only event in the Heraean Games, represented an ancient fertility rite to give thanks for a good harvest.

Figure 8.9   Girl runner. Courtesy of the National Archaeological Museum, Athens.

It is believed that such harvest races were formalized into the Heraean Games before the Olympic Games. According to legend, one woman from each of the sixteen Elean city-states was sent to arrange a peace in a time of war. They settled the peace satisfactorily and were ordered to weave a gown for the statue of Hera every four years and to hold games in her honor. Pausanias describes the games:

> The games consist of footraces for maidens. These are not all of the same age. The first to run are the youngest; after them come the next in age, and the last to run are the oldest of the maidens. They run in the following way: Their hair hangs down, a tunic reaches to a little above the knee, and they bare the right shoulder as far as the breast. These too have the Olympic stadium reserved for their games, but the course of the stadium is shortened for them by about one-sixth of its length. To the winning maidens they give crowns of olive and a portion of the cow sacrificed to Hera. They may also dedicate statues with their names inscribed upon them. . . The games of the maidens too are traced back to ancient times.[23]

Other evidence of women competing in athletic festivals dates from the first century A.D. Inscriptions commemorate the daughters of Hermesianax, a citizen of both Athens and Delphi, who made the following dedication to Pythian Apollo:

> Hermesianax, son of Dionysius, Caesareus of Tralles (also from Corinth), for his daughters, who themselves have the same citizenships.
> 1) Tryphosa, at the Pythian Games with Antigonus and Cleomachis as judges, and at the Isthmian Games, with Juventius and Proclus as judges, each time placed first in the girls' single-course race.
> 2) Hedea, at the Isthmian Games with Cornelius Pulcher as judge, won the race in armor, with her chariot: at the Nemean Games she won the single-course race with Antigonus as judge and also in Sicyon with Menoites as judge. She also won the children's lyre contest at the Augustan Games in Athens with Nusius son of Philinus as judge. She was first in her age group . . . citizen . . . a girl.
> 3) Dionysia won at . . . with Antigonus as judge, the single-course race at Asclepian Games at the sanctuary of Epidaurus with Nicoteles as judge.[24]

Another inscription from Patras on the Gulf of Corinth reads, "I, Nicophilus, erected this statue of Parian marble to my beloved sister Nicegora, victor in the girls' race."[25] Even later in the third century A.D. a traveler described girls wrestling with boys, but one author suggests that this is not serious history but scandalous gossip of cafe society.

Changes in the Function of the Festivals

The purposes of the ancient athletic festivals changed gradually in the course of centuries. Originally, sport or athletic events honored the gods or heroes of a family and when contests between clans began, the victor brought honor to his clan. Later, winning a wreath at an athletic festival was a mark of social distinction. Robinson notes that the list of victors at Olympia reads "like a page from the Social Register. It is to be expected that wealthy aristocrats and tyrants would be entering four-horse chariots in contests; but in these centuries future statesmen, generals, sons-in-law of wealthy tyrants and the like were also fighting hard pancratium matches of a far from gentle type of boxing and wrestling and were sprinting in the footraces at Olympia during the stifling heat of August."[26] Although the victor received only a wreath at the festival, he was treated like a hero and received other honors, such as having his statue erected at Olympia or having a poem dedicated to him, like the following Pindaric ode celebrating the 460 B.C. victory, in a mule-car race, of Psaumis, from the city of Kamarina:

OLYMPIAN 5

Receive, daughter of Okeanos,
the fairest reward of lofty achievements
and of garlands gained at Olympia—
the gift of Psaumis and his mule car
   drawn by undaunted hooves:
      graciously receive it.

Kamarina, whose town he exalted
at the greatest
of all festal gatherings, with sacrifice
at the six double altars,
   and in the whirling races
      of the fifth day,

the chariot, the mules, the single horse.
Victorious, he has secured
luxuriant renown
for you,
   having his father Akron acclaimed
      together with his city, risen again.

He comes from the lovely grounds
of Oinomaos and of Pelops,
singing, Pallas Polias,
of your sacred wood,
   of the stream Oanos
      and the lake nearby,

of Hipparis, whose channels
bring pure water to this city;
raising her houses as a lofty grove,
he swiftly lifts his people
   back into the light
      from their ruin.

Always, in the contest for excellence,
expense and labor
struggle to achieve an exploit
whose end
   lies veiled in danger—though the public
      thinks it sees wisdom in success.

Zeus, savior in the high clouds,
dweller on the Hill of Kronos,
glory of broad Alpheos
and Ida's sacred cave,
   to the music of Lydian flutes
      I come, beseeching you

to adorn this town
in the splendor of her brave men—
and may you, Psaumis,
who look with joy
   on the steeds of Poseidon,
     bring your life to completion

in good cheer, with your sons
standing beside you.
If the wealth a man tends and cares for
be sound,
   his house ample, and his name renowned as well,
     let him not envy the gods.[27]

As the city-states grew in importance, athletes represented their cities in the festivals rather than their families. The cities expressed their gratitude to victors by giving them food at public expense and presenting them with costly gifts. Gradually, men realized that they could gain personal profit from entering athletic contests, and the athlete as a professional performer became an accepted part of the festivals. These men, frequently specializing in only one event, earned their living by traveling from festival to festival much as today's pros "play the circuit" in tennis or "play the tour" in golf. However, in ancient Greece, because these men were no longer from the socially elite, the professional athlete was looked down on by some aristocratic Greeks who considered professionalism undesirable. Isocrates reminds his listeners that his father "disdained the gymnastic contests [at Olympia]; for he knew that some of the athletes were of low birth, inhabitants of petty states, and of mean education, but turned to the breeding of race-horses, which is possible only for those most blest by Fortune."[28]

By the first and second centuries A.D. professional athletes were organized into guilds much like today's unions. These organizations became powerful and could exact from Roman notables such as Mark Antony promises of "exemptions from military service, public duties, billeting of troops, a truce during the festival . . . , guarantee of personal safety, privilege of the purple. . ."[29]

The changes from religious athletic events honoring the gods to secular professional athletics entertaining multitudes took place over hundreds of years. Many scholars of the ancient festivals have considered the rise of professionalism to be the ruin of the Greek athletic festival; but today's concepts of professionalism and amateurism did not exist at that time. Authors of antiquity accepted the fact that there would be material benefits from Olympic victories. Finley and Pleket explain:

If there was any change over the centuries, it was only the growth from the vanity of a small number of aristocratic champions to the more loudly proclaimed vanity of a far larger number of champions, many of whom, though by no means all, had been born among the lowest social classes in the later Greek world.

ROME   In the beginning of the second century B.C. Rome became a major world power and continued in that position for nearly eight hundred years. The city boasts of its founding about the eighth century B.C. Etruscan kings in the sixth century B.C. built city walls and encouraged residential building. During the next several centuries local magistrates, both patricians and plebians, ruled over the Roman Republic, which became powerful, first locally, then in Italy, and after the Punic Wars, in the Mediterranean world. At its height the Roman world extended east to Persia, west to Spain and France, north to England and Germany, and south into Africa.

The Roman Empire, as it conquered local tribes, spread Roman language, law, and customs. In the farthest corners of the Western world and the Mediterranean countries people still use solidly constructed Roman bridges, roads, aqueducts, and arenas built for public amusement. In the city of Rome itself, aristocrats resided in their elegant homes in the winter but summered on their rural estates or in seaside resorts like Pompeii, where they swam, hunted, rode horseback, and discussed the latest plays. The Romans adapted the Greek palaestra, the place for exercise and wrestling, by adding enormous "baths" which provided bathing and swimming facilities. Many of these baths boasted separate pools for hot water, tepid water, and cold water; massage rooms; promenades with shops; and areas for playing ball or talking with friends.

The Campus Martius in Rome, a vast area for driving chariots, riding, ball games, wrestling, and playing, was set aside for the people. Extremely large facilities called *circuses* were built expressly for the most popular amusement, chariot racing. The largest, the Circus Maximus, built about 329 B.C., accommodated about 250,000 spectators, who came for a day's sport watching four chariots race simultaneously, seven times around the circuit, which was about six football fields long.

In the *Aeneid,* a classic of Roman literature, Virgil followed Homer's example in describing elaborate funeral games to honor the father of the hero, Aeneas, who was led by the gods to leave Troy and found Rome. Many of the events are similar to the funeral games for Patroclus in the *Iliad.* A "swift footrace" attracts many entrants, who upon the signal "stream out like a storm cloud." When the man in front slips and falls, he just happens to trip the second-runner, in order that his friend, in third place, can win. The boxing match is a challenge event: a retired champion is urged to fight a young challenger with "massive shoulders." The archery contest, with the target a fluttering live dove tied to a ship's mast, demonstrates remarkable shooting: one archer cut the cord, another brought down the bird as it flew away, and the last competitor's arrow, shot up into the sky, became a shooting star—sure sign of the gods' approval of the games. As a rousing finale a group of boys, sons of the Trojan warriors, perform an extended demonstration of disciplined close-order drill, on horseback, before their proud fathers.[30]

Funeral games are said to be the origin of gladiator contests, in which two men fought until death or, at times, a man fought an animal. The first account of a public fight of this nature occurred in 264 B.C. when men fought to honor the spirit of Pera's father. In the course of time more and more such public contests took place. As the Empire declined and the citizenry became dissatisfied because of unemployment or military defeats, public officials provided increasingly bizarre and brutal spectacles free of charge, to keep the Roman populace's attention diverted from public issues. By 80 A.D. when the Emperor Titus opened the Colosseum, the celebration observed one hundred days of gladiator fighting, wild beasts, and other spectacles. When the Christians became part of the Roman population, they protested the gladiatorial exhibitions, but it was not until about 400 A.D. that public fighting discontinued.

Their vanity . . . was accepted by society at large as a legitimate human quality. . . . If . . . they worked hard and lived moderately, they could count, after their retirement, on a life of affluence from "the fruits of their victories." Olympic wreaths and affluence remained part of one and the same complex to the very end of the thousand-year story.[31]

The athletic festivals and games declined slowly during the first centuries of the Christian era. During the second century A.D. the major festivals experienced a revival and many features were added for the comfort of the athletes and spectators. Eventually, however, the festivals and games came under the attack of Christian bishops and Roman rulers. The official banning of the Olympic Games is usually attributed to Emperor Theodosius I in 393 A.D. Early in the fifth century A.D. Theodosius II and Emperor Honorius of Rome ordered the destruction of all places dedicated to Greek gods. This ruling coupled with earthquakes the following century completed the destruction of Olympia. By 551 A.D. Olympia was in ruins and the festivals in the ancient sacred stadium were over.

The Modern Olympic Games

Beginnings

The modern Olympic Games were initiated through the efforts of one man, Pierre de Frèdy, Baron de Coubertin. However, Coubertin was not the first to consider reviving the ancient Olympic Games. From the time of the Renaissance and a rekindled interest in all things Greek, the idea of the Games appears in literary and educational works. For over two centuries, 1610 to 1860, the "Olympick Games" of England were conducted at Dover's Hill. Initiated by Captain Robert Dover, the games, also referred to as the Cotswold Games, lasted two days: "They were somewhat akin to a protest movement against the growing Puritanism in English life. The widely known games, conducted on Dover's property, consisted of wrestling, field hockey, fencing, jumping, and throwing the pole, hammer, and javelin."[32] Also in the nineteenth century other games were held in England near Wenlock in Shropshire by Dr. W. P. Brookes. Coubertin attended these games on one of his visits to England and became friendly with Brookes. Beginning in 1859 the Greeks themselves occasionally conducted modern games, called the National Greek Olympics. "The opening ceremony was a combination of religious rites, the playing of an Olympic anthem and the swearing of an Olympic oath. Parallel to ancient traditions, the athletes were required to train together daily for three months prior to the Olympics. . . . The Games were also conducted in 1875 and 1889 and in each instance included athletic competitions, gymnastic exercises and shooting."[33]

Interest in the modern Olympic Games was further stimulated by archaeological developments in Greece. The first attempts to uncover Olympia began in 1829 by the French. Later the Germans, from 1875 to 1881, uncovered the remains of the temples of Hera and Zeus, the palaestra, gymnasium, the entrance to the stadium, and other buildings in the Altis. Again in 1937 the Germans led an expedition that unearthed items revealing the history of Olympia.

The early German excavations took place during Coubertin's boyhood and perhaps suggested to him the means to achieve his avowed purpose in life—improving mankind and promoting peace through a broad use of sport. Coubertin has been described as a visionary, a passionate patriot, a fervid Anglophile, and a man of action. Born on January 1, 1863, to Charles Louis Baron Frèdy de Coubertin and Agathe Gabrielle de Crisenoy, his childhood was shadowed by France's defeat in the Franco-Prussian War. As a boy he read *Tom Brown's School Days,* and the Rugby School's system of sports and games, as well as Dr. Thomas Arnold, the Rugby headmaster, became a guide for Coubertin's developing ideas. By the age of seventeen Coubertin had become aware of the need for reform in French education and started preparing himself to become involved in that reform. Studying at the Jesuit College of the rue de Madrid and taking further courses in law and political science, Coubertin visited England and became an even stronger proponent of English public school sport. He saw the revival of the ancient Olympic Games as "the logical consequence of the cosmopolitan tendencies of the period: a general awakening of a taste for athletics, inventions such as railroads and telegraphs; exhibitions, assemblies, and conferences [bringing] together people of similar backgrounds in science, literature, art and industry."[34]

Coubertin's first public proposal to establish the modern Olympic Games, made at the Unions des Sports Athlétiques at the Sorbonne in November, 1892, was not well received. He carefully planned his second attempt. He organized an International Congress of Paris for the Study and the Propagation of the Principles of Amateurism to be held at the Sorbonne in June, 1894, and sent invitations to sport associations all over the world. Not leaving anything to chance, Coubertin traveled to the United States and England in an effort to gain support for his plan. Coubertin organized the program together with the secretary of the Amateur Athletic Association of Great Britain, C. Herbert, and a Princeton University professor of history, William Sloane. During the week of meetings helpful suggestions on amateurism were made, other sport-related items were discussed, and slowly the idea of the revival of the Games developed. It was the last item on the agenda of the Congress: "He must have known how to cast a spell over the seventy-nine delegates from twelve countries. There were poems, music and songs. And after every delegate had heard the hymn to Apollo, discovered at Delphi in 1893, set to music by Gabriel Fauré and sung by Jeanne Remacle from the Paris Opera, the assembly, unanimously and by acclaim, decided to restore the Olympic Games."[35]

Organization

The International Olympic Committee

An analysis of the modern Olympic Games reveals Coubertin's understanding of both the ancient games and the world of his time. He selected certain timeless concepts from the ancient games and recast them into a complex structure in which a neutral, nonpolitical, self-perpetuating body, the International Olympic Committee (IOC), governed the Games. Whereas the ancient Games were conducted by the men from Elis, Coubertin's governing body was to be a select group of men from all over the world, who then would proceed to choose their own additional members. Coubertin believed that this system would create a body of administrators who could be influenced neither by national interests nor by sport organizations and, thus, would be impartial in any disputes concerning the Games. The original members were personally selected by Coubertin himself. He picked fourteen men, from Great Britain, France, Greece, Russia, Sweden, Bohemia, Hungary, Italy, Belgium, Argentina, New Zealand, and the United States of America. Members were originally appointed to the Committee for life, but, for those elected after 1965, retirement has been mandatory at 75. Counting Coubertin, the first IOC numbered fifteen men from twelve countries, and in 1986 the IOC consisted of eighty-six men and five women from more than eighty countries. Representing neither a country nor a sport, the members must be interested in promoting amateur sport, reside in a country which has a National Olympic Committee, speak either French or English, and be prepared to contribute an annual fee. In the fall of 1981, the IOC elected its first women, Piryo Haggman of Finland and Flor Isava Fonseca of Venezuela, to membership.

The aims of the International Olympic Committee are stated as follows:

—to promote the development of those physical and moral qualities which are the basis of sport,

—to educate young people through sport in a spirit of better understanding between each other and of friendship, thereby helping to build a better and more peaceful world,

—to spread the Olympic principles throughout the world, thereby creating international goodwill,

—to bring together the athletes of the world in the great four-yearly sport festival, the Olympic Games.[36]

The term Olympiad refers, as it did in ancient times, to the four-year period between the Games; however, in the modern Games it is not used in reference to the Olympic Winter Games, which were initiated in 1924. Coubertin believed firmly that, as opposed to the ancient Games being held only at Olympia, the modern Olympic Games should be celebrated in cities in various parts of the world. He considered this idea a further effort to remove the Games from national political influences. Thus, every four years the Games are awarded to a city, not a country, selected by the IOC. The IOC is responsible for the overall supervision of the Games including financial arrangements, television contracts, and the development of the Olympic Movement.

Eight men have been President of the IOC, perhaps the most influential position in amateur sport. From 1894 to 1896 Demetrius Vikelas served as president, followed by Baron Pierre de Coubertin from 1896 to 1925. During World War I the president was Baron Godefroy de Blonay. In 1925 Count Henri Baillet-Latour became president and served until 1942. Following World War II Sigfrid Edström held the position from 1946 to 1952, when Avery Brundage took over until 1972. Lord Killanin was president from 1972 to 1980. Juan Antonio Samaranch was elected president at the Moscow Games.

Originally, it was anticipated that the IOC business would be conducted from the country celebrating the coming Games, but in 1915 Coubertin decided to move the IOC headquarters to Switzerland to protect its political neutrality, and it has been in Switzerland since that time. Business is carried on at the Lausanne headquarters by a permanent staff, the executive board of the IOC, and by commissions which are appointed to deal with specific aspects of the program.

The Olympic Games are open to all eligible athletes. Eligibility is established by the IOC under the jurisdiction of the international sport federation (IF) for each Olympic sport. According to the IOC, athletes must be citizens or nationals in a country or territory with a recognized National Olympic Committee (NOC). The charter states: "No discrimination in them [the Games] is allowed against any country or person on grounds of race, religion, or politics." It should be noted that the antidiscrimination clause of the IOC does not include "sex." There is in fact a special rule, Rule 28, concerning women's participation: "Women are allowed to compete according to the rules of the IF concerned and after approval of the IOC."[37]

To be recognized by the IOC, National Olympic Committees must have affiliated with them at least five national sport federations that are members of international sport federations with a minimum of three governing Olympic sports. The NOC's are responsible for the development of the Olympic Movement in their countries. The committees are expected to be free from political ideology and influence. The IOC prescribes that the membership of the NOC include IOC members who reside in the country and representatives of national federations who are members of their respective international federation; the IOC further suggests that delegates from a variety of sport bodies serve on the committee. Beginning in 1965 the NOC's formed a general assembly to examine issues of mutual concern.

Whereas the NOC's deal with the development of the Olympic Movement in their countries and are responsible for the athletes, the international sport federations retain the responsibility for the selection of sport events, the rules, and the conduct of events. For each sport the IOC must recognize one international sport federation which, in turn, recognizes one national governing body (NGB) in each country. By 1986, thirty-two international federations were recognized by the IOC.

Athletes must be members of their country's national governing body, which plans the competitive program for that sport. For example, a U.S. archer would join and compete in the National Archery Association, which is affiliated with the International Archery Federation. A cyclist would join the U.S. Cycling Federation, affiliated with the International Amateur Cycling Federation, and a gymnast would compete nationally through the United States Gymnastics Federation, an affiliate of the International Gymnastics Federation.

Thus, the path of an athlete to the Olympic Games may be visualized as follows:

In the United States an athlete joins and competes in a sport through a NGB such as the National Archery Association or the United States Gymnastics Federation. That NGB must be affiliated with the appropriate international federation, which in turn must be recognized by the IOC. The NOC recognizes the NGB affiliated with the IF.

The United States Olympic Committee

In the United States the national Olympic committee is the United States Olympic Committee (USOC) which has been in existence since 1896, under various names. James E. Sullivan, one of the founders of the Amateur Athletic Union (AAU), formed the first Olympic committee, known as the American Olympic Committee (AOC). Evolving from a small group of interested men, it was responsible for the development of the early United States Olympic teams. In 1921, following World War I, the AOC became more formally organized as the American Olympic Association (AOA), including other national amateur sports associations in its organization. The AAU was the most powerful of these associations. The National Collegiate Athletic Association

(NCAA), after its formation in 1906, held jurisdiction over collegiate sports and the many men who competed in them. Beginning in the 1920s disputes between the AAU and NCAA over the control of athletes and competitive events created problems with the development of Olympic sports in this country.

In 1950 Congress passed Public Law 805 incorporating the United States Olympic Association (USOA), which adopted a new name in 1961, the United States Olympic Committee (USOC). Internal disputes among the sports organizations continued, impairing the ability of the United States to reach its potential in Olympic sports. The United States always fielded a team, but not without internal struggles. Finally, in 1975, President Gerald Ford appointed the President's Commission on Olympic Sports whose findings resulted in the Amateur Sports Act of 1978. This act broadened the scope of the USOC and established it as the organization for the Olympic Movement in the United States and as the coordinating body for amateur sports in international competition. The USOC is generally responsible for coordinating amateur athletics in this country, from elite competition in the Olympic Games to programs for people with special needs; it also serves as the coordinating agency for international amateur athletics competition. According to the 1985 Constitution and Bylaws, the USOC recognizes national governing bodies for United States sports in the Olympic and Pan American Games; it represents the United States in all negotiations with the IOC; it facilitates the resolution of conflicts among amateur athletes and sports organizations; and in general it promotes amateur sport in this country.[38]

The United States Olympic Committee is made up of representatives of five classes of membership: Group A (national sports governing bodies), Group B (national multi-sport organizations), Group C (affiliated sports organizations), Group D (state Olympic organizations) and Group E (national disabled in sports organizations). For each sport eligible to be included in the Games, the USOC recognizes one national amateur sport governing body, which has complete jurisdiction over the conduct of that sport in the United States and which is recognized by the appropriate international sport federation, which in turn has been recognized by the IOC.

National sports governing bodies, which comprise Group A, must be open to all athletes and must not discriminate on the basis of religion, age, sex, color, creed, or race. At least twenty percent of the membership of the governing board for the sport must be athletes or former athletes who have participated within the past ten years. The membership must be open to all appropriate athletes, coaches, trainers, and administrators. In Group B are multi-sport organizations, those that hold national programs or national championships in two or more sports eligible for the Games but who are not eligible for membership in Group A. Included in Group B are organizations such as the Catholic Youth Organization; U.S. Armed Forces; and the American Alliance for Health, Physical Education, Recreation, and Dance. Group C includes national sports organizations that are not affiliated with the Games but that might be included in future Games. Group D consists of the Olympic organizations from each state. The responsibilities of the state organizations include promoting the United States Olympic Movement and raising funds for the conduct of Olympic programs. Group E is made up of amateur sports organizations not eligible for other groups that conduct national competitions or programs in two or more Olympic or Pan American sports for individuals with special needs. This structure of the USOC serves not only Olympic sports but the broad area of amateur sport in the United States. Like the IOC, the USOC does not discriminate on the basis of race, religion, politics or gender. Unlike the IOC, the USOC documents include the word "sex" in their anti-discrimination clause.[39]

When the Olympic Games were revived in 1896 international competition and international sports federations did not exist as they do today. This section has detailed the early organization of the Games under the IOC and the present structure with its complex relationships of the international federations, NOCs, and NGBs. From the beginning Coubertin recognized the importance not only of international organization, but also of symbols, rituals, and ceremonies in his concept of the modern Olympic Games. These are discussed in the next section.

Symbols, Rituals, and Ceremonies

The ancient Olympic Games originated as a religious, athletic festival to honor the Greek god Zeus. Symbols such as the laurel wreath for the prize, rituals such as the sacrifice before the Games, and other ceremonies were essential features of the ancient Games. Coubertin carefully designed the modern Games to embody "religious" qualities; however, his actual meaning of "religion" in reference to the Games is unclear:

> Coubertin . . . never precisely explained the sense in which he used the term "religion." In contrast to the genuine and traditional meaning of the concept . . . one could etymologically interpret "re-ligio" in a secularized manner. This interpretation would morally pertain to institutionalized rituals, rites and social ideologies not based on transcendent beings. Whereas the Games of antiquity certainly belong to the first category, Coubertin most likely had the second type in mind. Thus, the so-called religious significance of the Modern Games would radically differ from that of the ancient ones. Being a symbol of festive emotions, deep engagement, and human accomplishment at peak performance the Olympic Games incarnate the idea of actively achieved human excellence. . . . Rather than being magic and naturalistic, it is a historically developed myth of a sporting climax of life, and of sportsmanship institutionalized and symbolized by conventional social rules.[40]

Today the Games are characterized by symbols, rituals, and ceremonies which create, both for the spectators and for the athletes, some shared emotional experiences, although they may vary in intensity from the thrill of watching the torch bearer arrive in the stadium to light the Olympic flame, to the victorious athlete's transcendent sensation when the ribbon with the gold medal is slipped over the head.

The Olympic hymn, officially adopted in 1958, was composed for the first modern Games in Athens by the Greek Spyros Samaras with words by Costis Palamas. The Olympic emblem, five interlaced rings, was adapted by Coubertin from an emblem at Delphi to symbolize the five continents of the world. The Olympic flag was designed with the rings in five different colors, yellow, black, green, blue and red, set against a field of white. These six colors encompass the colors in the flags of the participating nations. The flag was first flown in 1914 and incorporated into game ceremonies in 1920.

The Olympic motto, *Citius, Altius, Fortius* (Faster, Higher, Stronger) is ascribed to a Dominican friar, Father Henri Didon, who had influenced Coubertin. A second statement, "the most important thing in the Olympic Games is not to win, but to take part," now widely associated with the Olympic Games, was adopted by Coubertin after he heard it in a sermon delivered during the celebration of the 1908 Olympic Games in London.

Immediately following World War I in 1920, doves, signifying peace, became a part of the opening ceremony. The symbolic flame and the torch relay from Olympia were planned for 1928, but the relay did not take place, and was first used in the 1936 Berlin Olympics. The athletes' oath in the opening ceremony and the symbolic medal for victory are further examples of Coubertin's desire to emphasize the religious components of the Games.

From the beginning the head of state in the host country has opened the Games. Officially, the president of the IOC arrives with the head of state and "supervises" the ceremony. The athletes parade by nation, saluting or acknowledging the president and head of state. Each delegation carries its country's flag, all of which are equal in size. The head of state recites the opening lines, "I declare open the Olympic Games of ___city___ celebrating the ___number___ Olympiad of the modern era." The Olympic hymn is played, the Olympic flag raised, the pigeons or doves released, and the Olympic flame lit by the final torch bearer from Olympia. A representative athlete of the country where the Games are held takes the oath on behalf of the athletes, and the host-city's national anthem is played. Then, the Games are officially underway. In recent years the host-city has staged a display that completes the opening ceremonies.

The victory ceremony is designed to honor the winning athlete with a symbolic prize. The first, second, and third place winners mount the podiums— the first place the middle one, the second to the right of the first place, and the third to the left. The president of the IOC or his representative slips a ribbon with the proper medal over the heads of the victors, and the flag of the winner's country is raised and the national anthem played.

The closing ceremony is altogether different from the opening ceremony and fulfills a different function. The athletes do not march by country, but instead walk together, eight to ten abreast, with the countries intermingled, thus signifying friendship through international sport. With the president of the IOC presiding, the Greek flag is raised on one of three flag poles. Next the flag of the host-city's country is raised and that national anthem played. Finally the flag of the country where the next Games will be celebrated is raised and that anthem played. The president of the IOC declares the Games ended, the trumpets sound, the Olympic flame is extinguished, the Olympic anthem played, the Olympic flag lowered, and the athletes march out.

Athens, 1896

Coubertin's original idea had been to hold the first modern Games in connection with the 1900 Paris World's Fair. However, Vikelas from Greece requested that the first modern Games be held in Athens in 1896. The 1894 Paris Congress approved Vikelas' proposal and preparations began immediately. Reconstructing the necessary facilities presented a severe financial strain on the Greek government, and Coubertin had to travel to Athens to lend his support to the Olympic idea and publicly acclaim the Greek origin of the Games. Finally, a commission of citizens, with Crown Prince Constantine as its honorary president, undertook the organization and conduct of the Games.

The major difficulty was finding the money to reconstruct the ancient Panathaenean Stadium so that it could be used. The Greek architect Metaxes, also a member of the commission to organize the Games, designed the reconstruction. Prince Constantine contacted a wealthy Alexandrian and Greek citizen, George Averoff, who made a gift of about one million drachmas for the stadium. The Greeks raised the other necessary funds in a variety of ways: "The issue of the first stamps dedicated to the Olympic theme, brought in 400,000 drs. Much of the required money was provided by the distribution of commemorative medals and the sale of tickets."[41]

The first Games of the modern Olympics were simple but ceremonial. On Easter Sunday, April 6, 1896, King George of Greece opened the Games and the Olympic hymn was sung while the athletes stood in the center of the stadium. Many of the athletes travelled informally to Athens, not in teams as they do today. Most of the United States athletes were members of the Boston Athletic Association or students from Princeton University. From the beginning Coubertin had planned that the events in the modern Olympics would reflect contemporary sport. While the modern Games included more athletic (track and field) events than any other sport, thus reflecting the ancient Games, there were also events in sports such as cycling, shooting, and tennis.

Events in the 1896 Games[42]

Sport	Number of Events	Sport	Number of Events
Fencing	3	Shooting	5
Weight Lifting	2	Swimming	4
Athletics	12	Tennis	2
Cycling	6	Gymnastics	8
Wrestling	1		

The modern Olympic events brought some remarks from an American magazine:

> An ancient Greek, had he come to life again, would have missed some of the events of his old games. The pancration, with its brutalities, was happily lacking. Even boxing was omitted. He might have asked with some reason why the pentathlon was not retained as a test of general athletic excellence. He would hardly have acquiesced in the substitution of the boat-races at Phaleron for the ancient chariot-races, and would doubtless have thought the pistol and rifle shooting a poor substitute for throwing the javelin. But of all the additions to his old list of games he would have found lawn-tennis and bicycling most removed from ancient athletics. Considering, however, not the shades of ancient Greeks, but the modern world, ought not the patrons of the contest to have persuaded Englishmen and Americans to add the sports games of football and baseball?[43]

There was one event that had been specially designed for the occasion. In contrast to the ancient Games, which did not include a marathon race, Coubertin included a race to honor the Greek who ran almost twenty-five miles from Marathon to Athens in 490 B.C. to tell the Athenians that they had won the Battle of Marathon. As the Games progressed, the Americans captured most of the events in athletics and the Germans in gymnastics. No Greek had won an event until, to the delight of everyone, Spiridon Loues, a Greek shepherd, came in first in the marathon, followed by two other Greeks. A traveler described the scene as Loues finished the race:

> It is impossible to describe the enthusiasm within the Stadium—nay, in the whole city of Athens—over the result of this the most important contest in the games during these ten days. The Stadium packed with over 50,000 people; the walls around it, the hills about, covered with a human crowd that from the distance looked like bees clustering over a comb; and this mass of humanity rising in one great shout of joy with the advent—the one runner who was first to cross the line within the Stadium, caught in the arms of the Crown-Prince, who led him before the King, embraced and kissed by those who could get near him; all this and much more sent a thrill through every heart which few could have experienced before with the same intensity. It might almost have been Philippides [sic] of old bringing to the anxious inhabitants of Athens the news of their glorious victory, the salvation of their country and home.[44]

Countries Represented by the 1896 Athletes[45]

Country	Number of Athletes	Country	Number of Athletes
Australia	1	Greece	230
Bulgaria	1	Great Britain	8
Chile	1	Austria	4
Denmark	4	Sweden	1
Germany	19	Switzerland	1
France	19	Hungary	8
U.S.A.	14		

From the beginning of the modern Games, nationalistic attitudes about which countries should compete have plagued the IOC. For example, in 1894 Germany had not been invited to the Congress in Paris because the French Gymnastic Union had threatened to leave if it were invited. However, in 1895 Dr. W. Gebhardt from Germany became a member of the IOC and it appeared as if Germany would compete in Athens. Later the Germans announced that they would not compete, but through the continued efforts of the German Olympic Committee and Gebhardt, nineteen Germans finally took part in the first modern Games.

Coubertin did not want women in the Olympics, and no events were planned for women in 1896. However, there is a story that one woman, Melpomene, ran the marathon race in the Games at Athens. She had trained herself for the event and applied to enter the race but was refused. According to accounts, she ran alongside the male athletes and completed the race. Thus it appears that women may have participated in some fashion throughout the modern Olympic Games.

The first Games of the modern Olympics were clearly a Greek observance. In spite of the early difficulties the Greek people took great pride in the Games and also staged performances of two famous Greek dramas, *Medea* and *Antigone,* presented concerts, gave receptions, and created an atmosphere of festivity in the city. Coubertin remained in the background, with the satisfaction of seeing his dream of modern Olympic Games come true.

The Period of Organization, 1900–1912

The modern Olympic Games were not firmly established until 1912. By that time international sport federations were in existence, the techniques and performance of the sports had improved, better methods of measuring and judging had been developed, and the idea of international sport was generally accepted. The modern program was not as stable as the ancient games, and sports were added and dropped depending on the country and the available facilities.

For Coubertin, both the 1900 and 1904 Games were failures, because they were held in conjunction with world fairs and had difficulties during the preparation period. Neither at Paris, the site of the 1900 Games, nor at St. Louis in 1904, were the events considered the serious competition that Coubertin had envisioned.

The 1900 Games, planned for Paris, immediately had difficulties in organization. From 1897 to 1899, differences over the conduct of the Games, changes in personnel, and bickering took place, until Coubertin resigned from the Union of French Athletic Associations, in whose hands the organization had been placed. The Games reflected this background and were described as casual. They were held in various parts of the city, with many contestants not realizing the nature of the Olympic Games. The events occurred from May to October, in poor locations, on bumpy tracks and in muddy swimming water. In spite of the conditions and confusion, over one thousand men and eleven women participated.[46] Tennis and golf, Olympic sports at that time, permitted women to compete, and thus from 1900 on records of victors include women.

The Games in 1904 were held in connection with the St. Louis World's Fair, which celebrated the one hundredth anniversary of the Louisiana Purchase. It had been understood that the third Games of the modern era would be held in the United States. The first consideration was given to Buffalo, then Chicago, and finally St. Louis. Only twelve nations participated, with most of the athletes from the United States. Again, the events were held during several months of the year and the issue arose as to which events of the many athletic and sport competitions held in St. Louis that summer were official. One report stated that "the International Olympic Committee expressed desires that all athletic competitions under the auspices of the Universal Exposition of 1904 bear the name, 'Olympic.' "[47]

Coubertin did not attend the 1904 Games and was even more disappointed than he had been in the Paris event when he learned of the "Anthropological Days" held in St. Louis in which the emphasis was placed on the origin of the competitors rather than on performance. The athletes were Patagonians, Filipinos, Ainus, Turks, native American Sioux Indians, and Syrians. The one highlight of the 1904 Olympics was the excellent athletic facilities used at Washington University.

For several reasons "interim" Games were held in Athens in 1906. Very few Europeans had competed in St. Louis, and Coubertin did not want the idea of international sport to be forgotten. Both the Paris and St. Louis Games had dismayed Coubertin and he wished to reestablish the idea of serious sport competition in relation to the Olympic ideals. The 1906 Games were held without fanfare, and while not considered "official" they were successful. Even though they were not well attended, Coubertin believed they permitted the modern Games to continue in the direction he hoped to establish.

The 1908 Games had been planned for Rome, but that city was unable to keep its commitment. British members of the IOC were approached about the possibility of holding the 1908 Games in London and agreed to do so. With years of sport tradition, an Amateur Athletic Association over three decades old, and the experience of conducting the Henley Royal Regatta, the London Games were the best example of modern international sport in the modern era. Experienced in conducting sport events, the British established rules for each event and distributed them in English, French, and German. In an effort to establish comparable status of the athletes, all competitors had to enter the Olympic Games as a member of a country's "team." Also, for the first time, an athletic complex of special sport facilities was built expressly for the Games. The stadium was used for athletics, fencing, gymnastics, swimming, and wrestling. The fact that all the officials were British led to many disputes, especially between the United States and British representatives. These confrontations led to changes. "After the quarrelsome episodes at London, management of the athletic events was delegated to the international governing body for each particular sport."[48] Women entered three sports in 1908, tennis, archery, and figure skating, and also presented exhibitions in swimming, diving, and gymnastics, that were favorably received.

With the 1912 Games in Stockholm, Coubertin believed that the modern era of the Olympic Games would be successful. Twenty-eight countries sent 2,504 athletes. There were no ugly incidents between athletes or countries, and the events were held in a spirit of serious sport competition and international goodwill. By this time more sports were governed by international federations that had had several years experience with international rules. At least three countries, Germany, Sweden, and Great Britain, coached their teams especially for the Games. The United States also had developed its unique approach to athletics, with "inter-collegiate competition, professional coaching and sports scholarships."[49]

Three sports were of special importance in the 1912 Olympics. One was swimming, in which women entered for the first time through the suggestion of the international federation. Second, equestrian events were held for the first time. They were first suggested by Count Clarence von Rosen at the 1908 Games but could not be included at that time. Third, a dream of Coubertin to identify the ideal all-round athlete was fulfilled in Stockholm when the modern pentathlon was inaugurated. It consisted of running, riding, swimming, fencing, and shooting. Coubertin explained the rationale:

The thread combining all five events is that of the military messenger who is dispatched with vital orders for the front line: his horse is shot away from under him after clearing certain obstacles, he fights his way through with his sword which in turn breaks and he is forced to turn to his revolver. Forcing his way to the river bank, he dives in to evade his captors and finally delivers the vital message on foot, like Pheidippides, the original runner in 490 B.C. from Marathon to Athens.[50]

The Period of Political Development, 1920–1936

The 1916 Games were not celebrated because of World War I, but the 1920 Games were held soon after the cessation of the conflict. The Games were awarded to Antwerp in recognition of the sacrifices which the Belgians had made during the war. Perhaps the most significant overall achievement of the period from 1920 to 1936 was that the Games became a major world event in their own right. The modern Olympic Movement demonstrated it could not be deterred by a world war that lasted longer than an Olympiad. The 1920 Games were modest, but by the 1924 Games in Paris there were forty-four nations which entered over three thousand athletes. The Games were international in character and victors emerged from a variety of nations. Uruguay's team was the Olympic champion in association football (soccer) and athletes from Argentina won two gold medals. A Japanese athlete won a gold in the triple jump, and both South Africa and Egypt had gold medalists. Three important developments occurred during this period. First, women were admitted to athletics (track and field) events. Second, the Winter Games were initiated, and finally, the Games emerged as part of the international political arena.

Coubertin continued to resist efforts to include women officially. However, the result of an almost ten-year struggle ended with women officially in the athletic events of the Olympic Games. After World War I European women became interested in track and field or athletic competition and joined the newly formed Fédération Sportive Féminine Internationale (FSFI), which had been established by Mme. Millait. International competitions in some fifteen events with distances as great as 1500 meters were held, and before the 1920 Games, Millait tried unsuccessfully to have women's athletic events added to the Olympic program. To demonstrate women's ability to engage in athletics, she organized and conducted the First Women's Olympic Games, held in 1922 and planned for the midpoint of each subsequent Olympiad.

The Women's Games were successful and preparations were underway for the second Women's Games when negotiations with the International Amateur Athletic Federation led to a plan to control women's athletics and to recommend an Olympic program of five events for women. Millait attempted to increase the number of events but was unsuccessful. The British women protested the meager program and refused to compete in the 1928 Games.

However, the five-event program was eventually accepted and, for the first time, women competed officially in the athletic events in the 1928 Games at Amsterdam. Even these few events were jeopardized when some of the contestants barely finished the 800-meter race. The FSFI proposed fifteen events for 1932, but only six events were approved and the 800-meter race was deleted. Throughout the period arguments continued over the possible harmful effects of athletics on women. Those opposed believed that athletics "threatened harm to future mothers" and "that sport for women should not be severely competitive."[51]

The United States women physical educators objected to women in the Olympic Games, not so much on the grounds of health, but because of the cost and attention given to a few highly skilled athletes rather than instruction to a great many women. In 1928 and again in 1932, United States women physical education associations protested women's participation to the IOC.

Millait continued to hold the Women's Olympic Games, changing the name to Women's World Games. From the beginning they were planned to honor a country as the winner; the first two Games honored Great Britain and the last two Germany. The Women's Games were held in Paris in 1922; Gothenburg, Sweden in 1926; Prague in 1930; and for the last time in London in 1934.

While the controversy over the entry of women into the Games ended in 1928, the problem was not completely resolved. The questions of the extent to which women could participate and their role in the sport-governing federations remained unsettled.

Just as Coubertin was opposed to women in the Games, he also objected to the idea of Winter Games. He believed they would detract from the summer Games, but finally, convinced of the increased popularity of winter sports, he joined with the IOC in approving the Winter Games with certain stipulations. The name "Olympiad" is not used for the winter cycle. While the country in which the summer Games are staged may also offer the Games, the location may be somewhat distant from the summer city. The Winter Games began with a modest program of five sports: ice hockey, figure skating for men and women, speedskating for men, four-man bobsled, Nordic crosscountry skiing for men, and ski jumping. Sonja Henie was a young competitor in the first Winter Games.

Although the VI Olympiad had to be cancelled because of World War I, the ability to celebrate the VII Games was an important factor in the postwar Olympic Movement. The unpretentious 1920 Games were organized in a very short period of time, but their very celebration supported the Olympic ideals. The later Olympiads of the period reemphasized the increasingly international nature of the Games. In Amsterdam at the 1928 Games forty-six nations entered 2,971 athletes. Although the Los Angeles Games were smaller, the 105,000-seat stadium itself was the largest Olympic stadium yet built, representing the city's efforts to create a mammoth sport entertainment spectacular.

Amid the growing size and importance of the Olympic Games many men and women made their contributions to sport through their Olympic performances. Form improved, technical aids were invented and utilized, and sport organizations helped to regulate national and international competition.

In men's athletics the Finns were among the outstanding athletes. The famous Paavo Nurmi suffered a defeat in his first Olympic event, but went ahead to win the 10,000-meter race. That was in 1920 and he continued to dominate the men's 1500- and 5000-meter races in 1924 and 1928. Although in the twenties Charles Paddock was the United States' best sprinter, perhaps the most exciting track and field star in the 1932 Games was Mildred "Babe" Didrikson. Coming from Texas she qualified for the AAU championships in Chicago as a one-woman team and in Los Angeles took two gold medals and missed a third when she was disqualified for form in the running high jump.

In swimming, Duke Kahanamoku continued to excel in the various events and child star Aileen Riggin won the gold in springboard diving. Kahanamoku and Johnny Weismuller were the famous United States swimmers of the period with Weismuller winning the 100-meter gold in 1924 and 1928 after Kahanamoku had won the event in 1912 and 1920. In 1932 Helene Madison and Eleanor Holm turned in outstanding performances while the Japanese men shattered records in several events. Although Sonja Henie had placed last in the 1924 Winter Games as a child, in 1928, 1932, and 1936 she took gold medals. She was the first woman to win three consecutive gold medals in the Olympics. The 1928 Winter Games were held at St. Moritz and the 1932 Games at Lake Placid, where snow had to be trucked in from nearby Canada.

Throughout this period the Games became increasingly politicized. In the first few Games athletes from both large and small nations won gold medals. The prestige such a victory brought to a small nation became apparent and the athletes vied for victory to bring honor to themselves and to their country. Although Coubertin believed in honoring only individual winners, the addition of team sports made identification of winning countries a necessary component of the Olympics. Thus, more attention was paid to the country winning team events. Sports reporters and sportscasters devised an unofficial point system and the publicized "points" further identified countries rather than individuals. An additional factor introduced in Los Angeles was the civic pride displayed by the city as it produced a sport extravaganza for foreign visitors.

Added to this was the intensifying international political scene in which power over men's and women's opinions played a major role in the new totalitarian governments. Berlin had been awarded the 1936 Games in 1931, two years before Hitler came to power. Although Coubertin and the IOC placed the Olympic Games above political maneuvering and power plays, it was during such a period that plans for the 1936 Games were formulated. By 1936 the Games had moved from the control of the German Olympic Organizing Committee to that of Hitler and the Nazi Party. Goodhue emphasizes the fact that "One cannot detach 1936 from the previous Olympic Games. It was not simply an aberration. The conditions that made 1936 possible were apparent in the development of the Games from 1900–1932."[52]

The Nazi Olympics, 1936

In 1933 Hitler became head of the German government and initiated his oppressive Nazi edicts. As the web of control over the average citizen became evident and as the Nazi systematic extinction of Jews was announced and put into effect, people from other countries were first dismayed and then horrified. Although these policies appeared to be in direct contradiction to the Olympic regulation forbidding discrimination on the grounds of race, politics, or religion, plans for the Games to be held in Berlin proceeded. However, some countries became concerned and indicated they might not participate in the 1936 Games. As early as 1933 the United States AAU passed a resolution against entering the Berlin Games unless Germany complied with the IOC policy of not discriminating on the basis of race or religion.

During the 1933 IOC meetings, the committee was assured by the German IOC members that they would remain on the German Organizing Committee, thus maintaining the political neutrality of the Games. The German government also agreed that German Jews would not be "excluded from the German teams for the 11th Olympic Games."[53]

Brundage, President of the American Olympic Committee (AOC, former name of USOC), toured Germany in 1934 and decided that the German sport programs were in compliance with the letter and spirit of Olympism. Although the AOC had not yet accepted the invitation to participate in the 1936 Games, they voted to enter the Berlin Olympics after Brundage's reassurance. This did not stop the controversy over the entry of the United States athletes and in 1935 the situation was exacerbated when Hitler proclaimed further restrictions on German Jews. The movement against participation in the Olympics gained strength from organizations such as the National Council of the Methodist Church and the American Federation of Labor; magazines such as *Commonweal;* and papers such as the *New York Times* and the *New York Daily News.* As late as 1935 the AAU remained opposed to sending teams to Berlin. Those in favor of the United States entering the Games countered with arguments based on principles such as Coubertin's belief in the importance of holding the Games regularly, his creed of Olympism, and hopes of promoting international understanding.

The situation was finally resolved at the December, 1935, meeting of the AAU:

> Both sides gathered rhetorical ammunition for a great debate at the national convention of the Amateur Athletic Union which opened in New York in early December. The proponents of a boycott were armed with resolutions to that effect from regional associations of the A.A.U. The delegates met tensely, but the expected battle was never really joined. The executive committee of the A.A.U. met at the Hotel Commodore on Sunday, December 8, to listen to five hours of speeches for and against participation. The moguls of American amateur sport were hungry and tired when

time for a vote came. The executives (who had weighted voting rights) defeated the proposed resolution against sending an American team by 2 1/2 votes. The narrow majority then succeeded in passing a motion in favor of participation, adding the specific rider that their affirmative action was not to be "construed to imply endorsement of the Nazi government."[54]

As a result of the action Mahoney, president of the AAU, resigned and Brundage was elected the AAU president. In his now dual role of president of both the AAU and the AOC, Brundage went ahead with plans for the United States athletes to compete in Berlin.

The boycotts and furor over the Nazi regime resulted in the planning of the "Peoples Games" or "Workers' Games," in Barcelona, Spain, just prior to the Berlin Olympic Games. Athletic teams from many countries were in Spain to boycott the official 1936 Olympic Games and to protest the policies of Hitler, when on the eve of the alternative games the Spanish Civil War broke out.

In spite of the turmoil, the 1936 Berlin Olympic Games were celebrated in an elaborately staged sport spectacle during which athletes and visitors alike enjoyed the carefully planned German hospitality. As if to discredit Hitler's theory of Aryan superiority, the star of the Games was the black American Jesse Owens. One of seven children, he grew up in Cleveland, Ohio, where one of his teachers suggested he try running to improve his health. He was found to be incredibly fast, and soon he was training for several track events. As an Ohio State sophomore in the 1935 Big Ten track and field championships, he broke four world records. In Berlin, Owens won gold medals in the 100-meter and 200-meter sprints, the long jump, and the 400-meter relay.[55]

There was no question that the athletic events were well organized and that the athletic performances were the best the world had seen. The IOC gained more worldwide publicity than it had had in the past, but it also lost some of its credibility. While the preceding Games had become increasingly political, the 1936 games clearly represented political manipulation. For the first time, the host country moved the control of the Games from the organizing committee to its own government. The Berlin Olympic Games thus became the instrument of the Nazi government, and although later Games would again be conducted by organizing committees, the Games themselves would never be the same.

Ten Successive Olympiads, 1948–1984

Demonstrating the importance of the Olympic movement as a worldwide phenomenon, the IOC awarded the 1940 Games to Tokyo. But, because of conflicts on three continents, culminating in World War II, neither the 1940 nor the 1944 Games were celebrated. As soon as possible after peace was declared the 1948 Olympics in London brought together 4,062 athletes from 58 countries. The world character of the modern Games was emphasized by the fact that athletes from 42 of these 58 countries competed in the finals. Still recovering from the war, London had to utilize many temporary and improvised facilities. With the exception of the closed circuit telecast in Berlin, this was the first time provision was made for televising the Games. Throughout this period, performances continued to improve due to better training, better health, better technical equipment, and a greater number of qualifying athletes from which to select Olympic contenders. Many of these factors were the results of what Coubertin had foreseen as part of the modern Olympic Movement.

The London Games were the first in a series of ten successive Olympiads, the longest continuous series in the modern Olympic era. The USSR, invited to enter the 1948 Games, declined but sent observers to London. Athletes in the Games varied from seventeen-year-old Bob Mathias from California to Holland's Fanny Blankers-Koen. After just three weeks' coaching young Mathias had entered a regional decathlon meet, which he won. He then went on to the nationals where he earned a berth on the Olympic team, and later won the gold medal in the decathlon. In contrast, Blankers-Koen had competed in the 1936 Games and twelve years later, at almost thirty years of age, won four gold medals: the 80-meter hurdles, the 100- and 200-meter sprints, and as a member of the 4 $\times$ 100-meter relay. London saw the first appearance of Emil Zatopek, the Czechoslovakian runner, who competed again in 1952. Twenty-eight countries competed in the 1948 Winter Games at St. Moritz. Alpine skiing was introduced as a full-fledged event although there had been some competition in this area in 1936. The United States' Gretchen Fraser took first in the special slalom and Dick Button starred in the figure skating.

The Helsinki Games in 1952 were conducted with more dignified ceremony than the London Olympics but without the prewar pageantry of the 1936 Berlin Games. Almost all events reflected the increased attention given to sports in the Olympic countries after World War II. Soviet athletes entered the Olympic Games in 1952 for the first time in forty years. They prepared very carefully for the Games, organizing a central sport authority that arranged mass competitions in schools and provided for the athletes selected to compete. The Soviets began their practice of finding positions for adult athletes in which time was made available to prepare for and participate in international competitions.

Even though the next Games were held half-way around the world in Melbourne, Australia, athletes from sixty-seven countries competed. The Games were celebrated in an atmosphere of world political unrest due to the 1956 unsuccessful Hungarian rebellion against the Soviet Union, and other international incidents. Although the fighting continued in Hungary, the Hungarians managed to send a team. The Netherlands and Spain, however, withdrew in protest of the conditions in Hungary; Egypt and Lebanon did not participate because of a Middle East crisis; and the People's Republic of China refused to compete because the Republic of China (Taiwan) entered athletes in the Games.

Figure 8.10   Seventeen-year-old Bob Mathias, Olympic decathlon champion in 1948 and 1952. Wide World.

Despite the dampening effect of international disputes the Games were considered successful. The Hungarian athletes who managed to reach Melbourne received a standing ovation as they marched into the stadium for the opening ceremonies. The United States men dominated the track events, taking the gold, silver, and bronze medals in four events. Young Wilma Rudolph earned her first Olympic medal, a bronze in the 4 ×100-meter relay. One of the outstanding women athletes was Australia's Betty Cuthbert, who won the 100- and 200-meter sprints. The Australian swimmers, working under innovative coaching techniques, won many of the medals in swimming. Dawn Fraser won the 100-meter freestyle, a feat which she repeated in 1960 and 1964. The

Figure 8.11   Wilma Rudolph winning the 200-meter dash at the 1960 Olympic Games in Rome. Wide World.

most talked-about event was the USSR-Hungary water polo game, described as a replay in the swimming pool of the Hungarian rebellion. In marked contrast with the reality, Hungary won, 4–0. USSR athletes, on the whole, were well prepared for the Games and won five more gold medals than the United States, thirty-seven to thirty-two, and twenty-four additional medals, including silver and bronze. With the USSR and the United States recognized as major world powers, the press and many individuals interpolated political and ideological competitions into the rivalry in sport.

In 1960 at the Rome Games, the United States long domination of men's track and field events ended when athletes from New Zealand, Poland, Germany, and Italy won gold medals. Of the ten women's track events, the USSR women took six, but the favorite woman athlete of the Rome Games was Wilma Rudolph, who won three gold medals. The United States swimmers reversed the Melbourne records and won eleven gold medals, breaking five world records. In boxing, Cassius Clay (Muhammad Ali) was awarded a gold medal in the light heavyweight division.

The 1964 Tokyo Games reflected the increasing size and complexity of staging modern sport competitions. Elaborate but functional facilities contributed to the excellent conduct of the Games and Japanese technology permitted live telecasts to thirty-nine countries by way of a satellite. The increased coverage permitted millions who previously had read about the Games or listened to them on the radio to become part of the crowd watching the Olympic Games. The viewers saw many athletes from previous Games who repeated or bettered their performances, including Bikila, the Ethiopian marathon

Figure 8.12   Bob Beamon at the 1968 Olympic Games. Wide World.

runner, swimmer Dawn Fraser, runner Snell from New Zealand, and gymnast Cáslavská from Czechoslovakia. By this time South Africa had been banned from the Olympics because of its *apartheid* policies.

When the 1968 Games were awarded to Mexico City apparently little thought was given to the effects of altitude on athletic performance. A great deal of research and planning on how to train for the 1968 Games occurred; nevertheless, athletes from countries with high altitudes had advantages in the endurance events. Some athletes who did not live in high altitudes trained away from home to learn to acclimate themselves to the thin air. Bob Beamon from the United States astounded everyone with his incredible jump of 29' 2 1/2''. Among the innovations in Mexico City was the United States Dick Fosbury's technique for the high jump, the famous "Fosbury Flop," with which he edged out his teammate for a gold medal. The "Flop" was viewed with disbelief as Fosbury approached the high jump bar, leaped across the bar on his back and landed, also on his back. His championship jump set an Olympic record of 7' 4 1/4''. Both the United States men and women set the pace in the swimming events and, in women's gymnastics, Cáslavská continued to dominate the events.

In the midst of the 1960s unrest over civil rights in the United States, a small group of black athletes threatened to boycott the Olympic Games to increase awareness of the problems of the black athlete. The boycott did not occur, but after taking the gold and bronze medals in the 200-meter sprint,

Figure 8.13   Peggy Fleming, 1968 Olympic women's figure skating champion. Wide World.

Tommie Smith and John Carlos stood on the winners' podiums and, as the national anthem was played, each raised his gloved fist in the "Black Power" salute. The shocked IOC debated on a suitable punishment and, at one point, it was decided by the IOC that the entire United States track and field team be removed from the Games. The United States team remained, but Smith and Carlos were suspended by the USOC and sent home. The IOC also suspended them from future Olympic competition.

The Munich Games for 1972 were planned to be as perfect as possible in every respect. Each sport facility incorporated the latest technical developments, from advanced, sweeping architecture to electronic measuring devices. Great care was taken with even the smallest details to create an atmosphere in which athletes could compete for the highest sport honors in the world. Almost six thousand men and over one thousand women entered events in twenty-one sports. The sports world turned its attention on Munich and watched the events on television, listened to the radio, or followed the events in the papers. Record after record fell as new Olympic champions mounted the podiums for the first time or repeated a victory from earlier Olympics. Mark Spitz from the United States won seven gold medals in swimming. Women stars included USSR gymnast Olga Korbut, who endeared herself to the world and sparked a growing interest in women's gymnastics; the German sprinter Renate Stecher; and Mary Peters from Great Britain, who won the pentathlon at the age of 33.

In team sports the United States lost the basketball tournament for the first time in history in a controversial game with the USSR. With three seconds to play, the United States was in the lead, 50–49, and the Soviet coach was trying to signal for a timeout. When the horn signaled the timeout the United

Figure 8.14   Mark Spitz, winner of seven gold medals at the 1972 Olympic Games in Munich. Wide World.

States' team believed the game was over and that they had won. The officials ruled that three seconds remained on the clock. The Soviets scored a goal, officially winning the game, 51–50, and the basketball tournament.

Intruding into the schedule of the closely fought games and the many well-contested events was a twenty-three-hour horror. The *New York Times* head-line on September 6 told the story:

9 ISRAELIS ON OLYMPIC TEAM KILLED WITH 4 ARAB CAPTORS AS POLICE FIGHT BAND THAT DISRUPTED MUNICH GAMES

MUNICH, West Germany, Wednesday, Sept. 6—Eleven members of Israel's Olympic team and four Arab terrorists were killed yesterday in a 23-hour drama that began with an invasion of the Olympic Village by the Arabs. It ended in a shootout at a military airport some 15 miles away as the Arabs were preparing to fly to Cairo with their Israeli hostages.

The first two Israelis were killed early yesterday morning when Arab commandos, armed with automatic rifles, broke into the quarters of the Israeli team and seized nine others as hostages. The hostages were killed in the airport shootout between the Arabs and German policemen and soldiers.[56]

Never before had the tensions of the world intruded into the modern Olympic Games to this degree. The IOC, the athletes, and the world were stunned. After a debate as to whether or not to end the Games, the IOC decided to continue them, thus reaffirming its position that the Games transcend politically motivated violence: "The International Olympic Committee and the West

Figure 8.15   Speed skater Sheila Young, gold medal winner in the 500-meter race at the 1976 Winter Olympic Games. Wide World.

German Olympic Committee will participate, together with the Olympic participants, in a memorial service for the victims tomorrow, Wednesday, at 10 o'clock in the Olympic Stadium. This service should make it clear the Olympic idea is stronger than terror and violence."[57] The memorial service for the slain athletes was attended by eighty thousand; later that afternoon the Games went on.

The 1976 Winter Games were held in Europe in Innsbruck, where live television coverage made the Games a worldwide sport spectacular. England's John Curry and Dorothy Hamill of the United States, popular gold medalists in figure skating, both turned professional after the Games. The United States Billy Koch's unexpected silver medal in the 30-kilometer Nordic ski race surprised everyone. Other outstanding performers included American speed skater Sheila Young.

After the tragedy in Munich, the Games of the XXI Olympiad, hosted by Montreal, Canada, were organized to provide maximum security. Helicopters hovered above the opening ceremonies over which England's Queen Elizabeth II presided. Watchful armed guards accompanied the athletes to and from the Olympic Village. Fortunately, no incidents occurred as the more than seven thousand athletes from one hundred countries competed.

Nadia Comaneci, a 14-year-old Romanian gymnast, astounded both the judges and the computer with scores of ten. By the end of her performances Comaneci had won three gold medals, a silver medal, and a bronze medal. Lasse Viren, the outstanding Finnish runner, again dominated track and field events. In both 1972 and 1976 he took first place in the 5,000- and 10,000-meter race. The United States regained the gold medal in men's basketball, and in the first appearance of women's basketball in the Games, the United States women lost to the Soviets in the finals. Whereas the United States swept the men's swimming events, it was the East Germans who took the women's swimming events. While the Montreal Games themselves displayed world-class athletes in competition to prove their athletic prowess, the near crises over completing the facilities and the technology of worldwide communication coverage for the Olympic Games underscored many problems that the IOC would have to face in planning for the future of the Games.

Another difficulty appeared before the start of the 1980 Winter Games held in Lake Placid, New York. On December 27, 1979, the government of the USSR sent military troops across its border into Afghanistan, and President Carter threatened a boycott of the summer Moscow Games. Other than a few signs of protest during the opening parade, however, the drama of the Winter Games was left to the athletes. Speedskater Eric Heiden of Wisconsin made an unprecedented sweep of all five men's contests. In a traditionally European-dominated event, eighteen-year-old American Heidi Preuss finished a strong fourth in the women's downhill ski race.

Most Americans will remember the 1980 Winter Games for the unexpected heroics of the United States ice hockey team, which triumphed over the stronger, older, and more experienced European and Soviet teams to claim the gold medal. When the collection of young collegiate skaters defeated the highly rated Czechoslovakian team in the second game and then, unbelievably, defeated the perennial world champions from the Soviet Union in the semifinal round, hockey fans and the American public erupted with joy.

That was, however, the last Olympic celebration of 1980 for the United States and its athletes. Public debate flared over President Carter's December proposal to boycott the summer Games in Moscow to protest the Soviet military action in Afghanistan. The government of the United States urged the IOC either to postpone the Games or else move them to another site, asking other nations to disregard the Moscow Games and instead, to compete in "alternative Olympics." The 1980 USOC House of Delegates voted not to send United States athletes to Moscow. As in the past, the IOC proceeded with the games of the XXII Olympiad as planned.

Eighty-one national teams took part in the Moscow Games, while thirty-six elected not to compete for various reasons. For the first time in the history of the modern Olympic Games athletes representing the United States were not present. Sixteen nations who chose to participate in the Games but also wished to indicate their protest of Soviet military actions refused to fly their own flags and instead made use of the Olympic flag and hymn for ceremonial purposes. The Eastern-bloc athletes dominated the Games. Although competition suffered in some of the less well-known sports such as equestrian and rowing events, there were many quality performances. Thirty-six world records were broken, including the pole vault, once the exclusive province of the

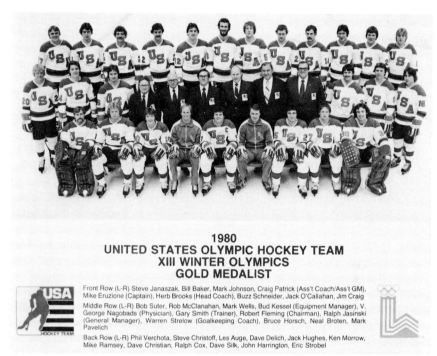

**1980
UNITED STATES OLYMPIC HOCKEY TEAM
XIII WINTER OLYMPICS
GOLD MEDALIST**

Front Row (L-R) Steve Janaszak, Bill Baker, Mark Johnson, Craig Patrick (Ass't Coach/Ass't GM), Mike Eruzione (Captain), Herb Brooks (Head Coach), Buzz Schneider, Jack O'Callahan, Jim Craig

Middle Row (L-R) Bob Suter, Rob McClanahan, Mark Wells, Bud Kessel (Equipment Manager), V. George Nagobads (Physician), Gary Smith (Trainer), Robert Fleming (Chairman), Ralph Jasinski (General Manager), Warren Strelow (Goalkeeping Coach), Bruce Horsch, Neal Broten, Mark Pavelich

Back Row (L-R) Phil Verchota, Steve Christoff, Les Auge, Dave Delich, Jack Hughes, Ken Morrow, Mike Ramsey, Dave Christian, Ralph Cox, Dave Silk, John Harrington, Eric Strobel

Figure 8.16 1980 United States Olympic Hockey Team XIII Winter Olympics gold medalist. Courtesy of the Amateur Hockey Association of the United States.

United States. Highlights of the Games included the Yugoslavian upset of the Soviet Union in men's basketball and the long-awaited duels between Britain's two world-record-holding middle distance runners, Sebastian Coe and Steve Ovett. Coe won the 1500-meter run and Ovett the 800-meter event.

For the athletes from the United States, 1980 was a summer of international competition and disappointment. Olympic trials were held in most sports and teams were selected. Many sport governing bodies held contests within the country and sent athletes to European meets following the Games. President Carter assembled the athletes in Washington and presented them with symbolic medals of appreciation.

The 1984 Winter Olympic Games were held in Sarajevo, Yugoslavia, amidst snow, fog, and winds that made the outdoor events very difficult. Athletes from seventeen different countries won medals. One young skier from the United States, William D. Johnson, did not appear to mind the weather and earned a gold medal in the men's downhill skiing. For the first time United States' men won both the downhill and slalom events with Johnson taking the downhill and Phil Mahre the slalom. The figure skating events went to United States' Scott Hamilton for the men, East Germany's Katarina Witt for the women,

USSR's Elena Valova and Oleg Vassiliev in the pairs, and Great Britain's exciting team of Jayne Torvill and Christopher Dean in ice dancing. The United States' men did not repeat their thrilling ice hockey performance of 1980; instead, the team lost in the pool play, and the gold went to the USSR.

The games of the XXIII Olympiad were awarded to Los Angeles, California, the site of the Games of the X Olympiad in 1932. To demonstrate the capability of private enterprise to finance the Olympic Games, the local organizing committee relied on television contracts and corporate sponsors for income. As has been true since the 1972 Munich Games, elaborate security measures were taken to insure the safety of the athletes and Olympic personnel.

In May, when the plans for the Games appeared to be progressing satisfactorily, the USSR announced that it would be unable to compete in the XXIII Olympiad because of the "lack of compliance with the Olympic ideals by the USA." With the exception of Romania and Yugoslavia, the Eastern bloc countries withdrew from the Games; for economic and political reasons, one or two other countries such as Cuba and Tanzania also chose not to compete.

Nearly eight thousand athletes from 140 countries marched in the elaborate opening ceremony. As might be expected, United States' athletes dominated the Games; but there were many good contests and the fans applauded gold medal performances from Canada's Alex Baumann and West Germany's Michael Gross in swimming. In weightlifting gold medalists came from China, West Germany, Romania, Italy, and Australia. Yugoslavia won the water polo competition. While the United States won the men's and women's basketball, Yugoslavia won the men's and women's team handball. Pakistan placed first in men's field hockey and the Netherlands in women's field hockey. With gold medalists from eleven countries, men's athletics seemed to portray the Olympic spirit; but one American, Carl Lewis, captured golds in four events. In gymnastics team competition the United States' men narrowly beat the Chinese men in an upset for the gold; the Romanian women gymnasts then passed the American women to win first place. Mary Lou Retton from the United States took the gold in the all-around gymnastic event with Ecaterina Szabo from Romania taking second.

New events for women attracted great interest, especially the women's marathon. Seventeen days before the tryouts, Joan Benoit of the United States underwent arthroscopic surgery on her right knee. She still entered, placing first in the trials. She also won the event in the Olympic Games with a time of 2 hours, 24 minutes, and 52 seconds. In synchronized swimming, another new event for women, the United States' Tracie Ruiz and Candy Costie took the gold in the duet, Canada's swimmers the silver, and Japan's swimmers the bronze. Ruiz also won the gold medal in the individual competition.

The Los Angeles organizing committee, under the leadership of Peter V. Ueberroth, made good its promise of a debt-free Olympic Games, showing a surplus of over two hundred million dollars which was shared with the USOC, who had guaranteed the Los Angeles Games. In spite of a number of potential problems, the 1984 Games proceeded smoothly. The general opinion seemed to be that the Los Angeles Games demonstrated the worth of the international four-year festival, the Olympic Games.

The Promotion of Sport

The USOC and the Promotion of Sport

Even a cursory examination of sports in the Olympic and Pan American programs reveals that, historically, many of them have not been among the most popular sports in the United States. Some, such as team handball and luge, enjoyed only limited popularity in this country. The sports eligible for the Olympic and/or Pan American programs are listed below:

> *Summer sports:* Aquatics (diving, swimming, water polo, synchronized swimming), archery, athletics (track and field), baseball, basketball, boxing, canoeing, equestrian, fencing, field hockey, cycling, gymnastics, judo, modern pentathlon, roller skating, rowing, shooting, soccer football, softball, table tennis, taekwondo, team handball, tennis, volleyball, weightlifting, wrestling, and yachting.
> *Winter sports:* Biathlon, bobsledding, figure skating, ice hockey, luge, skiing, and speedskating.

To develop athletes for the Olympic and Pan American Games and to acquaint the United States with these sports, the USOC undertook a number of specially designed programs in the 1970s. The USOC moved from New York City to Colorado Springs, Colorado, in 1978 where they established a comprehensive training center. The center included sport facilities, sport medicine laboratories, and living quarters for athletes, coaches, and trainers. Using the facilities constructed for the 1980 Olympic Winter Games, in 1983 the USOC opened a training center at Lake Placid, New York, designed primarily for winter sports.

Beginning in 1978 the USOC sponsored a National Sports Festival each year between the Olympic Games. In 1986 it was renamed the Olympic Festival. The festivals served to improve Olympic athletes' performances and to inform the American public about Olympic sports in general. In 1984 the USOC established a foundation to help the development of Olympic and Pan American sports. The USOC also assisted national sports associations in carrying out plans to develop their sports. It cooperated with educational institutions to increase the knowledge and understanding of the Olympic Movement in the United States.

To become a world class athlete in the 1980s required not only skill and dedication, but also financial resources frequently beyond the means of athletes and their families. To make it financially possible and attractive for men and women to devote their time to sport, national governing bodies, under the approval of the international federations, recognized a variety of programs such as trust funds, stipends, and flexible-time positions with corporations.

The IOC and the Promotion of Sport

The IOC is charged with promoting sport and the spirit of Olympism throughout the world. To accomplish this, the IOC grants patronage to selected regional games and an International Olympic Academy.

When the first request for sponsorship for games other than the Olympic Games was received, the IOC debated the issue and set a precedent by agreeing to sponsor the Far Eastern Games. Certain games were denied patronage because of government interference, while other games were planned but for a variety of reasons did not occur. Prior to the 1936 Olympics: "the proliferation of regional games was widespread. The I.O.C. was usually asked for its patronage, but not always. Games now held included the Balkan Games, the Colombian Games, the Central American Games, and several others. The situation was rapidly developing where several major 'Games' meets were held each year."[58] Regional games were disrupted by World War II, but following the war, other games such as the Pan American Games, the Mediterranean Games, and the Asian Games were introduced. These games follow the same general pattern of the Olympic Games, but do not always include the same program of sports. The Pan American Games are held in the fourth year of the Olympiad.

Additional Games have been introduced, not by region, but by educational institutions. Many Olympic athletes are students, and through the efforts of the International Union of Students and a group of western European educators, the Federation Internationale du Sports Universitaire (FISU) was established in 1948. The First World University Games were held in 1959 and have continued since that time.

One of Coubertin's ambitions was to establish a permanent site where sport and the Olympic ideal could be discussed and studied by sport scholars from all over the world. Various suggestions were made, but it was not until 1949 that the IOC gave permission for an International Olympic Academy. The academy, operated by the Hellenic Olympic Committee, is located in ancient Olympia, Greece, overlooking the ancient stadium. It opened in 1961 with thirty-one students from twenty-four countries and has grown to about 150 students. Academicians and sports leaders from many different National Olympic Committees lecture at the Academy. Each student must be from a country with a recognized NOC. The Academy meets for two weeks each summer to exchange ideas and consider contemporary applications of the Olympic ideals.

The growth of the modern Olympic Movement since 1896, the increase in international competition, new sports, and the improved performance of athletes have led to problems which could not have been anticipated by Coubertin, the founder of the modern Games. In 1986 the original concept of amateurism was under review not only by the USOC but also by the IOC. The issue had been raised again and again, especially since the 1960s. In 1985 the IOC voted to permit professional tennis, ice hockey, and soccer players to compete. In the 1980s the policy was to abide by regulations of the International Federations.

Commentary

The modern Olympic Games have become the most prestigious competition in international sport. With the world's attention focused on the Olympic Games for a few days during each Olympiad, they have been thrust into a role undreamed of by Coubertin, their founder. They have suffered at the hands of politicians and terrorists and have been exploited as a status symbol. For many, victory in the Games signifies national prestige among the nations of the world. For others, perhaps the majority, the modern Olympic Games still represent the search for human excellence in a complex world. In spite of the many difficulties, the modern Olympic Games fulfill a unique function in today's world and, to a large extent, have achieved the goals of the Olympic Movement.

Suggestions for Further Reading
1. "Ancient Athletics and Ancient Society," Special Issue, *Journal of Sport History* 11, no. 2 (Summer 1984).
2. Finley, M. I., and Pleket, H. W. *The Olympic Games: The First Thousand Years.* New York: The Viking Press, 1976.
3. Leigh, Mary. "Pierre de Coubertin: A Man of His Time." *Quest* 22 (Spring 1974): 19–24.
4. Mandell, Richard D. *The Nazi Olympics.* New York: Macmillan, 1971.
5. Segrave, Jeffrey, and Chu, Donald. *Olympism.* Champaign, IL: Human Kinetics, 1987.

Notes
1. Stephen H. Hardy, "Organized Sport and Community in Ancient Greece and Rome," Master's thesis, University of Massachusetts, 1975, 17.
2. From Homer, *The Iliad,* translated by Robert Fitzgerald. Copyright © 1974 by Robert Fitzgerald. Reprinted by permission of Doubleday & Company, Inc. 543–44.
3. Ibid., 544.
4. Ibid., 545.
5. Ibid., 546.

6. Ibid., 557.
7. Ibid., 558.
8. Ibid., 567.
9. Homer, *The Odyssey,* trans. by Robert Fitzgerald (New York: Anchor Press/Doubleday, 1963), 129.
10. William Harlan Hale, *Ancient Greece* (New York: American Heritage Press, 1970), 103–104.
11. *Pindar's Victory Songs,* trans. by Frank J. Nisetich (Baltimore: Johns Hopkins University Press, 1980), Olympian Ode 1, lines 4–10.
12. Ibid., Olympian Ode 2, line 5; Olympian Ode 3, lines 21–24, line 28.
13. Rachel S. Robinson, *Sources for the History of Greek Athletics* (Cincinnati: published by the author, 1955), 41.
14. Ibid., 42.
15. E. Norman Gardiner, *Athletics of the Ancient World* (Oxford: Clarendon Press, 1930), 224.
16. H. A. Harris, *Greek Athletes and Athletics* (London: Hutchinson, 1964), 68.
17. E. Norman Gardiner, *Athletics of the Ancient World* (Oxford: Clarendon Press, 1930), 152–53.
18. Ibid., 160–61.
19. Ibid., 177.
20. Rachel S. Robinson, *Sources for the History of Greek Athletics* (Cincinnati: published by the author, 1955), 216.
21. H. A. Harris, *Sport in Greece and Rome* (Ithaca, N.Y.: Cornell University Press, 1972), 162.
22. Rachel S. Robinson, *Sources for the History of Greek Athletics* (Cincinnati: published by the author, 1955), 69–71.
23. Ibid., 109.
24. Mary R. Lefkowitz and Maureen B. Fant, *Women's Life in Greece and Rome* (London: Duckworth, 1982), 160.
25. H. A. Harris, *Greek Athletes and Athletics* (London: Hutchinson, 1964), 181.
26. Rachel S. Robinson, *Sources for the History of Greek Athletics* (Cincinnati: published by the author, 1955), 58.
27. *Pindar's Victory Songs,* trans. by Frank J. Nisetich (Baltimore: Johns Hopkins University Press, 1980), Olympian Ode 5.
28. Rachel S. Robinson, *Sources for the History of Greek Athletics* (Cincinnati: published by the author, 1955), 120.
29. Ibid., 161.
30. *The Aeneid of Virgil,* trans. by Allen Mandelbaum (Berkeley: University of California Press, 1971), Book 5.
31. M. I. Finley and H. W. Pleket, *The Olympic Games: The First Thousand Years* (New York: The Viking Press, 1976), 125–27.
32. Horst Ueberhorst, "Return to Olympia and the Rebirth of the Games," in *The Modern Olympics,* ed. Peter J. Graham and Horst Ueberhorst (Cornwall, N.Y.: Leisure Press, 1976), 16.
33. Ibid., 15, 16.
34. Mary H. Leigh, "The Evolution of Women's Participation in the Summer Olympic Games, 1900–1948," Ph.D. diss. Ohio State University, 1974, 34.
35. Marie Thérèse Eyquem, "The Founder of the Modern Games," in *The Olympic Games,* ed. Michael Morris Killanin and John Rodda (New York: Macmillan, 1976), 139.

36. Comite International Olympique, *Olympic Charter* (Lausanne, Switzerland: International Olympic Committee, 1985), 6.
37. Ibid., 6, 18.
38. United States Olympic Committee, *Constitution and By-Laws* (Colorado Springs, 1985), 2, 3.
39. Ibid., 3–6.
40. Hans Lenk, "Toward a Social Philosophy of the Olympics . . .", in *The Modern Olympics,* ed. Peter J. Graham and Horst Ueberhorst (Cornwall, N.Y.: Leisure Press, 1976), 116.
41. Otto Szymiczek, I ATHENS 1896, in *The Olympic Games,* ed. Michael Morris Killanin and John Rodda (New York: Macmillan, 1976), 27.
42. Erich Kamper, *Encyclopedia of the Olympic Games* (New York: McGraw-Hill, 1972), 299.
43. Rufus B. Richardson, "The New Olympian Games," *Scribner's Magazine* 20, no. 3 (September 1896): 269.
44. Charles Waldstein, "The Olympian Games at Athens," *Harper's Weekly* 40, no. 3 (September 1896): 490.
45. Erich Kamper, *Encyclopedia of the Olympic Games* (New York: McGraw-Hill, 1972), 295–97.
46. The numbers of participants in the Olympic Games may be found in *Olympism* (Lausanne, Switzerland: International Committee, 1972), 27.
47. D. R. Francis, *The Universal Exposition of 1904* (St. Louis: Louisiana Purchase Exposition Co., 1913), 538.
48. George R. Matthews, "The Controversial Olympic Games of 1908 as Viewed by the *New York Times* and the *Times* of London," *Journal of Sport History* 7, no. 2 (Summer 1980): 52.
49. Tom McNab, "Athletics," in *The Olympic Games,* ed. Michael Morris Killanin and John Rodda (New York: Macmillan, 1976), 92.
50. James Coote, "Modern Pentathlon," in *The Olympic Games,* ed. Michael Morris Killanin and John Rodda (New York: Macmillan, 1976), 117, 118.
51. Betty Spears, "Women in the Olympics: An Unresolved Problem," in *The Modern Olympics,* ed. Peter J. Graham and Horst Ueberhorst (Cornwall, N.Y.: Leisure Press, 1976), 68.
52. Robert M. Goodhue, "The Development of Olympism, 1900–1932: Technical Success within a Threatening Political Reality," in *The Modern Olympics,* ed. Peter J. Graham and Horst Ueberhorst (Cornwall, N.Y.: Leisure Press, 1976), 30.
53. Arnd Kruger, "The 1936 Olympic Games—Berlin," in *The Modern Olympics,* ed. Peter J. Graham and Horst Ueberhorst (Cornwall, N.Y.: Leisure Press, 1976), 169.
54. Richard D. Mandell, *The Nazi Olympics* (New York: Macmillan, 1971), 79.
55. John Durant, *Highlights of the Olympics* (New York: Hastings House, 1965), 55–59.
56. David Binder, "9 Israelis on Olympic Team Killed," *New York Times,* 6 September 1972, 1.
57. Neil Amdur, "Games Suspended; Rites in Arena Set," *New York Times,* 6 September 1972, 18.
58. Jean M. Leiper, "The International Olympic Committee: The Pursuit of Olympism 1894–1970," Ph.D. diss. University of Alberta, 1976, 245.

Bibliography

"A Change of Attitude Has Taken Place." *The NCAA News* (January 14, 1987):1.

A Course of Calisthenics for Young Ladies. Hartford, CT: H. and F. J. Huntington, 1831. No author given; generally presumed to be Catharine Beecher's work.

Adams, Henry. *The United States in 1800*. Ithaca, N.Y.: Great Seal Books, 1955.

Addams, Jane. *Spirit of Youth and the City Streets*. New York: Macmillan, 1909.

Adelman, Melvin L. *A Sporting Time*. Urbana, IL: University of Illinois Press, 1986.

———. "Academicians and American Athletics: A Decade of Progress." *Journal of Sport History* 10, no. 1 (Spring, 1983):80–106.

———. "The First Modern Sport in America: Harness Racing in New York City, 1825–1870." *Journal of Sport History* 8, no. 1 (Spring, 1981):5–32.

Akers, Dwight. *Drivers Up: The Story of American Harness Racing*. New York: G. P. Putnam's, 1938.

Albertson, Roxanne. "Sports and Games in New England Schools and Academies, 1780–1860." Paper presented at the North American Society for Sport History, Boston, Mass., April 16–19, 1975.

Allen, Nathan. *Physical Culture in Amherst College*. Lowell, MA: Stone and Huse, 1869.

"Alliance Addresses Major Dilemma: Coaching Certification." *Alliance Update* (March, 1981):1, 5.

"Americans: Splurging in Big Ways, Cutting Back in Small Ones." *U.S. News and World Report* 82 (April 25, 1977):26–27.

"Ancient Athletics and Ancient Society." Special Issue. *Journal of Sport History* 11, no. 2 (Summer, 1984).

Anderson, William G. "The Early History of the American Association for Health, Physical Education and Recreation." *The Journal of Health and Physical Education* 12 (January, 1941):3–4, 61–62; (March, 1941):151–153, 200–201; April, 1941):244–245; (May, 1941):313–315, 340.

Applin, Albert G. "From Muscular Christianity to the Market Place: The History of Men's and Boy's Basketball in the United States, 1891–1957." Ph.D. dissertation, University of Massachusetts, 1982.

Armstrong, J. *A Disclosure Uttered in Part at Annauskeeg Falls in the Fishing Season, 1739.* Boston: S. Kneeland and T. Green in Queen Street, 1743.

Asinof, Eliot. *Eight Men Out: The Black Sox and the 1919 World Series.* New York: Holt, Rinehart & Winston, 1979.

Associated Press Sports Staff. *A Century of Major American Sports.* Maplewood, NJ: Hammond Inc., 1975.

Audubon, John James. "Kentucky Sports," from "Missouri River Journals (1843)," in *Audubon and His Journals,* Vol. II, ed. Maria R. Audubon. New York: Charles Scribner's Sons, 1897.

Aurther, Robert Alan. "Hanging Out." *Esquire* 84 (October, 1975):28, 54–58.

Baker, William J. *Sports in the Western World.* Totowa, NJ: Roman and Littlefield, 1982.

Baker, William J., and Carrol, John M., eds. *Sports in Modern America.* St. Louis: River City Publishers, 1981.

Ballintine, Harriet Isabel. *The History of Physical Training at Vassar College, 1865–1915.* Poughkeepsie, NY: Lansing and Bros., 19–?.

Bank, Theodore P. "Army Athletics." *Hygiea* 19 (November, 1941):876–880.

Barrows, Isabel C., ed. *Physical Training, A Full Report of the Papers and Discussion of the Conference Held in Boston in November, 1889.* Boston: George H. Ellis, 1890.

Barth, Heinrich. *Travels and Discoveries in North and Central Africa,* Vol. III. London: Frank Cass & Co., 1965.

Beck, Robert Holmes. *A Social History of Education.* Englewood Cliffs, NJ: Prentice-Hall, Inc., 1965.

Becker, Carl. *Everyman His Own Historian.* Chicago: Quadrangle Books, 1966.

Beecher, Catharine. *Letters to the People on Health and Happiness.* New York: Harper, 1855.

Benagh, Jim. *Incredible Olympic Feats.* New York: McGraw-Hill Book Co., 1976.

Bennett, Bruce L. "Christopher P. Linhart, M.D., Forgotten Physical Educator." *Research Quarterly* 35 (March, 1964):3–20.

———, ed. *The History of Physical Education and Sport.* Chicago: The Athletic Institute, 1972.

———. "The Making of Round Hill School." *Quest* 4 (April, 1965):53–64.

———. "Sports in the South Since 1865." *Quest* 31, no. 1 (1979):123–144.

———. "Sports in the South Up to 1865." *Quest* 27 (Winter, 1977):4–18.

Bennett, Charles E. *Three Voyages of René Laudonnière.* Gainesville: The University Presses of Florida, 1975.

Berenson, Senda. *Basket Ball for Women.* New York: American Sports Publishing Company, 1901.

———. "Editorial." *Basketball for Women.* New York: American Sports Publishing Company, 1903.

Berry, Robert C.; Gould, William B. IV; and Staudohar, Paul D. *Labor Relations in Professional Sports.* Dover, MA: Auburn House, 1986.

Berry, Robert C., and Wong, Glenn M. *Law and Business of the Sports Industries,* Vol. I. Dover, MA: Auburn House, 1986.

Berryman, Jack W. "The Animal in Sport: From Low Regard to Highest Esteem, 1778–1866." *Proceedings, 1973,* North American Society for Sport History, Columbus, Ohio (May, 1973):10–12.

———. "From the Cradle to the Playing Field: America's Emphasis on Highly Organized Competitive Sports for Pre-Adolescent Boys." *Journal of Sport History* 2, no. 2 (Fall, 1975):112–131.

———. "Sport History as Social History?" *Quest* 20 (June, 1973):65–73.

Betts, John Rickards. *America's Sporting Heritage: 1850–1950.* Reading, MA: Addison-Wesley Publishing Company, 1974.

———. "Home Front, Battle Field, and Sport During the Civil War." *Research Quarterly* 42 (May, 1971):113–132.

———. "Organized Sport in Industrial America." Ph.D. dissertation, Columbia University, 1952.

———. "The Technological Revolution and the Rise of Sport, 1850–1900." *Mississippi Valley Historical Review* 40 (1953):231–256.

Blake, Sophia J. *A Visit to Some American Schools and Colleges.* London: Macmillan and Co., 1867.

Blount, Roy, Jr. "Losersville U.S.A." *Sports Illustrated* 46 (March 21, 1977):74–77, 81–82, 84–86.

Boone, Daniel. "The ADVENTURES of Col. Daniel Boon; containing a NARRATIVE of the WARS of Kentucke, 1798," in *The Discovery, Settlement and present state of Kentucke,* ed. John Filson. New York: Corinth Books, 1962.

Bowen, Wilbur P. "Seven Years of Progress in Preparing Teachers of Physical Education." *American Physical Education Review* 27 (February, 1922):64–65.

Bowes, F. P. *The Culture of Early Charleston.* Chapel Hill: The University of North Carolina Press, 1942.

Boy's and Girl's Book of Sports. Providence: George P. Daniels, 1839.

Bradford's History "Of Plymouth Plantation." Boston: Wright and Potter Printing Co., 1898.

Brailsford, Dennis. *Sport and Society, Elizabeth to Anne.* Toronto: University of Toronto Press, 1969.

Bridenbaugh, Carl. *Cities in the Wilderness.* New York: Ronald Press Co., 1938.

Brown, Joseph. "R. Tait McKenzie, In Tribute." *Journal of Health, Physical Education and Recreation* 38 (May, 1967):27.

Bulger, Margery A. "Ali Ali in Free . . . The Games Children Played in Colonial America." *Early American Life,* August, 1975, pp. 48–49, 82.

Bulletin (1920–1921). Mary Hemenway Alumnae Association, Department of Hygiene. Wellesley College, Wellesley, Massachusetts.

Bulletin (March, 1927). Mary Hemenway Alumnae Association, Graduate Department of Hygiene and Physical Education. Wellesley College, Wellesley, Massachusetts.

Cady, Edwin H. *The Big Game: College Sports and American Life.* Knoxville: University of Tennessee Press, 1978.

Carson, Jane. *Colonial Virginians at Play.* Charlottesville: University of Virginia Press, 1965.

Carver, Robin. *The Book of Sports.* Boston: Lilly, Wait, Colman, and Holden, 1834.

Cassidy, Rosalind. *New Directions in Physical Education for the Adolescent Girl in High School and College.* New York: A. S. Barnes and Co., 1938.

Chalk, Ocania. *Pioneers of Black Sport.* New York: Dodd, Mead and Co., 1975.

Cheska, Alyce. "Ball Game Participation of North American Indian Women." Paper presented at The Third Canadian Symposium on History of Sport and Physical Education, Dalhousie University, August 18–21, 1974.

Chujoy, Anatole, and Manchester, Phyllis W., eds. *Dance Encyclopedia.* New York: Simon and Schuster, 1967.

Cogswell, Joseph C., and Bancroft, George. *Prospectus of a School to Be Established at Round Hill, Northampton, Massachusetts.* Cambridge, MA: 1823.

Colby, Gertrude. *Natural Rhythms and Dances.* New York: A. S. Barnes & Company, 1922.

Cole, Arthur C. "Our Sporting Grandfathers." *Atlantic Monthly* 150 (July, 1932): 88–96.

Collett, Glenna. "Golf We Women Play." *Saturday Evening Post* 200 (July 9, 1927): 12–13.

Collier, John. *The Indians of the Americas.* New York: W. W. Norton, 1947.

Constitution, By-Laws and General Rules. New York: United States Olympic Committee, 1977.

Comité International Olympique. *Olympic Charter.* Lausanne, Switzerland: International Olympic Committee, 1979.

Comité International Olympique. *Olympic Charter.* Lausanne, Switzerland: International Olympic Committee, 1985.

Coulton, G. G. *The Medieval Scene.* Cambridge: Cambridge University Press, 1959.

Cozens, Frederick W., and Stumpf, Florence. *Sports in American Life.* Chicago: University of Chicago Press, 1953.

Crepeau, Richard. *Baseball: America's Diamond Mind, 1919–1941.* Gainesville: The University Presses of Florida, 1980.

Cresswell, Nicholas. *The Journal of Nicholas Cresswell, 1774–1777.* New York: Lincoln MacVeagh, 1924.

Crowther, Samuel, and Ruhl, Arthur. *Rowing and Track Athletics.* New York: The Macmillan Co., 1905.

Culin, Stewart. *Games of the North American Indians.* New York: Dover, 1975.

Cumming, John. *Runners & Walkers: A Nineteenth Century Sports Chronicle.* Chicago: Regnery Gateway, 1981.

Cummings, Parke. *American Tennis: The Story of a Game and Its People.* Boston: Little, Brown and Company, 1957.

Czarnowski, Lucille; Schurman, Nona; Imel, Carmen; and Murray, Ruth Lovell. "Four Dance Pioneers." *Journal of Health, Physical Education and Recreation* 41 (February, 1970):23–31.

Damon, S. Foster. *The History of Square-Dancing.* Worcester, MA: American Antiquarian Society, 1952.

Danoff, Eric. "The Struggle for Control of Amateur Track and Field in the United States—Part I." *The Canadian Journal of History of Sport and Physical Education* 6, no. 1 (May, 1975):43–85.

————. "The Struggle for Control of Amateur Track and Field in the United States—Part II." *The Canadian Journal of History of Sport and Physical Education* 6, no. 2 (December, 1975):1–43.

Danzig, Allison, and Brandwein, Peter, eds. *Sport's Golden Age.* New York: Harper, 1948.

Davidson, Basil. *The African Past.* London: Longmans, 1964.

Davidson, Judith. "Sport for Women in the Thirties." Unpublished paper, University of Massachusetts, 1977.

Davis, Edwin Adams. *Plantation Life in the Florida Parishes of Louisiana, 1836–1846.* New York: Columbia University Press, 1943.

Davis, Thomas R. "Puritanism and Physical Education: The Shroud of Gloom Lifted." *The Canadian Journal of History of Sport and Physical Education* 3, no. 2 (May, 1972):1–7.

Davis, William S. *Life on a Mediaeval Barony.* New York: Harper & Brothers, 1923.

De Borhegyi, Stephan F. "America's Ballgame." *Natural History* 69 (1960):48–59.

Degler, Carl N. *Out of Our Past.* New York: Harper & Row, 1957.

DeGroot, Dudley S. "A History of Physical Education in California (1848–1939)." Ph.D. dissertation, Stanford University, 1940.

Demarest, William H. *A History of Rutgers College.* New Brunswick: Rutgers College, 1924.

de Tocqueville, Alexis. *Democracy in America,* Vol. II. New York: Alfred A. Knopf, 1945.

De Witt's Base-ball Guide for 1869, ed. Henry Chadwick. New York: Robert M. De Witt, Publisher, 1869.

De Witt's Base-ball Guide for 1875, ed. Henry Chadwick. New York: Robert M. De Witt, Publisher, 1875.

Dickey, Glenn. *The History of Professional Basketball.* New York: Stein and Day, 1982.

Division for Girls and Women's Sports. "Statement of Policies for Competition in Girls and Women's Sports." *Journal of Health, Physical Education and Recreation* 34 (September, 1963):31–33.

Driver, Harold E. *Indians of North America.* Chicago: University of Chicago Press, 1970.

Dulles, Foster Rhea. *America Learns to Play.* New York: D. Appleton-Century, 1940.

Durant, John, and Bettman, Otto. *Highlights of the Olympics.* New York: Hastings House, 1965.

⸻. *Pictorial History of American Sports.* New York: A. S. Barnes and Co., 1952.

Durant, John, and Rice, Edward. *Come Out Fighting.* New York: Duell, Sloan and Pearce, 1946.

Eastman, Mary F. *The Biography of Dio Lewis.* New York: Fowler & Wells, 1891.

Eitzen, Stanley D., and Sage, George H. *Sociology of American Sport.* Dubuque, IA: Wm. C. Brown Publishers, 1982.

Elyot, Sir Thomas. *The Boke Named the Governour,* Vol. II, ed. H. H. S. Croft. London: C. Kegan Paul & Co., 1880.

Emery, Lynne Fauley. *Black Dance in the United States from 1619 to 1970.* Palo Alto, CA: National Press Books, 1972.

Encyclopedia International. New York: Grolier Incorporated, 1975.

Espy, Richard. *The Politics of the Olympic Games: With an Epilogue, 1976–1980.* Berkeley: University of California Press, 1981.

Eyler, Marvin H. "Some Reflections on Objectivity and Selectivity in Historical Inquiry." *Journal of Sport History* 1, no. 1 (1974):63–76.

Fage, J. D. *An Introduction to the History of West Africa.* Cambridge: Cambridge University Press, 1955.

Federal Register 40, no. 108 (June 4, 1975):24141–24143.

Fidler, Merrie A. "The All-American Girls Baseball League, 1943–51." *Proceedings, 1975,* North American Society for Sport History, Boston, Massachusetts (April 16–19, 1975):35.

―――. "The Development and Decline of the All-American Girls Baseball League, 1943–54." M.S. thesis, University of Massachusetts, 1976.

Fielding, Lawrence W. "War and Trifles: Sport in the Shadows of Civil War Army Life." *Journal of Sport History* 4, no. 2 (1977):151–168.

Finley, M. I., and Pleket, H. W. *The Olympic Games: The First Thousand Years.* New York: The Viking Press, 1976.

Finley, Ruth E. *The Lady of Godey's: Sara Josepha Hale.* Philadelphia: J. B. Lippincott Co., 1931.

Fleming, Rhonda K. "A History of the Department of Physical Education at Winthrop College." M.S. thesis, University of North Carolina at Greensboro, 1973.

Flint, Timothy. *Recollections of the Last Ten Years,* ed. C. Hartley Grattan. New York: Alfred A. Knopf, 1932.

Forbes, Clarence A. *Greek Physical Education.* New York: The Century Co., 1929.

Forsythe, Lewis L. *Athletics in Michigan High Schools: The First Hundred Years.* New York: Prentice-Hall, Inc., 1950.

Francis, D. R. *The Universal Exposition of 1904.* St. Louis: Louisiana Purchase Exposition Co., 1913.

Franklin, Benjamin. *The Art of Swimming Rendered Easy, Dr. Franklin's Advice to Bathers.* Glassow: Printed for the book sellers, 184–?.

―――. *Benjamin Franklin on Education,* ed. John Hardin Best. New York: Bureau of Publications, Teachers College, 1962.

―――. *Proposals for the Education of Youth in Pennsylvania, 1749.* Ann Arbor: William L. Clements Library, 1927.

Fuess, Claude M. *Amherst.* Boston: Little, Brown, 1935.

Fullerton, H. S. "Baseball—the Business and the Sport." *American Review of Reviews* 63 (April, 1921):417–420.

Furnas, J. C. *The Americans: A Social History of the United States.* New York: G. P. Putnam's Sons, 1969.

Gallico, Paul. *The Golden People.* Garden City, NY: Doubleday, 1964.

Gardiner, E. Norman. *Athletics of the Ancient World.* Oxford: Clarendon Press, 1930.

Garraty, John A., and Gay, Peter. *The Columbia History of the World.* New York: Harper & Row, 1972.

Georgetown College, 1814. Georgetown University Library.

Gerber, Ellen W. "The Controlled Development of Collegiate Sport for Women, 1923–1936." *Journal of Sport History* 2, no. 1 (Spring, 1975):1–28.

———. "The Ideas and Influences of McCloy, Nash, and Williams," in *The History of Physical Education and Sport,* ed. Bruce L. Bennett. Chicago: The Athletic Institute, 1972.

———. *Innovators and Institutions in Physical Education.* Philadelphia: Lea & Febiger, 1971.

Gerber, Ellen W.; Felshin, Jan; Berlin, Pearl; and Wyrick, Waneen. *The American Woman in Sport.* Reading, MA: Addison-Wesley Publishing Company, 1974.

Gilbert, Bill, and Williamson, Nancy. "Are You Being Two-Faced?" *Sports Illustrated* 38, no. 22 (June 4, 1973):44–48, 50, 53–54.

———. "Programmed to Be Losers." *Sports Illustrated* 38, no. 23 (June 11, 1973):60–62, 65–66, 68, 73.

———. "Sport Is Unfair to Women." *Sports Illustrated* 38, no. 21 (May 28, 1973):88–92, 94–98.

Goodsell, Willystine, ed. *Pioneers of Women's Education in the United States.* New York: McGraw-Hill Book Company, 1931.

Govett, L. A. *The King's Book of Sports.* London: Elliot Stock, 1890.

Graham, Peter J., and Ueberhorst, Horst, eds. *The Modern Olympics.* Cornwall, NY: Leisure Press, 1976.

Grimsley, Will. *Golf: Its History, People and Events.* Englewood Cliffs, NJ: Prentice-Hall, 1966.

———. *Tennis: Its History, People and Events.* Englewood Cliffs, NJ: Prentice-Hall, 1971.

Gulick, Luther. *Physical Education by Muscular Exercise.* Philadelphia: P. Blakiston's Son & Company, 1904.

———. "Physical Education in the Y.M.C.A." *Proceedings,* American Association for the Advancement of Physical Education, 1891.

———. "What the American Young Men's Christian Associations Are Doing for the Physical Welfare of Young Men," in *Annual Autumn Games.* Young Men's Christian Association of the City of New York, October 13, 1888.

Gutek, Gerald. *An Historical Introduction to American Education.* New York: Thomas Y. Crowell, 1970.

Guttmann, Allen. *From Ritual to Record.* New York: Columbia University Press, 1978.

———. *The Games Must Go On: Avery Brundage and the Olympic Movement.* New York: Columbia University Press, 1984.

Hale, Creighton J. "What Research Says About Athletics for Pre-High School Age Children." *Journal of Health, Physical Education and Recreation* 30 (December, 1959):19–21, 23.

Hale, William Harlan. *Ancient Greece.* New York: American Heritage Press, 1970.

Haley, Alex. *Roots.* Garden City, NY: Doubleday, 1976.

Handlin, Oscar. *Truth in History.* Cambridge: Harvard University Press, 1979.

Hardy, Stephen H. *How Boston Played: Sport, Recreation, and Community.* Boston: Northeastern University Press, 1982.

———. "The Medieval Tournament: A Functional Sport of the Upper Class." *Journal of Sport History* 1, no. 2 (1974):91–105.

———. "Organized Sport and Community in Ancient Greece and Rome." M.S. thesis, University of Massachusetts, 1975.

Harper's Weekly 23 (September 13, 1879):73.

Harper's Weekly 29 (February 14, 1885):109.

Harris, H. A. *Greek Athletes and Athletics.* London: Hutchinson, 1964.

———. *Sport in Greece and Rome.* Ithaca, NY: Cornell University Press, 1972.

Hart, Albert Bushnell. "Status of Athletic Sports in American Colleges." *Atlantic Monthly* 66 (July, 1890):63–71.

Hartwell, Edward M. *Physical Training in American Colleges and Universities.* Bureau of Education Circular of Information No. 5, 1885. Washington, D.C.: Government Printing Office, 1886.

———. *Report of the Director of Physical Training.* Boston: Press of Rockwell and Churchill, 1895.

Hazelton, Helen W. "The University of Minnesota Plan for Freshmen Work." *Bulletin* (September, 1927). Mary Hemenway Alumnae Association, Graduate Department of Hygiene and Physical Education, Wellesley College, Wellesley, Massachusetts.

H'Doubler, Margaret. *The Dance and Its Place In Education.* New York: Harcourt, Brace & Company, 1925.

Henderson, Edwin B. *The Negro in Sports.* Washington, D.C.: Associated Publishers, 1949.

Henderson, Edwin B., and the Editors of Sport Magazine. *The Black Athlete—Emergence and Arrival.* New York: International Library of Negro History, 1968.

Henderson, Robert W. *Ball, Bat, and Bishop.* Reprint. Detroit: Gale Research Co., 1974.

―――. *Early American Sport.* 2nd ed. New York: A. S. Barnes & Co., 1953.

Henry, William N. *History of the Olympic Games.* New York: G. P. Putnam's Sons, 1948.

Herskovits, Melville J. *The Myth of the Negro Past.* Boston: Beacon Press, 1958.

Hervey, John. *Racing in America,* 2 vols. New York: The Jockey Club, 1944.

Higginson, Thomas Wentworth. "Gymnastics." *Atlantic Monthly* 7 (March, 1861): 283–302.

Higgs, Robert J. *Sports: A Reference Guide.* Westport, CT: Greenwood, 1982.

Hill, Lucille Eaton. *Athletic and Out-Door Sports for Women.* New York: The Macmillan Co., 1903.

Hill, Phyllis J. "A Cultural History of Frontier Sport in Illinois, 1673–1820." Ph.D. dissertation, University of Illinois, 1966.

Hitchcock, Edward. *The Power of Christian Benevolence Illustrated in the Life and Labor of Mary Lyon.* Northampton, MA: Hopkins, Bridgman, and Company, 1852.

Hitchman, James H. "Origins of Yacht Racing in British Columbia and Washington, 1870–1914." *Proceedings, 1976,* North American Society for Sport History, Eugene, Oregon (June, 1976):30–31.

Hoepner, Barbara J., ed. *Women's Athletics: Coping with Controversy.* Washington, D.C.: American Association for Health, Physical Education, and Recreation, 1974.

Hole, Christina. *English Sports and Pastimes.* London: B. T. Batsford, 1949.

Hollander, Phyllis. *100 Greatest Women in Sports.* New York: Grosset & Dunlap, 1976.

Holliman, Jennie. *American Sports (1785–1835).* Durham, NC: The Seeman Press, 1931.

Holmes, Oliver Wendell. *The Autocrat of the Breakfast Table.* Boston: Houghton, Mifflin and Company, 1904.

Homer. *The Iliad,* trans. Robert Fitzgerald. New York: Anchor Press/Doubleday, 1975.

―――. *The Odyssey,* trans. Robert Fitzgerald. New York: Anchor Press/Doubleday, 1963.

Honour, Hugh. *The European Vision of America.* Kent, OH: The Kent State University Press, 1975.

"Hooping It Up Big in the Cornbelt." *Time* 109 (March 28, 1977):85.

Hopkins, Charles Howard. *History of the Y.M.C.A. in North America.* New York: Association Press, 1951.

Hoy, James F. "The Origins and Originality of Rodeo," in *Sports and Recreation in the West,* ed. Donald J. Mrozek. Manhattan, KS: Sunflower University Press, 1978.

Hughes, S. F. *Letters and Recollections of John Murray Forbes.* Boston: Houghton Mifflin, 1899.

Huizinga, Johan. *Homo Ludens: A Study of the Play Element in Culture.* Boston: Beacon Press, 1955.

Isaacs, Neil D. *All the Moves: A History of College Basketball.* Philadelphia: J. B. Lippincott Company, 1975.

Jable, Thomas. "The English Puritans: Suppressors of Sport and Amusement?" *Canadian Journal of History of Sport and Physical Education* 7, no. 1 (May, 1976):33–40.

———. "Pennsylvania's Early Blue Laws: A Quaker Experiment in the Suppression of Sport and Amusements, 1682–1740." *Journal of Sport History* 1, no. 2 (November, 1974):107–121.

Jacobs, Edwin E. *A Study of the Physical Vigor of American Women.* Boston: Marshall Jones Company, 1920.

Jensen, Oliver. *The Revolt of American Women.* New York: Harcourt, Brace and Co., 1952.

Johnson, Elmer L. "A History of Physical Education in the YMCA." *69th Proceedings,* National College Physical Education Association for Men (December 28–31, 1966):20–21.

Johnson, Harold. *Who's Who in Major League Base Ball.* Chicago: Buxton Publishing Co., 1933.

Josephy, Alvin M., Jr., ed. *The American Heritage Book of Indians.* New York: McGraw-Hill Book Company, 1961.

Journals of Congress, Vol. 1. Philadelphia: Folwell's Press, 1800.

Journals of the Continental Congress, Vol I, 1774. Washington, D.C.: Government Printing Office, 1904.

Kamper, Erich. *Encyclopedia of the Olympic Games.* New York: McGraw-Hill Book Company, 1972.

Kaye, Ivan N. *Good Clean Violence: A History of College Football.* Philadelphia: J. B. Lippincott and Company, 1973.

Kelley, Robert F. *American Rowing: Its Background and Traditions.* New York: G. P. Putnam's Sons, 1932.

Kellor, Frances A. "Ethical Value of Sports for Women." *American Physical Education Review* 11 (September, 1906):160–171.

Kennard, June A. "Maryland Colonials at Play: Their Sports and Games." *Research Quarterly* 41 (1970):389–395.

Kenyon, Gerald, and Loy, John. "Toward a Sociology of Sport." *Journal of Health, Physical Education, and Recreation* 36 (May, 1965):24–25, 68–69.

Kerman, Joseph. *The Beethoven Quartets*. New York: Alfred A. Knopf, 1967.

Killanin, Michael Morris, and Rodda, John, eds. *The Olympic Games*. New York: Macmillan, 1976.

Kirkpatrick, Curry. "There She Is: Ms. America." *Sports Illustrated* 39 (October 1, 1973):30–32, 37.

Kirstein, Lincoln. *The Book of the Dance*. New York: Garden City Publishing Company, 1942.

Knight, Madam. *The Journal of Madam Knight*. Edition of 1825. New York: Peter Smith, 1835.

Korsgaard, Robert. "The Formative Years of Sports Control and the Founding of the Amateur Athletic Union of the United States." *67th Proceedings,* National College Physical Education Association for Men (January 8–11, 1964):65–70.

———. "A History of the Amateur Athletic Union of the United States." Ph.D. dissertation, Columbia University, 1952.

Kozar, Andrew J. *R. Tait McKenzie*. Knoxville: The University of Tennessee Press, 1975.

Kozman, Hilda Clute. "Building the General Curriculum in Physical Education for College Women." Report of the Second Workshop for College Women Teachers, sponsored by the National Association for Physical Education of College Women, Estes Park, Colorado, June 18–27, 1947.

Kraus, Richard. *History of the Dance in Art and Education*. Englewood Cliffs, NJ: Prentice-Hall, Inc., 1969.

Kroll, Walter P. *Perspectives in Physical Education*. New York: Academic Press, 1971.

Kroll, Walter P., and Lewis, Guy M. "America's First Sport Psychologist." *Quest* 13 (January, 1970):1–4.

———. "The First Academic Degree in Physical Education." *Journal of Health, Physical Education, and Recreation* 40 (June, 1969):73–74.

Krout, John A. *Annals of American Sport,* Vol. XV of *Pageant of America*. New Haven: Yale University Press, 1929.

Lattimore, Richmond, and Grene, David. *The Complete Greek Tragedies*. New York: Modern Library, 1960.

Lawler, Lillian. *The Dance in Ancient Greece*. Middletown, CT: Wesleyan University Press, 1964.

———. "Terpsichore: The Story of the Dance in Ancient Greece." *Dance Perspectives* 13 (Winter, 1962):1–56.

Leacock, Eleanor Burke, and Lurie, Nancy Oestreich, eds. *North American Indians in Historical Perspective.* New York: Random House, 1971.

LeCompte, Mary Lou. *"Charreada:* The First American Rodeo." Paper presented at the Annual Conference of the Western History Association, October 11, 1985.

―――. "The First Rodeo in Texas." *Proceedings, 1980,* North American Society for Sport History, Banff, Alberta (May 24–28, 1980):2–3.

LeCompte, Mary Lou, and Beezley, William H. "Any Sunday in April: The Rise of Sport in San Antonio and the Hispanic Borderlands." *Journal of Sport History* 13 (Summer, 1986):128–146.

Lee, Mabel. "The Case for and Against Intercollegiate Athletics for Women and the Situation Since 1923." *Research Quarterly* 2 (May, 1931):93–127.

―――. "Of Historical Interest." *Journal of Health, Physical Education, and Recreation* 39 (January, 1968):29–31.

―――. *Memories of a Bloomer Girl.* Washington, D.C.: American Alliance for Health, Physical Education, and Recreation, 1977.

Lefkowitz, Mary R., and Fant, Maureen B. *Women's Life in Greece and Rome.* London: Duckworth, 1982.

Leigh, Mary. "The Evolution of Women's Participation in the Summer Olympic Games, 1900–1948." Ph.D. dissertation, The Ohio State University, 1974.

―――. "Pierre de Coubertin: A Man of His Time." *Quest* 22 (Spring, 1974):19–24.

Leiper, Jean M. "The International Olympic Committee: The Pursuit of Olympism 1894–1970." Ph.D. dissertation, The University of Alberta, 1976.

Leonard, Fred E. *A Guide to the History of Physical Education.* Philadelphia: Lea & Febiger, 1923.

Leonard, Fred E., and Affleck, George B. *A Guide to the History of Physical Education.* Philadelphia: Lea & Febiger, 1947.

Lewis, Dio. *The New Gymnastics for Men, Women and Children.* 8th ed. Boston: Ticknor and Fields, 1864.

Lewis, Guy M. "Adoption of the Sports Program, 1906–39: The Role of Accommodation in the Transformation of Physical Education." *Quest* 12 (May, 1969):34–46.

―――. "America's First Intercollegiate Sport: The Regattas from 1852 to 1875." *Research Quarterly* 38 (December, 1967):637–647.

―――. "1879: The Beginning of an Era in American Sport." *72nd Proceedings,* National College Physical Education Association for Men (January 8–11, 1969): 136–145.

―――. "The Muscular Christianity Movement." *Journal of Health, Physical Education, and Recreation* 37 (May, 1966):27–28.

————. "Sport and the Making of American Higher Education: The Early Years, 1783–1875." *73rd Proceedings,* National College Physical Education Association for Men (December 27–30, 1970):208–213.

————. "Sport, Youth Culture and Conventionality." *Journal of Sport History* 4, no. 2 (1977):129–150.

Lewis, Guy, and Redmond, Gerald. *Sporting Heritage.* New York: A. S. Barnes, 1974.

Lincoln, C. Eric. *The Negro Pilgrimage in America.* New York: Bantam Pathfinder, 1967.

Livermore, Mary A. *The Story of My Life.* Hartford, CT: A. D. Worthington, 1899.

Lockhart, Aileene S., and Spears, Betty. *Chronicle of American Physical Education, 1855–1930.* Dubuque, IA: Wm. C. Brown Company Publishers, 1972.

Lohse, Lola L. "One Hundred Years of Teaching Physical Education Instructors." *Journal of Health, Physical Education, and Recreation* 37 (November–December, 1966):26–28.

Lowenfish, Lee, and Lupien, Tony. *The Imperfect Diamond: The Story of Baseball's Reserve System and the Men Who Fought to Change It.* New York: Stein and Day, 1980.

Loy, John W., Jr. "The Nature of Sport: A Definitional Effort." *Quest* 10 (May, 1968):1–15.

Loy, John W., Jr.; Kenyon, Gerald S.; and McPherson, Barry D. *Sport, Culture and Society: A Reader on the Sociology of Sport.* 2nd ed. Philadelphia: Lea & Febiger, 1981.

Lucas, John A. "A Prelude to the Rise of Sport: Ante-bellum America, 1850–1860." *Quest* 11 (December, 1968):50–57.

————. *The Modern Olympic Games.* New York: A. S. Barnes and Co., 1980.

Lucas, John A., and Smith, Ronald A. *Saga of American Sport.* Philadelphia: Lea & Febiger, 1978.

Lumpkin, Angela. "Elementary School Physical Education: 1950–1985," in *The History of Elementary School Physical Education: 1885–1985.* Reston, VA: National Association for Sport and Physical Education, 1985.

————. *Women's Tennis: A Historical Documentary of the Players and Their Game.* Troy, NY: Whitston, 1981.

MacLeod, Duncan. "Racing to War." *Southern Exposure* 7, no. 2 (Fall, 1979):7–10.

Maetozo, Matthew G. "Athletic Coaching: Its Future in a Changing Society." *Journal of Physical Education and Recreation* 52 (March, 1981):40–43.

Magriel, Paul, ed. *Chronicles of the American Dance.* New York: Henry Holt and Company, 1948.

Main, Jackson Turner. *The Social Structure of Revolutionary America.* Princeton, NJ: Princeton University Press, 1965.

Malcolmson, Robert W. *Popular Recreations in English Society 1710–1850.* Cambridge: Cambridge University Press, 1973.

Manchester, Gertrude B. "Physical Education in the High School." *Bulletin* (1924–25). Mary Hemenway Alumnae Association, Graduate Department of Hygiene and Physical Education. Wellesley College, Wellesley, Massachusetts.

Manchester, Herbert. *Four Centuries of Sport in America, 1490–1890.* New York: The Derrydale Press, 1931.

Mandell, Richard D. *The Nazi Olympics.* New York: The Macmillan Company, 1971.

———. *Sport: A Cultural History.* New York: Columbia University Press, 1984.

Marks, Joseph E. *America Learns to Dance.* New York: Exposition Press, 1957.

Martens, Rainer. *Joy and Sadness in Children's Sports.* Champaign, IL: Human Kinetics Publishers, 1978.

Matthews, George R. "The Controversial Olympic Games of 1908 as Viewed by the *New York Times* and the *Times* of London." *Journal of Sport History* 7, no. 2 (Summer, 1980):40–53.

Mawson, L. Marlene. "The Origin and Development of Movement Education." *Canadian Journal of History of Sport and Physical Education* 6, no. 1 (May, 1975):1–11.

Maynard, Olga. *The American Ballet.* Philadelphia: Macrae Smith Company, 1959.

McCracken, Harold. *George Catlin and the Old Frontier.* New York: Bonanza Books, 1959.

McGeehan, W. O. "Our Changing Sports Page." *Scribner's Magazine* 84, no. 1 (July, 1928):56–59.

McKelvey, Blake. *American Urbanization: A Comparative History.* Glenview, IL: Scott, Foresman and Company, 1973.

McKinney, G. B. "Negro Professional Baseball in the Upper South in the Gilded Age." *Journal of Sport History* 3, no. 3 (1976):273–280.

Menke, Frank G. *The Encyclopedia of Sports.* 5th ed. New York: A. S. Barnes and Company, 1975.

Metheny, Eleanor. *Movement and Meaning.* New York: McGraw-Hill Book Company, 1968.

Metzner, Henry. *History of the American Turners.* Rochester, NY: National Council of the American Turners, 1974.

Michener, James A. *Sports in America.* New York: Random House, 1976.

Middleton, Lorenzo. "NCAA Toughens Rules, Says Athletes Must Complete 12 Credits Each Term." *The Chronicle of Higher Education,* 19 January 1981, pp. 1, 6.

Miller, Kenneth D. "Stearns, Hitchcock, and Amherst College." *Journal of Health, Physical Education, and Recreation* 28 (May-June, 1957):29–30.

Mills, Paul R. "William Andrus Alcott, M.D. Pioneer Reformer in Physical Education, 1789–1859." *76th Proceedings,* National College Physical Education Association for Men (January 6–9, 1973):29–34.

Milnor, W. *Historical Memoir of the Schuylkill Fishing Company.* Philadelphia: Judah Dobson, 1830.

Mook, H. Telfer. "Training Day in New England." *New England Quarterly,* December, 1938, pp. 675–697.

Moolenijizer, Nicolaas J. "Our Legacy from the Middle Ages." *Quest* 11 (December, 1968):32–43.

Moore, Kenny, and Swift, E. M. "Detour on the High Road." *Sports Illustrated* 53 (July 7, 1980):26–38.

Morgan, Edmund S. *Virginians at Home: Family Life in the Eighteenth Century.* Williamsburg, VA: The Colonial Williamsburg Foundation, 1952.

Morison, Samuel Eliot. *The Great Explorers.* New York: Oxford University Press, 1978.

————. *The Oxford History of the American People.* New York: Oxford University Press, 1965.

Morton, Richard L. *Colonial Virginia,* Vol. I. New York: Van Rees Press, 1960.

Mungo Park's Travels in Africa. New York: Dutton, 1969.

Murphy, E. Jefferson. *History of African Civilization.* New York: Thomas Y. Crowell, 1972.

Naismith, James. *Basketball, Its Origin and Development.* New York: Association Press, 1941.

National Section on Women's Athletics. "Desirable Practices in Athletics." Washington, D.C.: American Association for Health, Physical Education, and Recreation, 1949.

Nevins, Allan. *The Emergence of Modern America 1865–1878.* New York: The Macmillan Company, 1927.

Nevins, Allan, and Commager, Henry Steele. *A Pocket History of the United States.* New York: Washington Square Press, 1966.

Newcomer, Mabel. *A Century of Higher Education for American Women.* New York: Harper & Brothers, 1959.

"1976 Sports Participation Survey." Elgin, IL: National Federation of State High School Associations, Nov. 13, 1974.

Noll, Roger G., ed. *Government and the Sports Business*. Washington, D.C.: The Brookings Institution, 1974.

North, Helen. *Sophrosyne*. New York: Anchor Press/Doubleday, 1963.

Novak, Michael. *The Joy of Sports: End Zones, Bases, Baskets, Balls, and the Consecration of the American Spirit*. New York: Basic Books, 1976.

Nye, R. B., and Morpurgo, J. E. *The Growth of the U.S.A*. Baltimore: Penguin Books, 1955.

Offenberg, R. S. "American College Football: Its Growth and Significance, 1869–1914." Paper presented at the North American Society for Sport History, Boston, Massachusetts, April 16–19, 1975.

Olaudah, Equiano. *The Interesting Narrative of Olaudah Equiano, or Gustavus Vasa, the African* (2 vols., London, 1789), in *Africa Remembered,* ed. P. Curtin. Madison: The University of Wisconsin, 1967.

————. *The Life of Olaudah Equiano or Gustavus Vassa, the African,* Boston, 1837, in *The Negro in American History,* ed. M. J. Adler. Encyclopedia Britannica Educational Corporation, 1969.

Olsen, Jack. *The Black Athlete: A Shameful Story*. New York: Time-Life Books, 1968.

The Olympic Games. New York: United States Olympic Committee, 1970.

Olympism. Lausanne, Switzerland: International Olympic Committee, 1972.

"One Hundred Years of Baseball." *Amherst Alumni News,* October, 1958, p. 4.

O'Neill, William L. *Everyone Was Brave*. Chicago: Quadrangle Books, 1971.

Orlick, Terry, and Botterill, Cal. *Every Kid Can Win*. Chicago: Nelson-Hall, 1975.

Osterhoudt, Robert G. "In Praise of Sport History: An Argument for its Study." *Canadian Journal of History of Sport and Physical Education* 10, no. 1 (May, 1979):1–6.

Owen, Janet. *Sports in Women's Colleges*. New York: *New York Herald-Tribune,* 1932.

Painter, Ruth E. "Tavern Amusements in Eighteenth Century America," in *The Leisure Class in America,* ed. Leon Stein. New York: Arno Press, 1975.

Painter, Sidney. *Mediaeval Society*. Ithaca, NY: Cornell University Press, 1951.

Park, Roberta J. " 'Embodied Selves': The Rise and Development of Concern for Physical Education, Active Games and Recreation for American Women, 1776–1865." *Journal of Sport History* 5, no. 2 (Summer, 1978):5–41.

————. "History and Structure of the Department of Physical Education at the University of California with Special Reference to Women's Sports." Unpublished paper, University of California at Berkeley, 1976.

Parker, Garland G. *The Enrollment Explosion*. New York: School & Society Books, 1971.

Paul, C. Robert, and Moran, R. Michael, eds. *The Olympic Games.* Colorado Springs, CO: United States Olympic Committee, 1979.

Paul, Joan. "The Health Reformers: George Barker Windship and Boston's Strength Seekers." *Journal of Sport History* 10, no. 3 (Winter, 1983):41–57.

Paxson, Frederic L. "The Rise of Sport." *Mississippi Valley Historical Review* 4 (1917):143–168.

Perham, Margery, and Simmons, J. *African Discovery.* London: Faber and Faber, 1957.

Pesavento, Wilma J. "Sport and Recreation in the Pullman Experiment, 1880–1900." *Journal of Sport History* 9 (Summer, 1982):38–62.

Peterson, Harold. *The Man Who Invented Baseball.* New York: Charles Scribner's Sons, 1973.

Peterson, James A., ed. *Intramural Administration: Theory and Practice.* Englewood Cliffs, NJ: Prentice-Hall, Inc., 1976.

Peterson, Robert. *Only the Ball Was White.* Englewood Cliffs, NJ: Prentice-Hall, Inc., 1970.

Phillips, Thomas. "A Journal of a Voyage to Africa and Barbadoes," in *A Collection of Voyages and Travels,* Vol. VI, ed. Churchill. London: 1732.

Pierce, Bessie Louise. *A History of Chicago,* Vol. I. New York: Alfred A. Knopf, 1937.

Pindar. *Pindar's Victory Songs,* trans. and with an introduction by Frank J. Nisetich. Baltimore: The Johns Hopkins University Press, 1980.

Potter, Robert E. *The Stream of American Education.* New York: American Book Company, 1967.

Proceedings of the Third Annual Convention of the Intercollegiate Athletic Association of the United States (January 2, 1909).

Proceedings of the 7th Annual Convention of the National Collegiate Athletic Association (December 27, 1912).

Proceedings of the 13th Annual Convention of the National Collegiate Athletic Association (December 27, 1918).

Proceedings of the 25th Annual Convention of the National Collegiate Athletic Association (December 31, 1930).

Proceedings of the 34th Annual Convention of the National Collegiate Athletic Association (December 28–30, 1939).

Professional Sports and the Law. Washington, D.C.: United States Government Printing Office, 1976.

Prospectus of the Vassar Female College. New York: Alford, 1865.

Rader, Benjamin G. *American Sports: From the Age of Folk Games to the Age of Spectators.* Englewood Cliffs, NJ: Prentice-Hall, 1982.

———. *In Its Own Image: How Television Has Transformed Sports.* New York: The Free Press, 1984.

Rainwater, Clarence E. *The Play Movement in the United States.* Chicago: University of Chicago Press, 1922.

Records of the Court of Assistants of the Colony of Massachusetts Bay, 1630–1644, Vol. II. Boston: County of Suffolk, 1904.

Redmond, Gerald. *The Caledonian Games in Nineteenth-Century America.* Rutherford, NJ: Fairleigh Dickinson University Press, 1971.

———. "Sport History in *Academe:* 1930 to the Present." Paper presented at the North American Society for Sport History, Banff, Alberta, May 24–28, 1980.

Reiss, Steven A. *Touching Base: Professional Baseball and American Culture in the Progressive Era.* Westport, CT: Greenwood, 1980.

Remley, Mary L. "From Sidesaddle to Rodeo," in *Sports and Recreation in the West,* ed. Donald J. Mrozek. Manhattan, KS: Sunflower University Press, 1978.

Richardson, Rufus B. "The New Olympian Games." *Scribner's Magazine* 20, no. 3 (September, 1896):267–286.

Richter, Frank C. *Richter's History and Records of Base Ball.* Philadelphia: Francis C. Richter, 1914.

Riess, Steven A. "The Baseball Magnate and Urban Politics in the Progressive Era: 1895–1920." *Journal of Sport History* 1, no. 1 (May, 1974):41–62.

Rinhart, Floyd and Marion. *Summertime, Photographs of Americans at Play, 1850–1900.* New York: Clarkson N. Potter, Inc., 1978.

Robinson, Rachel S. *Sources for the History of Greek Athletics.* Cincinnati: published by the author, 1955.

Rodney, Walter. *A History of the Upper Guinea Coast 1545–1800.* Oxford: Clarendon Press, 1970.

Rogosin, Don. *Invisible Men: Life in Baseball's Negro Leagues.* New York: Atheneum, 1983.

Rooney, John F., Jr. *A Geography of American Sport.* Reading, MA: Addison-Wesley Publishing Company, 1974.

Rosenberger, F. C., ed. *Virginia Reader.* New York: E. P. Dutton & Company, 1948.

Rowse, A. L. *The Use of History.* New York: Collier Books, 1963.

Russell, Fred, and Leonard, George. *Big Bowl Football.* New York: Ronald Press, 1963.

Rust, Edna and Art, Jr. *Art Rust's Illustrated History of the Black Athlete.* Garden City, NY: Doubleday, 1985.

Sachs, Curt. *World History of the Dance.* New York: W. W. Norton and Company, Inc., 1937.

Sargent, Dudley Allen. "Athletics in Secondary Schools." *American Physical Education Review* 8 (June, 1903):57–69.

———. *An Autobiography,* ed. Ledyard W. Sargent. Philadelphia: Lea & Febiger, 1927.

———. "Interest in Sport and Physical Education as a Phase of Woman's Development." *Mind and Body* 22 (November, 1915):830–833.

———. "The Physical Development of Women." *Scribner's Magazine* 5, no. 2 (1889):172–185.

———. *Physical Education.* Boston: Ginn & Company, 1906.

Savage, Howard J. *American College Athletics.* New York: The Carnegie Foundation for the Advancement of Teaching, 1929.

Schleppi, John R. " 'It Pays': John H. Patterson and Industrial Recreation at the National Cash Register Company." *Journal of Sport History* 6 (Winter, 1979):20–27.

Schlesinger, Arthur M. *The Rise of the City, 1878–1898.* New York: The Macmillan Company, 1933.

Schneider, Gretchen Adel. "Pigeon Wings and Polkas: The Dance of the California Miners." *Dance Perspectives* 39 (Winter, 1969):1–57.

Schollander, Don, and Savage, Duke. *Deep Water.* New York: Crown Publishers, Inc., 1971.

Schwarz, Marguerite. "The Athletic Federation of College Women." *Journal of Health and Physical Education* 7 (May, 1936):297, 345–346.

Scott, Gladys. "Competition for Women in American Colleges and Universities." *Research Quarterly* 16 (March, 1945):49–71.

Scott, Jack. "Sport and the Radical Ethic." *Quest* 19 (January, 1973):71–77.

Scott, Phebe, and Ulrich, Celeste. "Commission on Intercollegiate Sports for Women." *Journal of Health, Physical Education, and Recreation* 37 (October, 1966):10, 76.

Sefton, Alice A. *The Women's Division, National Amateur Athletic Federation.* Stanford: Stanford University Press, 1941.

Segrave, Jeffrey, and Chu, Donald. *Olympism.* Champaign, IL: Human Kinetics Publishers, 1987.

Seymour, Harold. *Baseball: The Early Years.* New York: Oxford University Press, 1959.

———. *Baseball: The Golden Years.* New York: Oxford University Press, 1971.

Shakespeare, William. *King Henry the Fifth.*

Shults, Frederick D. "Oberlin College: Molder of Four Great Men." *Quest* 11 (December, 1968):71–75.

Silvia, C. E. *Lifesaving and Water Safety Instruction.* New York: Association Press, 1960.

Singleton, Esther. *Dutch New York.* New York: Benjamin Blom, 1968.

———. *Social New York under the Georges, 1714–1776.* New York: D. Appleton, 1902.

Sklar, Kathryn Kish. *Catharine Beecher.* New Haven: Yale University Press, 1973.

Smelser, Marshall M. "The Babe on Balance." *The American Scholar* 44 (Spring, 1975):299–307.

Smith, Michael D. "Origins of Faculty Attitudes toward Intercollegiate Athletics." *Canadian Journal of History of Sport and Physical Education* 2, no. 2 (December, 1971):61–72.

Smith, Page. *Daughters of the Promised Land.* Boston: Little, Brown and Company, 1970.

Smith, Robert A. *A Social History of the Bicycle.* New York: American Heritage Press, 1972.

Smith, Ronald A. "Harvard and Columbia and a Reconsideration of the 1905–06 Football Crisis." *Journal of Sport History* 8, no. 3 (Winter, 1981):5–19.

Snodgrass, Jeanne. "The Development of the American National Red Cross Aquatic Schools with Special Reference to Camp Kiwanis." M.S. thesis, Smith College, 1953.

Somers, Dale A. *The Rise of Sports in New Orleans, 1850–1900.* Baton Rouge: Louisiana State University Press, 1972.

Spalding, Albert G. *Base Ball, America's National Game.* New York: American Sports Publishing Company, 1911.

Spear, Ruth E. "A Study of the Needs and Provisions in Physical Education of Women Students in Selected Negro Colleges." M.S. thesis, Smith College, 1950.

Spears, Betty. "The Emergence of Women in Sport," in *Women's Athletics: Coping with Controversy,* ed. Barbara J. Hoepner. Washington, D.C.: American Association for Health, Physical Education, and Recreation, 1974.

———. "Influences on Early Professional Physical Education Curriculums in the United States." *Proceedings,* The Second Canadian Symposium on the History of Sport and Physical Education, Windsor, Ontario (May 1–3, 1972):86–103.

———. "The Influential Miss Homans." *Quest* 29 (Winter, 1978):46–57.

———. *Leading the Way: Amy Morris Homans and the Beginnings of Professional Education for Women.* Westport, CT: Greenwood, 1986.

———. "The Olympic Movement and Physical Education." *The Academy Papers,* No. 14, The American Academy of Physical Education (December, 1980):65–72.

————. "Success, Women and Physical Education," in *Women as Leaders in Physical Education and Sport,* ed. Gladys M. Scott and Mary J. Hoferek. Iowa City: The University of Iowa, 1979.

Spicer, Edward H. *A Short History of the Indians of the United States.* New York: Van Nostrand Reinhold Co., 1969.

Staley, Seward C. "The Four Year Curriculum in Physical (Sports) Education." *Research Quarterly* 2 (March, 1931):76–90.

Starnes, Richard. "An Unprecedented Economic and Ethical Crisis Grips Big-Time Intercollegiate Sports." *The Chronicle of Higher Education,* 24 September 1973, pp. 1, 6.

State of Michigan, Joint Legislative Study on Youth Sports Programs. *Agency Sponsored Sports, Phase I.* November, 1976.

Statistical Abstract of the United States, 1976. United States Department of Commerce, Bureau of the Census.

Stillman, Agnes C. "Senda Berenson Abbot: Her Life and Contributions to Smith College and to the Physical Education Profession." M.S. thesis, Smith College, 1971.

Stow, John. *A Survey of London.* Reprinted from 1603. Oxford: Clarendon Press, 1908.

Struna, Nancy L. "E. P. Thompson's Notion of 'Context' and the Writing of Physical Education and Sport History." *Quest* 39 (1986):22–32.

————. "The Declaration of Sports Reconsidered." *Canadian Journal of History of Sport* 14 (December, 1983):44–68.

————. "The North-South Races: American Thoroughbred Racing in Transition, 1823–1850." *Journal of Sport History* 8, no. 2 (Summer, 1981):28–57.

————. "Sports and Colonial Education: A Cultural Perspective." *Research Quarterly for Exercise and Sport* 52, no. 1 (March, 1981):117–135.

————. "Sport and the Evolution of Massachusetts Bay Puritan Society, 1630–1730." M.A. thesis, University of Maryland, 1975.

————. "Sport and Societal Values: Massachusetts Bay." *Quest* 27 (Winter, 1977):38–46.

Struna, Nancy, and Remley, Mary L. "Physical Education for Women at the University of Wisconsin, 1863–1913: A Half Century of Progress." *Canadian Journal of History of Sport and Physical Education* 4, no. 1 (1973):8–26.

Strutt, Joseph. *The Sports and Pastimes of the People of England.* London: William Tegg, 1867.

Swanson, Richard A. "The Acceptance and Influence of Play in American Protestantism." *Quest* 11 (December, 1968):58–70.

————. "American Protestantism and Play: 1865–1915." Ph.D. dissertation, The Ohio State University, 1967.

————. "Elementary School Physical Education: 1920–1950," in *The History of Elementary School Physical Education: 1885–1985*. Reston, VA: National Association for Sport and Physical Education, 1985.

————. "The Evolution of the NCAA, the NAIA, and their Educational Goals." Paper presented at the Third Annual Symposium of the NASPE History Academy, American Alliance for Health, Physical Education, Recreation, and Dance, New Orleans, March 15, 1979.

Swett, John. *Public Education in California*. New York: American Book Company, 1911.

Tappan, Lilian. Report to the President, 1877. Vassar College, Poughkeepsie, New York.

Terry, Walter. "The Legacy of Isadora Duncan and Ruth St. Denis." *Dance Perspectives* 5 (Winter, 1960):1–60.

Theberge, Nancy. "Analysis of Women's Professional Golf." Ph.D. dissertation, University of Massachusetts, 1977.

Thompson, James G. "Ancient Greek Attitudes on Athletics." *Canadian Journal of History of Sport and Physical Education* 5, no. 2 (December, 1974):56–62.

Tilghman, T. F. "An Early Victorian College St. John's, 1830–1860." *Maryland Historical Society* 14, no. 4 (December, 1949):251–268.

Tingling, Marion, ed. *The Correspondence of the Three William Byrds of Westover Virginia, 1684–1776,* 2 vols. Charlottesville: The University Press of Virginia, 1977.

Trevelyan, G. M. *A Shortened History of England*. New York: Penguin, 1942.

Tuchman, Barbara A. *A Distant Mirror*. New York: Alfred A. Knopf, 1979.

Tunis, John R. "Changing Trends in Sport." *Harper's Monthly Magazine* 170 (December, 1934):75–86.

Twombly, Wells. *200 Years of Sport in America: A Pageant of a Nation at Play*. New York: McGraw-Hill Book Company, 1976.

Umstead, Elizabeth C. "Elementary School Physical Education: 1885–1920," in *The History of Elementary School Physical Education: 1885–1985*. Reston, VA: National Association for Sport and Physical Education, 1985.

U.S.A. 1776–1976, NCAA 1906–1976. Shawnee Mission, KS: National Collegiate Athletic Association, 1976.

United States Department of Health, Education, and Welfare. *HEW Fact Sheet*. June, 1975.

United States Office of Education. *Annual Report of the Federal Security Agency, 1947*.

United States Office of Education. *Biennial Survey of Education in the United States,* 1944–46.

United States Olympic Committee. *Constitution and By-Laws.* Colorado Springs, CO: United States Olympic Committee, 1985.

Van Cleef, Joy. "Rural Felicity: Social Dance in 18th Century Connecticut." *Dance Perspectives* 65 (Spring, 1976):1–45.

Van Dalen, Deobold B., and Bennett, Bruce L. *A World History of Physical Education.* 2nd ed. Englewood Cliffs, NJ: Prentice-Hall Inc., 1971.

VanderZwaag, Harold J., and Sheehan, Thomas J. *Introduction to Sport Studies.* Dubuque, IA: Wm. C. Brown Company, 1978.

Van Dyne, Larry. "College Sports Enforcement Squad." *The Chronicle of Higher Education,* 7 March 1977, pp. 1, 14.

———. "The South's Black Colleges Lose a Football Monopoly." *The Chronicle of Higher Education,* 15 November 1976, pp. 1, 8.

Vassar, Matthew. "Communications." June 25, 1867. Vassar College, Poughkeepsie, New York.

Vaughan, Linda. "A Century of Rowing at Wellesley, 1875–1975." Paper presented at the North American Society for Sport History, Boston, Massachusetts, April 16–19, 1975.

Vendien, Lynn C. "FISU (Federation Internationale du Sports Universitaire) and the World University Games." *Quest* 22 (Spring, 1974):74–81.

Vernam, Glenn R. *Man on Horseback.* New York: Harper & Row, 1964.

Virgil. *The Aeneid of Virgil,* trans. by Allen Mandelbaum. Berkeley: University of California Press, 1971.

Voight, David Q. *American Baseball,* Vol I. Norman: University of Oklahoma Press, 1966.

———. *American Baseball,* Vol. II. Norman: University of Oklahoma Press, 1970.

———. "Reflections on Diamonds: American Baseball and American Culture." *Journal of Sport History* 1, no. 1 (May, 1974):3–25.

Wagner, Peter. "Puritan Attitudes Towards Physical Recreation in 17th Century New England." *Journal of Sport History* 3, no. 2 (Summer, 1976):139–151.

Waldstein, Charles. "The Olympian Games at Athens." *Harper's Weekly* 40, no. 3 (September, 1896):490.

Wallace, William N. *The Macmillan Book of Boating.* New York: Crown Publishers, Inc., 1973.

Walters, M. L. "The Physical Education Society of the Y.M.C.A.'s of North America." *Journal of Health and Physical Education* 17 (May, 1947):311–312, 357–358.

Walton, Izaak. *The Compleat Angler.* New York: The Heritage Press, 1938.

Wayman, Agnes R. *Education Through Physical Education.* Philadelphia: Lea & Febiger, 1934.

———. "Women's Athletics—All Uses—No Abuses." *American Physical Education Review* 29 (November, 1924):517.

Weaver, Robert B. *Amusements and Sports in American Life.* Chicago: University of Chicago Press, 1939.

Webb, Bernice Larson. *The Basketball Man: James Naismith.* Lawrence: The University Press of Kansas, 1973.

Webb, Walter Prescott. *The Great Frontier.* Austin: University of Texas Press, 1964.

Webster, F. A. M. *Athletics of Today for Women.* New York: Frederick Warne and Co., Ltd., 1930.

Wecter, Dixon. *The Saga of American Society: A Record of Social Aspiration, 1607–1937.* New York: Charles Scribner's Sons, 1937.

Wedgwood, C. V. *The Sense of the Past.* New York: Collier Books, 1960.

Welch, J. Edmund. "George J. Fisher: Leader of Youth." *Journal of Health, Physical Education, and Recreation* 39 (May, 1968):37.

———. "The Origin, Development, and Effect of YMCA Junior Leaders Schools on Physical Education in the United States and Canada." *71st Proceedings,* National College Physical Education Association for Men (January 10–13, 1968):172–179.

Welch, Paula D., and Lerch, Harold A. *History of American Physical Education and Sport.* Springfield, IL: Charles C. Thomas, 1981.

Westermeier, Clifford P. "Seventy-five Years of Rodeo in Colorado." *Colorado Magazine* 28 (January, 1951):13–27; (April, 1951):127–145; (July, 1951):219–231.

Weston, Arthur. *The Making of American Physical Education.* New York: Appleton-Century-Crofts, 1962.

Whited, Clark V. "Sport Science, The Modern Disciplinary Concept of Physical Education." *73rd Proceedings,* National College Physical Education Association for Men (December 27–30, 1970):223–230.

Wiggins, David K. "Good Times on the Old Plantation: Popular Recreations of the Black Slave in Antebellum South, 1810–1860." *Journal of Sport History* 4, no. 3 (Fall, 1977):260–284.

———. "The Play of Slave Children in the Plantation Communities of the Old South, 1820–1860." *Journal of Sport History* 7, no. 2 (Summer, 1980): 21–39.

———. "Sport and Popular Pastimes: Shadow of the Slavequarter." *Canadian Journal of History of Sport and Physical Education* 11, no. 1 (May, 1980):61–88.

Williams, John. "William Ellery Channing's Philosophy of Physical Education and Recreation." *Quest* 4 (April, 1965):49–52.

Willis, Joseph D., and Wettan, Richard G. "Social Stratification in New York City Athletic Clubs, 1865–1915." *Journal of Sport History* 3, no. 1 (Spring, 1976):45–63.

Wilson, Elizabeth. *Fifty Years of Association Work Among Young Women, 1866–1916.* New York: National Board of the Young Women's Christian Associations, 1916.

Wilson, Kenneth L., and Brondfield, Jerry. *The Big Ten.* Englewood Cliffs, NJ: Prentice-Hall, Inc., 1967.

Wilson, S. S. "Bicycle Technology." *Scientific American* 228 (March, 1973):81–91.

Wilson, Wayne. "Social Discontent and the Growth of Wilderness Sport in America: 1965–1974." *Quest* 27 (Winter, 1977):54–60.

Wind, Herbert Warren, ed. *The Realm of Sport.* New York: Simon and Schuster, 1966.

Windship, George B. "Physical Culture." *Massachusetts Teacher* 13 (April, 1860):132.

Winks, Robin W. *The Historian as Detective.* New York: Harper & Row, 1968.

"Women's Play-off Paid Attendance a Record 15,514." *The NCAA News* (January 8, 1987):16.

Wood, Thomas Denison. *Ninth Yearbook of the National Society for the Study of Education.* Chicago: University of Chicago Press, 1910.

Woodhouse, Margaret K. "A History of Amateur Club Rowing in the New York Metropolitan Area 1830–1870." *Canadian Journal of History of Sport and Physical Education* 11, no. 2 (December, 1980):72–91.

Woodmason, Charles. *The Carolina Backcountry on the Eve of the Revolution,* ed. R. J. Hooker. Chapel Hill: University of North Carolina Press, 1953.

Woods, John. "Two Years' Residence in the Settlement on the English Prairie, in the Illinois Country, United States," in *Early Western Travels,* 1748–1846, Vol. X, ed. R. G. Thwaites. Cleveland: The Arthur H. Clark Company, 1904.

Woody, Thomas. *A History of Women's Education in the United States.* New York: Science Press, 1929.

———. *Life and Education in Early Societies.* New York: Macmillan, 1949.

World Almanac and Book of Facts. New York: Scripps Howard, 1986.

Wright, Louis B. *The Atlantic Frontier.* New York: Alfred A. Knopf, 1947.

———. *The Cultural Life of the American Colonies.* New York: Harper & Row, 1957.

Wynne, Shirley. "From Ballet to Ballroom: Dance in the Revolutionary Era." *Dance Scope* 10, no. 1 (Fall/Winter, 1975/1976):65–73.

Yee, Min S. *The Sports Book.* New York: Bantam Books, 1976.

YMCA Training School Catalogue, 1890–91. Springfield, Massachusetts.

Yoder, Paton. *Taverns and Travelers*. Bloomington: Indiana University Press, 1969.

Young, Alexander J., Jr. "The Rejuvenation of Major League Baseball in the Twenties." *Canadian Journal of History of Sport and Physical Education* 3, no. 2 (May, 1972):8–25.

———. "Sam Langford, 'The Boston Tarbaby.' " *Proceedings,* The Second Canadian Symposium on the History of Sport and Physical Education, Windsor, Ontario (May 1–3, 1972):45–67.

Zaharias, Babe Didrikson. *This Life I've Led*. New York: A. S. Barnes & Co., 1955.

Zaslavsky, Claudia. *Africa Counts*. Boston: Prindle, Weber, & Schmidt, 1973.

Zeigler, Earle F., ed. *A History of Physical Education and Sport in the United States and Canada*. Champaign, IL: Stipes Publishing Company, 1975.

Zuckerman, Jerome; Stull, G. Allan; and Eyler, Marvin H. "The Black Athlete in Post-Bellum 19th Century." *The Physical Educator* 29 (October, 1972):142–146.

Index